Fireball

Also by Robert Matzen

Dutch Girl: Audrey Hepburn and World War II

Mission: Jimmy Stewart and the Fight for Europe

Errol & Olivia

Errol Flynn Slept Here (with Michael Mazzone)

Fireball
Carole Lombard and the Mystery of Flight 3

Robert Matzen

GoodKnight Books
Pittsburgh, Pennsylvania

GoodKnight Books

Published by GoodKnight Books, an imprint of Paladin Communications, Pittsburgh, Pennsylvania

Printed in the United States of America

Library of Congress Control Number: 2016913765

ISBN 978-0-9962740-9-8

Book and cover design by Sharon Berk

For the one who, when I said, "I need to climb one
of the roughest mountains in the United States,"
responded without a second's hesitation,
"Me too. When do we go?"

Contents

Contents

Prologue

All Uphill

The book that became *Fireball* began with a mention of the fact that much of the wreckage of TWA Flight 3, a commercial airliner carrying Hollywood star Carole Lombard and twenty-one other people on the evening of January 16, 1942, still today lies strewn across the side of Mt. Potosi, Nevada. I said this to my friend and colleague John McElwee, author of *Showmen, Sell It Hot!* and host of the Greenbriar Picture Shows website. Most people don't know that the engines, landing gear, and various twisted chunks of fuselage remain entangled in brush, rest against trees, and, in general, litter the surface of some of America's most inhospitable real estate within sight of Las Vegas, Nevada.

Some months after our conversation, John suggested lunch with my wife, Mary, and me at a film convention in Columbus, Ohio, because he wanted to hit me with an idea, an inspiration for a book. This book would juxtapose a modern-day climb of the mountain to that remote crash site with the events of 1942, Carole Lombard's last days, her decisions on the trip from Indianapolis, Indiana, where she went to sell war bonds, and husband Clark Gable's reaction to the loss of his wife. John and I both knew that the story dripped irony and that such a book would be what he called "dynamite." Then he jabbed a finger in my direction and said, "And you are the only one to do it."

Mt. Potosi (an Indian word pronounced POE-tuh-see) rises to an elevation of 8,200 feet above sea level and looms over the desert west of Vegas. There are no roads to the crash site and no trails. Nothing much lives up there because even a mountain goat would have better sense than to scale grades so steep.

It took some months to get the climb organized, equipment rented, and guide secured. Mary and I set out to climb Potosi toward the end of October when the desert would be cool and the snakes charmed. By that time I itched to write the story that had been laid out, but I knew I must make the climb before I could feel any entitlement to set down a word of this book, and I had to accomplish this feat over the route that first responders took, and Clark Gable *tried* to take, when all still believed that survivors might be found up on the mountain.

A local conservationist named Jim Boone guided us that day. We started out in a four-wheel drive Jeep with hubs locked, and after an hour bouncing along old mining roads, we unfolded ourselves from the Jeep on scrambled legs and began our hike that turned into a climb, a dangerous passage that left me bloodied before the first mile had passed.

Mary, who is plenty tough, surrendered halfway up, and Jim led me on, climbing with annoying ease while I grunted and clawed behind him. It took four-and-a-half hours all told to ascend the mountain on foot, and after all the climbing, stumbling, and bleeding, I wasn't prepared for the experience of *being* at the spot of the crash. A fair amount of DC-3 number NC 1946 does indeed remain scattered over the side of the steep mountain slope, so much so that every footfall caused a tinkle of aluminum in shards and chunks. It's a place where twenty-two people departed this earth in one flaming second, and that hit me very hard.

When Jim found a bone that had been part of somebody's hand, I understood that this wasn't just Carole Lombard's story. It was the pilot's story and the copilot's and the stewardess's. It was the story of fifteen Army Air Corps personnel who perished, men as young as nineteen and as "old" as twenty-eight, and it was the story of three other civilians, all of whom died right *there*, on the spot where I stood shivering in the fading October sunshine at 7,700 feet.

I started writing on the plane ride home and haven't stopped since. I have had extreme good fortune in my research, accessing the complete Civil Aeronautics Board investigation, including the exhibits and testimony. I have examined the U.S. House of Representatives investigation, and TWA's complete, never-before-seen crash files. I found a passenger who flew across the United States with Carole Lombard on Flight 3 and left the plane before it crashed. And I have learned of some of the contents of the FBI files. I spoke to a number of relatives of Flight 3 crash victims, pored over hundreds of newspaper accounts and unpublished manuscripts, and sifted through raw research data, including previously unpublished interviews about Carole Lombard and Clark Gable.

With the assistance of Lombard/Gable expert Carole Sampeck and many others, I have been able to debunk some legends and verify others and make some conclusions about the people and events. The result is equal parts biography, rescue effort, and mystery; it's also a love story and an unimaginable tragedy that continues to haunt me, as it may haunt you.

Robert Matzen
Pittsburgh, Pennsylvania
August 2013

1

A Perfectly Routine Friday Night

It was after six o'clock on the evening of January 16, 1942, when Pfc. Tom Parnell first learned that a TWA airliner intended to stop at McCarran Field in Las Vegas. Private Parnell worked the tower of the Army airfield that evening, and it was going to be a cold one, temperature down around forty. McCarran had been leased to Transcontinental and Western Airlines, or TWA, and Western Air Express for use as a commercial field, which meant that the place saw more action than if it had been occupied by the Army alone. Parnell hadn't been expecting to work this evening, but a buddy, Private Craft, had asked him to switch so he could go to the pictures, and Tom said yes because maybe he would need a favor himself down the line.

Now, at 6:26, Parnell received a radio call from TWA Trip Number 3 inbound from Albuquerque asking for wind speed and a runway assignment. Parnell had been handling these duties for only a week and knew he needed some practice with his radio calls. He hoped his inexperience couldn't be heard as he radioed, "Winds are calm from the east. No traffic at this time. Captain's choice of runway." McCarran Field had two landing strips, a north-south runway and a diagonal northeast-southwest runway.

Three minutes later Parnell spotted the twin beams of forward landing lights on a DC-3 as it swung to come in from the southwest, and TWA Flight 3 eased into a smooth landing. It was a new DC-3 with a polished aluminum body. A red TWA emblem outlined in black showed on the left wing surface, and the plane number NC 1946, also in red, appeared atop the right wing. In red script above the eight rectangular passenger windows along the fuselage read the words, *The Lindbergh Line*; an arrow next to the script pointed forward, toward the nose of the plane and the limitless horizon beyond.

With the plane safely landed and taxied to the station, Parnell stood down on an otherwise quiet evening. He knew nothing about the plane and didn't much care. With a glance he noticed Army guys piling out, which was usual these days with the war on. Parnell cared only that the plane had landed safely, and once he saw that it took off safely in a few minutes, his job would be done.

On the runway thirty-one-year-old TWA station manager Charles Duffy walked from the station into the cold night air. He pushed aluminum steps on wheels out to the cabin door of the plane. The door swung open and there stood the air hostess, a good-looking brunette with dark eyes. Duffy moved the steps into place, locked the wheels, and climbed up to receive from the hostess a card that contained cargo and passenger information. She smiled as she handed it down and made eye contact that could have been flirtatious; he didn't know.

Duffy moved down next to the stairway and watched a number of Army men step off the plane, one set of striped, khaki pants after another. It was his habit to make sure each passenger descended the steps smoothly without mishap, so he watched legs and feet. Legs and feet. Suddenly a very different leg appeared; a shapely leg in stockings and high heels. He held out his hand instinctively to help a lady off the plane and looked up into the face of a pretty young woman with dark hair. She smiled, thanked him, and moved past. More Army men stepped down. Bang. Bang. Bang. Precise masculine strides, one after another.

Then another toned leg appeared beneath another hemline. Duffy caught the glint of an ankle bracelet and saw a black high-heeled shoe. He held out his hand again. A gloved hand took his, and when he looked up he was staring into the sculpted face and topaz-blue eyes of motion picture actress Carole Lombard. No mistaking it; she was a distinctive-looking woman. Duffy attempted to hide the fact that his heart had skipped a couple beats— to show that he was startled would be seen as unprofessional. The movie star managed a faint smile, forced it he thought, as she stepped off Flight 3 into the cold desert night. It was funny how the brain worked. In the split second that he had made eye contact with this woman he had never met, he could tell she was exhausted. Her makeup had worn off hours earlier revealing pale skin and circles under the eyes the color of storm clouds. Two other passengers seemed to be with her, a middle-aged man and a much older woman, and all proceeded into the station to stretch their legs and warm up while the plane refueled. Notables routinely appeared at the little Las Vegas airfield because of its proximity to the bigger air terminals at Burbank and Los Angeles to the southwest. Just ninety minutes of airspace separated Las Vegas from the movie capital of the world.

Flight 3's block time was 6:36, and Duffy followed the last of the passengers, one more cluster of soldiers, into the station. His was a high-pressure job, handling all the paperwork and cargo for the flights en route as well as passenger questions and final clearance with TWA control in Burbank. He heard the fuel truck being driven into place and knew that things were moving smoothly. Trip Number 3 was a transcontinental flight that had begun at LaGuardia in New York City the previous day, then stopped at Pittsburgh, Columbus, Dayton, Indianapolis, St. Louis, Kansas City, Wichita, Amarillo, and Albuquerque. The flight crew would have changed over a couple times by now, along with all the passengers, so the DC-3 itself and some of its cargo and mail contents were the only constants from New York City all the way to lonely Las Vegas.

Out at the plane, young Floyd Munson, not yet eighteen, leaned a ladder against the fuselage, and Ed Fuqua, the cargo man, climbed up on the wing and sticked the fuel tanks. He scribbled numbers on a slip of paper and handed it down to Munson, who walked the paper inside and stuck it in Duffy's palm before ambling back to his duties at the plane.

As Chuck Duffy processed paperwork, some of the Army personnel from the plane stood in a group, smoking and talking. Others sat quietly, one of them already slumped asleep in a chair. They were various ages, up to thirty he thought, but mostly they were young, barely shaving, and full of enthusiasm. Carole Lombard shared none of their energy or good spirits. All the while, she paced in front of the two other people, the businessman with slicked-back hair and the elderly lady who had followed the actress off the plane. Duffy glanced at the passenger list. Otto Winkler was the only civilian male he saw on the list, and there were two women passengers, a Mrs. Elizabeth Peters and a Mrs. Lois Hamilton. He wasn't sure who was who, but nobody looked happy. The actress was pale and thin and wore a sour expression, not at all what he might expect from a star of comedy pictures. The elderly woman sat rigidly in her seat and stared at nothing. Nobody said a word. After a while the businessman approached Duffy and asked to send a telegram. Duffy handed him a Western Union form, and the man scribbled some lines and handed the form back along with a quarter.

Out the corner of his eye, Duffy saw the pilot edge up to his desk. "Say, is Flight 3 going on to Long Beach?" the pilot asked. Duffy replied that he didn't have that information and the captain would have to check upon landing at Burbank. Wayne Williams was the captain's name, one of the veteran TWA pilots but a recent addition to this route, about forty years of age and a nice guy.

The captain nodded and motioned toward the plane. "Fill the

oil tanks to 20 gallons each, will you?" Duffy said he would see it done. He told Captain Williams that his man had sticked the tanks and there were 125 gallons of fuel remaining on the plane at landing. Chuck said he had ordered 225 gallons to be added for a total of 350. Capacity was more than 800, but Duffy was concerned about weight because he could see from the hostess card that the plane was already maxed out on passengers and cargo. Williams nodded his approval of the addition of fuel.

A few feet away Carole Lombard, dressed in a pink suit and wrapped in black fur, stopped pacing and stared out at the plane, watching Ed Fuqua continue to work. She fumbled for a cigarette, lit it, and took a deep drag. She huddled up and began pacing again, arms folded tightly about her. She pulled a bit of tobacco off the tip of her tongue with her fingers, and then continued to smoke and pace. Duffy thought her a tight little firecracker about ready to go off. The turnaround was longer than he would have liked, this quick service job that should have been ten minutes at most and was now more than twenty. No cargo or mail was being added to or removed from the plane, which should have made turnaround a snap. Floyd Munson, the young cargo assistant, simply had to work with the TWA hostess still aboard the plane to remove the remnants from a dinner served to passengers in the air between Albuquerque and Las Vegas, and that should have been done by now.

Outside, Fuqua worked as fast as he might. Western Air employed him and he preferred the smaller Western fuel truck. But the Las Vegas terminal served both Western Air Express and TWA, and by agreement he serviced the TWA ships too, and on those occasions he was forced to use the unwieldy TWA Texaco truck with too many levers and gauges. He was up on the wings adding gas to the mains, and then down, up again, and then down. The second time he almost bumped into a soldier who had strayed near the wing, obviously the guard assigned to watch the plane while it remained on the ground. They were just forty days past

Pearl Harbor after all. McCarran Field was an Army facility, and they had the place buttoned up tight, with guards at every entrance and by every plane.

Finally, Fuqua was done adding gas and oil. Munson confirmed that he had removed the meal service. Fuqua brought the maintenance sheet inside and handed it to Chuck Duffy. Chuck then prepared Flight 3's final clearance and gave it to Captain Williams. Pilot and copilot returned to the plane. Duffy was conscious of the delay and hurried over to the door to the station, calling for passengers to line up by seat assignment. He led them outside and stood by the portable aluminum stairway as the large group of Army personnel and the few civilians began to file past and climb aboard. By the order of boarding, Miss Lombard was sitting in the center of the plane. He held out his hand and she took it as she climbed the steps, her high heels clomping on aluminum. She thanked him for his help and seemed a bit less high voltage getting onto the plane than she had been stepping off. Then Duffy helped the elderly lady make the climb and set foot inside the plane.

When all were aboard, he swiveled the door into the hands of that pretty uniformed stewardess, who gave him a smile and a thank you. "Happy landings," he said, and she smiled again and pulled the door closed. He heard the lock catch inside the plane. He pulled his steps away and returned to the station, his work for the day now finished. Flight 3 hadn't been scheduled to land at McCarran and had been on its way to Boulder City to the south, but the flight was well behind schedule and had run out of daylight, and Boulder airfield didn't have runway lights. Flight 3 then had made the call to McCarran and the airfield had accommodated. Now Chuck Duffy was bushed and anxious to get home to dinner.

Up in the control tower, Private Parnell was once again engaged. Word hadn't reached him about Carole Lombard, and so all he cared about was getting Flight 3 airborne without incident.

He watched the pilot turn over one propeller, and then the other, and the twin-engined bird started to run up those big Wright Cyclone engines to takeoff speed.

The pilot radioed for permission to taxi to the northern edge of the north-south runway, and Parnell gave him the OK. The engines were practically screaming by now. Parnell was used to the throaty growl of the Western DC-3s, but this TWA airship had two engines that seemed to be working hard. A DC-3 was a DC-3, so why would the engines sound so different? He couldn't understand it, but then he was new and shrugged to himself that he didn't know what he didn't know.

Flight 3 began to move north to south along the runway. It continued to gain speed without getting off the ground, past the intersection with the diagonal runway. A streak of flame trailed each engine, which Parnell found a spectacular sight, like Independence Day fireworks. The ship didn't seem to be in any hurry to leave the ground, he thought, as she kept rolling along the runway, down and down. As quickly as he grew concerned, there she went, easing into the air and gaining altitude. The flame of the engines illuminated the plane enough for him to see the wheels start to retract.

Parnell glanced at his watch and grabbed his clipboard to write down the departure time. From downstairs he heard the maintenance man's voice—Parnell didn't know his name—as he called up suddenly, "What was that just took off, an AT-6? What's a trainer doing taking off at night?"

The engine of the AT-6 Texan made a terrific high and distinctive roar, a sound heard all day every day around McCarran since Pearl Harbor. That's what the engines of Flight 3 had sounded like; they were working hard to get off the ground because of a heavy load.

"Nope," Parnell shouted down the stairs. "It was a DC-3."

There was a pause. "Huh," said the operations man, as if a little embarrassed to have guessed wrong.

At about two miles downrange to the south or southwest, the TWA ship radioed back, "TWA Flight 3 takeoff time, seven zero seven," and Parnell acknowledged.

On the radio he heard Air Traffic Control talking to TWA Control: "Traffic for TWA 3 is northeast-bound Western 10, estimated Daggett 7:59, climbing to 9,000."

"K.F.," had come the response from ATC.

In Las Vegas tower life had grown quiet again, and Parnell thought about his buddy at the movies and envied him that little bit of Hollywood excitement. As it was, the private settled back and waited for Western Flight 10 on what was in all respects a perfectly routine Friday night in January.

2

Perpetual Motion Machine

Aboard TWA Flight 3 on takeoff from McCarran Field, the soft-hearted, hard-charging, caffeine-fueled, self-promoting, profanity-laced, nicotine-addicted, business-oriented, and usually optimistic sexpot and perpetual motion machine known to the world as Carole Lombard could finally see the end of the road. A Hoosier from Fort Wayne, Indiana, she was born Jane Alice Peters, the third child of Frederick and Elizabeth Knight Peters. Fred had money courtesy of his father, John C. Peters of the hardware Peters. Bess came from money courtesy of the Knight banking interests. Money would practically grow on every tree in the vicinity of Carole Lombard her whole life, symbolized in childhood visits to the mansion of old J.C. on West Wayne Street and the larger-still plantation-style home of Charles Knight across the Maumee River on Spy Run Road. These were the playgrounds of Jane and her big brothers during her first six years of life. But having money didn't mean the kid had it easy.

"I always had the feeling that I couldn't keep up," she said of a youth spent in the shadow of her brothers, which is odd considering that Carole Lombard gave the appearance all her Hollywood life of being comfortable in her own skin. Whether posing in a negligee or bathing suit (and nobody in the 1930s struck more cheesecake poses than Lombard), dancing on-screen, shooting skeet, attending the Academy Awards dinner, camping in long johns, or launching *Gone With the Wind* with 150,000 people looking on, Lombard always seemed on the verge of saying, "You bet your ass I belong here."

But she had good reason *not* to grow up a powerhouse. Before Fred Peters and Bess Knight had married, he had nearly been killed in an industrial accident at the manufacturing plant owned by his father, J.C. Fred had been mashed up badly and nearly lost a leg. But it was the head injury that would plague him the rest of his life, and after his marriage to Bess and the birth of their three children, headaches crippled him, and then came seizures so frightening that Bess feared she would have to take the children away. The episodes didn't seem to be spells of epilepsy, the "falling sickness," but more on the order of blind rages for which there was then no cure, no warning, and absolutely no defense. Testing for chronic traumatic encephalopathy was generations away, but this condition may have been responsible for Fred's erratic, dangerous behavior.

It was the dark cloud in an otherwise bucolic turn-of-the-century life in Fort Wayne. Jane grew up idolizing her two big brothers, Freddy, nicknamed Fritz, and Stuart, known as Tootie after Jane's early attempts at Stuart. Endless tagging along with Fritz and Tootie hardened Jane into a tomboy the likes of Scout in Harper Lee's *To Kill a Mockingbird*.

Before her sixth birthday, Jane was packed up with brothers and mother for a vacation west to California, the farthest point in the United States from Fred and his problem. As funded by Bess's family, and later by Fred Peters himself, the group of four found an apartment in Los Angeles, and the vacation turned into a lifestyle.

Jane was a quiet child, fair haired, blue eyed, with no hint of the raucous and profane personality of her adult life. She was a thoughtful girl and a follower, easy to laugh, quick with a joke, and possessing a love of the silent pictures that drew her in and spawned ambition.

Mother Bess moved the family to a big house on South Harvard in the affluent Wilshire Boulevard district of Los Angeles, just around the corner from the Ambassador Hotel. Future director Delmer Daves was a childhood friend of Fred and Stuart Peters. "We were front-door friends," said Daves. "We sat on the steps and talked about whatever boys talked about. And Carole was the kid sister and really beneath our attention. She teased me about it later." Daves' expression grew sour and he added, "Carole at that time was not an attractive girl. She was scrawny."

In this neighborhood that Daves described as "rather elegant," the entire Peters family mingled with the Hollywood crowd. For Jane Peters, it was a magical place to grow up. "I can remember myself as a little girl," said Carole Lombard later, "standing at the corner of Hollywood and Vine watching my idol Gloria Swanson." Jane decided then, "I, too, was going to have a screen career, and I've never deviated from my purpose."

In 1921 at age twelve, Jane landed a role in a motion picture production called *A Perfect Crime* directed by up-and-coming Allan Dwan, then just three pictures away from directing action-adventure hero Douglas Fairbanks in *Robin Hood*. *A Perfect Crime* starred Monte Blue, an actor so successful in the movie business that by 1921 he had already appeared in nearly fifty pictures, including bit parts in three of the most important epics of the early cinema: *Birth of a Nation*, *Intolerance*, and *The Squaw Man*. *A Perfect Crime* became a one-off with no print surviving, and Jane continued to dream of life in the picture business, with no direct route to stardom in view. But it didn't hurt to know Dwan, Blue, and *A Perfect Crime*'s leading lady, Jacqueline Logan.

It also didn't hurt that Jane lived in the middle of boomtown Hollywood. At Virgil Junior High she met other future film stars, girls like Sally Eilers, and became best friends with Dixie Pantages of the Pantages theater chain. During her years at Fairfax High School, Jane joined the jazz age and turned flapper. She dated many boys, including the son of newspaper magnate William Randolph Hearst and the son of film director Thomas Ince. She also made pictures after signing a Fox Films contract and began earning sixty-five dollars a week. She hit the big time co-starring with western hero Buck Jones in three features in rapid succession and taking bit parts in many other productions in 1925. Fox had ordered a name change from plain Jane Peters; thus was born, at age sixteen, Carole Lombard—her name including an *e* on the end of traditional Carol. But in billing, the *e* would come and go for the next six years, until stardom finally made it stick. At each step it was the girl's face that triumphed, or rather the combination of face, ash-blonde hair, blue eyes, and a natural comfortable *something* alluding to the fact that wherever she was, this girl belonged.

A near miss in casting involved rising director John Ford. Then John Barrymore, the famous Broadway star who had made a successful transition to Hollywood in pictures like *Dr. Jekyll and Mr. Hyde* and *Beau Brummel*, called Miss Lombard and wanted to meet her. If Barrymore didn't invent the casting couch, he was one of its earliest practitioners, which forced the sharp-beyond-her-years Carole to engineer her way through the meeting with virtue intact. Barrymore called her in for a screen test, acted with her, and then hired her to star opposite him in his newest production, *Tempest*.

Soon, everything went right. Director Howard Hawks was about to make a big picture called *The Road to Glory* at Fox starring popular leading lady May McEvoy, and Lombard was assigned to a nice supporting part. She didn't understand the irony of the story line of the Hawks picture just yet: A woman suffers terrible injuries in an auto accident and relies on prayer to live through the experience.

At the beginning of 1926, Carole Lombard may have been the happiest girl in southern California, just past seventeen and shooting scenes for Howard Hawks on the Fox soundstages while about to be the great John Barrymore's leading lady.

One evening early in the year, the ingénue went on a date with one of her wealthy boyfriends, this time Harry "Heinie" Cooper, fifteen-year-old son of John Titus "Jack" Cooper. Jack was a vice president and later chairman of the Security First National Bank in Los Angeles. Jack's wife Austeene was the niece of Leslie Coombs Brand, founder of the city of Glendale. This was the gang into which Jane-turned-Carole had inserted herself, and to her, Heinie was just another boyfriend and they were on just another date. All these beaus were brash, good-looking, all-American boys with money. All were well suited to the ash blonde with the striking face and topaz blue eyes. But this night and this date would be different.

The life story of Hollywood's queen of screwball can be broken down into four freak accidents. The first, before she was born, had crippled her father physically and emotionally and had caused Bess and children to migrate to California. On this evening in the winter of 1926, Carole experienced the second when young hotshot Heinie Cooper lost control of his roadster on Santa Monica Boulevard and struck another car. Upon impact, Carole rocketed forward off the front seat and her head punched through the windshield in what she would later describe as "a fireworks explosion." Shards of plate glass pierced her face and lodged in her cheek, sliced through the skin under her left eyebrow and cut to the bone, and nearly severed her upper lip. By the time she ricocheted back onto the seat, hot blood had blinded her and was pulsing down her neck, dribbling off her chin and the end of her nose. In an instant, all of Carole Lombard's legwork had been undone, and even if she lived, her dreamed-of career in pictures was most certainly over.

3

The Radiating Halo

The Blue Diamond Mine sat atop a high bluff guarding the entrance to Red Rock Canyon, southwest of the growing city of Las Vegas, Nevada. Almost 9,000 people now inhabited Las Vegas, and things were looking up further with the opening of a sprawling motor hotel and lodge called El Rancho Vegas, located on Highway 91 just south of town.

The strip mining operation at Blue Diamond produced gypsum for wallboard and had been in operation for sixty years. The mine's workers and their families lived in a collection of company structures generously called the "town" of Blue Diamond, which sat low in the valley below the strip mine in Red Rock Canyon.

Darkness had recently cloaked the diggings on the bluff. It had been a cold day and promised to be a colder night, a Friday night, with the sky clear and full of stars. Fifty-year-old watchman Danlo Yanich was on his rounds, which didn't amount to much in a location this remote. There was a war on now, and facilities across the nation had been ordered on high alert due to the dangers of sabotage, but that figured to be on the coasts where shipping proved to be vulnerable in the ports of Los Angeles and New York. Dan didn't have any reason to figure that saboteurs would come stumbling up to the Blue Diamond Mine. If anything, they might be tempted to try for the Hoover Dam fifteen miles to the southeast.

It was with some security that Dan Yanich guarded the Blue Diamond mining operation, where intruders usually took the shape of wild burros or rattlesnakes rather than Japs or Nazis. Yanich had emigrated from Yugoslavia, and with no formal education he counted himself lucky to find a job at the mine in 1916, half his life ago. Food poisoning had laid him low earlier in the year, and for the past five months he had worked guard duty. Now he was getting better, slowly but surely.

Going on 7:20, Dan saw a plane flying over a bit to the south and west, not too far off and not too high considering that the mine sat way up on the bluff. Dan couldn't hear the engines of the plane for the incessant drone of the machinery behind his ears, but he remarked to himself that this big baby was flying lower than he was used to, even considering the bombers and fighters that zipped past on their way to the classified area off to the southwest where Army maneuvers took place almost daily.

Far below the bluff and away from the machinery, Calvin Harper, the head loader in the loading department, *was* able to hear the plane fly over. Harper was down by the cook house at the gypsum plant below the mine and just moments from punching out for the night when he heard the mystery plane, lower and louder than other planes. He gave the airship a glance over his shoulder and saw a streak of flaming exhaust from the right engine—the plane was so low in the sky that the fuselage blocked his view of the left engine—but the peculiar thing to Calvin was the sound of the engines. One growled steadily while the other seemed to come and go. He would hear it, then it would sputter to silence, then he would hear it again. Harper had ridden planes a lot back when he lived in Los Angeles, and he was a motor man who loved to fool around with his car engine and keep it humming. He noticed motors and didn't like the sound of that sputtering engine.

By now the plane had flown over; Harper's shift was about done, and his attention returned to getting out of there and warming up on this cold night. He vaguely heard the piston engines of the plane growling away into the darkness, working hard, their frenetic drone bouncing off the nearby cliffs and echoing through Red Rock Canyon behind him.

Dan Yanich looked over at the silhouette of the plane and its wingtip running lights, one red, one green, and thought it a majestic sight, a big twin-engine number that he figured to be a bomber or a DC-3. TWA and Western Airlines planes flew out of McCarran Field up at the northern edge of Las Vegas, but so did all manner of Army planes; whichever this was, it was flying south-southwest, maybe toward Los Angeles. Because of the war and the new blackout rules, far fewer lights burned in the area at night, including signal beacons for air traffic. Dan could see the signal beacon due east over at Arden, and it seemed as if the plane flew right over it. But the beacons high up on 8,000-foot Potosi Mountain to the south no longer flashed their comforting beams at night. He could see Potosi's black mountaintops jutting up high in the distance, standing blacker than the velvety sky above. Very high, treacherous mountains they were, where even the prospectors didn't go because of the cliffs and the loose footing and the boulders. Snow blanketed those mountains all winter and gave them a picture-postcard appearance, but make no mistake: One wrong step up on Potosi Mountain, or any of those mountains, and even the surest-footed man would be found only when buzzards pointed the way in the spring.

The Army fliers didn't seem to mind the blackout and its darkening of the beacon lights, and the pilots of those big silver passenger planes didn't seem to give a care about new rules either. Didn't they fly by radio beam anyway? This pilot wasn't any different. That big plane climbed like it meant business, cutting purposefully through a skyful of stars that sparkled faintly behind high, light cloud cover.

Inside the Blue Diamond Mine business office, purchasing

agent Ora Salyer sat cleaning up some figures in his books and heard the plane roar overhead. Planes simply didn't fly so near the diggings at night, and so it was notable when he heard this one now. It was close enough and demanding enough that he gave it some notice, especially when he could feel vibration from the engines in his desktop. He half wondered what this plane's story was and in what direction it was heading. It had to be an Army plane, it just had to be. When the machines weren't running, the only sound in an hour's time might be the howl of a coyote. This was, after all, unforgiving country, part desert and part jutting mountains. Cactus grew in the parched earth, and Joshua trees, and yucca plants, and not much else. Hearty folks lived hereabouts—one had to be hearty to get by in southern Nevada. Then the sound of the plane receded, and Salyer's mind went back to his figures.

Yanich had moved on through the diggings down toward one of the conveyor belts, which were still in operation this late in the evening. Salyer kept at his bookkeeping, in the stillness of a perfectly ordinary, cold, and deepening January night.

Ten or so miles due south, off an old mining road in the foothills of Potosi Mountain, Charlie and Ruth Hawley had finished pitching their tent and now warmed themselves by a roaring campfire in preparation for spending the night in a desolate spot with high hills on either side. They were in the process of cutting firewood for the remainder of the winter and had half loaded their pickup truck when darkness settled in.

They sat in the quiet, the only sound the crackling fire, and stared into the flames. Ruth was about to retire to the tent when she heard a plane flying low overhead. The sound was loud enough that both looked skyward into the starry night but could not see an airplane.

"They're coming after us, Charlie," said Ruth deadpan, as she climbed to her feet.

"Well, they have to be wonderin' 'bout a fire in the middle of nowhere, I suppose," said Charlie. "We have to be the only people for miles."

"Not flying very high up, is it?" she said of the plane matter-of-factly, and left her husband by the fire. He kept looking heavenward.

"For the mountains, no, it sure ain't," Charlie murmured, but his wife was already gone. "Not high up at all." And then the plane came into view directly over their fire with a high-pitched mountain lion's growl that shook the ground, a rumble he could feel in his bones. The engines seemed to be working hard, very hard. And no, the plane wasn't as high up as a man would expect.

Charlie Hawley had a perfect view of it, looking straight up into its belly, and the entire time he watched, the plane seemed to be turning left, left, left. Not much of a turn, but a little—enough to be noticeable. He could see the twin glow of lights streaking forward from the plane, and he could feel those angry engines.

Inside the tent Ruth was too damn cold to go back outside and watch some airplane. She buried herself under her bedclothes and contented herself to wait out those loud motors and a vibration deep enough to rattle her teeth.

Charlie watched the plane fly on over yonder hill, and then the sound of the engines grew distant and the echo spread out and no longer sounded quite so angry.

Ruth began to relax a little as the bedclothes around her body warmed. She kept listening to a now-more-agreeable set of airplane engines out in the distance. It was almost peaceful. She had never been on an airplane; she didn't figure she ever *would* be on one. But somebody was up there heading someplace, and that was the sound of their progress, that plane now some distance downrange. It was kind of comforting, the thought of people around, even if they sat way up there flying around in the sky.

Then the sound stopped. Not as if it had faded away. It just stopped. Angry engines one second, and nothing the next. As if a light switch had been clicked, the engine noise was replaced by the dead silence of Potosi Mountain at night.

Strange, thought Charlie. The whole thing with that airplane: strange. Now all was still, so very still, when just a few moments ago there had been such commotion.

Ten miles north of the Hawleys, Dan Yanich had a different view. Yanich had seen a flash out the corner of his eye, and the ground trembled under his feet; the desk before Ora Salyer vibrated a bit more. Seconds later Salyer heard the faintest of rumbles in the distance. Like far-off thunder, except that it was a clear night and there weren't any storms.

Salyer was used to the reports of guns from hunters as he sat in the office, or from the Army boys practicing on the range to the south. It was always difficult trying to figure the origin of a gunshot or an explosion in the surrounding mountains, but whatever he had just heard tonight, and wherever, it seemed to be very distant but also sizable, as if maybe the Axis had dropped a bomb or dynamited the Hoover Dam.

Salyer scrambled up from his desk and slipped outside, joining Yanich there as the watchman frowned toward the south and said, his accent thick, "I think dat airplane maybe drop a flare."

Salyer stared off into the blackness to the south, and knew at once that this was no flare. He gaped at a fireball with flames licking upward into a high and spectacular orange beacon on Potosi Mountain. The view of both Ora and Dan was unobstructed, and that fire burned like something out of a nightmare, like something biblical, the flames reaching up what must have been hundreds of feet into the black sky, glowing yellow and orange, their light refracting off the smoke above, which gave the radiating effect of a halo. All around the fireball at center, the snow on the mountain glistened like gemstones, and Yanich saw the effect as utterly beautiful. They could make out trees burning as well, despite the fact that a storm had just dumped a couple feet of snow on the peaks of

Potosi, also known as Double Up Peak, also known as Double or Nothing Peak, and Table Mountain. It had lots of names because people respected it; it was a deadly place.

They wondered what in the world…

But deep down they knew, and their stomachs turned over: the growling plane that had flown past. Something had gone wrong with that plane. It didn't seem plausible because of the ferocity of the explosion and that fire up yonder, which seemed to burn much brighter and hotter than the aggregate of one airplane. It made no sense, yet something had set the jagged peak of Potosi aflame. And that big plane *had* just flown over. Only one explanation made any sense: It was an Army plane loaded with munitions.

Salyer ran inside and called the police station over in Las Vegas. All of a sudden, this particular Friday evening had become anything but ordinary.

4

The Long Road

What has this Cooper boy done to my beautiful daughter? thought Bess Peters—better known by now as Petey thanks to tempestuous Carole's nicknames—as the formerly pretty now bloody girl lay on a bed while a doctor dug shards of glass out of her face. But Petey was a woman who had endured years of life with a dangerous man, meaning she could handle this situation now. Before letting that doctor begin the task of sewing her daughter back together, Bess demanded answers to some tough questions. This girl is in pictures, and if you sew her delicate face up as you would an arm or a leg that's been cut, what will it look like? What about this plastic surgery business they're talking about? What can this type of surgery do for my girl? Who are these surgeons and where can I find one—there's no time to lose!

When the physician produced no ready answers, Bess got on the phone and worked her contacts and friends of friends. Finally, she was led to a plastic surgeon whom she managed to reach. She explained the situation. The doctor agreed to hurry in and operate, and he gave instructions by phone to the attending physician regarding preparation of the patient and operating room so that all would be ready when he arrived.

A long cosmetic surgical procedure followed without the benefit of anesthetic—Jane Peters turned Carole Lombard paid this exacting price after being advised that there was one chance, and a slim one, of saving that ingénue face from permanent disfigurement. The surgeon must sew with tiny stitches into a fully awake and alert patient to keep the facial muscles in proper position.

She endured stitch after stitch as the number of minutes went into two digits and then three. Through the length of the procedure and despite constant pain, she didn't crack or allow her jaw to slacken. At surgery's end, the doctor warned her not to get her hopes up; the odds were very long. He instructed her not to move her head—for months. It must be strapped down for optimal healing, he told her. The dressings would change but not the position of that blonde head if she were to have any chance to save her looks—and she was told to prepare for the worst: She was through; she would have no career in front of the camera.

A catharsis for Carole may have resulted from roots in the Baha'i faith, which Elizabeth Peters had practiced since early in her California tenure. Baha'i taught that all religions emanate from the same God and that people were put on earth to learn, to know God, and to serve humanity. Carole's acceptance of Baha'i teachings is documented as far back as 1922 and became a source of hope and inspiration during her torturous convalescence, head lashed down. She was limited to a liquid diet, with the doctor visiting daily to rub olive oil into the scars.

The part in Barrymore's *Tempest* came and went, and the Fox contract lapsed without renewal. Carole admitted that early on she wanted to die. She couldn't imagine being deformed. She didn't want to live without the dream of stardom that had taken hold deep in her brain, the thrill of seeing Gloria Swanson on a street corner; the imaginings that she *was* Gloria Swanson; the intoxication of meetings with John Barrymore.

The extent of Carole's injuries and the panic over their impact was revealed by the lawsuit filed by Petey and Carole against Heinie Cooper and his parents, Mr. and Mrs. John Cooper, claiming the injuries she received because of Heinie's negligent driving on Santa Monica Boulevard "permanently defaced her beauty and completely shattered her screen ambitions." And when suit was filed, this was precisely how the Peters women felt—that Carole's career was over. Petey also expressed no regrets for trying to tap into the Cooper and Leslie Coombs Brand empires to offset the substantial medical bills.

And yet, *were* Carole's screen ambitions shattered? Slowly her focus shifted from the likelihood that the surgery couldn't possibly succeed to the chance the surgeon had given her and the notion that she *might* be able to make it back. The dream that took hold involved rising up and out of her bed and getting on with life at full speed. At faster than full speed. Carole read biographies of great actresses as well as movie magazines and plays, and kept her mind active every day. On the long road to recovery, her ambition deepened.

She always had been a high-energy girl who could never sit still and now was forced to turn the energy inward, to healing, to wisdom. In the end, an inch-long scar dug up through one eyebrow, and the hair would never grow there. An inch-and-a-half-long scar resembling a misplaced dimple remained on her cheek, and a scar drew its way across her upper lip that "like Elizabeth Taylor's mole, only accentuated her beauty," said close friend Alice Marble. Carole would bear these scars for the remainder of her life. In some ways they would define her, force her to grow up, gaze into the mirror, and accept that sometimes bad things happen. As she would phrase it to Garson Kanin years later, "Another inch, half an inch maybe, a turn of my head and my whole fuckin' career could've been over." But she had had that inch to spare and she had not bled to death, which had been a real possibility. She had survived, this time. The "fireworks explosion" had come without warning. In a second her life had changed, in a second she had faced death, so who knew when death would need to be faced again? It was a strange sort of maturity for a girl about to turn eighteen, but it also caused her to make the days count for something.

Lombard biographer Larry Swindell credits Bess Peters with raising her daughter to be an independent thinker and a take-charge personality. The two had always been close but now formed a bond to see Carole through the crisis of losing all the ground she had made in Hollywood. When finally back on her feet, she learned how far and wide the news had traveled about her disfigurement. She was in a literal sense "damaged goods," with studio bosses and directors fearing that her talked-about facial scars would look like the transcontinental railroad and some sort of freak show on a theatrical screen.

Lombard knew better. She sought advice on makeup and on lighting and styled her hair into a bob that lessened the visual impact of the scar on her cheek. She hung out with her friends again, and dated, and visited her haunt of haunts, the Cocoanut Grove at the Ambassador Hotel on Wilshire Boulevard with a group of friends her age that included the well to do and would-be stars and starlets. "They were drinking and smoking and fooling around," said Carole Sampeck, director of the Carole Lombard Archive Foundation. "That's what they did."

It was here, through the social side of the business and not the pavement-pounding side, that Lombard got her break. Former schoolmate and actress Sally Eilers had a tip that Mack Sennett, king of the two-reeled comedies, was looking for a new girl for his Bathing Beauties concept pictures that had been invented by Sennett director Eddie Cline. Sally, who had been a classmate of Carole's during a weekly stint at the Nolkes Dramatic School years earlier, where both learned acting for the stage and camera, was going to see Sennett and wanted Carole to accompany her.

Mack Sennett, a towering man of six-foot-two, was one of the founding fathers of Hollywood. He had formed his Keystone Production Company in 1912, which included screen comedians Roscoe "Fatty" Arbuckle, Mabel Normand, and Charlie Chaplin. The bumbling, stumbling Keystone Kops were Sennett's brainchild, and soon he joined the other founding fathers of Hollywood, D.W. Griffith and Thomas Ince, in forming Triangle Films, where he first worked with the silent star Gloria Swanson. By the time Lombard met him, he was making Bathing Beauties comedies and continuing to perfect a model of eighteen-minute, two-reeled short subjects that would be followed by Laurel and Hardy and then the enduring surrealists, the Three Stooges. Comedy short subjects had evolved into a critical part of an evening's picture-show entertainment, along with serials, newsreels, and full-length features.

When Carole Lombard met Mack Sennett, she had never played comedy, and he didn't know if she had a funny bone in her scrawny, five-foot-four-inch body. This was Sennett's concern— could the girl play comedy? He shrugged off the scars in her cheek, lip, and eyebrow because they weren't shooting drama here with any sort of reliance on close-ups. When a member of the troupe slipped on a banana peel or took a pie in the face, it needed to be a wide or a medium shot. Sennett relied on those shots; only the reactions needed to be anything closer, and these were just full-on close-ups of the talent and not the romantic type of clinch close-ups that Lombard need worry about.

All she wanted, she told him, was a chance, and Mack Sennett gave it to her at $50 a week. It was even less than her modest Fox contract had paid, but it was paying work in the picture business for a scarred-up has-been of eighteen, and she gladly took it. After all, movie queen Gloria Swanson had gone on from working with Mack Sennett to make great pictures like *Zaza*, *Stage Struck*, and many others.

Lombard joined a comedy troupe that was more like a family and included girls who were pretty, or older, or short, or fat. Sennett needed them all for his physical brand of comedy, and Lombard attached herself to the "fat girl," Madalynne Field, just a year older, very tall, and naturally husky. The teens hit it off immediately, and formed a friendship that would endure. Carole had become a nickname fiend. Nicknames were fun and verbal shorthand for a girl who had lots of words to say all at once. Fred was Fritz and Stuart was Tootie. Then her mother, Bess Peters, became "Petey" or "Tots," and now Carole gave Madalynne Field the innocuous nickname of "Fieldsie," calling to mind a benign spirit. But the son born to Fieldsie ten years later would caution, "Mother was not one to be dominated," said motion picture and television director Richard Lang. "I called her Captain Bligh when I was growing up.... Mother was six feet tall and weighed 250. Being heavy's a very personal problem; when you're making a living off your infirmity, it gets to you after a while."

Sennett knew there was humor in pain, whether emotional or physical. If anything, he found this Lombard girl too glamorous for his players. He ordered her to gain some weight—Sennett liked his girls a deal curvier than natural athlete Carole. Depending on the role, her hair and wardrobe would be winsome or not, but she emerged in his two reelers as a personality that the camera loved. Audiences found her engaging as a heroine who overcame every comedic obstacle. By the end of their time together, Lombard had become Sennett's most versatile and valued player. One publicity photo of a scantily clad, sultry-looking Carole contained a caption that typified the selling of the ingénue at the time and the ongoing problem with spelling her name: "Miss Carolle Lombard is smiling. Why should she not? She has been chosen by Mack Sennett to act greater parts in his newest comedies and that's something. Wasn't Gloria once a Bathing Girl?"

Lombard would go on to make a steady line of Sennett pictures in the next two years. She would get paid to "work" when all she really did was hang out with a gang she grew to love, much of her time spent on the beach, a Bathing Beauty in a swimsuit. Between takes she paced incessantly, gabbed uncontrollably, growing into her personality. The Sennett shorts taught her timing, how and when to react, and how long to hold her take. She learned how to underplay, and overplay, depending on the situation. She learned about physical comedy from masters.

Finally, at the end of October 1927, the lawsuit against Heinie Cooper and family went before a judge. Carole was able to testify about Heinie's recklessness at age fifteen behind the wheel of a roadster and to show the scars on her face, and yet the initial panic of mother and daughter that Carole's career had been ruined by the scarring was mitigated by the fact that she now possessed a Sennett contract and had been working steadily for the past three months. The ruling held in favor of the plaintiffs, but the $35,000 in damages sought by the Peters was reduced to a settlement in the amount of $3,000 and life went on for all involved.

It was a time of technological advance, not just in the infant field of plastic surgery that had restored Carole Lombard's livelihood but everywhere. A young aviator of twenty-five named Charles Lindbergh flew nonstop from New York to Paris in May 1927 in a single-wing aircraft. Six pilots who had tried previously died in the attempt, but "Lucky Lindy" did it and claimed the Orteig Prize and its $25,000 cash award for flying across the Atlantic. Now "air mail" was zipping across the sky in planes, and it was envisioned that soon humans would be zipping across the sky as well, flying as paying passengers from city to city. Like on a train, but faster. Much faster.

Hollywood felt the crushing embrace of technology thanks to the four Warner brothers when sound came to previously silent pictures through the voice of Al Jolson in *The Jazz Singer*. Soon after Jolson drove audiences to a frenzy with his unexpected line "you ain't heard nothin' yet," Mack Sennett's empire crumbled, and Lombard nearly found herself in limbo once again as just another out-of-work actress—and a scarfaced actress at that. But with the resourcefulness of cliffhanger serial star Pearl White,

Carole managed to grasp a lifeline by landing a role at Pathé Pictures in a film called *Show Folks*, and once on the Pathé lot, the young blonde attracted the hormonal interest of Joseph P. Kennedy, later father of a U.S. president and two U.S. senators, and in 1928 a president himself, of Pathé Pictures. Kennedy brokered power in Hollywood at that time, and in the course of his dealings the "family man" had begun a well-documented affair with none other than Gloria Swanson.

Kennedy arrived on the Pathé scene with the studio foundering. His strategy for salvation: Follow the Metro Goldwyn Mayer Studios model and develop a young stable of stars with faces and voices for the sound era.

Carole Lombard, then nineteen and wise in the ways of Hollywood, managed to land a meeting with the big man in his office, but then Boston-born-and-bred Joe Kennedy had no reason *not* to meet with a good-looking and ambitious young starlet, if only to see what might develop. He was then thirty-nine and possessing the same hot blood that would get his sons in trouble decades later. The official version of the meeting had Lombard giving Kennedy what-for. When they began discussing a possible contract, Lombard's past biographers maintain that Kennedy said she needed to lose the weight Sennett had ordered her to gain. In turn, so the story goes, she offered in her wise-cracking style that Kennedy could also stand to drop a few pounds. It's a colorful legend and a less-than-credible yarn.

"I've always been uncomfortable with the Kennedy story," said Lombard expert Carole Sampeck. "It just doesn't make sense. She may have had the chutzpah then, as a basic part of her personality among friends, but you don't go for a job interview and set out to antagonize your potential employer. She wouldn't be throwing her professional weight around then, simply because she didn't really have any at that point."

However she arrived at a deal, Lombard walked out of Kennedy's office with a one-year (with options for more), $400-per-week Pathé Studios contract that took effect on her twentieth birthday, October 6, 1928. According to such contracts, the studio had exclusive rights to use that actor or to loan the actor to another studio, usually in trade for a player with a similar contract. During the next year, in a succession of pictures at Pathé and a couple on loan-out to the Fox Studios, she worked on a variety of projects that saw her through the transition from silents to sound, playing parts that showed a general progression toward importance.

During production of a picture called *The Great Gabbo* on the Pathé lot, Carole stopped by a set to watch the famous Prussian director Erich von Stroheim at work. The bald-headed Hussar, proponent of the casting couch, watched Lombard right back: "Today I went on von Stroheim's set," she reported, "and got myself introduced as if I were just a poor little girl trying to get along. Von didn't know me from Eve and offered to give me a few days' work as an East African tart—this is if I looked the part well enough in one of the costumes they had. It was a riot."

Lombard couldn't take von Stroheim up on his offer since she had already begun work as the top-billed female opposite leading man Robert Armstrong in a newspaper crime drama called *Big News*, so she didn't tart it up for the horny Prussian. Not that she would have minded—work was work, and it could never be too plentiful. Luckily, Joe Kennedy picked up the option on her contract for a second year and assigned her to Cecil B. DeMille, known even then as Hollywood's director of spectacular motion pictures. His body of work would ultimately include not one but two versions of *The Ten Commandments*. DeMille was in 1929 preparing his first talking picture, called *Dynamite*, to be made at Pathé Studios. Lombard's role wasn't big, but it was a DeMille picture and therefore the part could be important.

Another famous man also wanted Lombard. Howard Hughes, just a couple of years Lombard's senior, had been laboring on his flying epic of the Great War *Hell's Angels* for two years with Norwegian-born Greta Nissen his leading lady. As Howard waited weeks and months for just the right weather to stage his flying sequences, sound replaced silence and suddenly Nissen's part needed to be re-shot with an actress who could speak English well enough to be understood in the United States. Hughes saw a photo of Lombard and requested permission from Pathé to test the ingénue for *Hell's Angels*.

As usual, Howard got the girl, converting his social awkwardness and lack of conversation into a bad-boy asset that made women want to satisfy him in any way possible. Of course, the bad boy's wealth didn't hurt or the power he wielded in Hollywood. Whatever Carole's level of sexual sophistication prior to the onset of summer 1929, she certainly knew the ropes by Christmas. She fell hard for Howard Hughes and dearly wanted that female lead in *Hell's Angels*.

It was a time when Hughes ruled the skies, gobbling up every stunt pilot and flyable airplane in southern California. More than 2,000 miles away, Lt. James Doolittle was making aviation news of his own. A week after bailing out of his plane in an air race over Cleveland, Doolittle advanced the science of flight by years when he took off from Mitchel Field on Long Island, flew his plane straight and level, and landed safely on instruments alone, with no visual flight references and guided only by radio beam. The feat enabled commercial passenger flight in any weather because now pilots could either fly "contact," using ground references, or on "instruments," relying on their gauges and headsets to successfully navigate and land passengers and cargo. Thirteen short years later, this same James Doolittle, now a U.S. Army Air Forces colonel, would mastermind the first United States air raid on Tokyo, Japan, just four months after the bombing of Pearl Harbor.

Lombard the voracious reader might have seen a story about Doolittle in the newspaper. It's more likely she had her hands full with life at a studio the size of Pathé Pictures. Somewhere in this period, during her time under Pathé contract, she adopted the salty vocabulary of a dock worker, and according to her brother Fred Peters, she did it deliberately as a way to level the playing field with the men then in charge, most of whom were wolves at the least, with some of them full-fledged, unashamed sexual predators. In short, she intended harsh language to shut down unwanted advances, and she wore it like a suit of armor. Her friend Jill Winkler once asked Carole about the swearing and she replied, "Oh, that's not me swearing, honey. That's Carole Lombard. Jane Peters would never dream of using language like that." Carole believed that Jane Peters couldn't hold her own in Hollywood, whereas brash Carole Lombard could. As she once admitted in an interview, and it was a telling statement, "I try to be what people want me to be."

Said Margaret Tallichet Wyler, former actress and decades-long wife of director William Wyler, of Lombard's four-letter vocabulary, "Even then I understood that it had begun as a defense mechanism. She could tell stories about crazy parties as a very young girl, where she had been tossed into the wildest of surroundings. I felt then and feel now that it was a defense she built up not to be as vulnerable as she probably was." Wyler referred to Lombard's colorful language as "working jargon" and said, "I don't remember her talking that way when she was with her mother and brothers. You didn't feel that it was something she was born with. It was a tool she had adopted."

At Pathé, she began work on *Dynamite* and ran afoul of the autocratic C.B. DeMille right away. On this first production with bulky, uncooperative sound recording equipment, the director and his art director, Mitchell Leisen, proceeded with great uncertainty about capturing audio for their picture. DeMille shot one scene with Lombard but didn't like her voice or delivery. He also didn't care for her comfort on the set or the self-conscious foul language.

Particularly, the steady stream of foul language and her you-bet-your-ass-I-belong-here attitude annoyed him. Such an attitude didn't fly on Mr. DeMille's soundstage.

Said Lombard to the press, perhaps hopefully, "I'm getting accustomed to C.B. I'll say we get along just fine now, but at first I was awed by him." But Cecil B. DeMille never shared that awe and dumped Carole Lombard from the cast of his first "talking picture." In another few months, soon after the stock market crash of 1929, Howard Hughes dismissed Lombard from consideration for *Hell's Angels* when he beheld the even younger, blonder, ambitious young actress named Jean Harlow, face unscarred, who was working in two-reeled comedies for Hal Roach. Lombard was dumped, not just as DeMille actress but as Hughes girlfriend. Suddenly, the young starlet could claim the distinction of being fired by two Hollywood titans in succession. Upon reflection, she decided that both rejections cut as deeply as the glass of that exploding windshield.

Then Joe Kennedy made it a clean sweep. He wouldn't admit it and blamed the bad economy for failure to pick up the option for Carole's third year at Pathé, but in truth Constance Bennett, a new young, blonde star had come aboard from Broadway, and the studio needed to divest itself of other, similar blondes.

It was now the beginning of 1930, and Lombard found herself out on the street once again, but not for long. The girl with the easy-to-like personality had friends, contacts, confederates, and spies all over town. In short order, she made a lavish western with recent Academy Award winner Warner Baxter at Fox Studios and then secured a featured role in a comedy starring the popular and boyish leading man Buddy Rogers at Paramount Studios on Wilshire Boulevard in Hollywood. It was here that Lombard found a new home and would sign the most important document of her career, a standard seven-year studio contract that started her at $375 a week just months after the stock market crash known as Black Friday had wiped out lives and fortunes. She was now, and would remain for quite a while, the exclusive property of Paramount Pictures.

By this, her fourth studio contract, she knew how to pitch herself and how to bargain. She was a well-connected and politically savvy veteran of motion pictures and the Jazz Age. Having been a tomboy all her life, aligned closely with her brothers, she sported male sensibilities regarding everything from business to sports to carnal knowledge. She was building her brand organically and now had become a Paramount Player and a highly eligible and active bachelorette at age twenty-one while still living at home with her brothers and mother.

She counted among her lovers in the early Paramount days a young scriptwriter named Preston Sturges, who had done the screenplay for her picture *Fast and Loose*. The highly intelligent, well-to-do, ten-years-older Sturges fit Lombard's bill, as did fading publishing mogul Horace Liveright, twenty-five years her senior, with whom she had a short liaison before he was dismissed by Paramount.

Said Lombard, "I rapidly outgrew even older boys and gradually my escorts became men. Mature men. They were the only ones who could talk my language...."

At her new studio she appeared in a few light comedy features before stepping up to an "A," or major, studio picture called *Man of the World*, starring one of the hottest leading men in Hollywood, William Powell.

The arrival of sound in motion pictures had provided audience access to his caramel voice, suave delivery, and self-assured manner. Powell now began a string of pictures that would cast him as a jewel thief or other provocateur, or a tough-guy detective. In just three more years he would first play the most successful character of his career, Nick Charles, opposite Myrna Loy's Nora Charles in The Thin Man mystery series at MGM.

Sparks flew between Lombard and Powell from the first rehearsals, and a healthy infatuation catapulted them to the nearest bedroom. He was almost forty; she was twenty-two, making pictures by day and playing the field by night and determined not to marry. "I think marriage is dangerous," she told him. "It spoils beautiful friendships that might have lasted for years."

Anchored by a magnificent Paramount Pictures contract negotiated by his Hollywood superagent, Myron Selznick, Powell had the means to woo Lombard, and he didn't kid around with that wooing. Soon, she learned the true power of the mature man, if not with the imported perfume or the diamond-encrusted jade cigarette case, then surely with the Cadillac for Christmas. She tried to tell him: Sex was fine, but couldn't they agree to leave marriage out of the discussion?

She worked steadily and knocked off three more pictures at Paramount and then was cast with Powell again in another romantic drama, this one called *Ladies' Man*. The fact that the ingénue and the older sophisticate were now constant companions and obvious bedmates earned space in fan magazines and newspaper columns, and Lombard, now so obviously a sucker for the rich and the powerful, was sunk. The wedding took place at the end of June 1931, and the happy couple sailed off for a Hawaiian honeymoon. And then things went to hell right away.

Lombard got sick on the boat, either from working too hard for too long or from the nerves of being a bride. Or was it the boat? Or was it her own prophecy that they shouldn't marry? She stayed sick the length of the honeymoon with revolving ailments. When they returned to Hollywood, she remained ill with viruses of various sorts and pleurisy—she got what there was to get.

That was one problem. Beyond that, William Powell's closest friends included Hollywood's old guard of silent stars and their wives, some of whom had made the transition to sound pictures and some of whom hadn't. None of them took to the plain-talking Mrs. Powell; the lightweight; the gold digger with the foul mouth.

Then other difficulties presented themselves. Paramount Pictures hit the skids, and some of its stars went public with accusations that the studio had been cooking the books. Those madcap Marx Brothers found the situation quite unamusing, and Groucho, Zeppo, Harpo, and Gummo hopped a train east for a reckoning with the New York bosses. Soon, one of Paramount's biggest stars, William Powell, flew the coop for a lucrative $6,000-pcr-week contract at Warner Bros. of Burbank negotiated by Myron Selznick. Suddenly, Bill and Carole were no longer workplace comrades with a standing date for lunch.

In a deadly logical career move, Carole filled the void left by Bill's departure from Paramount by hiring as an accountant/personal assistant/secretary not some bookish prude, but pal Madalynne Field. Fieldsie's career as the "fat girl," the only movie work she was ever going to get, had died with the Sennett Studio, and Fieldsie was now out on the street. Seen with her sleek, blonde best friend, Fieldsie became the "what's wrong with this picture" aside and seemed harmless enough. But Fieldsie possessed a shrewd business sense and kept razor-sharp numbers. "She handled all the accounts," said son Richard Lang of his mother's lifelong affinity for balancing the books. "She had taken accounting somewhere along the line. Her checkbook wasn't a checkbook; it was a huge ledger. Every year she would demand from the IRS a letter saying everything was clear, and she'd frame it and hang it on the wall."

It would be misleading to call the hiring of Madalynne Field as Lombard's secretary the first of what would become many of "Carole's Causes"—the democratic spreading of love and generosity around town, the democratic helping of the down and out. Lombard benefited in many professional and personal ways from having Fieldsie close by as confidante and bodyguard.

Lombard also acquired another business partner at this time, or to be precise, Myron Selznick acquired Lombard as a client primarily because he represented William Powell, which made the signing of Lombard a favor to a successful client. The first thing Selznick did was to solidify Lombard's deal at Paramount. In effect, she now held a no-cut contract that didn't need to be renewed by option. Paramount was now married to Carole just about as legally as William Powell was. These three unlikely confederates—Carole, Fieldsie, and Myron Selznick—soon became a shrewd Hollywood think tank when it came to crafting Carole Lombard's career.

And they would need to be. Just after popular melodrama queen Kay Francis followed William Powell's path from Paramount to Warner Bros. because she sensed payroll might not be met, Paramount went bankrupt. A new regime assumed power and started making hard financial decisions. Lombard, a modest star but hardly a household name, was saved from unemployment only by the new ironclad contract that Myron had just negotiated for her. Paramount started shopping her around town to see if another studio wanted to assume her contract, but the attachment of a shark like Myron Selznick to Lombard's name assured lukewarm interest. She ended up on a one-shot loan-out at the Columbia studios on nearby Gower Street and portrayed a hooker in a risqué pre-Code drama called *Virtue*, which co-starred Mayo Methot, who would meet and then marry struggling actor Humphrey Bogart a few years later.

Pre-Code pictures include movies like *Virtue*, which featured a tawdry plotline and women in stockings and garter belts who "would do anything to get ahead." Lombard had already gained a reputation for going braless on-screen, acquiring cult status at the grindhouses for nipples poking through slinky dresses and displaying lots of leg. Fieldsie and Myron had caught on to what the public wanted from Lombard and advised her to play it sexy on-screen. The result: Carole had never enjoyed a certified hit; neither had her pictures lost money, which was saying something in an America gripped by a deepening Depression.

Back within the walls of Paramount, she portrayed a librarian in a romance called *No Man of Her Own* opposite MGM's thirty-one-year-old sensation, Clark Gable. A sort of *Music Man* without the music, *No Man of Her Own* concerned the reaction of the single, repressed librarian to a new con man in town. Gable's vibe at this early point in his Hollywood career was enacting a growling tough guy, usually named Ace, or Rid, or Rod, and this time Babe. It was his first picture after making MGM's sensational *Red Dust*, a sexy and saucy pre-Code picture that had teamed him with Jean Harlow, the blonde bombshell who had stolen Howard Hughes from Lombard.

No Man of Her Own became the only picture with both Clark Gable and Carole Lombard except for a silent comedy called *The Plastic Age*, starring sex symbol Clara Bow and featuring both Carole and Clark in bit parts. Clark didn't meet Carole back then, but she had been among the throng of Los Angelinos mesmerized by Gable's performance on the stage as a condemned convict in *The Last Mile* in 1930, and Carole and Clark certainly got along now as co-workers at Paramount. Clark Gable liked women, and Carole Lombard liked men. Each enjoyed the company of the other while making *No Man of Her Own*. Since both were married at the time, neither seemed to be interested in a "test drive," and they parted friends after Lombard presented Gable with a ham emblazoned with his star portrait. It was a move made for the fan magazines and brainstormed by the team of Fieldsie and Selznick.

By coincidence and not because of the temporary presence of Clark Gable, the marriage of Powell and Lombard finished the unraveling it had begun right after "I do." The sexual libertine spawned by anything-goes Hollywood and encouraged by her mother, the unconventional Petey, wasn't shy in saying that she found the union less than satisfactory. Soon she headlined the article "Carole Lombard Tells Why Hollywood Marriages Can't Succeed" for a fan magazine. With the brashness of youth, she shrugged that it might be easy for the garden-variety housewife "to put a fence around her heart," but in the picture business a woman was constantly in front of cameras with desirable men by the dozen and required to "syndicate her charm." With William Powell, a man sixteen years her senior whom she called "Popsie," she confessed to marriage making the walls press in around her until she found herself "breathless with the loss of freedom."

She also found her new husband lacking ambition for better work on-screen and believed that he had begun to "coast" at Warner Bros. When Harry Warner, the business mind, and younger brother Jack Warner, the on-site studio boss, hit rough financial waters and lost an astounding $14 million in 1932, they asked William Powell to take a thirty-three percent pay cut from $6,000 to $4,000 per week. He capitulated. Carole called him "lazy" in an interview, but Powell didn't need to work so very hard; he was William Powell. For his part, Bill found living with Carole Lombard no picnic. She was always down with something, whether seasickness or pleurisy or flu, or more flu, and Lombard's menstrual cycle was endless to the extent that she admitted maybe three days a month that were clear. "God has me built backwards," she would say. "There's only a couple of days a month I'm not bleeding." When she wasn't sick she was working at Paramount on one picture after another, and Powell rarely saw the woman who was supposed to be his wife. When he did, she wanted to hit the town, and suddenly the generation gap exhausted them both.

The separation, with Carole moving back to Petey's tudor-influenced home on Rexford Drive in Beverly Hills, was inevitable. Brimming with frustration, Lombard stated flatly that the Powell-Lombard exercise in marriage had been "a waste of time—his and mine." Trouble was, they liked each other; they always would.

Lombard kept working. She made a picture about racetracks called *From Hell to Heaven* with comic actor Jack Oakie, and then a paranormal spook show far ahead of its time called *Supernatural*, which dove deep into a tale of ghosts and possession. The thoroughly New Age Lombard, a believer in psychics and astrology, had no problem with the plot line of *Supernatural* but found the professionalism of director Victor Halperin so vexing that at one point she reached out her arms and shouted to the heavens, "Who do I have to screw to get off this picture?" Since that day in 1933, this plea uttered by Carole Lombard may hold a record as the most quoted on-set line in Hollywood history.

Despite a hurly-burly schedule of pictures at Paramount, Carole found time to engage the process of divorce from William Powell. She and brother Tootie took their first plane ride with famous aviator Roscoe Turner from Los Angeles airfield to Lake Tahoe to set up six weeks' residence in preparation for a "quickie" Nevada divorce. Living at Tahoe at that time was a thirteen-year-old boy named Bobby Stack with a mop of wavy blonde hair. Well-heeled Bobby took one look at the blonde movie star eleven years his senior and fell in love. During her six weeks at Tahoe, Carole spent time every day with Stack, an avid skeet shooter even then and soon to become national champion. With young Bobby Stack as her coach, Lombard learned the ways of the shotgun. It was a skill that would pay off later as would her association with the boy who would grow up to be Academy Award-nominated actor Robert Stack. Until the day he died, Stack would be in love with her and never attempt to hide it.

Lombard's day in court divorcing Powell had been scripted by Carole and Bill in tandem. She would agree to testify against him only if he agreed to every word, revealing an unorthodox level of respect and loyalty for two people ending their union. Before the judge she stated that William Powell had been cross and cruel, and in six minutes they became exes. She flew back to Los Angeles and grumped to her pals in the press, who wanted her to kid and vamp for photographs, "I'm not at all happy about this, you know, so I'm not going to give you a smile I don't mean."

She went back to work on one Paramount picture after another and returned to Columbia to work as well. Then she met a man. Not a "lazy" older man like Popsie Powell, but an intriguing younger man on his way to superstardom, a man full of passion and full of himself. Before long their relationship would result in Freak Accident Number Three, and even a tough cookie like Carole Lombard would find herself shattered.

5

A Long and Grim Weekend

Just south of the Potosi peaks sat a collection of shacks generously called the "town" of Goodsprings, Nevada. Local miners and ranchers inhabited Goodsprings, including miner and former high school football star Herbert Lyle Van Gordon, age twenty-seven, who had walked outside to warm up his car in preparation for driving himself and wife Elizabeth to a town social when he heard an explosion on Potosi Mountain. He wandered into the patch of inhospitable, parched earth that comprised their yard and there saw the mountain peaks to the north aglow around what he figured to be Potosi's saddle. Van Gordon was a quick thinker and ran to the phone to call the local sheriff and then hurried back out and stared at the soaring flames. He knew it was a plane; he had heard the humming engines right up until the sound of the explosion. Van Gordon's first impulse was to rush to the scene, but he knew the looming mountain well enough to understand there was no point to such rash action in the dark of night. That mountain didn't want people on it; that mountain would kill you easy as you please.

Fifty miles to the southeast of Potosi on a sprawling ranch called the Walking Box, owned by a star of the silent pictures named Rex Bell, retired movie actress Clara Bow, who had lived a very hard life and now loved being out of the limelight, was drawn to a west-facing window where she saw a distant radiating light above the McCullough Mountain range. With her view obstructed by the near ridge she couldn't see what was aflame, but the sky lit up in an orange glow that put her in mind of lights burning brightly for a movie premiere at Grauman's Chinese. For Bow the memory was bittersweet, of happy years as queen of the movies and also of incredible pain and the nightmares that had accompanied her stardom. She thanked her stars every day that she could live way out here at the Walking Box deep in Nevada desert and not think of Hollywood and the old days, although think she did, endlessly, and the distant glow above the mountains reminded her anew of long-lost vitality. Clara's young son, Rex Jr., noticed her staring outside and together they watched that haunting glow over the mountain ridge.

Up in the McCarran Field control tower, Pfc. Tom Parnell still manned his post and all was quiet. Then he heard some chatter on the radio. It didn't make any sense to him at first, but then he started to take notice.

He heard TWA Control in Los Angeles calling Air Traffic Control: "I haven't been able to contact TWA 3 on Silver Lake Check. Silver Lake is an authorized checkpoint—I mean, the required airways checkpoint, isn't it?" crackled a voice on the radio.

"That's right, yes," said a voice at Air Traffic Control. It was a calm, controlled voice.

A moment or two passed and Parnell kept listening. This time he heard the Las Vegas communications man. "I got a call from the Blue Diamond Mine near Arden beacon that they heard a plane go over and shortly after a crash, and there's a fire burning over in that section now."

Parnell grabbed his field glasses and looked southwest in the direction of the Arden beacon. The terrain around Las Vegas was perfectly flat, and from the tower he could see clear to Potosi Mountain. Through the blackness off to the southwest he could make out a pinpoint of orange light, inconstant, oblong, larger and then smaller. It did indeed seem to be a fire, like the radio chatter had said.

"I checked with TWA," said the voice of the Las Vegas man on the radio, "and their Flight 3 cleared here at seven-zero-seven. There's no reports since he left."

Parnell's throat tightened as he continued to listen to the people in thin air trying to sort things out. He wanted to believe this was a coincidence and that the distant light had nothing to do with Flight 3.

The tower phone rang and Parnell gave a start. He fumbled to answer. "This is the Las Vegas Police Station," said the man on the phone. "We're getting reports of a plane going over Blue Diamond and then some sort of crash. And now there's a fire burning over that way. Whaddya know about any of that?"

"TWA Flight 3 took off at 7:07," Parnell managed. "Everything was fine at that time—"

Vegas police cut him off and said, "Call you back," and the connection went dead. Parnell called the Officer of the Day. The Officer of the Day called Major Herbert W. Anderson, second in command at McCarran Field. In a few minutes Anderson gathered crucial details. TWA commercial flight, Blue Diamond Mine, Army personnel on the plane. He acted at once, dispatching the post surgeon, the provost marshal, and fifteen men to the mine to render aid. Then he grabbed the quartermaster, Major Taylor, and Taylor's assistant and hopped in a car heading for the mine because this was an Army Air Corps matter and he needed to be out there. Little did he know just how long and grim the weekend ahead would turn out to be.

6

Merely Physical

Ruggiero Eugenio di Rodolfo Colombo had Americanized his name to Russ Columbo in the hopes of avoiding Italian stereotyping. The move had worked, and in mid-1933 Russ was the hottest young thing in music. All of twenty-five, handsome as the devil, and a musical genius, Columbo took Hollywood by storm, having recently been announced for a featured role in a Fox musical called *Broadway Thru a Keyhole*. By now, Carole had established a pattern: She went after men who were prized. First there had been Howard Hughes, whose name was on everyone's lips for *Hell's Angels* in 1929. Then William Powell, a fresh screen sensation when they began dating in 1931. After their divorce, the new boyfriend was Columbia scriptwriter Robert Riskin, eleven years her senior and, according to Lombard, a different type of animal: a scholar. To keep up, she said, "I started in reading books. I don't mean just bullshit. I mean book books. Aldous Huxley and Jane Austen. Charles Dickens. William Faulkner. Because Bob, he was an intellectual…and I felt I had to keep up." They were seen at nightclubs; they were seen at the track.

Lombard enjoyed the exchange of sexual energy with this type of power player. She liked "real men." It was while out on a date with Riskin at the Cocoanut Grove that Lombard moved Columbo into the crosshairs. As big as rock stars are today, that's what a number of romantic male singers, or crooners, were in the early 1930s, when the demand for radios exploded and a Depression-ravaged nation sought cheap entertainment. The love songs of the "big three" crooners, first Rudy Vallee and then Bing Crosby and Russ Columbo, went straight to the heart. Columbo was soon referred to as the "Valentino of the Air" and the "Singing Romeo." And he earned these monikers with a rich baritone and torch-song lyrics capable of reducing women to puddles of desire.

Eye contact that September evening at the Cocoanut Grove between Carole Lombard and Russ Columbo sent sparks careening off the polished dance floor. Bemused screenwriter Riskin made no effort to compete with Columbo and predicted that Lombard soon should expect an inundation of roses. The next morning a dozen yellow roses hit Petey's Rexford Drive doorstep, attesting to Riskin's savvy and Columbo's interest.

But Russ Columbo had already become damaged goods by his mid-twenties, not long out of a devastating relationship with a married singer named Hannah Williams Kahn. Letters from their affair reveal what appeared to be Hannah's obsession with Columbo and hint at his for her. Embroiled as she was in a passionate affair with the Singing Romeo, Hannah headed to Reno for a quickie divorce and established residence in Nevada for the required six weeks at just about the time Lombard was there shooting skeet with Bobby Stack en route to divorcing William Powell. Kahn continued to write Columbo scorching love letters from Reno each and every day as he toured several Midwestern U.S. cities with the Russ Columbo Orchestra.

In one such letter, Hannah wrote, "It was simply heavenly hearing your grand voice again tonight. Oh honey, when I hear you say, I love you darling, I miss you so. I want you near me every second—it just breaks my heart. I can't stand, dearest, just cannot stand it, that's all. I must be near you always."

And then, just two days later, she took pen to paper again: "I'm so depressed. I doubt very much whether I shall be able to write a letter. Why, oh, why do we have to suffer like this? I promise you, darling, I'm going to do something desperate if it isn't settled one way or the other. I'm a nervous wreck. Everything I eat makes me ill. I go to bed early but cannot sleep. What am I to do, dearest?"

The Hannah Williams Kahn love letters ran thousands of words but never varied from these two themes: I adore you and I will die without you. Russ loved hearing such words because Russ Columbo sought to be adored. Nothing pleased him so much as a woman's attention. He expected it, because that's what Mama had given him all his life. He was Narcissus and did gaze into mirrors and loved his Echo, whoever Echo may be at a given moment, to tell him how desirable he was.

Hannah's psychology became clear by her next action: In a move that stunned Columbo to the verge of suicide, she dumped the crooner for boxer Jack Dempsey, a turn of events nobody saw coming, least of all an earnest Valentino of the Air who was known to possess a strong streak of childlike innocence. Evidence shows that Hannah had been two-timing Russ for the length of her stay in Nevada!

Columbo canceled the remainder of his tour, retreated to Beverly Hills, and went cold turkey from his treacherous lover. He folded himself into his music and vented his frustration in song lyrics that remembered a woman who "promises faithfully to become your wife" until she writes a letter and says "she loves some other guy."

"So the tears start to fall," wrote Russ, "and you threaten to quit, You're thinking of suicide, and you're having a fit, But you think you'll keep going, tho it kills you inside, And just say you're a new man, for the old guy has died."

In his own creditable way, Columbo soldiered on through the betrayal, with his large family and adoring mother circling wagons around him. Russ was the baby of a large brood and his mother's pride and joy.

Hollywood writer Adela Rogers St. John summed up Columbo in a nutshell: "Russ was a very unusual man—a boy he seemed to me." Fueled by his mother's lifelong praise, Russ loved to be photographed as a hero in costumed poses, whether emulating a Valentino-like sheik or a helmet-clad military officer. Most often, he was captured for the lens in the midst of overpowering a damsel, and in all cases his image was courtesy of close friend Lansing Brown, a Hollywood photographer of some reputation. Brown also knew and had photographed Carole Lombard, and soon the three would become involved in a fatal love triangle the depths of which Hollywood could not imagine or dare to bring to the screen.

In small-town Hollywood, Lombard may have met Columbo four years earlier on the set of DeMille's *Dynamite* prior to her dismissal, as Russ had played a bit part as the guitar-strumming character known as Mexican Boy. In truth, Lombard and Columbo traveled along the fringes of the same circle. Lombard's friend Sally Blaine, sister of Loretta Young, said she "used to go to the Grove just to sit and stare at the boy whose soft voice made one dream." Blaine and Columbo became more than friends, and there were off-and-on rumors of coming nuptials. In fact, Columbo got around, which made him all the more attractive to Carole. It was what she had imagined she was getting in Powell, the sexy seducer—except for the reality that Bill turned out to be, well, something of a lump.

In terms of both style and sanity, Carole Lombard knew she had a lot to offer Columbo. She understood how damaged he had been by Hannah Williams Kahn. Carole loved the fact that Russ was young, vital, ambitious, and in a fresher phase of life than Powell. Russ's skill as a lover and his tales of other conquests thrilled her, which was all part of Carole living on the edge with a man all the girls wanted. Right away she asked Russ to coach her through songs she must perform in the steamy Paramount melodrama

White Woman with brooding leading man Charles Laughton and romantic lead Charles Bickford. She found it a handy excuse to be close to Russ during the workday, as Columbo was now just getting familiar with soundstages; he had just finished up work on *Broadway Thru a Keyhole* at the Fox studios near Beverly Hills.

Lombard's next picture at Paramount sent worlds colliding. She starred with Bing Crosby, Columbo's bitter rival (although Crosby would later claim that he and Russ were "great pals") in a musical called *We're Not Dressing* that was notable for an incident on the Paramount soundstages. When Crosby gave Lombard a stage slap with camera rolling, something inside her snapped. The resulting melee demonstrated a dark side to Carole Lombard— she tore into Bing Crosby like an uncaged lion, striking out with blinding fury until he was cowering in a corner and minus toupee. Crew members finally pried her off.

Perhaps the relationship with Columbo was already getting to her. Yes, she knew how it felt to be jilted because Hughes had done it to her just as Kahn had done it to Columbo. Now, Carole found herself in the middle of a powerful sexual attraction as Columbo threw himself body and soul into an association that, when she stopped to think about it, scared the hell out of her. Soon each was calling the other "Pookie," just as he had called Hannah "Sweetch" and she had called Bill "Junior" and "Popsie." But as passionate and intense as the Lombard-Columbo relationship obviously was, Carole had her doubts. Something just wasn't right with Russ Columbo.

In the fall of 1933 she leased a 3,000-square-foot, two-story French Provincial house at the far end of Hollywood Boulevard and moved in there with Fieldsie, a combination that produced as many laughs as Laurel and Hardy. One writer noted that during a bridge party, Fieldsie sat idly eating chocolates, which she professed to dislike, "but I'm eating it to keep Carole's face from breaking out."

Their live-in situation rekindled old rumors around town that the two were lesbians. But Lombard didn't have women on her mind; she had Pookie ensconced there and reflexively sought out her ex, William Powell, as a sounding board when she experienced that familiar old "breathless with the loss of freedom" feeling.

Three months into Lombard's association with Columbo, Fieldsie dared to cross swords with Russ on Christmas Eve. He had called on Carole at the Hollywood Boulevard house, only to be met at the front door by Fieldsie who announced that Carole wasn't at home. No need to say where she was (at Bill Powell's house). A letter from Russ to Carole the next day indicates what happened afterward, with Columbo reacting badly to Carole being "out." The fiercely loyal Fieldsie had leveled her gaze on the not-singing-right-now Romeo and opined that what he and Carole had was "merely physical" and he needed to accept it for that only. Russ took this as a shot fired across his bow, not from the best friend, but from the girlfriend herself. And Carole got an earful for it.

"As I gathered from Fieldsie," he wrote bitterly, "I should have felt perfectly contented to take love as it was and enjoyed it and cherished the sweetness and loveliness when it was all over. Well—that's all nice and lovely—if I had known that you wanted me just that way, but I gathered from our earlier meetings that you wanted me for always...."

A month later, Carole failed to show for Russ's birthday party, and his letter to her echoed the excesses of Hannah Williams Kahn: "I worship you as the ancient worshipped their gods and goddesses. I have placed you on a pedestal, yes, and there I shall always keep you in my heart and soul, as my goddess—my infinite ideal."

The fan magazines and gossip columns led the nation to believe that Lombard and Columbo were the perfect young couple, and this version of the story has been accepted by her biographers ever since. But Carole had retreated early on from the pressure and obsessiveness of Russ's ardor. The sex was fantastic! But it came at a stiff price, and she knew now she had gotten what she wished for—a lover like she imagined Powell would have been in his prime, a man who could experience the heights of passion for her and take her along to those heights. That much Russ did, but to such excess that it drove her back into the protection of the dispassionate man who had alienated her in the first place.

She found the missing ingredient to be intellect.

Columbo poured his heart out in letters to his Pookie: "You know definitely in your mind that I do not meet your certain requirements, so therefore you look elsewhere for that. Physically you adore me and love me madly. But Angel, this is not a great love on your part. For if you loved me as greatly as I love you, there would be no requirement that you might demand from me, for a great love between man and woman demands nothing."

She could only write of not wanting to hurt him, of loving him in a reasonable manner without the necessity of falling on some sword or other every moment. But he would not be assuaged.

In hindsight, this was not the all-consuming love of Carole Lombard's life. Supposedly, Noel Fairchild Busch from *Life* magazine referred to Clark Gable as the love of her life in interviews with Lombard for an October 1938 cover story. This is the same Noel Busch who went on to gain acclaim as a World War II war correspondent and then as a biographer of not one but two Roosevelts, both Theodore and Franklin. The story goes that Carole's snippy response about Gable was to say that Russ Columbo, not Gable, was her great love, "and that is most definitely off the record." But her actions five years earlier, viewed through the prism of Columbo's anguished letters, speak loudly about who loved whom, and how much. They reveal a Carole Lombard who was backpedaling as fast as her size-four feet could manage from a character she found far too complex and oppressive. But Lombard's own brothers had good reason to plant a story that credited

Columbo and devalued Gable in the chronicle of their sister's life. The second-hand quote discrediting Lombard's feelings toward Gable would have legs for decades.

Says Lombard historian Carole Sampeck, "I think the whole *Life* magazine quote was indeed a plant by one of Carole Lombard's brothers. My feeling is that it was Fred, not Stuart. Stuart got along just fine with Clark Gable; Fred never really warmed up to him."

The situation between Lombard and Columbo grew so bizarre that Russ moved into a palatial Spanish villa on Outpost Circle, a moment's drive away from Lombard's Hollywood Boulevard home and five minutes away from the fortress on Iris Circle in Whitley Heights that Carole had shared with Bill and that Bill now occupied alone. But just how *alone* was Mr. Powell, Mr. Columbo wanted to know.

He began stalking Carole late at night with the brim of his fedora pulled low and the collar of his trench coat high, as proven by his journal, which contained such tidbits as the fact that on February 5, 1934, Lombard spent the night at Powell's house on Iris Circle. The next morning Columbo had it out with Lombard, prompting a later telegram from her that included a cynical, "Your faith and belief in me is most inspiring." Five days later Carole and Russ made up, and he reported in his diary's shorthand, "All beautiful again."

Lombard continued to work steadily at Paramount as the studio struggled to right its financial ship. Carole wore clothes well and received polite notices in picture after picture the likes of *White Woman*, the jungle drama; *Brief Moment*, a society drama; and *Bolero*, a dance drama. Then, out of nowhere came one of those lucky breaks that resulted from working six days a week for years with her name seen on marquees and billboards and movie posters.

Columbia studios had stumbled upon a hit picture with *It Happened One Night*, a zany comedy about a runaway heiress and a newspaper reporter on the road in Depression-plagued America. With returns so strong, Columbia pushed ahead with another surreal comedy, *Twentieth Century*. John Barrymore, a big star with a big drinking problem, was signed as Broadway producer Oscar Jaffe. Barrymore had transitioned from silent film to appear in some of the most prestigious pictures of the early sound era, including *Grand Hotel*, where he romanced the great Greta Garbo, *Dinner at Eight* with blonde bombshell Jean Harlow, and *Rasputin and the Empress*, appearing with his brother Lionel and sister Ethel.

As Lily Garland, Jaffe's protégé, Columbia chose Carole Lombard in a move that left insiders gasping. It had been nine years since Barrymore had chosen Lombard with such a flourish for *Tempest*, the part she lost after the car crash, and now Carole worked nonstop while Barrymore's looks and vitality slipped away. In *Twentieth Century* Lombard enacted shy, innocent shop girl Mildred Plotka, whom Jaffe turns into shrieking, stomping diva Garland in the course of three years. Carole would credit "Jack" with pulling out of her a performance nobody expected, purring one moment, beating her temples the next in exasperation at Oscar Jaffe's antics. The picture would endure as a clever, vivid adventure in theatrics, and upon release in May 1934, it re-molded existing impressions of Carole Lombard.

Said *Shadoplay* magazine, *Twentieth Century* presented a "Lombard like no other Lombard you've seen.... When you see her, you'll forget the rather restrained and somewhat stilted Lombard of old. You'll see a star blaze out of this scene and that scene, high spots Carole never dreamed of hitting."

Photoplay focused on "Carole Lombard's fiery talent, which few suspected she had." These backhanded compliments—praising her excellence here in contrast to all the pale dramatic work that had come before—indicated just how ineffective she had been and how badly she needed some reinventing. Barrymore had made amends for cutting her out of *Tempest* by co-starring graciously in *Twen-*

tieth Century. "It would take a book to cover all the things he did to help," she told one reporter. "But perhaps the greatest was the subtle way he built my self-confidence and flattered me into believing I was good."

To another she said that working with Barrymore was "experience with a Capital E." The truth was that at the start, the aging reprobate had been far from supportive.

More than anything, the secret formula for Lombard's success in the picture came courtesy of its director, Howard Hawks, the guy she had worked for just prior to the car crash. Hawks had been trying for weeks to cast the lead role of fictional Broadway star Lily Garland with no luck. Popular stage actress Tallulah Bankhead would have been right, but shied away from working with Barrymore. Silent star Gloria Swanson had been faltering at the box office but still said no, and so did fading leading lady Ruth Chatterton. Currently hot Miriam Hopkins fit the bill, but had already earned a reputation for being difficult to work with, which turned attention to the poor man's Miriam Hopkins, Carole Lombard.

With the success of the stage version of *Twentieth Century* and the pedigree of writers Ben Hecht and Charles MacArthur, with the participation of Howard Hawks, a director of some very popular pictures, and with the signing of John Barrymore, one of the most prestigious actors in the business, *Twentieth Century* would be an important film for Columbia. Casting of an actress capable of playing at Barrymore's level continued to produce heartburn, and nobody was sold on Lombard. "She was a great personality," said Hawks of the impression Carole had made on-screen, but "she couldn't act for a damn. She just became completely phony."

Hawks saw potential and signed her anyway, and then regretted it when shooting began. Hawks got the results he expected, a weak Lombard performance, and Barrymore was shocked at the transformation of fun-loving Carole into stiff and phony Carole when cameras rolled. Said Hawks of Barrymore, "He was kind of amazed, she was so bad. He held his nose behind her back." Hawks took Lombard into the depths of the soundstage where it was just the two of them and asked why she seemed so intimidated, why she didn't give Barrymore's Oscar Jaffe back the level of energy he radiated. Hawks asked her what she would do if a man spoke to her that way in real life. She said she would kick him in the nuts. Hawks said, then kick him in the nuts and if she didn't, he said, "I'm going to fire you and get another girl."

She looked up at him—*was this a gag?*—and said, "You're serious, aren't you?"

"I'm very serious," he said.

They returned to the set with the cast and crew and played the scene. Recalled Hawks: "They were just in a little compartment of a train.... She made a kick at him and he jumped back and started pointing his finger at her and she waved her arms. She got back on the seat in the compartment and was kicking with both feet up at him and he was dancing around and finally he exited out of the scene and I said, 'Cut, print it.' Barrymore came back and said [to Lombard], 'That was magnificent. Were you fooling me all the time?' And she started to cry and ran off the stage."

Hawks had made the connection in her brain between personality and character. It was a lesson she never forgot, and more than anything else, this created Carole Lombard, Queen of Screwball. She said of the experience of making *Twentieth Century*, "Somehow it seemed to loosen something that's been tied up in me all my life, and to release an entirely new source of energy."

Ironically, the picture didn't do big business in spite of its pedigree. Columbia expected another windfall like *It Happened One Night*, but *Twentieth Century* wasn't about salt-of-the-earth Americans; it was about theater people and the concept proved to be too highbrow for the "stix," as *Variety* would call it—the small towns that sometimes made or broke pictures like *Twentieth Century*. Jaffe and Garland seemed to be carrying on about nothing important given that people were starving in all corners of America. So *Twentieth Century* earned terrific reviews and made a little money, and life went on for all involved.

But the perception of Lombard's talent within Hollywood improved upon the picture's May 1934 release, just as Russ Columbo was getting hot and earning consideration for a star turn in the pending production of *Show Boat* over at Universal Pictures. Romantically, the lovers were beginning to settle down and had pledged exclusivity to the other—or did he merely wear her down and obtain the appearance of surrender? Lombard and Columbo continued to enjoy sexual chemistry and spent a seemingly peaceful summer. He made his next picture at Universal, a musical called *Wake Up and Dream*; she made a melodrama at Paramount with rising stud Gary Cooper and six-year-old sensation Shirley Temple called *Now and Forever* and then an endearing screwball comedy at Columbia called *Lady By Choice*.

Under the surface Columbo kept another problem a secret: money troubles. He had run afoul of some shady characters, like songwriter Con Conrad, who would dog Russ for years demanding a portion of the crooner's salary for services rendered.

During summer 1934 Carole got to know the Colombo family with its intense Italian culture and found herself at sea. She wasn't Catholic; she was happily Baha'i and had no desire to become Catholic. She loved her friends, she loved her career, and her pets, and her family, but she never experienced anything like the intensity of *this* family; the Colombos seemed to be passionate about everything. Suddenly, she understood why Russ was the way he was, and he was learning that maybe he should distance himself from his ethnic heritage or he might risk hitting a glass ceiling in Hollywood. Lombard biographer Larry Swindell stated that Columbo was "devoted to his Old World family but embarrassed by their overt ethnic stripe." For her part, Carole kept quiet her doubts about marrying into the midst of these people, and contented herself with the sex and adoration.

Then, sometime in August, she began to feel some vague little something that all was not well in the cosmos. It grew into a feeling of dread that bad luck lurked ahead. She had always been intuitive and she always would be, and even Russ picked up on it to the extent that he drew up a will and spoke with his priest.

Carole and Russ approached the upcoming Labor Day holiday with trepidation. On Friday, August 31, Russ and Carole attended a sneak preview of his new picture *Wake Up and Dream*. On Saturday morning, while Columbo attended to a number of appointments, including studio recording, Carole, Petey, and Fieldsie drove two hours up to Lake Arrowhead for some R&R. Lombard had just wrapped the only picture of her career made at MGM studios, *The Gay Bride*, and was, as usual, coming down with something.

The next day she relaxed in the Arrowhead sunshine and finally began to unwind. Then came a phone call out of the blue: Russ Columbo had been shot.

7

A Perfect Flying Experience

Capt. Arthur Cheney loved to fly and on this fine evening lifted his Western Airlines DC-3 up and away from Burbank heading north-northeast for the run to Salt Lake City via Las Vegas. He had been airborne twenty minutes when Western Airlines Dispatch was in his ear. "Flight 10, we have you over Daggett at 7-5-7, is that correct?"

"This is Flight 10," said Cheney. "Affirmative, Dispatch. We passed Daggett at 7:57." Daggett signal beacon stood just east of Barstow heading into the Mojave.

"Flight 10," said Dispatch, "any sign of TWA 3? ATC should have had them over Daggett at 7-5-8."

Art Cheney looked at his copilot, got a wag of the head. They both scanned the clear horizon. There was a thin cloud deck above, but the stars were brightening as night settled in. Winds calm. A great night for flying. "Negative on TWA 3," said Cheney, and Western 10 continued on toward Vegas.

For the next thirty minutes Captain Cheney had Flight 3 on his mind and kept eyes peeled for any sign of the ship. Western 10 passed into Nevada airspace and wall-to-wall desert below. Desert and endless, empty black. Night runs in the void of desert were pleasant enough but never routine because a pilot always had the mental exercise of flying by instruments. Visual checks were all well and good, but a pilot lived by the instruments and what they read. Vertigo was real and vertigo was deadly, and Art Cheney knew enough never to let his guard down at night. They were also supposed to fly by radio beam and the copilot would handle that; weather over the desert was most often perfect or CAVU, ceiling and visibility unlimited, and closer to Las Vegas, flying was by visual reference.

Ahead and to the left, Cheney made out the blacker silhouette of the mountains of the Charleston Range from forty miles off. Above, he could see some stars and high clouds. At a cruising altitude of 9,000 feet, he came in safely south of those looming mountains. Ahead lay Las Vegas. Cheney swung his ship around signal beacon 23A, now darkened by the blackout rules, and banked left at 6,300 on approach to Las Vegas Municipal Airport, known generally as McCarran Field, home of the TWA and Western Airlines hangers. It had been a milk run of a flight, just perfect; still, that call regarding Flight 3 nagged at him. He wondered who the pilot was and tried to remember who was on for TWA but couldn't. Williams maybe. It could be Williams, a very well-known pilot among the brotherhood and a new man to the TWA western region, but Cheney wasn't sure.

Up ahead Cheney could see the beacon 24 with its powerful revolving lamp and knew that below him sat the village of Arden. Flight 10 skimmed over some scattered lights below. Such a beautiful machine to fly, the DC-3 was. The two 1,200-horsepower Wright Cyclone engines hummed at his fingertips, so responsive to the controls. Just one of the Cyclones would keep the ship afloat, but he had the luxury of two, and he often wished he could let his wife sit in the left seat, or his kids, just once to let them feel the perfection of the Douglas-crafted flying machine and all the power he had at hand.

He flew over beacon 24 with its revolving light and now could see the glow of Las Vegas way ahead on the broad plain of desert floor surrounded by mountains on all sides. But the highest and most daunting of those mountaintops, Potosi Mountain, was already past Western 10's position, and Cheney was happy to have that granite giant safely behind him. He settled his ship into a power glide for the final approach to Vegas.

"Western Air Dispatch to Western 10," came a call over the radio.

"Western 10," said the copilot.

"Hey, listen," said Dispatch, "we've got a request from KCT to check out a fire in the vicinity of Potosi Mountain or Spring Mountain. Can you handle?"

KCT was TWA Control in Burbank. Cheney cut in and said, "Dispatch, we are on final approach to Las Vegas."

"Understood, but need you to check out a fire."

Cheney and his copilot looked at one another. "Can you confirm—a *fire*?" said Cheney, not quite understanding. They both strained to look hard left out the side cockpit window, and sure enough, up on one of the peaks at a distance of maybe twelve miles they saw steady sheets of flame rising from some source on the mountaintop.

"That is affirmative," said Dispatch. "A fire on Potosi Mountain. Please report by interphone when you arrive Las Vegas."

It was by no means routine to take such a request with a load of passengers on board, and Captain Cheney suspected what this was about. He banked left and boosted the RPM to 2,050 for a climb back to 9,000, heading toward the visible flames. At an air speed of 190, Western 10 approached the peak of Potosi Mountain. Cheney was wary of this beast of a mountain and at a distance of five miles switched on a landing light, which threw forward nicely and would provide a visual reference of the approaching cliffs. In another mile he flicked on the other landing light, giving him twin spots on the mountain and the fire. At 9,000 he was safely above the peak and made sure he remained in level flight.

With the fire directly ahead and below him, he dipped to the right, then back to the left to see what was aflame. On first inspection Cheney thought he was looking at a good-sized bonfire, as if a college fraternity had convened on the lonely mountaintop and dug a campsite out of the deep snow. But his view was all too brief, so he banked left at about twenty degrees and came in again, giving the fire a wide berth of a quarter mile.

Cheney dimmed the lights of his control panel to provide an unobstructed view out the side window. At night, the glow could bounce off the windscreen and the side windows—one of the few things that pilots didn't like about the sleek DC-3s.

With landing lights on, Cheney banked in as low as he could over the spot and now could see, down in what appeared to be a ravine below the mountain peak—

—exactly what he had hoped not to see: a glint of silver metal. He gaped down at the tail section of a DC-3, upside down in the snow on a steep mountainside below the main fireball, spots of flames licking up off of its gleaming aluminum at a high cliff wall. His training took over, and he locked his attention on the task at hand.

In a moment the radio crackled: "Las Vegas calling Western 10. What is your position?"

"Western 10, circling in the vicinity of Spring Mountain."

"What is your ETA to Las Vegas?"

"Eight minutes," said Cheney and banked away from the fire and back toward beacon 24.

"Be advised," said Vegas, "you have Western 11 southbound approaching your position."

In a moment Western Flight 11 was on the radio. Cheney recognized the voice of Capt. Marshall Wooster, another veteran pilot. It was evident there had been talk in the station about the situation on the mountain because of the nature of Wooster's message: "Eleven to Ten. We are southbound over Las Vegas at 4,800." And then Wooster added, "Uh, see anything?"

Cheney let out a breath. "Yeah," he said into the microphone. He forced himself not to think about his unsettled stomach.

"Where?" asked Wooster.

"You'll see it when you get a little closer," said Cheney as he headed due east to pick up his normal approach and steer well clear of Flight 11 as it made the passage south over the usual flight lane and then banked southwest once it had cleared the mountains— the flight path that TWA 3 *should* have taken but for some reason hadn't.

Arthur Cheney now understood the directive to report over the interphone and not to put anything out over the airwaves. His report would wait another six minutes until they were wheels-down and at the blocks.

But between the calls flooding the Las Vegas police station about a fire on the mountain and the fact that Flight 3 still hadn't passed into California airspace, Burbank Air Traffic Control already knew exactly what the situation was.

8

Inflexible Fate

It would be difficult to imagine a freakier freak accident than the one that killed Russ Columbo: shot through the eye by a ricocheting bullet discharged from an antique percussion-cap pistol that the owner didn't even know was loaded. But that was apparently what had happened because *there* was the crooner on the floor of Lansing Brown's library in his modest little Los Angeles bungalow on Lillian Way, just off Melrose, and over *there* was the mark of the ricochet on the mahogany desktop. Brown's parents had been in the next room and were witnesses that the house was otherwise quiet and the two men were alone and, claimed the elder Mr. and Mrs. Brown, not angry with each other.

Columbo's mind had been weighed down this Sunday afternoon. His beloved mother had just suffered a stroke, and the family was reeling. Lansing, Russ's best friend, had not showed up at the sneak preview of *Wake Up and Dream*, and a hurt Columbo wanted to know why. Con Conrad, the songwriter and former Svengali of Columbo's life, was again pressing Russ for money. And of course the subject *du jour* was, as always, Pookie Lombard. Every single conversation Lansing and Russ shared for a solid year had ended up with an analysis of Lombard and her latest display of cold feet. Russ Columbo was a man obsessed. Lansing Brown was Russ's advisor and therapist as William Powell was Lombard's. Paranoid, sensitive, easily wounded, Columbo pressed Brown endlessly for answers to his romantic troubles with the far-too-practical actress. Today was no different.

Lansing Brown provided a chilling account of the moment of violence. "All of a sudden," he said, "there was a deafening explosion. You have no idea how terrific it was."

He had put a cigarette in his mouth and then struck a match on the hammer of one of two pistols on his desk. What were the odds that there was a percussion cap on the pistol in the first place or a slug in the barrel? What were the odds that, even though the pistol wasn't even pointed at Russ, that said slug, traveling at extreme low velocity, would strike the desktop and bounce into the one place that could prove lethal: Russ Columbo's eye socket? Had it hit him anyplace in the body with bone underneath, a superficial wound would have resulted and nothing more, but the lead ball punched through his eye and just far enough into his brain to cause a mortal wound.

He was rushed to the hospital, where doctors saw the case as hopeless. In that time his close friend Sally Blaine arrived at the hospital to sit by his bedside until the last moment. Columbo lingered for five hours and then expired. Carole, Petey, and Fieldsie packed up and started home. Fieldsie drove, Petey in the front passenger seat and Lombard in the back with her Alaskan Husky named Pookie, a gift from Columbo.

Carole said, "I knew on the way down the very instant Russ died. My dog, which loved Russ, was sitting in the back of the car. Suddenly he began to whimper. He crawled over to me and put his muzzle against my neck. Later I checked on the time—Russ had died in that very second."

Despite the outlandishness of the death of a twenty-six-year-old singing sensation just entering the prime of life, the idea that the shooting had been intentional was looked at and dismissed. A reconstruction of the event, the position of the two men, and particularly that ricochet mark on the desktop, seemed to indicate just how mundane a moment it was. Mundane and horrifying.

Carole Lombard's psyche was shattered. She was beset with equal parts grief and guilt. She *had* withheld and backpedaled and lugged doubts around with her. And when the end came, and she had sensed it coming, she was hours away and could do nothing, not even say good-bye. Now he was gone for good, this boy in a man's body, this innocent in heartless Hollywood.

Lombard hated funerals and vowed not to attend Columbo's. What could it help? But in the end she knew it was her obligation to Russ, to all the good things, and no amount of sidestepping would get her around it.

Three thousand people turned out for the funeral of Russ Columbo at the imposing, Spanish mission-styled Church of the Blessed Sacrament on Sunset Boulevard in Hollywood. Lombard put obvious agony on display as she sat through the funeral mass with Columbo's large family. Afterward, his body was taken to Forest Lawn Memorial Park in Glendale for interment in the Great Mausoleum.

She said nothing to the press until she granted one interview about Columbo, and one only, to young stringer Sonia Lee, then still a newcomer to the job of reporting in Hollywood. Lee was an early beneficiary of Lombard's generous heart and would label the interview "amazing." It appeared in *Movie Classic* magazine under the title "We Would Have Married—" and in it, Carole gave many clues concerning her reticence, which resulted from Columbo's obsessive nature. Said Lombard, "Russ and I loved one another. Eventually, I believe, we would have married. How soon, I don't know. His love for me was the kind that rarely comes to any woman. I never expected to have such worship, such idolatry, such sweetness from any man." The use of the word *eventually* was key. That Columbo level of idolatry had early on and many times thereafter given her pause. "He was completely content to sit of an evening and just watch me—without saying a word, without moving. He had no life apart from me. He was lost if we were not together."

She talked about the sensational sex in veiled terms, and offered an oblique reference to Columbo's emotional immaturity: "I loved Russ not only as a man, but as a mother would love her child."

She also indicted Lansing Brown for his failure to support Russ at the premiere of *Wake Up and Dream*, which became the catalyst for Columbo's death, as the fragile Russ had been forced by his nature to confront Brown about his failure to show on this critical night: "Russ depended on Lansing's judgment and considered his criticism extremely valuable," reported Lombard. "He had said to me, 'If Lansing doesn't get back in time to call me tonight, I'm going over to see him tomorrow.'"

Lombard also mentioned her intuition in the interview as she recounted her drive to Lake Arrowhead on the day before Columbo died. "On the drive from Hollywood," she recalled, "I almost turned back twice. It seemed as if something were calling me, telling me not to go up there. I dismissed my fears as foolish."

Most important, in this interview Lombard explored her own belief system, which would be applied on January 16, 1942. "I am convinced," she told Sonia Lee, "that if he had not met his death through that ricocheting bullet, he would have met it some other way—in an automobile accident, perhaps. His number was up." She summed up by saying, "I believe that everything that happens is determined by an inflexible Fate. I believe that Russ's death was pre-destined. And I am glad that it came when he was so happy—so happy in our love and in his winning of stardom."

Those who knew Lombard, Fieldsie and others, would make similar statements eight years later.

The man who held the pistol, Lansing Brown, would never recover from his involvement in the death of Russ Columbo.

Lombard ultimately urged him toward self-forgiveness. Carole also participated in subterfuge for Russ's frail and incapacitated mother, who was never told of her son's death. Instead, a lavish European tour was dreamed up, and Russ would send her letters from exotic locations that spoke of his latest successes, while his remains settled into a crypt in the Great Mausoleum at Forest Lawn Glendale.

9

Jimmy Donnally Lands His Plane

Pawnee, Illinois, sat smack-dab in the center of the state. Looked at from north to south on a map or from east to west, Pawnee represented the bull's-eye in the middle. In June 1930 Pawnee made headlines because of a boy who stood in a field. He stood there every day after school for months watching the horizon for a hero he had read about in a storybook, a brave and virtuous pilot named Jimmy Donnally.

Each afternoon when a particular green-and-silver biplane thundered over the Castle family farm just outside Pawnee, eight-year-old Charles Castle held the perfect vantage point because his farm sat on high ground, and he positioned himself right under the flight path so he could hear the roar of the engine and feel its pulse as it growled overhead, savoring the vortices created by the plane that would swirl down around him and tousle the field grass. His special thrill was *seeing* the pilot, seeing Jimmy Donnally in his open cockpit, goggles down and scarf flapping as he rocketed past on his daily rounds.

At lunch one Saturday, Charles decided to take a chance and get his mother's opinion on what he was sure he already knew. "Mother," Charles began in his high, thoughtful voice, not making eye contact and pushing baked ham and scrambled eggs around the plate, "I wonder if that pilot carrying the mail over our house isn't Jimmy."

Careworn, forty-one-year-old Maude Castle looked over her shoulder at the very earnest Charles, sitting between younger sister Nell and younger brother James. On the inside she smiled; on the outside she said, "It may be, son." She said it with gravity to match that of her boy. "It may well be."

Wow! thought Charles, who eagerly scraped up all the eggs in gulping bites and downed some fresh bread whole and drank some milk that had come straight from the family cow, then banged out the screen door to take up his post. Maude could see him out there on the gentle rise where Sam had planted wheat this year. Charles was always in sight, never a worry, because that spot was where the plane would go over, and when on this morning it finally did, Charles leapt and waved and shouted so loud that even she could hear it near to a quarter mile away, and then for Charles the day had ended, and he would slink back to the house with his shoulders slumped, and he would do his chores and then get ready for bed, already anticipating tomorrow's flight.

In coming weeks Charles convinced his mother to make him a flight uniform like he imagined Jimmy would wear, and Charles himself crafted wings—all proper pilots wore a pin in the shape of wings—out of cardboard. One night at bedtime he said his prayers differently. He rattled off names of family members that God should bless, and then paused and riffed, "God? I need you to help me on a big adventure, maybe the big one of my whole life. I want to meet..." he stopped to think. He thought so loud that Maude could hear it. Then he continued, "I want to meet, to be friends with, and to *fly* with Jimmy Donnally."

Maude's heart skipped a beat and she thought, Uh-oh. She knew then that her boy was rising for a fall, thinking foolish thoughts about some airmail pilot swooping out of a storybook and down out of the sky to gather him up for a ride in some damn dangerous plane.

Every day Charles shouted and waved, and every day the plane passed over the Castle farm, the flight path varying, but the indifference of that pilot constant. At a subsequent lunch over sandwiches, the conversation was less positive. "Mother?" Charles began. "Jimmy don't see me, Mother. If he did I know he'd come down in the big pasture."

More days passed, and finally Charles knew he must sit down and write a letter. His careful pencil carved:

Dear Jimmy:

I see you go over every day in your airoplane. I see you if you didn't go I would almost cry.

I love to watch you fly by. Some day won't you come down and take me up in the sky with you I want to fly like you. Will you please Jimmy? Do you know where my Daddy's pasture is—the big one? Could you come down there?

Have you a boy? What is his name? How old is he? I will be nine (9) years old groundhog day. Did you bring Santa Claus to my house Xmas in your plane?

I'm looking for you to come see me every day Jimmy. Good-by Jimmy.

And he signed it boldly: *Charles Castle.*

There was something magical about a child's innocence that could make a mother do crazy things, and as she kept an eye on Charles up there on the wheaty rise, Maude Castle sat down and penned a hasty letter of her own, this one to the Springfield newspaper. It read, "You try and find Jimmy for my little Charles. Jimmy pilots that big green and silver double-winged plane. I know there must be more than one pilot, but Charles insists that 'Jimmy pilots all these ships.' When you find him please send him this letter from Charles."

Maude stuffed her letter into an envelope along with his and sent both off to Springfield, and then she waited as the overflights continued. The weather grew bad, and Charles worried aloud about Jimmy's safety.

Weeks passed, and then came a wrapped package by the rural route mail carrier. "It's Jimmy, Mother!" Charles shrieked as he bounced off every wall of the farmhouse carrying the parcel under his arm like a football. "It's Jimmy!"

He tore open the package and there found a stiff-backed photograph of a confident, smiling young pilot in goggles. The photo was inscribed, *To my friend, Charles Castle*, and there was the signature, *Jimmy Donnally*. An accompanying short note asked if Charles really wanted a plane ride; if so, Jimmy could meet him at the Springfield airfield. Not only had Charles' prayers been answered by God, but so had Maude's, by the *Illinois State Register* newspaper in Springfield.

The reply of Charles Castle was instant and heartfelt:

Dear Jimmy:

I got your picture and I want to thank you. I love to look at you. I love your airoplane. You bet I want to ride with you. Will you show me how you do it? May I sit beside you up there? I love you Jimmy and so does Nellie and James. You know Nellie and James are my little sister and brother. Don't forget to come soon. Please be careful in this bad weather. I love you Jimmy.

Your friend Charles

After this exchange of letters, every single day that Charles stood in the field, the pilot would wave down to him, goggles over eyes and scarf trailing in the wind. It was glorious!

Finally, the day arrived for Charles to meet Jimmy Donnally at the Springfield airport. There, Springfield Postmaster William Conkling escorted the eight year old, and the newspaper noted:

"There came a roar of motor—far away, then closer and closer.

'It's Jimmy!' Charles yelled, as he danced about in his great excitement. Santa Claus in person would never have been afforded such an eager welcome.

"Hope and faith had won. Charles was about to realize a dream, to see the fulfillment of his prayers. He stared as down swooped the great green and silver plane and then up to circle the field. Then down to a swift and graceful landing, and to taxi up to the waiting crowd.

"Firm hands held the excited child. As Jimmy cut off his power the little lad was released and he sped to the plane's side and into Jimmy's arms with a wild cry. Later came the ride. Little Charles climbed into the plane with Jimmy. The motor roared and the craft swept down the field, into the wind, and was up and away. Jimmy headed due south to Charles' home and school.

"A little loving mother wept with joy, meanwhile waving a towel to her son there above her as the plane circled the home. In the field was the father at his task of coaxing a living from the soil for his little brood.

"'There's Mother,' the lad screamed into his idol's ear. 'There's Daddy!' Over the home and the school Jimmy swung his craft low and in wide circles so that the faces of the beloved mother and father were plain to the excited boy."

Charles was presented with gold wings by Jimmy and not to be outdone, the boy gave the cardboard wings that adorned his little natty flying suit to his Jimmy. Charles thought Jimmy would be his to keep—to take to school for show and tell and to teach him about flying every day—but as the hero himself said, "The mail must go through." And so he took off, leaving Charles, the postmaster, and a conclave of press behind.

After a chicken dinner for half the village of Pawnee, with all the fixin's and ice cream to boot, Charles was asked for a quote by unusually respectful newspapermen. He said, "It was great! Believe me, my Jimmy knows how to fly a plane—and he showed me all

71

about it."

In conclusion, wrote the newspaper reporter covering the event, "Following came the secret, but assuredly the promised prophecy that one day Charles and Jimmy will be flying the air lines together."

One half of the prophecy did come true. Jimmy Donnally did fly the airlines, except that the young airmail pilot who landed that June 1930 day in Springfield, Illinois, for the benefit of the postmaster, the press, and eight-year-old Charles Castle was really a young ex-Army flier named Wayne Clark Williams, then twenty-eight and full of the devil, if one could say that the devil made pilots feel like they could conquer not only the skies but the entirety of the world, including the imaginations of eight-year-old boys. That innocent day when flying was new, Wayne Williams created a memory to last a lifetime for several farm folk in the dead center of Illinois and crafted a story that would be remembered by newspaper reporters in January 1942.

10

Calculated Mayhem

Jack Frye became president of TWA in December 1934 at a time when the innovative DC-2 went into service and the company sought ways to fly "over weather." TWA had just created its first three-stop, eighteen-hour transcontinental flight, in theory anyway, using the new DC-2, but all manner of delays resulted in nobody actually flying coast to coast in anything approaching eighteen hours, or just three stops. Frye and TWA owner Howard Hughes now had a vision and sought effective means to get people from coast to coast with alacrity and in comfort.

Around this same time, Carole Lombard sought a different kind of comfort and leaned on her ex-husband for support after the shooting death of Russ Columbo. She also continued to be seen with friend and lover Robert Riskin. Through production of a romantic dance picture at Paramount called *Rumba*, Lombard diverted her attention with co-star George Raft. A year earlier they had appeared together in the smoldering, moderately successful dance drama *Bolero*.

George Raft was a pint-sized, tough-talking New Yorker out of Hell's Kitchen. He had made his mark as the henchman of murderous gangster "Tony" in the original 1932 version of *Scarface* and would go on to play variations on this gangster theme for decades. He was seven years Lombard's senior, with a bad-boy vibe and dark good looks. How could Carole resist? Raft would later say, "I truly loved Carole Lombard," and he truly did. Carole loved the sex, and his warmth, and his *lack* of turning every interaction into high drama, as Russ had seemed determined to do. When *Rumba* wrapped, the emotionally spent Lombard asked for a leave of absence from her employers at Paramount to get away from Raft and from the pressures of nonstop six-day weeks. The studio said yes.

Then grim news arrived from back home. Frederick Peters, Petey's husband and Carole's father, had lived out the final stage of his nightmarish life in Ann Arbor, Michigan, where a last-ditch effort was made via brain surgery to relieve his seizures. Once under his skull, doctors discovered cancer that had metastasized from *somewhere*. Further examination revealed his right lung as the culprit. Fred lived only five days past the craniotomy and died of lung cancer on February 20, 1935. Carole had last seen him in 1930 on a visit to Fort Wayne and realized then that he was a stranger. She now found it impossible and pointless to travel 2,000 miles to attend another funeral. She claimed that her participation would turn his service into a spectacle, but the fact was she couldn't face any more death. On the contrary, she decided to devote herself to pleasure today because there might not be a tomorrow.

Wounded on the inside, she projected all the more passionately on the outside. She threw herself into redecorating the leased Hollywood Boulevard house and brought in "Billy" Haines to help. William Haines had been a leading man in the silent era and an early casualty of the transition to sound when his effeminate speech patterns brought his sexual orientation to the forefront. All of a sudden, acting work dried up. He became one of Carole's causes when she asked him to employ his hobby of interior decoration at her new house. He offered advice, some of which she took and some she didn't, and she paid him for his services even though he told her he wouldn't cash the check—and he never did. The notoriety that accompanied her support of a gay actor meant more than cash anyway and helped to launch a forty-year decorating career.

Petey tried to redirect her daughter into new interests. One of Petey's close friends was Elinor Tennant, the first woman tennis player in the United States to turn pro. The forty-five-year-old Tennant had become a tennis instructor in L.A. and hung out with Petey—nobody in the gang called Bess by her name anymore; to everyone she was Petey. Tennant and Petey played in the same bridge club and shared practice of the Baha'i religion and a belief in numerology and mysticism. Lombard fell in with this crowd and soon spent her mornings on the tennis court, learning from the best instructor in the game. As with everything she took on, Carole obsessed over tennis hours a day, every day of the week.

During a break on the court, Tennant fretted to Lombard about a star pupil, twenty-year-old Alice Marble of the American Wightman Cup team, who had collapsed at Roland Garros stadium in Paris a year earlier and now was wasting away in a tuberculosis sanatorium in Monrovia, east of Pasadena. Tennant said that Marble possessed all the talent in the world but, frankly, she was morose and bitter at being diagnosed with TB and wanted to die. Her weight had ballooned to 175, and she had given up any hope.

Remembering the ordeal of 1925, Carole took pen and paper in hand and sat down to write Alice Marble a letter that read:

Dear Alice,

You don't know me, but your tennis teacher is also my teacher, and she has told me all about you. It really makes very little difference who I am, but once I thought I had a great career in front of me, just like you thought you had. Then one day I was in a terrible automobile accident. For six months I lay on a hospital bed, just like you are today. Doctors told me I was through, but then I began to think I had nothing to lose by fighting, so I began to fight. Well—I proved the doctors wrong. I made my career come true, just as you can—if you'll fight.

Carole Lombard

Marble said, "I kept the letter in front of me for days, trying to think: How can I fight? How can anyone who is ill fight?"

Alice Marble regained enough strength to move from the sanatorium to the home of Elinor Tennant's sister in Beverly Hills. She said, "Every time I was ready to give up, I remembered Carole's letter, [and] my obligation to Miss Tennant. Every day I was a little stronger and closer to my goal. I had to get well." One day Tennant told Marble they were going to dinner at Lombard's house on Hollywood Boulevard. There Alice met Carole and also Fritz, Tootie, and Petey, who, according to Marble, "ordered her three children around just as if they were five-year-olds."

Marble wanted nothing to do with tennis courts, but Lombard cajoled her to at least go and watch Elinor's lessons with the movie stars. By now, Carole had, inevitably, dubbed Tennant with a nickname: "Teach." Soon the formal name of Elinor had been dropped and the instructor became simply Teach Tennant, and Alice found herself shagging balls during Lombard's lessons.

"Carole found a general practitioner," said Marble. "She told me, 'This is a marvelous man. I like this man; he treated Petey.' He said, 'Miss Marble, I don't think you ever had tuberculosis. You don't have scars on your lungs.'"

The doctor believed that Marble had suffered a combination of anemia and pleurisy and that if she could drop fifteen to twenty-five pounds, she might play tennis again. "The day arrived," said Marble, "and my coach and Carole challenged Louise Macy and me to three games of doubles. I felt so shaky, but loved every minute of it...."

As with Teach Tennant, everyone in Carole's universe had a nickname, and Marble became "Allie." Lombard took an intense interest in everything Allie did, hoping the enthusiasm would be contagious. Reported Marble: "Carole would say, 'What did you eat today, honey?' I began to lose weight. I lost forty-five pounds and we began to talk about clothes. She sent me to USC and I took a course in costume design. Even though I was twenty-one, I had bad acne from all the medication. She sent me to a dermatologist and she always said, 'You'll pay me back,' but then when I tried, she'd say, 'Oh shit, forget about it!'"

Marble became a regular at the Peters home on Rexford Drive. Carole's entourage included Fieldsie and two psychics who, said Allie, were "the real thing" and so accurate they could make Marble's "hair stand on end…. They liked Carole…. She'd have them over for dinner. They never did it for pay; they just did it."

In 1937 Lombard cheered Marble on as she claimed the California state singles title, and the tournament organizer asked Carole to present the trophy to Allie. Lombard said, "Congratulations, Champ. The next trophy will be for winning the national championship." Marble did just that, capturing the U.S. Open Women's Singles title at Forest Hills. Wimbledon titles followed, including a clean sweep in 1939 in singles, doubles, and mixed doubles. With Alice Marble back on her feet, attempts to repay Lombard for all the sportswear purchased and all the doctors consulted were always met with that same refrain: "Oh shit, forget about it!"

Said Allie, "She was always embarrassed when people wanted to thank her. So whenever I won a championship I'd give her a silver tray. I must have given her twenty-five over the years."

On the Hollywood courts Carole met other Tennant protégés, including Bobby Riggs and Don Budge. "I play tennis now two and three hours a day," said Lombard. "I'm working harder at it than I have ever worked at anything."

But the sponsorship with Marble went deeper as Lombard sent the tennis star to Paramount for drama and dancing lessons. Allie went along with the idea but knew she didn't have the natural talent to take it anywhere. One thing she *could* do, and loved to do, was belt out a song in a voice much like Kate Smith's. It was with ambivalence that Marble saw Lombard take over her life, and within the entourage, discord bubbled.

"Teach was a funny person," said Marble. "She loved Carole, but hated anything that took me away from tennis. I was the closest thing to a daughter she ever had [but] Carole was very persuasive."

Lombard had found her way past the death of Russ Columbo and all its conflicts and mysteries. A mystic from India who visited Hollywood, Swami Daru Yoganu, took one look at Carole Lombard and "the emanation of her Karma, or life force," and labeled her "an old soul" whose life force went back 900 or 1,000 years. It would be all too easy to dismiss such a story as the work of Paramount's publicity department—except to those who knew Carole and experienced the breadth of that soul, her easy manner and generosity of spirit all packed inside a woman just twenty-five years of age.

She was always in motion, always doing something, always devoted to a cause or sweating on a tennis court or investigating ways to buy publicity to further her career. In the Hollywood of 1934, elaborate parties were all the rage, and Lombard reconceptualized that entire fad by planning and hosting parties. Not just cocktail parties for the Hollywood elite, but a series of lavish, raucous theme parties at the Hollywood Boulevard house that included the hillbilly party, with a complete barnyard motif that included live cows and flailing chickens, and the hospital party, with waiters dressed as doctors and supper served on operating tables, and yes, in bedpans. Unfortunately, the hospital party flopped because guests in formal attire refused to change into hospital gowns, leaving the hostess with egg on her face. Her biographer, Larry Swindell, said that Lombard admitted becoming "a madcap party-giver with rank calculation, courting the kind of publicity that would identify her, personality-wise, with the roles she wanted to play."

Lombard made no apologies for being a performer at heart. "What a ham," exclaimed Alice Marble. "What a *ham!*" The professional personality suited her natural energy level and gregarious nature. Of course, all Hollywood knew what Lombard was up to, and many bought in while others resented the power grab and the press's subservience to the overt manipulations of a marginal star.

She capped a year of these parties by renting the entire Venice Amusement Pier at Oceanside Park for an evening and inviting most of Hollywood to come have fun at her expense. She staged the party in honor of real estate developer Alfred Cleveland Blumenthal. The Paramount Pictures crowd dominated, including Marlene Dietrich, Claudette Colbert, Randolph Scott, and Cary Grant, but Hollywood A-listers Richard Barthelmess and Clive Brook were there, along with Josephine Hutchinson, Toby Wing, Constance Talmadge, Warner Baxter, Regis Toomey, and Louella Parsons. French actress Lili Damita showed up as well without really knowing or caring what an amusement park was. She wanted to be seen, and so she dressed to the nines and brought a young Aussie unknown named Errol Flynn, wide-eyed and fresh off the boat from England. Another awestruck newcomer in attendance was Fox contract player Henry Fonda, just in from New York.

The Venice Pier party would mark Lombard's swan song in over-the-top entertainment and end a half year away from soundstages. Her return to Paramount Pictures would be supervised by Ernst Lubitsch, the new general production manager at the financially troubled studio. The German-born writer-producer-director was already known for "the Lubitsch Touch," his particular talent for crafting elegant, bewitching scenarios. It was no secret that Ernst Lubitsch had become a Lombard fan. After reviewing her performances in *Twentieth Century* and *Lady By Choice*—both of which had been made away from Paramount—Lubitsch wanted to give direction to Lombard's career by capitalizing on her Sennett-schooled affinity for comedy because, frankly, she could open a roadside stand selling eggs, she had laid so many in melodrama. Carole had earned the unflattering nickname of the "Orchid Lady" after an earlier melodrama called *No More Orchids* and a subsequent string of melodramatic performances in clinkers. Hence the party campaign of 1934–35 and its focus on the kind of madcap themes found in *Twentieth Century*. Reviewers suddenly treated her like a shiny new star, and the brain trust—Carole, Fieldsie, and Myron Selznick—believed this comedy thing could become something uniquely Lombardian.

The script chosen now by Paramount boss Lubitsch for Lombard was *Hands Across the Table*, about a manicurist dreaming of marrying a rich husband but falling for a young playboy whose family had been wiped out by the Depression. The story had been purchased for Claudette Colbert, the star of two 1934 blockbusters, DeMille's *Cleopatra* and director Frank Capra's *It Happened One Night*. Claudette didn't need a hit. Carole did, so the self-assured Lubitsch ordered the *Hands Across the Table* script rewritten for Lombard, then assigned Mitchell Leisen, former assistant of Cecil B. DeMille, to direct and dashing newcomer Fred MacMurray to co-star alongside Carole.

She was in the right place at the right time as a new genre, the screwball comedy, took hold after *It Happened One Night* earned Oscars for Colbert, for her male lead Clark Gable, and for director Capra and the picture itself.

Suddenly, *everybody* wanted to see comedy with a zany touch, and *Hands Across the Table* stood at the forefront. Lombard's popularity spiked. But Carole, or possibly Fieldsie, or possibly Myron Selznick, realized the impact on Hollywood of the recently enforced Motion Picture Production Code, a set of rules governing morality in movies. This set of edicts fell upon the studios like a nun's habit in response to the sex and violence in Depression-era pictures. Main catalysts for change were two overtly sexual actresses, Jean Harlow and Mae West. Now with pejorative rules in place, Lombard tested the edicts to attract attention and build her brand. She seized every press opportunity, showing as much leg in publicity shots as decency allowed. She went braless in the slinkiest costumes that could be designed and worn on-screen, iced her nipples before cameras rolled, and jiggled when possible. She did whatever she could to ascend to the role of sex symbol. Just because she had veered into comedy didn't mean she wanted to stop being sexy because, as everyone knew, sex sold tickets.

Following completion of *Hands Across the Table*, Lombard proceeded to another screwball comedy with Fred MacMurray called *The Princess Comes Across*.

After making ten pictures at Paramount in his first year there, the lanky MacMurray had ascended to star heights at the studio and was offered Dressing Room 1. After a quick tour he declined, muttering, "Too big. I'd rattle around." He was the kind of guy to pair with Lombard—a couple of working-class stiffs—and MacMurray would remain her friend to the end, and beyond.

It didn't matter that their boss, Ernst Lubitsch, was fired right about now as head of production at Paramount. Lombard had found her place in Hollywood and it was in comedies, in being the loud but lovable one in the group. Thus ensconced, she began to prepare for the first event of the 1936 Hollywood social season, January's exclusive White Mayfair Ball, which would be held in Beverly Hills for an exclusive 300 movie-colony A-listers.

The Mayfair Club had been created by the Hollywood moguls for movie people, and toward the end of 1935 Lombard was acknowledged by the group for her imaginative recent social events and asked to serve as hostess for the kickoff Mayfair event of 1936. Unspoken was a vote of sympathy for Carole as something akin to comeback player of the year in the wake of the Columbo tragedy.

The White Mayfair Ball was a prestigious event, held this time at the large and elegant Victor Hugo restaurant at Wilshire and Beverly Drive in tony Beverly Hills. At the time of the ball, on January 25, 1936, Carole Lombard was a veteran of fifty-seven pictures and sixteen months past Russ's death. She decked herself out in white chiffon and went on the arm of Cesar Romero, busiest escort in town and also a friend who wouldn't mind the fact that she was official hostess and out of pocket for most of the evening.

The 1936 White Mayfair Ball would be scandalized by the fact that an attention-seeking and, some whispered, *fading* MGM star Norma Shearer infuriated hostess Lombard by showing up not in dress-code white but in form-fitting scarlet, a move that would be memorialized by Bette Davis in the Warner Bros. picture *Jezebel* two years later. But even *that* became nothing in terms of the historical reporting on the 1936 White Mayfair Ball. No, this night would become famous when a slightly drunk and technically married Clark Gable made an overture to a tipsy Carole Lombard and the hostess and the Hollywood stud suddenly disappeared. They were spotted rushing off to his suite at the Beverly Wilshire Hotel. And so on a chilly January night in 1936, Carole Lombard's fireball life would begin its final segment.

11

Flight 3 Is Down

In the village of Goodsprings, Nevada, south of the base of Potosi Mountain, local mine employee Lyle Van Gordon and his wife Elizabeth continued to stare up open-mouthed at the glow of the fire high above them in the northern sky. Lyle's given name was Herbert, but he had opted for his middle name early on and was glad he had chosen Lyle when tearing up the local gridiron a decade earlier. "Bull" Van Gordon he had been called back then. Lyle was a man of action, barrel chested, quick tempered, and just now his skin crawled at the idea that a plane had crashed up there in wilderness. He had heard the plane fly over, and then he had caught the sound of the muffled explosion on impact. He stood transfixed as the glow of the flames rose high in the northern sky, and Elizabeth watched with him; she had taken hold of his considerable bicep in her hands and squeezed as they shivered together in the night, from both the cold and the thought of the poor pilot up there. Lyle was another who figured it was a military plane with at most a pilot and copilot. All day long he heard the Army planes flying over and the distant pop-pop of gunnery range activity.

After a while Elizabeth went inside their shack when she heard eighteen-month-old Nancy crying over something or other, and Lyle's mother-in-law, known to all as "Gonga," wandered out and stood with him, watching. It was while talking with Gonga that

Lyle began to think: big mountain, small crash site, deep snow. How would rescuers ever find the site come daybreak once the snow had smothered it? So he set down a broomstick pointing straight at the flames. It was just about then that he and Gonga heard that other plane come into range. They watched it circle the fire on the mountain, once, and then twice. It didn't hang around too long before skedaddling off toward the northeast.

Such a cold January night, and yet Lyle's blood boiled; there were people up there on that mountain and he wanted to help them. He wanted, no, he *needed* to act. He didn't know that the pilots could have survived, but he didn't know otherwise, either, and if they had bailed out or crawled away from the fire, they wouldn't last long up there in the snow and cold.

But the hell of it was, there were no roads up to the peaks of Potosi. There never had been, because there was nothing up there worth getting to. Anybody going up after that plane would be blazing a trail and praying to be able to find the crash site. Lyle had been working the local mines as a geologist, and he knew that area well enough, up the cliffs above Ninety-Nine Mine Road. He had never had reason to go all the way up, but he already knew as he stood there and watched the fire consume all the gas and oil the plane had carried, that he would be going up after it. After another half hour the phone rang. In a moment Elizabeth called him inside to talk to one of the cops who said there was a rumor that it wasn't a military plane but a DC-3 full of people that had gone down and that one of the passengers on the plane was the movie star Carole Lombard. Lyle had to find a chair and sit down and think about that one. He remembered seeing her in the picture show over in Henderson not long ago. Some comedy with, who was it? Robert Montgomery.

He hung up the phone, walked back outside, and began to pace the brittle desert by the Van Gordon shack and think, think about what he would need to take with him. A thermos of coffee, of course, sandwiches, a knife, a length of rope. He paused to look up one last time at the dying fire, then he went inside and started to gather his things for tomorrow and what he suspected was going to be the toughest day of his life.

Twenty miles away on North Seventh Street in Las Vegas, Chuck Duffy had finally sat down for supper at his home when the phone rang. It was McCarran Field calling to say that Flight 3 was down in the mountains southwest of Las Vegas, that there was a fire visible on the mountain. *Oh, God, no*, he thought. Not that plane. Not her and all those other people. The crew—the Army men. A chill raked his spine and he sat there a long moment before his mind would work again. He looked at food he no longer wanted and said he'd be right there. On the drive back to McCarran he could see the little point of fire on the opposite mountaintop more than thirty miles away. Brush fire? No, not in deep snow. Somebody's bonfire? On Potosi Mountain? Who was he trying to kid.

No, the unthinkable had somehow happened, and Flight 3 had bought the farm up on the mountain, and only by some miracle were any of the souls aboard her still alive. Maybe it had been a crash landing. Maybe they had scrambled out before the fuel caught and that was their fire for survival. Maybe, maybe, maybe.

He grabbed his phone and called TWA in Burbank. "Flight 3 is—" the words caught in his throat, "—down west of here. What do you want me to do?"

Silence deafened at the other end of the line. Finally, he heard a breath, and the voice at the other end of the line said, "Nothing. It's being taken care of. The only thing I would like you to do is not to allow the information to be released. I've already told that to LQ."

LQ was code for Las Vegas Communications Center. "OK," said Duffy. He thought of Carole Lombard, and her party, and the flash of bare leg. Carole Lombard. He forced himself to focus. "We have to launch a ground search. You know—survivors will—"

Pause. Muffled conversation. "Not right away," said the voice.

Duffy gave his own pause. Why on earth wouldn't they get rescue parties going right away? Now? This made no sense to him, and he could feel the sweat breaking out on his forehead and under his arms. He finally said, "Then you're saying that everything is under control?" He found bitter humor in his own question, as nothing seemed to be under control.

"Yes," said the voice, "Burbank has it under control." There was a click, and that was that.

12

A Man in a Man's Body

He was born William Clark Gable in 1901 in a hellacious section of eastern Ohio, a rural place of endless hills and hollows and a few terrible hairpin roads. His mother, the former Addie Hershelman, had died when Clark was ten months old of a debilitating illness that began at childbirth. And there right away was the event that marked him. Clark Gable, known from birth as "Billy," became motherless before he could walk, before he could talk, before he was even done breastfeeding. In a sense he would always be cut off and distant from everyone, particularly women, bearing the pain of abandonment by his mother silently and stoically.

His father, William Gable, was the kind of hard man that Gable would sometimes portray: two-fisted and no nonsense. But unlike those Clark Gable movie characters who turned out to possess extraordinary depth, or developed it by the last reel, Will wasn't warm as fathers go. Will remarried quickly, in part to assure that the baby boy would be cared for, and how Jennie Gable did care for her adopted son, loving him unconditionally but unsuccessfully because of that distance he brought to every relationship and especially the stepmother relationship, perhaps some instinct for self-preservation so he would never be hurt again by the level of abandonment felt by a ten-month-old infant.

He matured early into a broad-shouldered, reticent teen who

worked various jobs, including some in the oil fields with his father. He also worked at a lumber company and as a mechanic and
at other odd jobs, but settled on acting because it allowed him to
be other people who could project emotions he never would; who
lived happy and successful lives and were heroes and who loved
deeply and got the girl. In fact, he got a girl of his own, a slightly
older woman, very pretty, petite, dark haired, named Franz Doerfler, from a stock acting company that he joined in the northwest-
ern United States. Billy Gable and Franz Doerfler were deliriously
happy but always broke. In fact poverty and hunger were frequent
adversaries of young Gable, and his complexion was so yellow, perhaps from jaundice or hepatitis, that people pitied him. The lack of
money he experienced in the late 1910s and early '20s would scar
him forever and produce a tight-fisted money grubber.

He proposed marriage to Franz in 1923, but she refused to accept until he could assure a steady income. Instead she urged him
to seek out a drama coach, a woman named Josephine Dillon who
could improve Billy's skills so he might earn a living as an actor.
Before long, forty-year-old Dillon became twenty-three-year-old
Gable's lover, and all of a sudden Franz Doerfler was out. For the
first time Gable loved and left a woman, a practice he would repeat
often as he climbed the ladder of success and forever sought the
approval of the mother-type he had missed in infancy.

Josephine Dillon helped Gable get rid of his too-high-pitched
voice in favor of more of a growl, and she helped him relax a fur-
rowed brow that made him play older than his years. The Clark
Gable of later Hollywood was in large part the invention of the
earnest acting teacher. Billy learned from Josephine how to be a
master of affectation, and soon the quiet fellow with no discernible
personality had reconstructed himself into what appeared to be a
force of nature. In gratitude, Billy married Josephine and then re-
billed himself as Clark Gable and hit the road seeking acting jobs
in the theater. The character she had created became something of

a Frankenstein's Monster, and his carousing far from home caused her to write at the time, "Thank God I'm not in love with him."

Thank God indeed, because Gable divorced Josephine in 1929 and married up very soon, this time to Maria Franklin Prentiss Lucas Langham, three times married, one time widowed, aged forty-six and extremely wealthy, having married up herself at every opportunity. Known as Ria, she fell for the Clark Gable created by Josephine Dillon the way all women seemed to, hearing that growling voice and instantly reaching the melting point. Yes, they fell for the voice, and the smirk, and the vibe, and the broad-shouldered, narrow-waisted frame that displayed clothes just so. But there was always distance and vulnerability in his eyes, and vacancy in his attention. Some translated this as lack of intelligence. Many a woman found Gable as the ultimate in cool, yes, but also as a man that needed rescuing.

Clark worked hard to learn to act on the stage and appeared in plays all over the country and in bit parts in the movies, including Clara Bow's 1925 picture, *The Plastic Age*. But Gable didn't make much impact until he appeared as Killer Mears in *The Last Mile* on the stage in Los Angeles in 1930, at which point he became the next big thing. Suddenly a famous agent, Minna Wallis, came calling and from there his picture career took off. Maybe the scales balanced out when the motherless guy landed a contract at the best possible movie studio in Hollywood, Metro Goldwyn Mayer. He rose meteorically after his teeth had been fixed and eyebrows plucked, and after he had grown fully into unusual facial features including wide-set eyes and a round face with prominent jug ears. Then he had everything going for him that Dillon had instilled, plus everything that MGM re-engineered. Suddenly, Gable had star power.

He met Howard Strickling, a top man in the MGM publicity department, a fast thinker and a fast talker, and stutterer, whose first impression was, "He was the biggest guy I ever knew, and I would say one of the most powerful."

Musical star Betty Garrett met Gable at MGM years later: "He walked into my dressing room and just literally filled it up—at least that's how it seemed to me. He was bigger than life: his head, his hands, everything about him was bigger than life. And he really did exude something that was so powerful."

Part of Gable's power emanated from his ability to turn the tables on people he met, to deflect attention from himself. He would make strong eye contact and begin asking questions of everyone, co-workers, members of the press, everyone. "If you walked in and started talking to him," said Strickling, "before you knew it you were talking about yourself."

"He was a great listener if you found a subject he liked," said Gable's pal, Steve Hayes.

When asked what it would have been like for a woman to meet Gable, actress Ursula Theiss described it this way: "He would have made you feel twice the woman than you think you are, because he did like the ladies. Intellectually, you might have expected more of him, but you would have been charmed…. He would have given all the attention you expected, and more."

To which Gail Strickling added, "He flirted outrageously!"

Underneath Gable's charisma, that million-dollar smile and those sparkling gray eyes, was his desire *not* to have attention directed at what he knew to be a wounded, vulnerable soul. By now he was obsessively clean. He could sleep on a set of sheets only once, even at home, and he showered three or four or five times a day. However clean he got, it was never clean enough. He liked things to be tidy all right. For example, he did not wish to discuss his fiancée, discarded in the great northwest, or his first wife the acting teacher, discarded and in poverty. In a few more years, he would similarly not discuss his bastard child, who wasn't merely discarded but unrecognized while Gable walked the earth, or in his will.

At the beginning of his MGM career he was typecast and playing all manner of gangsters like Killer Mears, but then the public demanded that the new star branch out. He worked long hours six days a week at the studio and returned with nothing left for Ria and her two older children by a previous marriage. The same ambition he had experienced in 1923 still burned a decade later. He started to make money and hoard money, and he joined a new crop of "movie stars" of the era of talking pictures, who were in reality outcasts much like Gable and had managed to find the right time and the right place to be successful.

Among them was Joan Crawford, at twenty-four a hard-working leading lady who had struggled her way up from silent westerns to become a new queen of MGM melodrama. Joan was a straightforward woman who sought control on her pictures by seducing her director and her leading man and taking very, very good care of them. Crawford played big on the screen but she stood all of five-one. The physically powerful Gable could have broken Joan in half but instead found in her a kindred spirit who was, like him, a wounded soul and a believer that career was all. He thought she was a beautiful woman; she thought he was a beautiful man. She was also on the Hollywood "A" list, and Gable was ambitious. Their love affair would foreshadow much that occurred in 1941 and '42. Gable lost himself in the role of romantic lover, as did Crawford, who called it all "glorious and hopeless," with these two self-involved souls enacting what was for each the most passionate of scenarios: perfect humans, he the prototype male, she the prototype female, meeting and making glorious, perfect love.

As Joan said of their studio sessions making *Possessed* in 1932, "All day long we'd seek each other's eyes." But Ria was a respected woman in Hollywood, and so MGM studio boss Louis B. Mayer ordered the Gable-Crawford liaison to be nullified—at least they concurred that it would be nullified. But they continued to make pictures together and rumor was they continued on as lovers.

Not long after the "official" termination of the Gable-Craw-ford affair, MGM loaned him out to Paramount in central Holly-wood for a little picture called *No Man of Her Own*, pairing Clark Gable with a dame about Crawford's age—and another gal he fig-ured for a sexual athlete. What else *could* he think with the way the woman swore and carried herself. She never even wore a bra for chrissake! Carole Lombard was married to William Powell at the time but wasn't shy about telling everyone, and loudly, that they were great friends and lousy spouses and already she spouted the business about how Hollywood marriages couldn't last. Ga-ble still had eyes for Crawford and smarted from Mayer's dressing down, so he finished the little picture at Paramount with his pants buttoned and went on his way. Gable wasn't ready for Lombard; Lombard wasn't ready for Gable.

A divorce (Lombard's), a shooting death (Columbo's), an Oscar (Gable's), a separation (also Gable's), and three-and-a-half years later, both were ready. They struck up a conversation at the Vic-tor Hugo during the White Mayfair Ball, sparks flew, and neither looked back from that night on. Lombard had matured quite a bit, and Clark found a lot behind those topaz-blue Lombard eyes that hadn't been there while making the little picture at Paramount. Carole seemed to respect him for the Academy Award he had earned for *It Happened One Night*, and she also took the time to notice that little boy's vulnerability underneath the big star's sex appeal. Clark liked the fact that they looked good together because publicity was everything in Hollywood and the candids would be socko, but much more than that, he found in her an answer to life's romantic mystery that he hadn't known previously, even with Crawford. Back then he had thrown himself into passion under-standing that it was all make-believe. Now, at the White Mayfair Ball and beyond, he found Lombard to be quite a different animal from Miss Joan Crawford. Crawford was all pretense, all the time. Joan was full of shit—he knew it and she knew it. Lombard showed ambition, sure, and just by way of casual conversation, he realized she was a walking, talking issue of *Box Office* magazine. Still, Lombard managed to be as down to earth as the lemon trees, and she had this odd quality to her that he couldn't begin to figure out, but it was a quality he liked. A lot. Carole Lombard had the capacity to love, not like a sucker, not like some doormat. She was an honest-to-God warm human being. Somehow, a real live woman had managed to survive in Hollywood and he had found her.

For a while Carole kept quiet about Russ Columbo. He could tell the relationship had scarred her. She described Columbo as a boy in a man's body. Well, Gable had been bedroom-hopping Hollywood for five, six years now and knew damn well that he was all man in a man's body. He didn't even have to work at being great shakes in bed because he knew that dames found him perfectly beautiful to look at and touch and be close to and surrounded by. He wore his Clark Gable suit like armor and enjoyed its protection from having to reveal the real him.

Gable held a dark secret tight to his breast, something he seems never to have revealed even to Lombard. Gable was a father, having engaged in an affair with actress Loretta Young while on loan-out to Fox for the Alaskan adventure *Call of the Wild* in 1935. It was a long, cold location shoot, and the two stars found a great way to pass the time, with only one complication, a baby girl named Judy who was born after Loretta Young dropped out of sight for several conspicuous months after *Call of the Wild* wrapped. Later the single Loretta would decide to "adopt" a baby to make her life complete—her own infant daughter Judy. For such a delicate little girl, Judy Lewis would represent an enormous skeleton in Gable's closet. He would never acknowledge his paternity despite an uncanny facial resemblance and a smoking-hot trail of circumstantial evidence. His conduct regarding his own daughter showed an unsettling ability to shut people out, no matter who they were or how obligated he should feel. He had always been a scrapper who did whatever it took to survive. Whatever it took. Gable always saw poverty as being one or two bad pictures away, or one or two paternity suits away. He had been poor, and now he was rich and successful. No power on earth could take away what belonged to Clark Gable.

A related realization knocked Lombard over. She didn't see it coming, and she couldn't resist it. Clark Gable was a big kid, a lot like she was a big gee-whiz kid herself. He liked toys, the simplest guy things. She could give him gold cuff links and that would be nice; but a passing motorcycle? That produced a gleam in his eye. Gable's hard life and his struggles had led to appreciation. Of Gable with Lombard, Howard Strickling said, "It's the first time I think he ever really played in his life. He'd had a very serious life when you stop to think about it—his early life, his father, his step-mother. He had to make his own way. Nobody gave him anything on a silver tray. He earned every dime he made."

Gable had never seen anyone like her—a dame this naturally energetic, this naturally *up*. "She laughed all the time," said Hollywood director Delmer Daves, and soon Gable was laughing right along with her.

Says Richard Lang of the Gable that emerged, "He had great fun; he laughed. He was a great kidder. That's why they always had fun and kidded each other."

Looking back on the pair, Loretta Young said, "They were always way up in the air or way down—they were real people."

True, Lombard was damaged goods and so was Gable, but together they made one spectacular package and after the 1936 Mayfair Ball they became an item. In fact they became *the* item in Hollywood, just as Pickford and Fairbanks Sr., and Valentino and Negri, and Crawford and Fairbanks Jr. had once been the item in Hollywood. The press ate up the unexpected romance of MGM's top heartthrob and Paramount's glamour girl. Clark and Carole protested endlessly that they wanted nothing but a quiet life together well out of the spotlight, yet somehow managed to find their way in front of every news camera within range of Southern California and grab every possible headline for five full years. They couldn't resist it. They knew they sparkled and got a kick out of the reaction they earned together. They were seen at the fights, at the tennis matches, at Santa Anita for the horse-racing, at nightclubs, at her place, at his, shooting skeet, hunting in the wilds, at movie premieres (his, hers, and others), and at awards ceremonies, with candids of the couple plastered across articles in fan magazines, and newsreels plastered across the silver screen.

They became known for gag gifts; she wanted a kitten so he bought her a cougar cub. He liked high-end automobiles so she bought him broken-down jalopies. When they fought, and they fought often, she got into the habit of sending a peace offering of live doves, and the move always worked—but the caged doves piled up at her place and had to be cared for.

Their careers boomed, especially that of Gable, who made hit after hit. But Lombard got lucky as well, not just at the Beverly Wilshire that first night, but at Universal, which requested her for the screwball part of a lifetime in a hot property called *1011 Fifth Avenue*, a novella written by Eric Hatch of *The New Yorker* with script adaptation by Hatch and Morrie Ryskind, pedigreed comedy writer by way of work on three of the Marx Brothers' best pictures. The part came Lombard's way in circuitous fashion. Universal wanted William Powell on loan-out from MGM. Powell said he would agree to make the picture only if Lombard was his co-star. When offered, she said yes in a heartbeat for two critical reasons: Ex-husband Powell remained her closest male friend in the world. More important, her entire party spree had been built around re-branding Carole Lombard as a madcap comedienne, and she found the part in *1011 Fifth Avenue* to be as good as, or maybe even better than, Lily Garland in *Twentieth Century*.

The resulting picture, renamed *My Man Godfrey*, was a send-up of the upper class in Depression-plagued New York City, the daffy Bullock family with Lombard as flighty daughter Irene to former Broadway star Alice Brady's equally mad mother. Set against the two are the growling, put-upon father played by Eugene Pallette and Irene's canny, scheming sister played by Gail Patrick. Godfrey, portrayed by Powell, is a society guy who drops out of sight after a bad romance and ends up living with hobos at the pier. Godfrey is "found" by the Bullocks during a high society scavenger hunt, and they retain him as their butler, thinking they're giving him a break. Irene falls for Godfrey with screwball consequences, of course, but the writers imbued Godfrey with such heart that he soon brings the flighty Bullocks down to earth, which enables them to discover their own souls. Upon release in November 1936, *My Man Godfrey* would become one of the most revered pictures of the 1930s and earn six Academy Award nominations in the categories of Best Actor (Powell), Best Actress (Lombard), Best Supporting Actor (Mischa Auer), Best Supporting Actress (Brady), Best Director (Gregory LaCava), and Best Writing/Screenplay (Hatch and Ryskind). All this from a studio, Universal Pictures, most famous for unleashing *Frankenstein*, *Dracula*, and *The Mummy* on a receptive movie-going public.

For the second time in three years, Lombard had been in the right place at the right time. Suddenly Academy Award nominated, she became a hot commodity and returned to Paramount for several star vehicles that took her through the completion of her seven-year deal in 1937. Myron Selznick then began shopping Carole around town. His reasoning was sound: Why tie yourself down to one studio when you could freelance and have them all bidding for your services? Myron parlayed her popularity into a contract with the Selznick Studios (operated by his brother, David O. Selznick) that kicked off with the biting comedy *Nothing Sacred*, filmed in Technicolor and featuring Lombard to great advantage as Hazel Flagg, a girl misdiagnosed with radium poisoning who, when thought to be dying, accepts a trip to New York and becomes a media sensation, only to later be exposed as a fraud. The screenplay by Ben Hecht featured what the *The Spectator* of London pinpointed as "a fundamental distaste for humanity" and included a dig at American culture with every scene, with enough of a surrealist touch added by director William A. "Wild Bill" Wellman to boost it into the screwball zone.

Wellman was a man's man who disliked actors because all they could ever do was *pretend* to be manly, although he did appreciate Clark Gable's genuine masculinity when the two had worked together a couple of years earlier. But then, as Wellman remembered of Gable, "We had trouble on *Call of the Wild*, big trouble, on top of a mountain. He wasn't tending to business, not the business of making pictures. He was paying a lot of attention to monkey business, and I called him for it, lost my easy-to-lose temper, and did it in front of the company."

Wellman was referring to Gable and Loretta Young. But far from embarrassing Gable, the confrontation before not a friendly MGM crew but a Twentieth Century Fox location crew, strangers all, proved that Wild Bill was Gable's idea of a director, tough as nails and no nonsense, and Wellman said that Clark was "a nice guy, and my kind—not *too* nice."

Wild Bill disliked actresses as a rule—they were delicate, primping prima donnas who too often held up production, but Lombard won him over on *Nothing Sacred*. Production went well enough that at the cast party, Lombard talked Wellman into a straitjacket where he remained for the duration, resulting in zany news photos and a fistful of press releases generated by producer David Selznick's publicity hound, Russell Birdwell.

In typical fashion, Selznick kept adding lavish ingredients to his tidy and sadistic comedy until the production cost for just seventy-five minutes of running time bulged to $1.3 million, meaning that the picture was assured of losing money and did, despite a stout $1.1 million in domestic box office. Lombard always devoted time to reading the trades—*The Hollywood Reporter, Box Office, Variety*—and cared deeply whether her pictures made money or not.

One fact she readily accepted: All the publicity around *Nothing Sacred* and the fact that she had appeared in a Technicolor production proved a tremendous boost to her name recognition and earning potential. She was now, to use modern vernacular, trending.

She resonated with ticket buyers in part because her pictures represented social commentary; her blossoming career had its foundation rooted in a scathing examination of the morals and hypocrisy of the nation and the need for social consciousness raising. In *Twentieth Century* she had portrayed a shop-girl turned actress who had lost all semblance of self, and in *My Man Godfrey* the dizzy rich girl who failed to see the suffering all around her. In *Nothing Sacred* she played the innocent fool manipulated by the press into a darling of fickle masses. In all cases what the character lacked was a soul, which had been infused by fade out. Lombard confirmed the difficulty in playing these roles, saying of Irene Bullock, "Irene in *Godfrey* was, I'd say, the most difficult part I ever played. Because Irene was a complicated and, believe it or not, essentially a tragic person."

Variety agreed. In comparing the roles of Carole Lombard and William Powell in *My Man Godfrey*, *Variety* said, "Miss Lombard's role is the more difficult of the two, since it calls for more pressure acting all the way.... It's Powell's job to be normal and breezily comic in the madcap household, and that doesn't require stretching for him."

In fact, the characters that Lombard portrayed in all of these critical successes were flawed figures who survived only by crafting alternate realities. It was all part of that "new energy" she had tapped thanks to director Howard Hawks, a screwball formula that aligned with her own unusual life and set of madcap friends and lovers.

Soon after hooking up with Gable, Lombard found it necessary to ditch her high-profile Hollywood Boulevard party house for an address in labyrinthian Bel Air, where lived far more shrubs and vines than people. She found a brick and stucco, Tudor-influenced one story with a barn along with orange and lemon trees and signed a lease for three years; by paying in advance she earned a $300 discount, which didn't mean much to Carole but it meant the world to the practical Fieldsie.

Carole ordered new stationery with an address that read simply "The Farm," and she knew that disorienting Bel Air with its infernally winding roads and hedgerows would provide some breathing room for the lovers.

Lombard the rescuer/nurturer proceeded to populate the Farm with Fieldsie, who continued to live with Carole, and with animals: six doves, two ducks, Edmund the rooster, Ellen and Eleanor the hens, several dogs, three goldfish (unnamed), and Josephine the cat, who came with the house. While making a picture, Carole kept to a strict routine: just work, study, eat, and sleep. When not on a production, she stayed up to all hours talking to Fieldsie or playing with the animals. Her biggest animal and rescue effort, Clark Gable, also became a more-than-part-time resident of the St. Cloud Road address of Carole Lombard.

13

The Plane That Fell

Calvin Harper, the head loader at the Blue Diamond Mine, never figured to punch out at the end of his shift and embark on an errand of mercy, but Ora Salyer had taken a call from the Clark County sheriff and soon there Harper went, down into Red Rock Canyon to the Wilson Ranch to round up some horses for the rescue party that would soon set out to reach that plane on the side of Potosi Mountain.

Harper drove down a long, dusty road to the ranch and rapped his knuckles against the screen door of the ranch house. The house was dark; it was going on ten at night.

Inside the house, fifty-two-year-old Willard H. George stumbled half asleep to the door and opened it to behold a young man who was wide-eyed enough and breathless enough that it made George cautious. "I'm from the Blue Diamond Mine," said the fellow through the screen door. "Have you got any horses?"

George was foggy in the head and had to think a moment. "Yes, I have horses." The sound of his own voice awakened him more than he wanted. "What do you want them for?"

The young man said the strangest thing. He said, "Well, the sheriff telephoned and said there was a plane fell on the mountain up here, and they want some horses and some riders to go up there."

George processed the information and ciphered up what he knew. "Well, I have four horses and two riders."

"OK, thank you," said the young fellow, who hurried off.

Alone again and in the dark, Willard George started to really think about the evening. He had seen some strange things. First was an object in the southern sky, hovering a quarter mile above the mountain. It offered a steady light and seemed to be a few feet in diameter. Later, right at bedtime, he saw a plane that had acted strangely. He was out draining his radiator to keep it from turning into a block of ice in the winter air. Standing there in the dark he had seen a plane fly over, or rather it was the engines racing at top speed that drew his attention; they were really roaring. He wondered what in Sam Hill a plane was doing this far north of the beam. Willard George knew the routes the planes took; the San Francisco planes flew right over the ranch house, back and forth. The Los Angeles planes flew six or eight miles south of the ranch. But this plane had followed neither course; it had meandered across the sky dipping and swerving like a porpoise and then crossed over behind the sandstone butte, and George hadn't seen it anymore. He figured the plane had made the grade and crossed the mountains, so he drained his radiator and prepared for slumber on a night that called for warm bedclothes and retiring early.

Inside the house he had recounted the view of the plane to his wife, Florence, and figured it to be an Army ship from McCarran. "I never saw a plane set so peculiar as this plane out here," he told her. "It was doing all kinds of things."

A little later he had seen an orange glow over the ridge and remarked, "If this was back forty years when I was a kid, I would think it was the Indians in the mountains building a big fire because in the fall of the year they would go up to gather pine nuts and build big fires and roast the pine nuts." But this wasn't the turn of the century; this was the beginning of 1942 and a civilized age, and Willard had seen an orange halo glow in the sky over the near foothills before heading off to bed.

Now Willard H. George was wide awake, and on instinct he climbed into his clothes from the day, thinking about all he had seen this night, when there came another knock at his door. This time the screen door separated him from the same young man, now accompanied by Army officers in uniform.

"I'm Major Anderson from McCarran Field," said a fellow in a fancy green uniform with an official-sounding voice. Out beyond the porch, George could see some other men that he didn't know. He figured them for tourists.

"How do we get up *there*?" asked Major Anderson, pointing up in the direction of Potosi Mountain. "On top of *that*?"

George took a moment to grasp what the stranger was asking. "There is nobody can find the way up *there*," he said patiently. "You've got to have a guide." The officer named Anderson said again that a plane had gone down and they needed to reach a spot up on the mountain.

"Just a minute," said Willard George. He nudged past the men on his porch and shuffled out across the parched earth to the bunk house of the Wilson Ranch and there roused his Piute Indian boy, Jim Wilson, who wasn't a boy at all but a wiry old man, age seventy-five, who was nicknamed "Tweed," a quiet, ancient fellow and an old hand with the horses from back in the day when Indians were wild and ruled the range.

George explained to the sleepy-eyed Native American what was going on, about the plane and the crash and the strangers at the door. After a moment, the Indian said, "The only way you can get up the mountain is on horses."

With that, George relinquished his four horses to the Army-led posse, and his Indian, and one of his cowboys. Then Willard went back to bed, wondering what in the blazes was really going on, but not really caring because sleep soon overtook him and that was it for the night.

14

Somber Hymns and Cold Marble

In the 1930s women were coming a long way, baby. In 1931, just eleven years after passage of the Nineteenth Amendment granting women the right to vote, Jane Addams became the first woman to win the Nobel Prize for her work benefiting the poor in Chicago. A year after that, Amelia Earhart became the first woman to fly the Atlantic Ocean, and a year after that, Frances Perkins became U.S. Secretary of Labor, the first woman to sit in the cabinet of the president of the United States. In the 1930s about one in four women in the United States worked at a job outside the home, meaning that three out of four were "homemakers" and central to holding families together during the Great Depression. Carole Lombard counted herself in the minority, and by 1937 reigned as one of the highest-paid women in America and spoke stridently of her beliefs that the sexes were different and yet equal.

Carole Lombard and Clark Gable would find 1937 to be a tough year. First came a federal trial against a woman named Violet Norton from the United Kingdom who tried unsuccessfully to extort money from Gable. She claimed he had impregnated her in 1923 and brought to court a thirteen-year-old named Gwendoline to prove it, with the only problem being that Gable wasn't in the U.K. in 1923 as Violet Norton claimed. For the first time, Franz Doerfler emerged from the shadows of Oregon to testify on Gable's behalf, and given the circumstances of his abrupt 1924 Doerfler-dumping, it proved to be an uncomfortable day. FBI files reveal that Gable was a frequent target of blackmail and extortion, and that he followed a regular process of turning letters and other evidence over to the studio, which would then contact the FBI.

The other watershed event of 1937 was the death of the blonde bombshell Jean Harlow. She had been Gable's pal since they broke in playing supporting roles at MGM in *The Secret Six* in 1930 and since then had made huge hits together like *Red Dust*, *China Seas*, and *Wife vs. Secretary*. Fireball Lombard and passively sweet Harlow made for quite a contrast, and Lombard wanted to dislike the girl who was Gable's friend and had become William Powell's lover, but there was no disliking the sweetheart that everyone called "the Baby." Harlow possessed a gentle, acquiescent soul and proved entirely lovable.

Bill's relationship with the Baby mirrored Carole's with Russ, but in reverse: Columbo and Harlow were the earnest pursuers, and Lombard and Powell the wary prey. Bill Powell liked Jean Harlow just fine as a girlfriend, but he balked at marrying again, a situation that came to a head soon after the March 4, 1937 Academy Awards when *My Man Godfrey* was shut out despite five nominations and the Powell-Harlow comedy *Libeled Lady* lost for Best Picture. But Powell had appeared in three Best Picture nominees, the third being *The Great Ziegfeld*, which did take Best Picture. Gable and Lombard and Powell and Harlow had spent the evening together, celebrating and commiserating. Harlow was just over a serious bout of influenza and soon would have trouble with her wisdom teeth and her man. William Powell was adept at attracting blondes but had trouble keeping them around because he tended to grow aloof. Powell did a lot of taking and little giving, much like Gable, which occasionally caused trouble for Lombard as well.

Later in March, Harlow underwent surgery to extract her wisdom teeth and, according to her biographer David Stenn, almost died on the table. Her health never recovered. She began another picture with Gable, the horse racing romance *Saratoga*, and struggled through the month of May 1937 on the set, her looks sliding by the day and her energy shot, until finally she was forced to retreat to a sick bed. At the beginning of June she was critically ill at home on Palm Drive in Beverly Hills when Gable visited. Leaning down over her bed, he took in the foul odor of disease and would later say, "It was like kissing a dead person, a rotting person. It was a terrible thing to walk into."

According to Stenn, Harlow's home became a "virtual hospital" of equipment and nurses so that Harlow's domineering mother could continue efforts to control the situation. But Jean Harlow's body was shutting down due to chronic kidney degeneration that Stenn traces back to a 1925 bout of scarlet fever. Now, a secondary kidney infection spread. Jean Harlow was doomed. Bill Powell, who legend says adored Harlow, failed to grasp the seriousness of the situation until the end. Jean Harlow died on June 7, 1937.

No one could believe it. The vibrant, sexy, twenty-six-year-old, box-office queen of the movies was gone, not from a horrible accident or a violent crime. She had simply withered up and died.

It was still spring, the time of year when Southern California became paradise with beautiful weather and the landscape an explosion of blooms. But Hollywood mourned, and braced for a funeral unlike anything since Valentino. With the Columbo interment all too recent, Carole Lombard wanted to avoid Forest Lawn at all costs. Life was for the living, not the fallen. And as much as Lombard courted the press and encouraged fandom, she resented the intrusion of reporters *and* fans at such events. It made for another compelling reason to stay away.

She wasn't alone in dreading the Harlow funeral. Despite the fact that Clark Gable looked on the Baby as a sister, which was rare for a male always on the prowl, he also didn't want to attend the funeral because that was Gable's nature, not to want to do things that others wanted him to do, even things he knew he should do. Louis B. Mayer demanded that Gable go because to do otherwise would imply disharmony at MGM, and that was not allowed. Yes, Gable would go, and since that was a fact, then Lombard would be there to support her man.

Gable and Lombard believed they had already paid their dues with this type of Hollywood spectacle when they had attended the funeral of Irving Thalberg less than nine months earlier. Always in poor health, MGM's "Boy Genius" had died at just thirty-seven years of age, a turn of events that rocked MGM more profoundly than any earthquake. As much as Gable owed to Thalberg, he hadn't wanted to go to that funeral, and neither had Lombard. But both had attended, along with all the other heavyweights in town.

Photographs tell the story of the couple's Forest Lawn morning spent at the Wee Kirk O' the Heather Chapel attending the service for Jean Harlow in a foursome with Fieldsie and her boyfriend, director Walter Lang. Gable wore a black suit, as did Lombard, who covered it with a black fur cape. In one photo they climb the stone path leading to the chapel prior to the service. In another they descend the path afterward. Clark's hand under Carole's arm conveys strength and hints at protection as they look ahead with frowns on their faces, no doubt scrutinizing some sacrilegious act by the press or a crazed fan. In an hour Harlow would be interred in a crypt in the Great Mausoleum, mere yards from the remains of Russ Columbo in one direction and Irving Thalberg in another. The crypt inside Harlow's tomb would be marked simply, Our Baby, and a guilt-ridden William Powell would sit with her often and soon develop rectal cancer and suffer terribly.

The death of Harlow, piled on all the other deaths of young Hollywood people, changed the playing field for Lombard and Gable. The fatalist Lombard had no use for spectacle, especially at funerals, and murmured to Gable in the limousine after the Baby's service that when Carole died, no public unpleasantness must occur. Oh, she knew she never was and never would be a blonde bombshell and box-office sensation in Harlow's class. Sex sold, and Jean Harlow was so sexy that she made nearly every line of dialogue into the Kama Sutra. Lombard was, well, Lombard, and whatever that was, it involved celebrity and her death would invite the morbidly curious. She told Gable that when her time came, the service must be brief, simple, and private. Pragmatist Gable groused at such talk; he was years older and he would go first. But she extracted a promise from him that day, and he would be bound to honor it a lot sooner than he ever might have imagined.

Just to prove the fragility of life in general and of famous women in particular, less than a month after Harlow's death, hotshot pilot Amelia Earhart, age thirty-nine, and navigator Fred Noonan disappeared over the South Pacific in her Lockheed Electra airplane during a spectacular failure of an attempt to circumnavigate the earth by air. Losses like Earhart were the price paid by society for great advances in aviation. On the plus side, a new commercial airplane called the DC-3 was changing the lives of the well to do, including the Hollywood set. Suddenly they could travel anywhere, seemingly everywhere, not in terms of weeks or days but by the hour. Those dreaded personal appearances in Salt Lake City and Des Moines and Fargo no longer needed to be endured by train but could be checked off the list via the amazing new DC-3 with service that included the Sky Sleeper with fold-down seats and the Sky-Club with full meal service and other comforts. All at once the glamorous air travel promoted in RKO's musical *Flying Down to Rio* moved from fantasy to glorious reality.

For Lombard, 1937 wasn't all court cases, somber hymns, and the cold hand of death. Professionally, she was rolling. She made a musical drama at Paramount, *Swing High, Swing Low* with Fred MacMurray that would go on to be highly profitable. Tongue in cheek, she referred to *Swing High, Swing Low* as her "come-back picture." But as the reporter noted upon hearing the statement,

"Every picture Carole makes is her 'come-back picture.' She discusses her 'return to the screen' as if she had been off it for years." This from a woman signed to make three pictures in 1937 alone. It was shtick; it was always shtick with Lombard, who was her own best audience. Sometimes it didn't matter if those around her got the humor as long as she herself laughed. If Carole got the joke, that was enough.

Before *Swing High, Swing Low* wrapped, Lombard sat on a Paramount soundstage for an interview with a newspaper reporter. The reporter was ushered in by a twenty-two-year-old brunette office assistant named Margaret Tallichet who said in her buttery voice and Texas drawl, "My job was to take these visiting people out to the sets. I'd introduce them to the stars so they could get their interviews. As I recall it, this was one of the first times I had done this. I didn't know the protocol, whether I was to sit with them or go back to my office. So I stayed."

The reporter looked at Tallichet and said to Lombard, "This is a pretty girl. Don't you think she should be in pictures?"

Lombard said later, "Something about her struck me as unusual. Her personality, rather than any exceptional beauty.... I had the sudden hunch that this girl, if given a little help, might go places." Indeed there was nothing spectacular about Tallichet's looks; what captured Lombard's attention was the girl's sweet disposition and that lilting Texas flavor to every word she spoke.

Carole leveled her ice-blue eyes on the startled publicity assistant. "Yes I do," said Lombard, "and I'm going to do something about it."

Tallichet remembered, "And it wasn't a week until she did."

Carole arranged for the girl she nicknamed "Talli" to sign with up-and-coming agent Zeppo Marx, whom she knew from his days working on the Paramount lot with his three better-known brothers, Groucho, Harpo, and Chico. In one of those lucky coincidences that seemed to happen around Lombard, her latest cause caught fire thanks to David Selznick's epic in the works, *Gone With the Wind*, still two years from cameras rolling. Selznick's head of publicity Russell Birdwell, known as "Birdie," saw in the Lombard-grooming-Tallichet story an opportunity to prove to David Selznick his abilities as a publicity man.

"At Carole's behest," drawled Tallichet, "Zeppo took me to Selznick International and introduced me there. I got one of those stock contracts. Selznick was pleasant; I was terrified. I was a jelly of fear."

Birdwell asked his boss to let Tallichet do a walk-on with a line of dialogue in the Selznick picture then in production, *A Star Is Born*. Birdwell's press release labeled the girl Lombard's "discovery," and while the publicity man sought only placement in the papers, Carole's interest was genuine and ongoing.

Lombard invited Talli to the Bel Air farm, and also to Petey's house in Beverly Hills where the newcomer met the Peters crowd. Carole gave Talli a boost inside Paramount's walls by being seen with her often, arms locked, carrying on. Lombard, probably at Birdwell's urging, served as Tallichet's makeup girl when it came time to shoot her *A Star Is Born* walk-on, but the final gesture was all Carole. Said Tallichet, "I remember going with her to see John Engstead shoot a series of still photos of her." Engstead was, with George Hurrell, among the most sought-after portrait artists in Hollywood. As they chatted during the session, it occurred to Lombard that Engstead portraits would benefit Talli, so Carole made the appointment and paid for the session.

"She was kind and generous, unbelievably so," said Tallichet years later with undiminished astonishment. "This combination of energy and generosity."

David Selznick soon sent Margaret Tallichet off for a year of dramatic lessons, and when she returned to Hollywood, she met and fell in love with director William Wyler. Her film career would consist of a half-dozen pictures, only one of which is remembered today. Tallichet played the endangered female lead in *Stranger on the Third Floor*, a thriller made at RKO in 1940 starring Peter Lorre in one of his creepiest roles. Many consider it the first *film noir* picture ever, although Tallichet was loath to remember *Stranger* afterward and lived out her life better known as Mrs. William Wyler in a marriage that produced four children and endured until William Wyler's death in 1981. It was a path that Lombard set Talli on, and the would-be ingénue remained forever grateful.

15

Hoping Against Hope

By nine o'clock on the night of January 16, 1942, telephone lines were lit up all over Las Vegas. The police had now received calls from the Blue Diamond Mine, from men working the trains in Arden, from several other citizens across the Las Vegas area, and from the constable down in Goodsprings. Las Vegas police sent a response team directly to Blue Diamond where police cars, ambulances with doctors and nurses, and even an army truck roared in with sirens screaming over Blue Diamond Road to the mine itself, and Dan Yanich and Ora Salyer could but watch the parade of rescue vehicles careen up the treacherous access road and pull to a stop in their facility. The pair stared blankly and pointed at a distant blob of flame ten miles off to the south in the deepened night and observed shocked reactions of the responders.

Some of the first would-be rescuers stayed behind, including Las Vegas Mayor Howell "Hal" Garrison—also the local undertaker—and others headed back to town. One of these was Clark County road supervisor Jack Moore, who also served as a deputy sheriff. Back in Las Vegas, Moore entered a police station buzzing with activity, men drinking coffee and poring over maps, smoking cigarettes, many offering opinions about where the plane was and how it should be accessed. Faces were drawn and gray, and the name Carole Lombard hung on the air as Moore nudged his way through the crowd.

After seeing the flames from the Blue Diamond, Jack Moore had a good idea where the plane was up on the ridges of Potosi Mountain, and he figured that the only way to get to that spot was by way of Goodsprings. Now, he learned new information: A pilot had just flown over the crash scene and landed at the airport. Moore dashed north to the terminal and had to show his badge to gain admittance at the outer gate. As he climbed out of his car he could still see a pinpoint of flame on the distant mountain. He rushed into the TWA and Western Airlines station at McCarran Field to find that pilot.

Capt. Art Cheney and some airport men, including Chuck Duffy, stood around a map, and Cheney was pointing at the site of the crash when Moore walked up. The spot under the pilot's finger was well southwest of Arden and above Goodsprings. In other words, it was the no man's land of Potosi Mountain. A fellow in the group who serviced the airplane beacons in that area was adamant: The only way in was over the Goodsprings Road to the old Ninety-Nine Mine Road. It was rough going all the way by any sort of vehicle, and at some point that road would be washed out and impassable. Then God help anyone continuing on by foot and then trying to climb the cliffs to the place where that plane probably went down. According to Captain Cheney it was in the saddle of the mountain up near the peak, against sheer rockface.

Jack Moore piped up and asked if there was any road at all to the peak of the mountain. "Nope," came the answer. Moore wasn't a supervisor and a deputy for nothing. He was a man who got things done. He searched the room for a phone, found one, and called the sheriff's office and asked that a message be forwarded to Sheriff Ward, wherever he was, and to Mayor Garrison out at Blue Diamond. Moore said both men must be told that the plane hit Potosi Mountain above Goodsprings and that Deputy Sheriff Jack Moore would be taking a party in by that way. By Goodsprings. He hung up the phone.

"Well, boys," said Moore, "that's our play." He grabbed Deputy Sheriff George Bondley and a couple of other fellows. They stuffed as many sandwiches and tangerines in their pockets as would fit and then grabbed some flashlights, shovels, and rope, threw these in the trunk of Moore's car and then they piled in. Robert Griffith of the Las Vegas Chamber of Commerce came rushing up and asked to go along. Moore hesitated—this was a businessman—but he said OK, and with the four other men he sped off toward the highway for the trip south to Goodsprings.

Ideally, he could grab a Caterpillar tractor to blaze a trail when the road ran out, but there wasn't time. Nobody knew if there were survivors up on the mountain. That Western Airlines captain had painted a grim picture, but nobody knew for sure if any of the passengers on the plane had spilled out into deep snow before the explosion. The drifts up there could hit fifteen or twenty feet in places and any survivors could freeze to death pretty fast. It had already been three hours since impact had been reported. Three long hours, way too long, and help was still hours away, he knew, because Jack Moore was the help and here they were, speeding along but far from their objective.

It was a pitch-black, moonless night, and in places the drive was illuminated only by the headlights of his car. It was twenty-five miles to Goodsprings and seemed to take forever, with all the men silent in contemplation of a hard experience ahead. They finally pulled up at the sheriff's office in Goodsprings and there learned of a local man named Lyle Van Gordon who had reported the crash and fire to the sheriff and who claimed to know the exact spot where rescuers should go.

"Are you talking about *Bull* Van Gordon?" asked the deputy.

The sheriff said yes, one and the same. Moore asked the sheriff to get Bull on the phone, and then when the connection was made asked Van Gordon if he was certain where the crash had happened.

Lyle said that he had watched the fire, marked the spot, and knew exactly where it was. Moore asked where Van Gordon lived—he could pick him up in a few minutes and—

The sheriff interrupted the conversation. There was no point starting off for that mountain in the dead of night; no good could come of it. They could wait in the office and pick Van Gordon up before dawn. So that's what they did, looked over maps, drank coffee, made plans, and waited until five, still well before dawn, at which point they drove to Lyle Van Gordon's shack, one of many that dotted Goodsprings.

Moore knocked on the front door, and Van Gordon fairly burst out, filling the doorway as he passed through. He was a powerfully built man and seemed like he could make the climb up any mountain and then some. Van Gordon hopped in his truck and pulled out in front of Moore's car and up to the rock-strewn dirt road leading to the old mines of Clark County. It was a long, slow, eleven-mile crawl over rutted paths, dodging washouts and boulders, all the while hoping against hope that they might yet find Miss Carole Lombard and the brave Army men on that TWA flight still alive.

16

Certified Bombs

Carole Lombard enjoyed everything about being Clark Gable's paramour. Well, everything except maybe the sex because, after all, Gable had his limitations. He was a heavily engineered piece of machinery, built for show by Josephine Dillon and then by the MGM publicity department. He hadn't been road-tested for performance. Among his problems were dentures from the extraction of most of his teeth a few years earlier. This apparatus became problematic during the rigors of lovemaking. Plus Gable was in the habit of *being* Clark Gable, which meant that anything he contributed to the lovemaking ritual should be good enough. He seemed to share with fellow Hollywood lover Errol Flynn, or so rumor said, the problem of racking up numbers and not necessarily assuring satisfaction at the end of the evening.

Yeah, well, Carole Lombard had different ideas. Lombard had proven herself to be an athlete, sexual and otherwise, so Gable's reputation could take him only so far. But her ballsiness was something that Gable actually *liked*. He liked being told when his performance didn't pass muster. He liked and relied upon strong women; the kind of women he had married twice already. "I knew every wife he had," said Delmer Daves. "I think probably the psychological thing behind all this was, he needed a mama."

Jean Garceau, who would become a Gable employee in 1938

and remain one for twenty years, said, "He liked a woman with a lot of guts, vim and vigor, humor particularly."

Carole played by a man's rules and he respected her for it. She wasn't like other dames; she wasn't like any dame he had met. This girl played the game of life for high stakes, and she gave the impression that at any time she could scrape back her chair and walk away from the table. She even *talked* tough, her language as salty as advertised, but at all times slangy, informal, real. "Yah, yah, I get you," she'd say as she listened, intently listened, to what he had to say. When something was satisfactory, she'd say, "It's OK by me!" and mean it.

Yes, to Gable Carole Lombard seemed to believe that she belonged at the high-stakes table. For once Gable's admiring grin wasn't for show. He truly did admire this dish.

He especially enjoyed Lombard's practical jokes at his expense. He knew it was all about building the reputation of the screwball girl, and he also found something funny in the tearing down of the revered Gable persona. Of all her stunts, the attempted bombing of MGM with leaflets tickled him. He had just made his biggest dud of a picture at Metro, *Parnell*, the screen biography of Charles Stewart Parnell, Irish nationalist hero of the nineteenth century. Gable broke out of his successful formula of wise-cracking tough guys to attempt something in the realm of Warner Bros.' Paul Muni, and Gable had been skewered for it. Nowhere had the ribbing been less merciful than on his own lot, among his actor colleagues. Spencer Tracy, one of the studio's most talented actors, had been especially snide.

Gable's own girlfriend got into the act when she learned that *Parnell* had become a success in, of all places, China. She huddled up with publicity wiz Russell Birdwell, "Birdie," and developed a leaflet announcing, **PARNELL: 50 Million Chinamen Can't Be Wrong**. It was a beautiful gag in theory, so good that Gable actually laughed when he heard, but it proved a dud in execution. No pilot would fly low over the studio and lose his license, so she hired boys to stand in front of the MGM gates and distribute the leaflets one at a time. But a Culver City ordinance rendered the distribution of handbills illegal as well, so the boys were paid and sent home and the leaflets never did circulate.

It was a power-mad move by the publicity-mad team of Lombard and Birdwell, but it typified the early portion of the Lombard-Gable association, with Lombard having found a real man, not a gentleman like Powell or a tender child like Columbo or an egghead like Riskin. She had caught the big game, biggest of all, and he had revealed himself to be, well, fun! But then clouds formed on the horizon as all that talk of filming *Gone With the Wind* turned Hollywood on its ear. From the beginning the word was that Gable must portray the self-serving hero, Rhett Butler, which he never wanted to do, and from the beginning Carole Lombard very much wanted to portray spoiled Southern belle Scarlett O'Hara, a part that in no way suited her. No, she would never play Scarlett, but he was cursed to portray Rhett, and the result was the most famous motion picture of the twentieth century.

"I read *Gone With the Wind*," reported a deadpan Gable. "My reaction was enthusiastic and immediate. 'What a part for Ronald Colman,' I said. I was sincere."

Even before shooting of *Gone With the Wind* had commenced, Gable was voted the King of Hollywood by legions of fans, with Myrna Loy his Queen in name only and Lombard his consort of the flesh. In terms of her own career, Carole had taken her eye off the ball as she focused so hard on Gable, and paid a price. There had been the Technicolor hit for David Selznick, *Nothing Sacred*, which had made box-office cash registers jingle. Then Carole laid an egg at Paramount with another screwball comedy called *True Confession* in which she portrayed a hard-to-care-about habitual liar. Lombard believed that she could pull off the disagreeable premise of *True Confession* with sight gags and mugging, but things went south fast and stayed there for the winter.

Matters weren't helped by Carole's latest cause, John Barrymore. The actor who had co-starred with Lombard in *Twentieth Century* just three years earlier was now drowning in liquor and in need of a break. She found a small part for "Jack" in *True Confession* and asked the writer to pump up a bit part into a feature role. Barrymore tried but failed to make the part work because *True Confession* had been ill-conceived from the start.

Lombard had made a strategic blunder, and trumped it with her next move. Now a free agent, she agreed to make a picture at Warner Bros., an unfunny studio known for social dramas and gangsters and now attempting a new direction in screwball comedy. For Carole, the direction turned out to be—down. She found herself overacting miserably to try to infuse energy into a lifeless cast, crew, and script that attempted to rework the *Godfrey* formula: Impoverished European nobleman becomes the butler of a movie star. Carole could measure the disaster by the length of the shoot, which dragged on for months as opposed to the usual six or eight weeks of a successful shoot. The most successful productions came and went all too fast, with an energy about them, a symmetry, but the making of this thing, *Food for Scandal*, seemed endless. Why had she signed with Warner Bros. in the first place, a studio led by the highly unusual Jack L. Warner. He was a charismatic, under-educated man, notorious for telling bad jokes, most of them off-color, which, if she thought about it, explained why he ran a studio that couldn't produce a comedy. Sometimes Carole had to wonder at her own judgment. Decisions came easy, but some were mistakes. Big mistakes. Huge mistakes. But, oh, how they had treated her like a queen, hiring her cameraman of choice, Ted Tetzlaff, and her wardrobe expert of choice, Travis Banton.

"Anything you want, Miss Lombard."

"We'll take care of it right away, Miss Lombard."

"Whatever you say, Miss Lombard."

Box office for the retitled *Fools for Scandal* said otherwise—she may have been a queen to Warner Bros., and she remained Gable's queen in waiting, but she wasn't box-office royalty to the critics. The *Photoplay* reviewer said this was the straw that would "break the back of that slapstick camel Carole Lombard's been riding so long," while *Variety* said, "this falls short of distinction and is in many respects pretty dull stuff." The *Time* reviewer cut to the chase by calling *Fools for Scandal* "unearthly."

Not that Lombard had stood pat and watched her career sink to the depths. She possessed that intuitive streak and had surrounded herself with smart people. Myron maximized each free-agent deal, and Lombard was the highest-earning woman in Hollywood; Fieldsie offered shrewd counsel; and Selznick International PR man Birdwell had intervened at a critical moment in 1937 and found a way to earn Lombard headlines that had propelled her through 1938. Carole happened to mention during production of *Nothing Sacred* that she had filed her tax return for 1936, earning nearly half a million bucks and paying all but twenty grand in taxes. But she shrugged and said something to the effect that, oh well, it's worth it to live in the good-old U. S. of A.

Birdwell's eyes lit up and in a week Lombard was earning headlines in papers across the country: **Highest Paid Actress Shrugs Off Huge Tax Bill**. The press release quoted Lombard as saying, "We still don't starve in the picture business after we've divided with the government. Taxes go to build schools, to maintain the public utilities we all use, so why not?" Coming at a critical moment in the Depression, Lombard's altruism as exploited by Birdwell earned praise nationwide, beginning with President Franklin Roosevelt.

Sometimes the Lombardian antics proved so wild that even Russell Birdwell couldn't dream them up. When a South American explorer gave Carole a gift of two shrunken heads, her psychic consultants said they were bad luck, so Carole and Clark drove to Benedict Canyon and threw the heads away. When advised that this was the worst possible solution, the tipsy, giggling pair went back to the canyon and searched for the heads on hands and knees. Ultimately, they buried the heads in her backyard in Bel Air and said a prayer. Imagine the surprise for the house's next tenant, Alfred Hitchcock, when Carole Lombard said, "Oh, by the way…"

The Screwball Girl rolled on with such career momentum that even certified bomb *Fools for Scandal* couldn't stop her. The week of October 17, 1938, Birdwell landed her the cover of the nation's most popular magazine, *Life*. In going for a memorable cover shot, photographer Peter Stackpole captured an unexpectedly pensive Lombard, and it was this moody face that stared out at patrons of every newsstand in America, and readers now got the inside scoop on her unorthodox personality. Writer Noel Busch described her method of conversation in terms of "screeches, laughs, growls, gesticulations, and the expletives of a sailor's parrot."

Yes, Gable was the king of Hollywood, nobody could argue that, but she was his lady and now a *Life* magazine cover girl. It was one thing to land covers of *Photoplay*, *Motion Picture*, and the rest—she had been doing that for the past seven years—and another to make the front of *Life*. No, Lombard couldn't presume to match Gable, but as she accepted the mantle of consort, she was holding her own. She had always loved powerful men and how she gloried in his status as the king. She loved it, which meant that to Lombard, nothing, absolutely nothing was too good for her sovereign.

It was a time of change in Carole Lombard's life. In April 1938 she officially joined the Baha'i Faith under direction of her teacher, Beulah Storrs Lewis. "The Carole who longed to meet and know her Lord, Abdu'l Bahá," said Lewis, "this Carole few people knew." The night of her appearance before the Los Angeles Assembly, through what was reported to be a torrent of happy tears, Lombard told Lewis, "This is why I was born." Baha'i teachings, the generosity of spirit, the positive outlook, the humble attitude, deepened in Carole moving forward.

There were other changes. Fieldsie married director Walter Lang on July 5, 1938, and the bride resigned as Carole's secretary. Carole hired Jean Garceau from the Myron Selznick Talent Agency as a replacement.

Said Carole Sampeck, "To function in Myron Selznick's office you had to be tough as nails, but you had to do it diplomatically or people would just go around you. You had to be discreet but take no prisoners, stand your ground, and make it look like you were planting flowers on that ground all the while."

So Garceau was a sharp cookie; not quite the head-on force of nature that Fieldsie had been, but sharp, competent, and loyal. Gable approved of her, which meant everything.

In career terms, Lombard knew she was down two strikes with screwball bombs in *True Confession* and *Fools for Scandal*. One more and she was out, so the stakes were high on what scripts she looked at. She decided to change it up and switch to drama. David O. Selznick produced her first picture of 1939. *Made for Each Other* paired Carole with rising MGM star Jimmy Stewart in a maudlin tale of newlyweds that featured a race against time to save their sick baby. Next, she teamed with popular RKO leading man Cary Grant and waning Warner star Kay Francis to make *In Name Only*, a hard-edged drama about a love triangle.

Made for Each Other lost some money, but the sassy soap opera *In Name Only* scored nicely in the black, putting Myron Selznick in a favorable position as he set up future picture deals for Miss Carole Lombard.

But a crisis loomed for Lombard and Gable at the end of 1938 when *Photoplay* magazine ran an article written by Carole's supposed pal, reporter Kirtley Baskette. Entitled "Hollywood's Unmarried Husbands and Wives," the piece detailed the couples in Hollywood shacking up without benefit of a marriage license. Among them were Carole and Clark, who now felt the indignation of a morally conservative America—and it no longer mattered how much Carole Lombard had paid in taxes. MGM came down hard on Gable for making the studio look bad.

In January 1939 Clark started work on *Gone With the Wind*, the most pressure-packed motion picture production in the history of Hollywood, while behind the scenes, MGM tried to settle what was known in the front office as "this Gable mess." Ria possessed what one Gable biographer called "an impregnable dignity." She had been humiliated by the carrying on of these two overaged teenagers. *Photoplay's* article was both a blessing and a curse to Ria. Yes, it exposed Clark and Carole to a scowling nation, but it humiliated Ria that her husband was flaunting convention at her expense.

In response to the article, a shaken Gable stated that he would seek a divorce from his estranged wife. An infuriated Ria then demanded an apology from the King—if anybody was going to divorce anybody, *she* was going to save face and divorce *him*.

Like always with its star, MGM did the apologizing for Clark, issuing a public apology in Gable's name in the nation's newspapers that read, "I regret bitterly that a short time ago a story was printed to the effect that I would seek a divorce from Mrs. Gable." The logjam broke. Ria's attorneys negotiated with MGM's attorneys and a divorce settlement came together. It would cost Gable $286,000, fronted by MGM and paid out over three years, to secede from an unhappy union.

In the meantime, Gable and Lombard shopped for a house in the San Fernando Valley, away from the press and the public. Carole's love of press now clashed with Clark's loathing; she decided she was through with prying eyes and lurking cameras.

It didn't take long to find their dream home: director Raoul Walsh's horse ranch with twenty acres in the sparsely developed Valley community of Encino. Gable talked Walsh into selling but was cash-strapped to make the purchase due to that ungodly divorce settlement. Lombard put up the $65,000 purchase price and at long last, things were looking up for America's dream couple.

17

The Plain, Black Night

Back around midnight, when it seemed nothing could be done amidst the clot of responders and a great deal of commotion and wasted effort at the Blue Diamond Mine, Maj. Herbert Anderson, his quartermaster, Major Taylor, and Taylor's aide set out to find the crash site on their own. They drove toward Red Rock Canyon and turned down Wilson Ranch Road, past the ranch and out-buildings into desert, heading toward Potosi. They drove along an old trail around the base of the mountain and finally ran out of navigable surface, as evidenced by the number of vehicles parked there, those of rescuers who had followed the same reasoning and the same path. The beam of their headlights showed men standing and talking in a group.

Taylor parked and shut off the engine. It was cold out there, dry, biting cold. On foot, the soldiers approached the huddle of men and discovered one man at the center holding a map. It was Mayor Hal Garrison with a number of civilians standing around him, including some of the local cowboys who yet roamed the range on horseback and wore ten-gallon hats, just like in the movies. A few of these men had seen the plane fly over and told how they had watched it head straight toward the mountain and strike it with no explosion that they could hear. One man said it had "burst into a large tongue of flame which kicked up frequently and burned for a total of about three hours."

Now, the fire on the mountain was long out and when the darkness had swallowed it, confusion began about where the crash was located and how it could be reached. Anderson would call this moonless night "one of the darkest I have ever seen, and I'm pretty well qualified on dark nights. It was so dark that those sharp ridges couldn't be seen, and they were only evidenced by the light of the stars. There was starlight but no light on the ground from the stars. It was a plain, black night."

Anderson felt duty-bound to press on, and he and the two others headed south by southwest along the foot of the mountain in the faint hope that they would pick up the scent of the still-smoldering wreck and it would guide them in. They passed a pack of wild burros and then found campfires and cowboys. "Did you see a plane fly over?" Anderson would ask. "Sure did," came the answer. "Flew right over, trailing bright orange flame out of the left wing."

The soldiers moved on, found another cowboy encamped. Same story—a streak of orange flame trailing the left engine as the plane flew over the desert.

"We would see a cowboy here and a cowboy there," said Anderson later. "They all clicked on this left engine. One man said he saw this orange flame and I asked him what he meant, if the flame was all over the engine, and he said, 'No, it was out of the exhaust.' I asked him why that appeared unusual to him, and he said it wasn't the normal blue exhaust. He said he was quite accustomed to these things."

The Army men walked another mile in the impenetrable night and realized they were on a fool's errand and would never reach the crash site this way. At somewhere around four in the morning they turned back toward Blue Diamond and stumbled along as batteries drained in their flashlights.

18

Malaise

At the end of March 1939, Carole and Clark eloped to Kingman, Arizona, found a Methodist minister, and made it through the marriage ceremony with MGM press agent Otto Winkler and two strangers as witnesses. Clark fumbled the vows; Carole's voice shook and she cried. Otto had driven them to the far-flung location for the ceremony and managed to keep the press in the dark throughout. It was the beginning of a short blissful period for the newlyweds, with Carole following the usual practice of nicknaming her mate. Once there had been Popsie, and then Pookie, and Gable became Pa or Pappy. And he called her Ma, names that became the stuff of filmland legend, perpetuated in part by Kodachrome home movies showing the new spouses clowning on hunting trips and generally appearing to be happy.

Lombard had reason to be in her glory in 1939, not just because she had landed a king, but because now she could establish a home for them at the ranch in Encino. The twenty acres featured stables, a workshop, barn, kennels, chicken houses, vineyard, alfalfa field, and citrus groves. In short order, under Carole's management, assisted by Jean Garceau, the Gables' ranch sold fowl to the MGM commissary and oranges and lemons through the Farmers Association. The Gables used alfalfa to feed the livestock and donated grapes to local hospitals.

Jessie, Carole's African-American cook, took over in Encino, as did Juanita, Carole's Hispanic maid. The screwball girl wouldn't entertain any other ideas. She told Gable he needed a valet, and the king groused he needed no such thing. But when Carole hired Rufus Martin to tend Gable's wardrobe and see to maintaining Clark's portion of the house, the groom had to admit that maybe a valet wasn't her worst idea.

Then Carole turned her attention to the property. She envisioned a grand, walk-in cage for the doves, which she had once sent to Gable as peace offerings and now had been brought over lovingly from Bel Air. She refurbished the living room of Raoul Walsh's former residence in Early American, painted the pine paneling white, and laid down canary yellow carpet. She bought oversized sofas, also yellow, and oversized green club chairs. The tables were maple and oversized—all the furniture was king-sized for her king. Gable shared with other movie stars the hobby of collecting 16mm film and made arrangements with MGM to obtain a print of each of his pictures for movie nights in the living room. All of his pictures except *Parnell*.

A downstairs bedroom became Jean Garceau's office, and the knotty pine den became Gable's gun room, featuring a thirty-foot built-in cabinet filled from ceiling to floor with his firearm collection. The gun room included enough leftover space for oversized chairs and smoking tables. It was here most evenings they hung out, playing backgammon. There were two bedrooms upstairs, his in brown and beige, and hers in blue and white. He didn't want a fancy bath, so his was modest; hers befitted a movie queen, with white marble walls, wraparound mirrors, and crystal and silver fixtures. Conspicuous by its absence at the Gable ranch was a guest bedroom because for all her many acts of kindness, Carole made no secret that she did not welcome overnight guests. It was a rule never violated.

Here in the sweltering heat of July 1939 she participated in the culmination of Alice Marble's comeback when Allie tore through the women's field and won Wimbledon—not just singles but doubles with partner Sarah Fabyan and mixed doubles with partner Bobby Riggs. In fact, Americans swept all six titles as Riggs also won the men's singles title and the doubles title with Elwood Cooke. Lombard knew them all and tuned in the championships on multiple radios, as she would the U.S. National Championships in September, and paced from set to set muttering, "Come on, Champ! Come on, Champ!" And the champ came through.

Back in Hollywood, Allie landed a singing gig at Club Lamaze on the Sunset Strip, and there were Carole and Clark to cheer her on—so what if Lombard had to drag Gable there? Carole and Allie had remained close and shared all each other's secrets. And there were secrets for Hollywood's dream couple. Gable had an insecure streak about his acting, a big, wide one. Actor Richard Gere looked in retrospect at Gable the actor and saw someone who rushed through his dialogue. Gere found Gable to be "not totally comfortable in being that big and butch, macho-whatever-thing Clark Gable was. It's kind of an interesting dynamic.... We identify with people who aren't totally comfortable. Very few of us are. Even in *Gone With the Wind*, this is a very fragile guy.... I think it works because he *is* so fragile."

Said Delmer Daves, who directed Gable with Gene Tierney in the 1953 feature *Never Let Me Go*, "He was not a flexible actor. There was a Clark Gable way of doing a scene."

Gable wasn't just insecure about his acting. He was insecure about money, like always. He didn't trust banks and carried thousands in cash at all times simply because he could; because he had to. He never knew when he would need it. When he walked into the Brown Derby for lunch he ordered the special to save a couple bucks. He didn't have what one would call an altruistic side; no siblings or close family ties, and he wasn't fond of Carole's brother Fred, whom he considered to be judgmental and humorless.

Clark didn't mind younger Stuart—Stuart liked to drink—but Gable never grew close to any of the Peters clan and thought of the brothers as freeloaders.

Clark tended to be thin-skinned about romantic rivals Howard Hughes, George Raft, and particularly Russ Columbo, who would forever have one up on the king. Columbo had been there first, and he had died in such a way that his memory would linger, despite the fact that the crooner had been, in Gable's eyes, a pansy.

From Lombard's point of view, Russ Columbo's death at such a tender age and in so sudden a manner made her appreciate Gable all the more and seek to give her all to married life. She actually acquiesced to a monogamous lifestyle, she who in 1933 had stated that "marriage fits neither human nature nor human needs." She didn't know how long she would continue to abide by a one-man rule, but for now it held firm.

"She had such enormous energy," said Margaret Wyler. "That was one of her main qualities. When she would zero in on something, that was it, and she wanted this relationship. On every level, she was a driving force, because I think she had more energy than he did. Maybe it was glandular or I don't know what."

But all the glands weren't performing, because Carole wanted to get pregnant and figured every month this was it, and it kept not happening. Fieldsie had no trouble—a year and change after her wedding, Carole rushed Fieldsie to the hospital and stood by for the birth of Walter Richard Lang. Fieldsie described Carole the delivery room coach as "completely adequate except that she turned pretty white," and after the birth, Fieldsie named Carole godmother. Lombard delighted in lavishing the baby with attention while wondering at the same time what the hell was wrong that she couldn't produce one of her own, an heir to the king, a new generation for the kingdom. Then, finally, it happened. At the beginning of December she missed her period and in the slang of the day, "the rabbit died" and Carole Lombard was a mother to be.

Every month the fan magazines had speculated, jumping at every hint of a Lombard pregnancy, and the timing was terrible with the Gables traveling to Atlanta, Georgia, for the ultimately glitzy premiere of *Gone With the Wind*, where 150,000 adoring fans showed up in the cold Georgia air for a parade, and there were Clark and Carole, oh so serene, oh so regal, lending so much elegance to the proceedings. She couldn't say anything to anyone, even Gable. They flew in on an American Air Lines DC-3, and Carole took Alice Marble along since Fieldsie was home with the baby. By now, they had grown so close that Allie had confided to Missy Carole that she ended each day with a prayer her mother had taught her, "God bless and angels keep." From then on they ended each phone call with Allie saying, "God bless," and Carole answering, "Angels keep."

In Atlanta Carole and Clark shared adjoining hotel rooms and plenty of downtime because, said Marble of Gable, "Every day he had to have some quiet time for himself, for though he loved Carole, she was a chatterbox." Especially in a new city. Especially with the hubbub of the premiere. She saw it as a kid on a wild ride; Gable found it agonizing, the culmination of a year of hell on a picture he never wanted to make, and the crowds—this renowned he-man withered at the thought of crowds and public speaking. He had to be coached every red-carpeted step by Lombard as he approached the microphone to say a few carefully crafted, long-rehearsed words before the show went on. But then Carole had plenty of experience. "Come on, Champ! Come on, Champ!"

As far as anyone knew that evening, all the stars on the red carpet were perfect. David Selznick, Vivien Leigh, Olivia de Havilland, Leslie Howard, Margaret Mitchell, tennis champion Alice Marble, and especially Lombard and Gable. Never had anyone been more elegant than these two, certainly not in America. Admirers searched the history books for something comparable and found Caesar and Cleopatra, maybe. But even in Atlanta there were intrigue and feuding, because Victor Fleming, who directed most of *Gone With the Wind*, felt slighted by Selznick's decision to split the "Directed by" credit between Fleming and George Cukor, who had been fired after only three weeks. Gable's loyalty was to Fleming, and Lombard's loyalty was to Gable, despite her love of David Selznick. The Gable contingent had taken one plane; the Selznick contingent another. Fleming had agreed to go on Gable's DC-3, but just prior to departure, the director's close friend, Douglas Fairbanks, Sr., had died. Fleming remained in Hollywood while the feud moved on without him. Atlanta grew chilly for more reasons than the onset of winter, as when Selznick publicity man Birdie Birdwell tried to pick a bar fight with MGM publicity chief Howard Strickling, and Gable squared his shoulders and sidled over to the two of them. Glaring at Birdwell, Gable asked his friend Strickling, "Is he giving you a bad time, Howard?" Birdwell retreated.

Gable was a handful all right. After spending months making David Selznick's epic, he was down on everything Selznick, including David's brother, who was Carole's agent—the one who had made her a couple of fortunes as the highest-paid woman in Hollywood. Carole had always been loyal to her friends, but now, to keep the peace, she sued Myron to get out of her contract. The two would part amicably, although Hollywood was a small town and found it puzzling. It would cost Carole, but that was one of the prices of being married to the king.

Another price was infidelity, because Pa was screwing around just as he had from way back in his barnstorming days. After he played Rhett Butler, there was no doubt that Gable had ascended to the most desired man in 1930s America, able to choose freely, cafeteria style, from just about any living, breathing woman. They literally fell at his feet in all shapes, sizes, and hair colors at MGM, from bargain-basement script girls to glamour queen Joan Crawford. Yes, Lombard was comfortable in her own skin, and yes,

Lombard attempted to look the other way. Intellectually, she knew his dalliances were necessary. He needed an ego; he needed women to fall over him. It was all part of a thriving Gable brand.

In particular, Clark found himself drawn to a delicate, five-foot-five, blonde screen hopeful named Virginia Grey, age twenty, and secured bit parts for her in his 1938 pictures *Test Pilot* and *Idiot's Delight*. Carole certainly knew about Virginia's rise to prominence in Gable's affection but somehow seemed to sense who comprised a threat and who didn't, and she picked her battles carefully as a result. Carole found herself disarmed by the sweet, very religious Virginia Grey and never made a fuss when Gable strayed in Virginia's direction. On the other hand, another chorine on *Idiot's Delight* prompted a rampaging Lombard to storm the set and scream, "Get that whore out of here!" The offender was dismissed.

"He was running around a lot," said Richard Lang, who grew up from the baby of 1939 to know Gable well and learn of Lombard from his mother, "which is not to say he didn't love her. With the drinking and the hunting, he was that type of guy. It's only wrong in the wife's eyes. I think she knew about most of his affairs, and gave him hell about it. In the normal course of events, she probably screamed at him every six, eight weeks, and he was a good boy for a while."

Of course Gable had that closed-off corner of his soul, dark, impenetrable, the one that had shut out his own kid, Judy Lewis. Lombard had not learned about Loretta Young and the resulting Judy from Gable. He would never discuss it, even with his wife. Carole learned about it because she lived for gossip and knew all the bedroom shenanigans in town. And this was frightening that Gable could harden his heart to such a degree—that he was at times dangerously aloof, that he could retreat easily and shut everyone out, even her.

Within a week of their return from Atlanta, page-one newspaper copy read: "The movie colony is as excited as a couple of maiden aunts over the persistent rumor that both Carole Lombard and Barbara Stanwyck are expecting babies. There's no denying that Miss Lombard isn't herself on the set these days. More than once she has displayed a Victorian fragility quite uncommon to her usual vivacious character by fainting during the filming of *Vigil in the Night*."

Then she miscarried. It was a lousy start to the year, and both were ready to crack, Carole from the personal tragedy of losing a child and Clark from the hellacious production of *Gone With the Wind* and the previous month's nightmarish string of premieres in Atlanta, New York, and Hollywood. But the Gables had a solution, one they had employed in the past and would employ in the future: escape.

She had just bought him a station wagon capable of going off road. Its sixty-five-gallon gas tank meant capabilities for long drives into wilderness. The food, supplies, blankets, water, guns, and other provisions on board meant roughing it would be no problem. Gable was also armed with a 16mm movie camera and a box full of film. They took nobody with them, gave few clues regarding their destination, and headed toward Mexico at the end of January 1940.

The weather turned foul and after four days with no contact, Gable's press man Otto Winkler was dispatched from Culver City with a cameraman to determine the Gables' location. An aerial search from Tijuana to Ensenada, their last known whereabouts, revealed no station wagon and no Gables. "I know Gable can take care of his wife and himself," said Wink after the day's search, "so I'm not alarmed." He vowed to keep looking until he found them.

Gables Are Missing Somewhere in Mexico read headlines that for once the MGM publicity department didn't need to dream up. In fact, MGM would have preferred that its $2 million investment (he had just signed a new seven-year contract) *not* abandon civilization and head out of the country.

Less than a day later, the Gables reappeared muddy but unbowed, having gotten the station wagon stuck in, and removed from, mud from recent rains in northern Mexico. It was with relief that MGM issued a statement and headlines announced, **Gables Reported Safe.** "They're supposed to be at the La Brea Gun Club today," said MGM's Ralph Wheelright (because Gable spokesman Winkler was still in the middle of nowhere looking for the lost Gables), "and we're sure that's where they'll be." Except MGM wasn't sure of their whereabouts at all.

Clark had become something of a loose cannon, and Carole didn't help. Their groupthink became antagonistic to any studio that tried to rein them in.

"Those people are on my nerves," he would growl.

"Yah, yah, I get you," she would respond, and off they would go, to Oregon, to Canada, to Mexico, with or without the usual hunting crowd but always in the trusty station wagon.

But 1940 was still a lousy year with—for Lombard—two more certified bombs. Both pictures she made that year were at RKO, the dramas *Vigil in the Night* and *They Knew What They Wanted*, and both went spectacularly belly up. The former was a story of British nurses and co-starred British leading man Brian Aherne; the latter paired her for a second time with Charles Laughton, then coming off his big success in *The Hunchback of Notre Dame*, and God, how she loathed that man, helped along by the fact that Gable despised him after the experience of *Mutiny on the Bounty* back in '35. Carole's reaction to Laughton, fed by the antipathy of Gable, earned the prickly Brit a place on her shit list, from which there was no return, and the story got all over town.

Young Orson Welles worked on the RKO lot during the making of *They Knew What They Wanted* and told of Laughton's visits. "He would come to my office, and sit down across the desk from me, and put his head on the desk and cry," Welles recalled in the 1980s. He quoted Laughton as saying, "I can't go on the way they're making fun of me on the set." Welles claimed he approached director Garson Kanin and Lombard, and said of Laughton, "You know, he is a great actor. Take it easy with him. You're gonna ruin your own picture."

But Lombard ruled the roost and had the clout not to stand for Laughton's self-aggrandizement. Garson Kanin had just scored a big screwball success directing *My Favorite Wife* with Cary Grant and Irene Dunne, a Lombard kind of a role that Dunne had landed instead even though she was miscast and the part had been perfect for Carole. Kanin was all of twenty-seven and just a kid, but a brilliant kid and just four years younger than was Lombard, so they got along well.

Kanin developed a crush on Lombard, like they all did. He wrote about her in one of his books and attempted to preserve for posterity the Lombard he knew:

"Don't be too hard on me," Carole said one day, when we were having difficulty achieving the necessary effect. "I'm pretty tired. I'm getting on, you know."

"Getting on, for God's sake. You're what?" I asked. "Thirty-four? Thirty-five?"

"Why you son of a bitch no good dirty bastard," she said. "Thirty-*one*. I'm thirty-*one*."

"You're thirty-two," I said.

"Oh, you knew that, huh?"

"Certainly. I know all about you."

"So if you knew I was thirty-two, why did you say thirty-four?"

"I wonder that myself, Carole."

"I know why," she said. "It's because you're nothing but a goddamn—man."

Another man, the famous Clark Gable, knocked her up again, and another miscarriage deepened her feelings of confusion over her aspirations—could she be wife, mother, and viable screen star? Could she even carry a pregnancy to term? She had always suffered heavy and long-lasting menstrual flows, and with her latest problems conceiving, a desperate Lombard sought help. She was referred to Dr. Richard W. TeLinde at Johns Hopkins University School of Medicine in Baltimore, Maryland. TeLinde was then gaining a national reputation for his work in the field of gynecology. Trouble was, Lombard didn't want the world to know her business, particularly this business, and here Howard Strickling and Otto Winkler stepped in to create a story that Gable would need to travel east to see about an old injury to his right shoulder dating back to production of the 1936 disaster epic *San Francisco*.

After the Gables' quiet Christmas at home, Winkler announced that they were heading east on December 26, 1940. They arrived in Washington, D.C., on Saturday the twenty-eighth, saw the sights along the National Mall and then toured Mount Vernon, where, according to Jean Garceau, "Carole had the best time of all." Lombard liked George Washington's style and wanted to take some Early American decorating ideas back to the Encino ranch.

"I knew this was going to cost me money," groused Gable.

The Gables accepted an invitation from President Franklin Delano Roosevelt to sit in on his Sunday evening, December 29, "fireside chat" radio broadcast on national security, what would become known to history as the Arsenal of Democracy speech. It was a long, grim monologue about the threat of the Axis powers, Germany, Japan, and Italy. Roosevelt discussed the raging Battle of Britain and said in small part, "If Great Britain goes down, the Axis powers will control the continents of Europe, Asia, Africa, Australia, and the high seas—and they will be in a position to bring enormous military and naval resources against this hemisphere. It is no exaggeration to say that all of us, in all the Americas, would be living at the point of a gun—a gun loaded with explosive bullets, economic as well as military."

FDR's tough talk to jolt Americans out of their isolationist malaise hit Lombard hard. She had been anti-war up to that point, but it was difficult *not* to see the handwriting on this particular wall, especially coming from the one man in the world she admired above all others.

The mood at the White House brightened later in the evening when FDR and First Lady Eleanor Roosevelt questioned Gable and Lombard "closely about the film industry and their careers," reported Garceau. "He was most interested, for he was aware of the publicity Carole had garnered in 1937 when she paid eighty-five percent of the $465,000 she earned that year in state and federal income taxes and announced that she was glad to do it because she was proud of being an American."

The next morning Gable and Lombard were driven to the Johns Hopkins University School of Medicine where they reported for study. By now Strickling and Winkler had managed to bungle the fabricated story, which started to unravel when the "shoulder injury" would require Gable to be hospitalized three or four days. In one release to the press, the shoulder injury occurred "several months ago," and in the next it was traced back to 1933. Somehow word leaked that Lombard was undergoing examination as well as Gable, leading the press to all new questioning. On Thursday, January 2, it was announced that Gable would have a tooth extracted to solve his "shoulder problem"; as reporters stood bewildered on that account, suddenly it was announced that Lombard would undergo a surgical procedure that same day, January 2. The dilation and curettage performed by Dr. TeLinde, his specialty, cleaned out tissue remaining from her early 1940 miscarriage and, she hoped, restored Carole's ability to conceive.

By afternoon that same eventful Thursday, Howard Strickling was denying that Lombard was having any sort of medical procedure, but she did, as confirmed by the fact that Lombard and Gable returned home less than a week later, but embarked Thursday, January 9, on a month-long hunting trip to Mexico during which, friends said, Carole jumped Clark's bones at every opportunity in earnest attempts to get herself in the family way once again.

19

Road King

At 3:30 in the morning, forty-five-year-old Warren Earl Carey, lugging his worn suitcase, pushed open the lobby door of the Hotel Amarillo and stepped to the curb. A cab sat there waiting and the driver hurried out, took Warren's suitcase, and set it on the front seat of the cab. He opened the door, and Carey eased his weary body into the backseat. There wasn't much to do at noon in Amarillo, Texas, let alone at 3:30 A.M.

The cabbie climbed into the car and closed his door. "English Field," Carey forced himself to say, and the cab pulled away from the curb. Carey had gotten a few hours' sleep in an otherwise brutal passage toward his home in Los Angeles after a safety conference in Washington, D.C. Flying was such a dicey enterprise these days, airlines flying here and there but often late. Recently, many flights has been delayed or diverted due to various security issues related to the war—restricted airspace, blackouts and signal beacons darkened, commandeering of civilian flights for troop movements, and spot fuel shortages. Now, he held a ticket on American Air Lines that would take him to Boulder City, Nevada, to catch a ride home to Los Angeles. Home. Home and Wilma awaited. He smiled at the very thought.

"Sad thing," called the cab driver over his shoulder. "Very sad."

Warren tried to engage his mind. He found the exercise like

trying to turn over an automobile engine on a frosty morning. His mind was as foggy as it should have been in the middle of the night after skipping from time zone to time zone for days. He couldn't figure out what this man was going on about. "You say something's sad?" Carey let out. "What's sad?"

"Why, the crash," said the cabbie in surprise, as if Carey should have known. As if everybody should have known. "The plane crash out in California somewhere."

Warren Carey awakened with a jolt. "Oh? A plane crash? I hadn't heard," he said, sitting up at attention, propping himself forward to hear.

"Oh, yeah," said the driver. "Some TWA plane went down in some mountains. Nobody knows where. That actress was on the plane. You know, the funny one. And a bunch of Army boys. From what they're saying, it looks bad."

Actress? Army boys? Carey wanted his mind to catch up, to rev into coherent thought but found it tough. Even through the cotton of his thoughts, Carey could imagine what lay ahead. All crashes were bad, all broke your heart, especially when your livelihood meant stepping into the middle of it and making sense of the nonsensical.

"Say, what takes you to the airport in the middle of the night?" asked the cabbie.

"I'm heading home," said Carey, and then corrected himself. "I *was* heading home, but I'm not now."

"You a businessman or somethin'?"

"Civil Aeronautics Board," said Carey. "Senior safety man."

The cabbie shot him a hot glance in the rear view mirror, and in the last faint lights of town before they headed into prairie, Warren Carey saw something in the cabbie's eyes. Sympathy, or awe, or something.

"Tell me what you've heard about this crash," Carey said. "Where? When? Anything you've heard."

"I saw a newspaper at the coffee shop," said the cabbie, "and heard some radio reports. A plane full of people and that actress, Carole Lombard, went into the mountains, oh, where was it. California—Nevada—somewhere near the border in rough country. They're out hunting for the plane right now."

It was no wonder that Carey hadn't heard; they wouldn't have known to reach him at the Hotel Amarillo because he hadn't known he'd be there. He looked about him at the ink-black Texas night. "How about stepping on it and get me out to English Field? I need to make some calls, find out what's going on."

"Sure thing, mac," said the cabbie, and the intake of gas into the Road King's six-cylinder engine smacked Warren Carey's back against his seat, and they flew the rest of the way to the airfield.

20

A Flame to Many Moths

Carole Lombard still couldn't get herself in a family way. Said the Gables' friend Buster Collier of Carole and Clark, "They spent a lot of time in the sack and tried every position to try to get pregnant." Carole entered 1941 in the third year of a career swoon. She witnessed the release of her two most recent RKO dramatic pictures and recoiled in horror at the results. *Vigil in the Night*, an overwrought hospital drama, lost an astonishing $327,000, and the Kanin-directed *They Knew What They Wanted*, about love and deceit in the California wine country, lost almost as much. Lombard and Kanin should have listened to the advice of Orson Welles, who warned they might ruin their picture. Once again the career waters had grown treacherous.

Even in the midst of her slump, Carole remained viable and desired as one-half of the most perfect couple in Hollywood. She had always been a competitor, and despite quotes to the press about retiring to raise a family, the failed attempts at conception, not to mention failed dramatic pictures, left her stuck in Encino at the farm more than she wanted. She conveyed to a reporter what burned in her blood: "There's been a lot of talk about me retiring from the screen, and I've thought a lot about it. There have been times when I thought I wanted to, but the only thing that could bring that about would be a baby. Even then, I really couldn't quit.

I've said I could, and now I know better. This business is in my blood. I don't mean acting, I mean making movies. God, I love it."

She found herself unable to stay away from the set. Said Garson Kanin of making *They Knew What They Wanted*, "On days when she wasn't required, she would drive in anyway, all the way from the Valley. The first time she turned up on one of those days, I panicked, certain there had been a mistake."

"What're you doing here?" I asked. "You're not called today."

"Piss off!" she said. "I'm on this picture."

Said Kanin, "She wanted to be around, to stay with the feel of things. She did not want to lose the momentum of the work."

Or as Lombard would describe when asked of her aspirations, "I grew up in Hollywood, and this is my culture. But produce [pictures], maybe, and don't laugh. If I had my choice of being anybody else, I think I'd rather be David Selznick."

The Hollywood of 1940 limited women to certain crafts— some wrote scripts or doctored them; others worked in wardrobe, hair and makeup, or script notation. Most often women in Hollywood worked in offices as secretaries and typists. But Lombard now considered moving *behind* the camera as a producer or even a director and spoke openly about "women emancipated from masculine domination" and "a different social order brought about by economic independence." It was all part of a Petey-influenced, progressive nature that would take Hollywood by storm a couple of generations later.

Carole's restlessness had become common knowledge around Hollywood, where her absence was felt at all the old haunts. "Where, oh where, has the Carole of yesterday gone?" a writer at *Modern Screen* magazine asked. "The Carole of the press gatherings, the portrait galleries, the Venice Pier, the Carole who was Hollywood's favorite Party Girl—what has happened to her? Days past you never had to look twice to find her. In headlines, at preview microphones, in most anyone's front parlor. She was always there, and conspicuously. But now Carole is the needle in the Hollywood haystack."

The "party girl" had also grown weary of Gable's constant taking, taking, taking, and unwillingness to give an inch. Rumors of separation found their way into print and onto radio, where a report by the closest thing to a shock jock in Hollywood at the time, Jimmy Fidler, particularly stung.

Now more than ever she threw energy behind her causes. She had struck up a friendship with young RKO contract player Lucille Ball, who had been kicking around the studio in smaller parts in "A" pictures and larger parts in "B's," for five years. RKO had made some important pictures and introduced Astaire and Rogers to the world, but more often made bad business decisions that resulted in red ink. Ball would later quote Lombard as advising, "Tell the sons-a-bitches to give you a break. You've got something. Tell them I said they're missing the boat again." Lombard advised Ball to follow the comedy path and gave her the playbook on "studio behavior," from how to negotiate off the casting couch to how to drop names. When Lucy married Desi Arnaz at the end of November 1940, the Gables threw a champagne supper party for the newlyweds at Chasen's on Beverly Boulevard, and visits by Ball and Arnaz to the ranch in Encino would influence their decision to establish a home in the San Fernando Valley.

Yet Lombard was at sea and shopping for good scripts with no success. At just the wrong moment, sashaying onto an MGM soundstage and into Gable's life was a five-foot-three, blonde-headed bundle of raw sexual need all of twenty-one years old named Lana Turner, co-star of the new Gable picture, *Honky Tonk*. Lana had been dubbed the "Sweater Girl" for obvious reasons and had already proved in Hollywood to be as easy to conquer as the Maginot Line.

Turner was an insecure girl who sought approval through sex, behavior practiced by Gable from his teens on. So potent a female

142

was Lana Turner that Lombard found it difficult to look the other way this time; Carole found Lana too young, too blonde, too perfect, and way too much on the make. Lombard understood because she had *been* Lana Turner not so long ago—an up-and-coming young starlet wielding formidable sexual power over the ruling male population of Hollywood. This wasn't another Virginia Grey, some sweet lost soul who recognized in Gable a kindred spirit; Lana Turner was trouble, and Lombard went to battle stations.

Carole and Lana butted heads because they now shared feelings of insecurity; Carole over passing thirty childless, her career sliding, and Lana over a lack of self-worth and hunger for validation. Said fellow Hollywood bombshell Ava Gardner, "Lana pushed too hard with men and pushed them away. I guess she felt needy somewhere inside."

Lana would never admit to an affair with Gable, but in her memoir she owned up to a fear of Carole when she told of rehearsing a clinch with Gable on the *Honky Tonk* soundstage. It was a moment they both enjoyed; Lana called it "a wonderful chemical rapport" with Clark Gable, lips to lips, for director Jack Conway's assessment prior to committing the scene to film. Conway called a break. Lana said she "turned around and froze. There was beloved Carole Lombard." The piercing stare of Lombard's icy blue eyes devastated Lana, who fled the soundstage.

When Lombard saw how effective the appearance had been, she kept showing up on the set and unnerving Turner until MGM brass asked the fireball to knock it off.

A chagrined wife looked on as *Honky Tonk* went box office in blockbuster style and assured a follow-up. Meanwhile, Carole's latest release, the comedy *Mr. and Mrs. Smith*, had scored in the black, and that's what mattered to Lombard, the bottom line. Alfred Hitchcock had attracted her to the property; Hitchcock was hot after his massive success with *Rebecca*, and Carole knew enough to ride coattails when she could, and even to exploit Hitch's attraction to blondes, which everybody knew about. He was an absolute sucker for the dames.

On the Hitchcock soundstage she had done her usual part to keep the on-set proceedings light, as when she directed Hitch's obligatory cameo—a simple stroll in front of a department-store building, walking through the frame. She asked him to repeat the walk over, and over, and over. He could never get it *quite right*, or so she kept telling him. It was good-natured payback for the director who had recently and famously said that actors were no more than cattle to be herded.

When *Mr. and Mrs. Smith* performed well at the box office, Carole admitted to herself that she did best in comedy and that's where the public accepted her. She saw reason now to hope for a career revival and decided to make herself more attractive to prospective employers. She instructed her new agent, Gable's good friend Nat Wolff, to offer her at a discounted rate and negotiate for a percentage of the net profit (if any) for the picture. Lombard had dreamed up the idea of profit participation a few years earlier, reasoning that a lower up-front salary and a cut of the profits would be a win-win for anyone hiring her. It landed her work all right, even if recent pictures had stunk up the joint. In another decade profit participation would be all the rage, particularly at Universal International, and make independent players like James Stewart a fortune.

For appearing in a new picture called *To Be or Not to Be*, about to go into production at United Artists, Wolff got Lombard a salary of $75,000 plus 4.0837 percent of the net profit from the picture. After that, she would make a comedy at Columbia called *He Kissed the Bride*, and then a picture at Universal with what she considered tremendous potential, a sequel of sorts to *My Man Godfrey* entitled, appropriately enough, *My Girl Godfrey* about a stage hopeful who is so desperate to audition for a Broadway producer that she becomes a maid in his household. Comedies one and all.

Although she considered comedy to be safe, as a concept, *To Be or Not to Be* involved risk. The plot concerned a company of Shakespearean actors in Poland as the Germans invade. The actors become freedom fighters against the Nazis and use their talents to stop a traitor before fleeing to England. Would audiences laugh at an aggressor nation that had already laid waste to Europe?

To Be or Not to Be was conceived by maestro producer-director Ernst Lubitsch, Carole's old champion from the Paramount days, and Lubitsch had seen Lombard as the perfect Maria Tura, a great stage actress who must rise above her own self-centered lifestyle to fight the Nazis.

Gable had long been suspicious of Lubitsch, whom he called "the horny Hun." And Clark reeled when Carole brought another one of her strays into the project, young Robert Stack, to portray her lover in the film. Carole considered Stack among her closer friends from way back in Tahoe, and now he was all grown up and handsome as the devil. By no coincidence, his presence on the picture would serve as a constant reminder to Clark about how it felt to watch your spouse in close quarters with a younger and very attractive co-star for days on end.

But Stack's relative inexperience in Hollywood had drawbacks. "I was so nervous in close-ups," he said. "I often moved out of range of my key light, the last thing an actor wants to do. She'd gently maneuver me right back into focus. This was a courtesy never repeated in my long and spotted career."

Lombard knew that Bob Stack was infatuated; she always knew the effect she had on men. She was a flame without apology to many moths during her entire Hollywood run and wielded her charms the way studio moguls wielded a cigar and a Montblanc pen. She didn't need to put out; she merely made that devastating blue-eyed contact and flashed the Lombard smile and touched an occasional forearm, and sweat broke out on men's foreheads and knees turned to butter.

Radio personality Jack Benny, king of comedic timing, made an unlikely co-star for Lombard in *To Be or Not to Be*, portraying her husband, the "great actor" Josef Tura. Benny fell for Lombard, from her impeccable timing to what he saw as a glorious soul. Benny's transition from radio to silver screen had been shaky, and his pictures had failed to capture the magic of the airwaves. He doubted himself as a motion picture actor and relied on the experience of Lubitsch and Lombard to see him through.

To Be or Not to Be became the highlight of Jack Benny's screen career. As a comedy it worked, and Lombard took pride in calling attention to the dangers of Axis oppression at a time when America sought to remain isolationist and not participate in a second world war. People needed to see why they must fight, and Lombard and Benny would serve them a spoonful of sugar with the medicine.

The bombing of Pearl Harbor in December 1941 occurred with Gable on hiatus from pictures and Lombard hard at work on *To Be or Not to Be*. War had been coming for years; it was simply a matter of where and when. The attack stunned the nation, and Hollywood's stars knew that their carefree lives were about to change. They would now have to pay up for all that adoration and all that income. They would become role models in a shooting war, which represented a different manner of hero—altruistic times were ahead. Some stars merely played along, while others, Lombard among them, sought an active role in the war effort.

The same Carole Lombard who had won hearts and minds with her 1937 proclamation about paying taxes now stood primed to take a leadership role in Hollywood's war effort. She found the prospect no different from planning the White Mayfair Ball or bringing the Encino ranch up to speed. She would just jump in and do it.

America changed overnight after Pearl Harbor. Boys aged eighteen, nineteen, and twenty suddenly became men, and mothers held them tight. Manufacturing shifted to the machinery of war, and raw materials became precious. Hollywood changed its working hours from the traditional nine to six to eight to five so that production would be wrapped for the day before mandatory blackouts commenced at dusk. The idea that an attack on the American mainland could be guided by the lights of homes and businesses was something new for the population, and the national mood turned somber.

Many American movie actors moved fast to enlist. Jimmy Stewart had already gone nine months back, and there was talk of others going or about to go, Robert Taylor, Robert Montgomery, Ty Power, Ronnie Reagan, Henry Fonda, and John Payne among them. Lombard wanted Gable to enlist, but at forty macho Clark Gable saw only his own limitations—and his own Encino farm fields. Lombard whipped up a telegram to President Franklin Roosevelt offering the service of Clark Gable and Carole Lombard in any capacity and made Pa sign on to the notion, but Gable let out a relieved sigh when FDR responded that the Gables should stay in Hollywood and make pictures and serve by entertaining the populace rather than worrying about manning any guns.

Patriotism in the wake of Pearl Harbor sprung up in every corner of the land. Hollywood formed a Victory Committee and, when looking for someone to lead it, settled on the ever-capable Rhett Butler himself, the biggest star in the stable of the biggest studio, Clark Gable at MGM. Never was a man less ready, willing, and able to lead, and Lombard jumped in to coach him through.

A continent away, U.S. Secretary of the Treasury Henry Morganthau approached MGM's New York head of advertising and publicity, Howard Dietz, asking for ideas that would help to sell war bonds and stamps to the American people, and Dietz said that getting Hollywood stars out on the road would sell the sizzle and the steak.

Dietz communicated the idea to Victory Committee Chairman Clark Gable, who passed it on to the movie stars on the committee. Bond tours could be easily accomplished with a star on hiatus between pictures. Home cities and home states would welcome the returning stars, and funds would be raised for the war effort. Hollywood's elite would become barnstormers. The idea caught fire in a day and Washington made one thing clear: No star could travel by air because of the vulnerability of airplanes in general and the susceptibility to sabotage in particular.

But who was on hiatus right now? Who could go on tour? Suddenly, the kickoff effort wouldn't involve just any star, but Chairman Gable's wife, screwball queen and freelance actress Carole Lombard, whose new picture had wrapped and was due to sneak preview on Monday, January 19, 1942. Both Carole and UA jumped at the chance to get her name in newspapers pending the sneak preview, final cut, and release of *To Be or Not to Be*.

The Monday screening back in Inglewood gave Carole just enough time to take a train to Indiana to sell war bonds in the capital of her home state and return by train for the preview. When Lombard asked Gable to accompany her on the trip, he told her no, that unfortunately he was due to travel to New York on business and then rush home to start a picture on the fifteenth. But it was more than a trip and a picture standing in the way of his participation. Gable's old fear of public speaking and public events precluded such a thing, and she knew it. It was his private prison, and there he was stuck in it with no thought of getting out, but his wife the "great ham" had no such reservations.

Carole shopped for a traveling companion. Fieldsie couldn't go and neither could Allie. But Petey was game because it afforded another opportunity to see the family back home—she had just visited Fort Wayne in November. Yes, she would go as long as no airplanes were involved. She hated the very idea of flying, as her daughter well knew. So Carole readily agreed, saying she had been told not to fly anyway, and the round trip would be by train.

As an independent, Carole employed no publicity people, so

MGM took over press duties for her tour, which was announced to the public on January 7, 1942, in a simple paragraph that appeared between pages six and ten of American newspapers. Lombard would be taking the City of Los Angeles streamliner over the northern route out of Los Angeles and change trains in Chicago for her final destination of Indianapolis. It was an item that achieved traction in three markets: Salt Lake City/Ogden, Utah, because these cities were on the train route and underappreciated by Hollywood; Chicago for the novelty of a Lombard visit; and Indianapolis because Carole was a Hoosier—no matter that she had left Indiana at age five. She was a double-barreled attraction—a sexy, glamorous movie star and much more important these days, wife of Clark Gable, star of *Gone With the Wind* and by far the hottest actor in the picture business.

Around New Year's, dark clouds appeared on Carole's horizon. She would leave for Indianapolis on January 12 and return early on January 19, while the picture that would keep Gable in Hollywood, the one starting to shoot on January 15 while she would be in Chicago, 2,000 miles away, would co-star none other than Lana Turner. With the government edict barring air travel in place, Carole had no choice but to endure a forty-hour train ride in each direction while her Lothario husband enjoyed the freedom to entertain any local troops of his choosing.

21

Fool's Errand

From his pickup truck, Lyle Van Gordon kept glancing up at the cliffs to his left as he led Jack Moore's trailing car off Goodsprings Road onto the horrendous Ninety-Nine Mine Road and inched along a rocky, rutted, washed-out path barely wide enough for a mulc, let alone a car. This was desert, which meant that roads held up longer than they did in other places of the country, but maintenance was spotty at best, and it took more than two hours to drive north over these bad roads within narrow cones of headlights, the drivers turning their wheels this way and that to avoid bottoming out while watching for mule deer as the Van Gordon and Moore vehicles crept along. The sun finally started to rise at about the time they ran out of road at a deep, rocky washout. Van Gordon pulled to a stop, and Moore did the same, the stillness oppressive as the men climbed out of their vehicles and slammed shut the doors. The group of men stood in the dusky emptiness of morning and looked about.

Cottonwood Pass was a spooky place at the best of times, the walls of the canyon dotted with yawning openings that carried picturesque names: Double Up Mine, Pauline Mine, Rainbow Quarries, Red Bluff Mine, Snowstorm Mine. Some had been worked in recent times and others not for fifty years or more. Mining always was and always would be a tough life the way they did it in Nevada, and bodies of men entombed in some of those old shafts proved it.

Van Gordon, Moore, Bondley, and the others gathered their supplies and started out. Above them 2,000 feet or more, somewhere on that wild mountain, lay the downed plane. They started up the road past the place it had washed out and walked a good half mile until they reached a jagged ravine. Nobody was saying anything, but their labored breathing said a lot. They had gradually, over the course of the eleven-mile drive, ascended steadily into the foothills of Potosi Mountain and kept a brisk hiking pace heading toward the cliffs. Already, they felt the cold and the altitude approaching 6,000 feet above sea level.

The light was gathering into something helpful as they made their way up a long rise through heavy brush beside the ravine. Cactus grabbed overcoats and pantlegs, so the men were forced into what was clearly a dry wash that would become a torrent of runoff during storms. This was rough going as well, the gully strewn with boulders, some of them ten feet high, offering the men nothing to hold on to. Suddenly, knees and heads were cracking against rock, and they might as well have been *crawling* toward the plane for the progress they were making. But Carole Lombard was up there, a beautiful, vulnerable woman and a great movie star who epitomized Hollywood glamour. Hearts pounded. Carole Lombard. They couldn't believe it. Here, in Nevada, and in trouble. The horrific thought of it haunted all the men: There were people, women, directly above them on that mountain. And so on they went up this seemingly endless, boulder-strewn crevice, toward cliffs that they hadn't yet figured out how to climb.

22

The VIPs

Otto Winkler had cut his teeth in communications working for the *Los Angeles Examiner* as a reporter on the city beat. A roundish little guy with slicked-back dark hair, Otto had accomplished the nearly impossible task of making many friends and no enemies while working with the cops, the D.A.'s office, and the publicity departments of the studios, because much of the crime and corruption in L.A. involved stars or studio employees. Hollywood people would get into scrapes; Otto would keep things hush-hush as needed. He didn't mind because he liked to do favors. Otto liked people and was always digging into his pocket for a dime for somebody down on his luck, doing what he could to make a life better, or at least a little less miserable. Fellow reporter for the *Examiner* Tom Devlin chided his friend every day it seemed, because there would be Winkler on skid row giving some bum a ride or lending his coat to some hooker who had been beaten by her pimp at three in the morning. "What're ya doin' here, Wink?" Tommy would say. "This is no place for you; let's vamoose." Devlin couldn't believe the size of Otto's heart, and he admired the little guy for always being stand-up, whatever the circumstances.

The studios noticed sharp guys like Otto, writers who could find the lead and not bury it, slant a story, and bang it out in minutes. And Otto could be trusted. When Clark Gable had been dragged into court in April 1937on a paternity charge by deranged Violet Norton, Wink had written it up for the *Examiner* to such a favorable degree to Gable that the star asked MGM to hire the reporter. At age thirty-four, Otto Winkler became the personal publicist of Clark Gable. Boy, was Wink now on the inside, toiling at the brawniest studio in Hollywood and working with the most beautiful people. Devlin and the old gang, the reporters and the city detectives, really gave it to Wink now but all in good fun because if anybody deserved a break like this, it was Otto Winkler. Not that Gable was easy. Gable wasn't easy at all, and he wanted Winkler within arm's reach every waking studio day and Wink never let the boss down.

In 1939 when MGM needed to settle "this Gable mess" once and for all by marrying off Gable and Lombard, it was Otto Winkler thrown into the fire, ordered by MGM publicity chief Howard Strickling to find a suitable spot for a quickie elopement.

Recently, Otto had met a girl, a good-looking blonde named Lucyle "Jill" Keeling who worked at the studio. They were head over heels for each other and began talking marriage. Jill looked enough like Carole Lombard to double for her, and in fact, she had. Jill stood five-foot five, an inch taller than Carole. Jill had danced on Broadway and opened a dance studio, then found work at Warner Bros. dancing in *Gold Diggers of 1937* and at Paramount in *College Holiday*. Her dancer's athletic body matched Carole's tennis-lean frame, and Jill even had the same blue eyes, as vivid a blue as the clearest summer day.

"He was the love of her life," said Jill's niece, Nazoma Ball, of Otto Winkler and Jill Keeling. "She'd given up her career to be with him." It was the second time around for both Jill and Otto, and the second time was always better. The bugs were worked out and it was a fresh start, a new opportunity to do things right.

Suddenly Howard Strickling had an idea: What if the studio gave Otto and Jill an all-expenses-paid elopement so they could sneak off to Arizona and conduct a dry run for Gable and Lombard at the quietest, most out-of-the-way spot Winkler could find in the desert—a place where two people might marry on the sly?

Otto and Jill sped off to Arizona and tied the knot on March 18, 1939, at Prescott City Hall. But the fact that Prescott even had a city hall, and a swelling population of 6,000, rendered it inappropriate for a clandestine *anything*. On a meandering drive back through the Mojave, in the general direction of home, they found a tumbleweed town called Kingman near the western border of the state. Here, Wink decided, was a hitching post fit for a king.

Ten days later, when the *Gone With the Wind* shooting schedule called for a break—after Gable had shot the scene with Vivien Leigh where Rhett leaves Scarlett and party in the wagon and goes off to fight in the war—Gable prepared for a wedding. The newly minted Mrs. Jill Winkler stood in front of Otto's Hermosa Beach cottage, down near the ocean, and watched Lombard and Gable squeeze into the interior rumble seat of Jill's new blue DeSoto, her husband Otto's wedding present to her. Gable wore hunting clothes, fedora, and sunglasses, and Lombard remained in hair curlers and wore no makeup. Jill stuck a picnic basket in Carole's lap and watched Otto drive them off.

"They were so madly in love," said Jill. "I had never seen two happier people."

For the next few days, Jill maintained the subterfuge, running errands in Carole's convertible, blonde hair held in place by a head scarf, hiding behind sunglasses, looking for all the world like the queen of screwball going about her weekly routine. The ruse worked. While the Hollywood press focused on a star-studded junket to the premiere of Fox's *Alexander Graham Bell* in San Francisco, Carole Lombard became Mrs. Gable in Kingman. But it proved costly: Gossip columnist Louella Parsons had carefully cultivated a friendship with Winkie and thought that when Gable and Lombard made their move, she could count on the scoop. But

Otto knew who buttered the bread and it wasn't the woman nick-named "Lollypops." Parsons spat nails over the incident, and in her mind Otto Winkler ceased to exist. Gable, on the other hand, admired Wink more than ever for outraging Louella, and with the king on your side, did it matter if you had one gossip-columnist enemy?

The coming of war made Otto glad that the family name had been changed from von Winkler. His heritage was Bavarian, but Winkler was safe enough a name for a true-blue American.

Otto and Jill had moved from Hermosa Beach to Wink's family home at 1106 North Wilton in L.A., the house his parents had left him when they died. Not long after, Howard Strickling gave Wink a tip about a piece of property across Louise Avenue from the Stricklings in Encino, just a mile from the Gable ranch. Otto made the purchase, and Carole paid for architectural drawings that she supervised with the girl Winkie called "Jilliepants." It would be a love nest built for two and hopefully more. By now, Jill wanted to open a restaurant with her sister Hazel, and there was endless talk of the dreamed-of place Otto dubbed "Jillie's Chili Joint."

In early January 1942 when the idea of a bond sale in Indianap-olis came up, Gable was happy to endorse such an idea—as long as he didn't have to go. He asked Wink to accompany Ma, and Otto hesitated on any number of grounds. He didn't like to fly; he wasn't an event planner; Lombard wasn't even one of the MGM players on his roster, or an MGM player at all! But Otto had gotten where he had gotten by saying "yes" to the stars and never "no." Sure, Gable took it for granted, but this was no time to make waves.

The Gables invited the Winklers to the ranch to plan. After cocktails and dinner, they sat around talking about the pending trip, and Winkler lobbied that they shouldn't go. They should stay put and do what President Roosevelt advised of the king and queen: Entertain people. Make pictures. Be satisfied with that. Let others fight the war.

"I was seated across from Carole," said Jill, "and Clark was seated in a big club chair. Carole was sitting on the floor, her arms resting on Clark's knees. I'll never forget this picture of beautiful Carole's lovely half-averted profile as she kept looking up at Clark, ignoring Otto's speech."

Winkler knew he was getting nowhere. He took a drink and said, "I swear, I'll never get used to you two and this obsession to do something for your country." He said Lombard was foolish—his word—"*foolish* for acting this way."

Carole had simmered to a sudden boil. She leapt to her feet and with arms upraised shouted, "Fuck it, Otto! I'm going!"

Silence fell upon the room. Winkler retreated and took a seat beside Jill. Gable smiled and winked at his wife. The tension of the moment eased. Otto leaned forward and began to speak. Lombard cut him off. "You're going into another speech that'll get you nowhere, Otto. Save your breath."

That week, with Carole's trip approaching, Jean Garceau prepared to leave the ranch at the end of her workday. Carole handed Jean a stack of folded pieces of paper and instructed her to give one to Clark each morning. They were love notes written to Pa, and they had a purpose. "She wanted to keep him on the right path," said Lombard archivist Carole Sampeck. "She wanted to be able to tap him on the shoulder and say, 'Hey, remember me?' She wanted to be there without being there. It was the longest they had been apart since they'd been a couple. It was like having her perfume in the room with him."

On Friday morning, January 9, Gable packed for a cross-country business trip to New York—Otto had booked him on the TWA transcontinental route of DC-3 stratoliners flying out that evening. Heading east wasn't bad given the favorable tail winds and with decent stops and no mechanical difficulties he'd be in New York Saturday morning. In all, counting his trip and hers, they faced ten days away from each other.

Carole wasn't quite packing for her trip but rather rounding up items to take, including a subdued wardrobe of blacks, grays, and pale pinks that befitted wartime, as designed by her favorite, Irene. She included a new black strapless gown that she would wear for her concluding appearance in Indianapolis, at a huge hall that supposedly seated 10,000. She couldn't imagine that many people turning out, but it was thrilling to think about.

This Friday should have been sunshine and doves for Mr. and Mrs. Gable. Instead, insecurity brewed up in her mile-a-minute head into a warning to Clark: Stay the fuck away from Lana while I'm gone. Such a statement violated their non-aggression pact about his dalliances, and a pitched battle ensued that sent the parties slamming into their separate bedrooms for final packing.

Clark likely said in return: Fine, then stay away from Mr. Bob Stack. Gable found Stack far too young, far too good-looking, and far too familiar with Carole, who clearly adored him. Ma's plan to teach Pa a lesson had worked like a charm.

Witnesses in Carole's family and many of her friends confirm that a loud argument preceded Gable's departure for the airport. He slammed out of the house, suitcases in hand, and was picked up by an MGM driver.

At the Winkler house on North Wilton two days later, early that Sunday long before dawn, Otto awoke with a start. His pajamas were soaked in sweat. He lay there awake and then carried dark thoughts with him through the day. At dinner with Jill that evening, he finally broke down. He admitted, tears in his eyes, that he had dreamed his own death. "If I get on a plane on this trip," he told his wife, "I won't be coming home."

Luckily, the plan didn't call for air travel at all. The party would depart Los Angeles by train on Monday evening January 12 and make a whistle-stop in Salt Lake City on Tuesday. They would arrive in Chicago on Wednesday for a press day, then take the train to Indianapolis, arriving there Thursday afternoon and heading straight into bond-selling action. They would depart Indianapolis Friday by train for the return trip to Chicago and then head west Saturday evening, make more whistle-stops on the way, and reach home Monday morning in time for the sneak preview of *To Be or Not to Be* at the Academy Theater in Inglewood the evening of the nineteenth.

Lombard also was disquieted after spending a subdued post-argument weekend at the ranch with Gable gone. She departed the ranch for her bond trip on Monday afternoon with Jean Garceau reporting, "She left on a very quiet and rather sad note—which was unlike her, usually so gay and lighthearted." Garceau also said, "Carole was not overly affectionate or demonstrative with her women friends, and had never put her arms about me or even kissed me until now. But when she was ready to leave, she hugged me hard, kissed me, and said: 'Take care of my old man for me, will you, Jeanie?'"

MGM sent a car to pick up Carole in Encino with some of her luggage; the rest would be hauled to the train station. Stuart drove Petey in and Jilliepants drove Winkie. All consoled themselves that the trip was only to be eight days. Carole boarded the train with the others, with no telegrams or flowers from her old man.

The Union Pacific streamliner, The City of Los Angeles, headed north through California to Sacramento and then swung east across northern Nevada toward Salt Lake City. Lombard was hard at work during the train ride composing a telegram to United Artists in response to plans to change the name of *To Be or Not to Be* to "The Censor Forbids." UA figured that *To Be* was way too highbrow a title for middle America, to which Lombard's boiling-mad telegram replied: "In the interest of a picture in which I am an investor as well as a participant, I feel that my investment is jeopardized by the proposed title change. I consider the title 'The Censor Forbids' suggestive and definitely question its good taste. It in no way conveys the spirit of the picture and is unbecoming to an organization as important as United Artists. So strongly do I feel about this that had the picture been offered to me under [that] title, I definitely would not have accepted the engagement nor would I have invested in the venture under any circumstances whatsoever. I strongly recommend that no change be made from the original title..., which in my opinion fits the picture, the story, and the situation."

As the train lurched to a stop in Salt Lake City, Lombard handed Wink the telegram and then stepped out of the Pullman and up to microphones for broadcasts through Salt Lake radio stations KDYL and KSL. She introduced Petey, and when asked about the purpose of her trip to Indianapolis, Lombard likened herself to a carnival barker. "I'll go out and say, ladieees and gentlemen, come on out and buy a bond!" The reporters chuckled; she had them at "good morning."

In remarks described by the local papers as "brief but punchy," the movie star cut to the chase: "This is a year we should all devote to our country. The morale of the country is the main thing. We've got to get out and get the boys pumped up!" She posed for pictures with local servicemen and with a small child who shyly dropped a ceremonial dime into the hand of the screwball queen and whispered, "Here's my dime for a stamp." Carole's face lit up.

After a few minutes, during which Wink sent the telegram to United Artists, Carole and Petey pushed their way to the steps of the Pullman as Winkler returned and helped them up. Lombard turned back and shouted from the moving train, "I don't have to tell you what to do: Go out and buy a bond!" She waved an apology for not being able to sign autographs, and the Salt Lake City train station receded into the distance.

Otto expressed concern about the lack of security in Salt Lake City and the potential dangers of allowing a movie star to be mobbed by crowds. As the train approached Ogden, he advised that Lombard conduct the next appearance from the window of the Pullman. This she did and took questions from reporters. She called out, "I think the wonderful thing about these defense bonds is that people are buying them so fast."

She was asked about Hollywood's part of the war effort. "We will go from place to place all year helping sell bonds," she said. As she spoke, autograph seekers handed papers in the window. She obliged, signing Carole Lombard Gable in a flamboyant script. She also revealed yet again a head for all aspects of the picture business, from production to distribution. "We're planning to make special shorts for the training camps, and other movies to be sent out through the regular houses advising people what to do in blackouts and other new conditions." She added, "Of course, movie companies have lost their European markets, but with new budgets they can make just about as much money in this country."

A mother lifted a boy who handed a piece of paper to Lombard. "Hello, cutie!" she said to the moppet and signed an autograph.

Finally, she was asked what were her favorite pictures to make. As the train departed the station she laughed and shouted, "Anything that's good!" With that, Carole Lombard whistle-stopped her way out of Utah.

The City of Los Angeles began its bisection of vast American spaces, giving Carole time to think and to buttonhole Otto for a heart to heart about the old man and their fight. After all, who better to talk to than Pa's friend and wrangler, a guy who also happened to handle press for Lana Turner? But Otto could only be pushed so far before he would clam up and invoke client privilege.

They pulled into the station at Cheyenne, Wyoming, for a ten-minute stop, and Carole hopped off the train and called the ranch, managing to get Gable on the line for a quick hello and confirmation he had made it safely back from New York.

After that, feeling better about her old man, she helped to kill a thousand miles of railway monotony by hanging out with fellow actor Pat O'Brien, also aboard the transcontinental train heading for New York City. He would remember the ride and Lombard in his memoir published a quarter century later.

"She was a remarkable girl," he said, "beautiful, down to earth and with a ready wit." He and Lombard went back a decade to the saucy pre-Code picture, *Virtue*. Lombard liked him because he had a balanced energy, didn't mince words, and wasn't on the make. She found his stories hysterical.

O'Brien had been under contract to Warner Bros. and mad mogul Jack Warner for years and spent hours talking shop with Lombard. And she needed distractions to take her mind off Gable and the fact that he would be reporting to MGM and Lana Turner at just about the time the train pulled into Chicago.

Lombard knew something about Warner Bros. from her experience making *Fools for Scandal* at the decidedly unfunny studio. O'Brien filled in many blanks for Lombard about the politics in Burbank, where Jack Warner served as warden to inmates that included Bette Davis, Jimmy Cagney, Humphrey Bogart, and Errol Flynn. Carole well recalled exchanging electric glances with bad boy Flynn in his Robin Hood costume as each headed to lunch in the Green Room and then back to the soundstages afterward.

Suddenly, the gabbing pair realized they were nearing Chicago, and Wink pulled Carole and Petey into a meeting to go over another tight schedule that included a platform appearance and photo op with the press and then a quick tour of radio studios for broadcast interviews. At the North Western Station in downtown Chicago, Carole and Petey set to the task of accounting for all their twenty-four bags and trunks in preparation for what lay ahead.

Carole asked Otto to check on the situation with the title change to her new picture. He returned with news that United Artists was "absolutely certain that the title *To Be or Not to Be* is not box office," but the company had relented and the name of the picture would not change.

Lombard squealed in delight, and just then, amidst the chaos of the moment, a young, quiet man edged into view carrying a camera, with a heavy leather bag slung over one shoulder. Wink introduced Carole to Chicago native Myron Davis, a *Life* magazine staff photographer assigned to cover the next two days' activities for a planned *Life* photo essay. By the look of him, Davis could barely shave, and had Pa's jug ears.

"Glad to know you, Myron," she said, and couldn't help but ask if he was new at *Life*.

He told "Miss Lombard" he had been on the job a few months.

"Just call me Carole," she said with a wave, and he would later recall, "I sensed from the start of working with her that she was a wonderful, down-to-earth lady. Being in Hollywood and being a star and being married to Clark Gable hadn't gone to her head."

The frozen air crackled with electricity, with Chi-town reporters and photographers gathered to meet the Hollywood VIPs. Carole chomped at the bit to get going, and the three of them stepped into frigid Chicago winds. Dressed in a gray suit with matching turban to protect her from the cold, Lombard strode inside the station house for a series of photographs by Myron Davis and a *Chicago Tribune* photographer as she posed beside a red, white, and blue war bond poster that bore the words, BUY A SHARE IN AMERICA. UNITED STATES DEFENSE SAVINGS BONDS & STAMPS.

She checked her watch and called MGM, managing to get Pa out of wardrobe fittings and on the line. Then she and Wink were placed in a car along with suitcases and hat boxes for a drive to the *Tribune* offices and another photo shoot while Petey headed to their hotel to settle in for a visit with family in from Fort Wayne.

The paper had asked to take photos of Lombard wearing a colorful hat, photos that would appear on the cover of the Sunday rotogravure section, and Carole had packed a gaudy number sporting red roses, green leaves, and black netting that would provide deep color for the feature section. She knew that some of her hats were ridiculous and that's why she liked them; it was sort of a joke on herself, and she especially enjoyed Gable's sour expression when he saw an offensive piece of millinery planted on her head. As she prepared to depart the Tribune's color studio, she autographed the dressing room wall with a sweeping signature, *Carole Lombard Gable*, and dated it *Jan 14-42*.

Next, Carole and Otto were whisked to the studios of WGN Radio, where Lombard sat for an interview by Marcia Winn of the *Chicago Tribune*. Or rather, Lombard paced, gesticulated, and joked her way through Winn's interview.

"Vivid, gay, she never stopped talking," said Winn of Lombard, "her comments as colorful as her hat." She described Lombard as "a flurry of mink cape, defense vigor, and Hoosier eloquence." In the WGN lobby Lombard pounded the tile under her feet as she paced and spoke passionately about the bond tour and the need to support the war effort. Suddenly, she spied Don Budge and Bobby Riggs, two of her court cronies via Teach and Allie, rushing past.

"Hello, sweetie!" she shrieked to Budge, and to Riggs, "Oh, Bobby dear!" Turning back to Winn she reminded that Riggs had won Wimbledon in 1939 and described him as "the Mickey Rooney of the tennis court." Then Carole mugged for both pals as they cowered their way past. Lombard had already told Winn that she had spent hours with Pat O'Brien on the train, and it seemed to the reporter that famous men were moths to Carole Lombard's flame. Winn described Carole as "constantly in motion and constantly talking and laughing."

When asked about the remainder of her schedule in Chicago and Indianapolis, Lombard reached into her purse and pulled out an envelope stuffed full of tri-folded pages. She rattled off everything that Otto had set up for her. She talked about the upcoming preview of her latest picture, and a radio appearance concerning the war effort in Latin-American countries later next week.

After the Marcia Winn interview, Carole went live on the air on WGN radio, where she turned serious and spoke about the war effort bringing the studios together. "This is the first unity Hollywood ever had," she said bluntly. "From now on it's sell a bond, sell a bond, sell a bond."

Winkler had packed the morning and early afternoon schedule, which Lombard didn't mind. But after a WBBM radio interview with Lorraine Hall and nothing further planned in Chicago, Carole second-guessed the hectic schedule of the next day that had her taking the train into Indianapolis and then proceeding through ten hours of activities. Instead, she ordered Otto to buy two plane tickets from Chicago to Indianapolis for the two of them, so she could check into the hotel and get some rest in advance of the bond sale. Petey could follow by train.

Marcia Winn had asked Carole whether she would fly from Chicago to Indianapolis. Her reply, said with a sly wink: "The governor of Indiana won't let me. Guess he's a pessimist." The fireball would *not* allow bureaucrats to tell her what she should do and not do, men who didn't have to participate in this brutal schedule. She knew that Otto disagreed about flying; she insisted anyway and he was obliged to ride shotgun wherever she went and however she got there.

Lombard and Winkler took a cab to the airport and flew south on Eastern Airlines Flight 7 at 6:45 P.M., arriving in Indianapolis after 162 air miles at 7:55. They checked into the Claypool Hotel in downtown Indianapolis knowing most of their luggage would arrive with Petey the next afternoon.

Dog-tired, they stepped into an elevator and Winkler told the boy what floor. On Lombard's mind was Gable's lack of availability to speak with her, and she wondered what it was all about, but in her heart knowing full well. It was now after six in the evening back home. The studio had closed down for the day and Pa was… where? At the ranch with Jean? Out with the boys? Or with Lana? At times, Lombard herself didn't understand why the idea of Lana Turner steamed her to such a degree. Carole knew Pa well enough;

he would never leave her for somebody else—never. Gable's name would be mud from coast to coast if he ever pulled such a stunt.

But she remained disquieted about the situation with the old man. Worse, she missed the bastard. She could take comfort only in the fact that at least the night's sleep would be stationary and not on a transcontinental train.

The next morning she prepared for another top-secret assignment, one never recorded in official history. Carole dressed early and she and Otto grabbed a cab to 3128 North Pennsylvania Street in the Meridian Park section of Indianapolis for a meeting with "scientific palmist" Nellie Simmons Meier, who was famous for her readings with world figures from Einstein to Eleanor Roosevelt to Walt Disney. Nellie was a longtime friend of Petey, and Carole had had a reading with Nellie in Hollywood in 1933. An amazing reading. Now Carole had lots of questions, dead-important questions: How would things turn out with Pa? Would she bear children? What would happen to her during the war?

Nellie, a diabetic in failing health, received her at Tuckaway, a rambling bungalow with walls gilded in gold. Nellie said she had chosen gold after seeing Coco Chanel's apartment in Paris and decided a similar look should be incorporated into Tuckaway.

During Carole's brief visit, Nellie looked into her palm and saw earmarks of danger. Nellie had studied Amelia Earhart's palm in 1933 and reported the findings in her book, *Lion's Paws*. In it, Meier spoke of aviators in general and Earhart in particular when she said, "Fear in the acute sense, that is shrinking from hurt to the point of avoidance of action, they do not know; their hands show it. All of them have in their hands significant characteristics that mark their owners as brave, courageous, audacious, aggressive. Any one of these words implies fear reduced to a protective minimum, reduced to the point where it cannot interfere with action. Not without fear, but with less fear than the average human being, these Lions of the air have taken their wings."

At about the time Meier's book containing this quote was going to press, Earhart was vanishing from the planet in the South Pacific. Nellie Simmons Meier was not a palm reader in the sense that she predicted the future. She merely reported the characteristics of palm prints and how the lines represented personality types, with results so stunning that even FDR had agreed to a reading. And many of the features of Earhart's palm could also be found in Carole Lombard's. According to Meier family history, with the experience of Earhart's death fresh in mind, Meier stood inside the massive oak door of Tuckaway and wished Carole good luck and also warned her to be careful. Bravery was one thing, but taking too many risks, especially now in wartime, was tempting fate.

Carole sped back to the Claypool, slipped on a black Irene dress, black slingbacks, a full-length sable cape, and a black feathered pillbox hat, and she and Otto hurried to the Indianapolis Union Station with its signature clock tower. Otto dragged Carole by the arm through a throng of confused reporters—*wait, where was Carole Lombard coming from and where was she going to?* Suddenly, she was side by side with Elizabeth Peters, newly arrived from Chicago aboard the Big 4. There they were greeted by today's presiding dignitaries: Indiana Governor Henry F. Schricker, Indianapolis Mayor Reginald H. Sullivan, Eugene C. Pulliam, publisher of the *Indianapolis Star*, Will Hays, censorship czar of Hollywood and Indiana native, and J. Dwight Peterson, Indiana businessman serving as state chairman of the Bond Sales Advisory Board.

Events kicked into gear with a short motorcade to the first large-scale fundraising event of the new world war. The three Southern Californians headed for West Washington Street for a two o'clock flag-raising ceremony at the Indiana State House. Newspapers, radio broadcasts, and placards in shop windows had been teasing local residents all week about the visit by Hollywood royalty, and when Carole and party arrived, a crowd of two thousand had congregated in the greenspace beside the building, with a line of prospective bond buyers numbering hundreds more stretching from the door of the east entrance, down the steps, and around the block, braced against bitter Indiana winds. Hopes that Clark Gable might show up with his wife fueled the swelling crowd.

Clark Gable was all thirteen-year-old Rosalynn Henricks of Indianapolis could think about. She was madly in love with Gable and had to be as close as possible to his wife. Rosalynn managed to shake school for the day, and as the instantly recognizable movie star appeared, the teenager wormed her way through the capitol plaza crowded to overflowing until, on the steps of the State House, Rosalynn said, "I was close enough to see Carole Lombard's beautiful smile and pretty blue eyes. She was very pleasant, very sweet." Rosalynn delighted in the glamour of Carole's black outfit and fur coat and felt the warmth of the Lombard personality on the "dark, gray, overcast day."

Carole descended the steps of the State House to a raised platform constructed on the lawn nearby. There, she looked down upon a line of military cadets and a crowd of still and newsreel photographers. Behind them, an energetic throng kept growing, a rippling sea of bundled faces stretching way off down South Capitol Avenue. She stood there with a number of dignitaries, all men, and listened as Indiana Governor Schricker introduced her as "the little Hoosier girl who made good in Hollywood!"

Lombard was led to a flagpole erected in the middle of the platform where she raised an American flag into the bitter winds. And it wasn't just any flag. This version of the Stars and Stripes had been flying over the United States Capitol Building when President Roosevelt formally declared war on Japan thirty-eight days earlier on December 8, 1941. All the dignitaries crowded in for posed photos with Lombard.

Will Hays of the censorship office, who had had fits over the years with braless Lombard and her jiggling breasts on the silver screen, would later look back on his time with this woman with raw admiration: "She threw herself joyously into every event of the crowded day."

Newsreel cameras turned in front of her as she read a short speech and called into the microphone, "Let's give a rousing cheer that will be heard in Berlin and Tokyo!"

A description to the crowd was made of the first cannon shot fired by U.S. forces in the Great War by Indiana boys, former Lt. Arthur Braxton and former Sgt. Alex Arch. "Applause rose as Sergeant Arch was presented to the crowd," said Hays, "carrying the shell from which the famous shot had been fired, and which was then autographed by Miss Lombard, the governor, the mayor, Mr. Pulliam, and myself—all with brief speeches."

After a demonstration of incendiary bomb technologies, the dignitaries and throng of onlookers moved inside the capitol building, to a spot off the rotunda near the governor's business office, for an hour of bond selling. J. Dwight Peterson of the Bond Advisory Board oversaw Carole's every move. Since this bond event was the nation's first, and there was no telling how a nervous public would respond, the goal had been set at a conservative $500,000 in sales of war bonds and stamps. But the line of people eager to interact with a real live Hollywood movie star had been building for more than seven hours, and hopes suddenly ran high.

Life magazine would later describe the event inside the State House as "jammed and hectic," with Lombard desperately handing out slips of paper to the deafening roar of a delirious throng as Myron Davis snapped photos. Each slip was a receipt that bore her picture, her personal printed thank you, and the stamped signature Carole Lombard Gable, bordered by red stripes and blue stars.

After an hour, with bond action still brisk, she was spirited away, through the governor's business office and down a back stairwell. A police cordon led to waiting cars that drove her the short distance back to the Claypool for another flag-raising ceremony, this one in the atrium of the hotel itself, location of an unlikely thirty-six-foot-tall flagpole. The flag-raising opened a new information booth for Army, Navy, and Marine Corps recruiting.

The breakneck pace continued. After a quick stop in her suite for a wardrobe change, she and Petey were driven north to the governor's mansion for a tea and reception with women of the Defense Savings Staff of Indiana, which was hosted by Mrs. Schricker. An attendee, Mrs. Lionel Artis, remarked on Carole's "hearty handshake" and called her an attentive listener who "looked directly into my face as if she were really glad to meet me and be where she was."

Mrs. Cleo Blackburn said, "Miss Lombard was very gracious and impressively natural. She was simple in her mannerisms and… I was impressed by her ability to remember people's faces and their names."

A reporter on hand took special notice of Petey and said, "Mrs. Peters was a refined and reserved woman and the contrast of she and her daughter was most vivid."

Carole addressed the group by saying in part, "I came here to experience Indiana people and your Defense program, and I am anxious to do every little thing that I can do, just as I hope that everyone here is willing to do everything you can do."

From there the famous duo rocketed back to the Claypool for a quick bath and wardrobe change. But when she turned the key on the door to her suite, a gasp was pulled from her chest and she leaned back into the frame of the door. A contented smile settled on her face.

Vases and vases of fresh-cut roses filled the room in an explosion of red, courtesy of Gable. If it had been one vase of roses, she would have suspected the work of Jean Garceau acting without Gable's consent, but for an expenditure this grand, no, it was Pa all right; Pa was saying, *Knock 'em dead, kid.*

Carole gathered her wits, took a quick bath, and pulled on the black velvet strapless gown created by Irene, along with black opera-length gloves and a whisper-delicate length of black lace about her hair and shoulders. Petey climbed into a V-necked black gown of heavy crepe with satin trim, and Wink into a tux. The three hurried down to the Empire Room of the hotel for a 6:30 formal dinner with Governor Schricker, Mayor Sullivan, Will Hays, Eugene Pulliam, and others. At that moment, eight blocks northeast, doors were opening at the Cadle Tabernacle, temple of popular evangelical radio personality Howard Cadle. People streamed into the cavernous wood-frame venue for a "pageant of patriotism" to kick off at 7 P.M. with a concert by the Indiana and Purdue University marching bands and the Culver Military Academy Drum and Bugle Corps.

The VIPs enjoyed a quiet supper of several courses and then made their way in a motorcade to the Tabernacle at New Jersey and Ohio Streets. As the car bearing Carole, Petey, and Otto arrived at its destination, Petey noticed relatives, part of a contingent of 1,000 from Fort Wayne, and pointed them out to her daughter.

"Hello, folks!" Lombard shouted warmly as she fumbled out of the car in her gown. "Hello, folks from home! Glad to see you from Fort Wayne! Hello! Hello!"

Inside, a well-beyond-capacity crowd continued to shoehorn in. Carole and Petey mingled with their large contingent of in-laws and cousins from Fort Wayne amidst the constant, deafening clatter of activity: One hundred soldiers from Fort Benjamin Harrison and sailors from the Naval Armory marched past; the Women's American Legion Auxiliary Drum Corps performed, and the Culver honor guard and color guard appeared. The Lord's Prayer was sung. The flag Lombard had raised earlier in the day was brought in and put on a display amidst a crossfire of spotlights.

Eugene Pulliam took the stage and presented Will Hays. Then the Purdue Symphonic Choir sang and a soloist performed God Bless America. Finally, newspaperman Pulliam took the podium again to say, "I've got some real news for you. Boy, this is hot news.

I almost got out an extra on this." He announced that Lombard's day of activities had resulted in sales of bonds not in the amount of $500,000, the initial goal, but in the amount of more than $2 million! The crowd went wild.

"It felt like an old-time political rally," said Will Hays, "and I thought what a joy it would be to any campaign manager to have such a candidate as this evening's star. She was the first principal I had ever seen go through such an occasion with never a single mistake; every time there was anything to be said or done, she said or did exactly the right thing. Her observations were all appropriate and at times absolutely brilliant. It was ad libbing at its best."

Governor Schricker approached the podium to introduce Carole Lombard. Interest in this duty had been great among "the boys," he explained to the audience in his most officious tone. "And so, as a measure of last resort, I had to issue an executive order authorizing the governor of Indiana to enjoy this great privilege."

The crowd erupted in laughter and applause. After a lengthy formal invitation, Carole approached the podium to sustained, thunderous cheers and wolf whistles.

"Oh!" she exclaimed breathlessly. "This has been a wonderful—a memorable day. Nothing could have made me happier than your kind invitation to share it with you and to be in Indianapolis tonight. In the true spirit of Indiana's bountiful hospitality, which I know so well, it was also kindly extended to include my relatives. However, I have not taken advantage of that because if I had, you'd all be moving out of this coliseum right now to let my relatives in."

With the audience laughing along, the ice was broken and her nerves began to abate. From the podium, she carefully read:

"I am here for one reason. It's the same reason you are here. It's the reason why one hundred thirty million Americans like us are united and determined to do a job that must be done. At first thought, we might say, 'Our job is to win a war.' That's true, but I'm sure it would be closer to the hearts of all of us to say, 'We are fighting a war to assure a peace—our kind of peace.

"We all know what this war is going to cost. But the peace it will bring is priceless. We know what an enormous task lies ahead. We know this because it has been told us in the plain and forceful language of our President, Franklin Delano Roosevelt. As Americans, we have the rare privilege of deciding for ourselves the direction we are to take. We have made that decision. Now our task is to provide more airplanes, more guns, and more ships than the world has ever seen before. That is our job: to give our fighting men the instruments for winning this war and insuring peace.

"There could be no greater tragedy than that we should send one soldier, sailor, marine, or flier to his death because we fail to give him the weapons with which to fight. I don't have to tell you what to do. You know what to do. Buy bonds. Buy stamps. Buy more bonds and more stamps. Keep buying them until this war is won. This is not only our duty—it's our right as Americans. I know there are people in this audience right now—men, women, and children—who are buying bonds and stamps regularly, day after day, week after week. People who are learning to do without their little luxuries in order to gain victory and peace. Can any of us do less than they?

"As a Hoosier, I am proud that Indiana led the nation in buying Liberty Bonds in the last war. I want to believe that Indiana will lead every other state again this time—and we will! We won the last war, and with your help, we will win this war!"

Carole then stepped discreetly away from the microphone to lead those in attendance in the singing of the *Star-Spangled Banner*, a tune she admitted terrified her. She had said in Chicago she would be lost if attempting that standard and said "the crowd would have to carry it." The crowd did, and her eyes welled with tears. Myron Davis and other photographers captured the moment of a straight-backed Lombard and an estimated 12,000 Hoosiers singing together. To an enormous roar of adoration, Carole was led offstage and the VIPs completed one last mingling session. Prior to the day's events, Lombard stated no public intention to fly home, although she had given Marcia Winn a sly wink when asked about flying. The official plan remained to board the train back to Chicago the following morning after an appearance at H.P. Wasson department store a couple of blocks up West Washington Street from the Claypool. But that Eastern Airlines hop down from Chicago the previous evening had been so convenient that she knew flying was the only answer to the question of how to get home. Mention of her situation to so many high-ranking officials (all of them men) led to easy solutions, and suddenly she was promised priority status for a plane trip west.

Finally, the party of three stepped into a waiting car and headed for the Claypool, or rather, to the Indiana Roof Ballroom next door, where she caused great confusion by surprising the large crowd of partiers who had been swinging to big bands on the 8,700-square-foot dance floor. Carole stepped to the microphone and pleaded with those in attendance to buy war bonds. Then, finally, she, Petey, and Otto dragged themselves inside the Claypool and made their way to Carole's suite. The entourage of other celebrities of the day followed behind.

"Back in the hotel," said Will Hays, "the governor, Gene Pulliam, and I stopped for a few minutes of final visit with the two ladies. They had to pack, but Carole still wanted to talk. She was full of the day's events. I doubt if she had ever been happier in her life."

After the three men said their good-byes, an ecstatic Will Hays stopped in the hotel lobby to wire Carole's husband in Encino: GREAT DAY HERE. CAROLE WAS PERFECT. REALLY SHE WAS MAGNIFICENT, AND THEY SOLD IN THIS ONE DAY $2,017,513 WORTH OF BONDS, WITH A QUOTA OF ONLY $500,000. EVERYONE DEEPLY GRATEFUL. I FEEL I MUST SEND YOU THIS EXPRESSION OF MY PERSONAL APPRECIATION.

The VIPs

In Carole's suite, she and Petey posed for a few more photos, ushered the press out, and held a brief get-together with all those Fort Wayne relatives. Long after midnight, the exhausted Lombard found strength to turn to Wink and say something he simply couldn't believe: "We're flying home."

23

Gleaming Silver

The foot of Potosi Mountain amounted to bad terrain, littered with boulders and cactus. The rescue party led by Jack Moore and Lyle Van Gordon spent an hour and a half climbing along a ravine in the cold, and soon they crossed the snow line.

Van Gordon kept picturing a forlorn band of survivors atop the mountain, bandaging each other and waiting in the snow beside a pitiful makeshift fire. Certainly, if there were Army men on the plane, they would have constructed a fire right away and offered Miss Lombard an overcoat. Sure, the burning mountaintop had looked terrible, but it might have been a crash landing, and perhaps the survivors had struggled clear of the wreck, or been thrown clear, before it caught fire.

At last they reached the top of the dry wash and now stared at three rows of cliffs directly ahead, each divided by patches of loose earth and pines. In all, the cliffs shot up 2,000 feet. It didn't even seem possible to climb all that way, but they started up anyway and found long stretches where the earth was loose under the snow. Somebody would take a false step and down they'd go, on stomachs, sliding thirty or fifty feet at a time. But each man would find his feet again and on they struggled, hanging onto boulders, some of them providing a moment of secure footing before giving way and bouncing toward the men climbing below. "Look out!" would call those above in warning to the other climbers. In places, the men moved tree to tree or rock to rock. They slipped, they fell, they clawed on.

Soon Lyle Van Gordon assumed a long lead, but then Bull had been capable of rushing for 300 yards in a single high school football game, so it was no wonder the others were fanned out behind him for half a mile. Van Gordon stayed out ahead, moving to the pounding of his heart, to the heaving of his chest, his rhythm steady up the nearly vertical mountainside of earth and rock. The snow became ever deeper, dry, powdery snow that had drifted this way and that and was inches deep in some places and over his head in others. All the men learned as they went to use the trees and rocks to pull themselves up, and when there weren't any trees or rocks, they clawed at the frozen earth just inches in front of their faces. As long as they kept moving they stayed warm, but if they stopped, the cold knifed into their flesh. Blood soaked through the knees of their pantlegs and stained the snow red. Dead branches on the pine trees speared them and tore at clothes, and feet kept slipping out from under them and they slid down precious feet and precious yards on their bellies and smacked into rock, only to scramble up again.

Another hour of visceral effort later, they hit the jagged promontory at the front of the mountain. It couldn't be much farther, they thought, gasping, but they couldn't know because the boulders and pines obscured their view. They crossed into another dry wash full of fallen timber and renewed their ascent. Or tried to. They found themselves boxed in by a ledge above, so they retraced their steps and crossed the terrain higher and moved into the ravine. When they paused to look back, they saw Nevada stretched out into the distance clear to Las Vegas thirty miles beyond. On any other day they would have remarked at the spectacular view.

Suddenly, Van Gordon could smell smoldering wood. His imaginings about the band of survivors moved front of mind and his body tried to respond, his legs pushing forward in the deep snow, muscles aching. He glanced behind, and none of the other searchers were in sight. He saw only his own breath forming clouds in the dry mountain air near 8,000 feet. He felt sweat accumulating under his coats. Lyle didn't want to admit it, and he knew the others would feel the same, but he was nearly played out and would soon need to sit down and rest but knew he couldn't because then the cold would close in and take him.

Through watery eyes, he saw a disturbed patch in the pristine blanket of snow twenty yards ahead. He didn't know how far off it really was. Everything was a blur. He staggered over that way, chest burning, reached down into the snow, and pulled out a jagged piece of aluminum a foot square. One side of the fragment showed a row of rivets. He looked up above him at a hellish confusion of rocks and fallen timber; through the rough terrain in the morning light, maybe seventy-five yards up above, he saw something silver gleaming in the rising sun.

"Hey!" the Bull called up into the ravine rising high above. His voice deadened into the fresh snow. "Is anybody up there?"

Nothing.

"Hellooo!"

He listened and heard only the rushing breeze, and the creak of distant pines. He never imagined he could be so alone anywhere in the world. He hadn't felt this alone deep in the Nevada mines, but he felt alone now, as some powerful, invisible force pulled him up and up through some of the most unforgiving terrain in the Western Hemisphere.

24

The Coin Flip

Carole's pronouncement about flying home froze both Otto and Petey. Elizabeth Peters had made it her business never to step onto an airplane in her life. The idea of sitting in a seat with nothing under her for thousands of feet terrified Petey, and her daughter knew it. But using the previous day's flight from Chicago to Indianapolis as a precedent, Carole saw only one goal now: to get home as fast as possible.

Ever since the exploding windshield, ever since the bullet in the eye, Carole Lombard had been a live-for-now kind of a gal, and she'd be goddamned if she would crawl back to Encino on a train when pretty silver planes criss-crossed the skies overhead, planes that would carry the three of them home in seventeen hours instead of forty. Wasn't that what the ads said: coast to coast in seventeen hours? What good was a half million a year in income if you couldn't actually use it when needed? And brother did she need it now.

Wink dug in his heels. He had been told by everyone not to take any airplanes. Gable had told him. Wink's boss at MGM, Ralph Wheelright, had told him. Wheelright's boss, Howard Strickling, had told him. Strickling's boss, Howard Dietz, had told him. Otto had already risked way more than he wanted by flying the short hop from Chicago to Indianapolis with Carole the evening before.

And now he was doing Lombard's evil bidding again, looking at flight options to southern California against the orders of all his superiors and the workings of his own brain and its premonitions.

Way back before leaving Los Angeles, Carole had looked him in the eye and *promised* she would take the train, and she knew why she must: Commercial passenger air service was less than ten years old and risky enough, and the danger existed of sabotage by enemies that may have infiltrated the United States and been drawn to the nation's first bond rally. In addition, whistle-stops had been planned for the return trip, and these were important opportunities to help the war effort. But Carole wasn't in listening mode; she meant business, and Otto knew if he crossed swords with the fireball now he wouldn't win, any more than he had won a couple of weeks earlier.

Wink was too bone-weary for a confrontation. He didn't like to argue anyway; he had made his living at MGM accommodating the stars, not making trouble for them. And Wink wasn't exactly alone as he sat in their suite at the Claypool at eleven at night, suffering sheer exhaustion of the day. Petey sat there in horror as well and could only look on as Otto dragged himself off to make inquiries with the Indianapolis airport about flights west.

Lombard paced her Claypool Hotel suite a dozen, fifty, a hundred times, a Coke in one hand and a cigarette in the other, before Otto came back looking gloomy, with pencil scribbles on the back of an envelope. The information she had supplied to Wink courtesy of the military brass at Cadle Tabernacle had led to three seat reservations on TWA Trip Number 3, a Sky-Club out of LaGuardia by way of Columbus that would be stopping in Indianapolis in a few hours, at about 3 A.M., and then flying on to St. Louis and points west, getting into Burbank at 7 P.M. Friday evening local time.

Carole hopped in glee and smiled a genuine million-dollar smile. Burbank yet! Pa could motor over Ventura Boulevard, pick them up, and everybody could be sleeping in their own beds by nine or ten Friday night. Carole reminded Otto that he could see Jill two days sooner! And, Petey—

Petey sat there hurt, terribly hurt by her daughter's betrayal but much more, frightened at seemingly innocent words Otto had said: Trip Number 3. Petey happened to be a student of numerology and knew 3 to be a hard-luck number. Theirs was a party of 3. Carole was 33 years old. Oh my God, 33 years and 3 months. This was bad, bad, bad.

"Petey—" Carole began.

What was the elder woman to do? She had nothing but pure love for this girl, joy in watching her and listening to her and marveling that "this is my child," the pure acceptance of the dynamo her kid had become and the pride of what she would accomplish next. Yes, pride in Jane Peters turned Carole Lombard, a thoroughly modern woman making her way in a man's world with both fists clenched and ready to fight. And it was this same hard-charging attitude that Petey faced now, this monster she had created.

Nellie Meier's plea for caution felt like it had come long ago, so incredible had the day been, and there was no reason for Carole to believe she wasn't being careful. She didn't know about Otto's premonition, or about Petey's dread of threes, but there was no missing their devastated faces. She tried to lighten a deadly moment. She offered to flip for it with Otto. She must have felt the weight of the offer—flipping for something this important when both these people sincerely wished to get home slowly and steadily and when calling it wrong meant the torture of that deadly train. But Lombard might lose too, and get home in three days while Pa was back there with *her*.

She told Otto to call it in the air. If he called it right, they'd go his way. If he called it wrong, they would fly.

Otto considered his options and he had none. He could get on the phone with the feds, or with his boss of bosses, MGM VP

Eddie Mannix, or with Gable, and in all cases he would be turning stool pigeon on Carole, and he knew he couldn't do that. Clark and Carole were family, and if he betrayed her now, she wouldn't forgive him for the rest of their lives.

"Tails," he said without enthusiasm.

She flipped the coin. It came up heads. She enjoyed the Lombard happy moment, that silly grin with tongue visible through teeth and the fast applause, and they all changed clothes out of their formal attire; Lombard slipped into a pale pink suit with a fur over it. In ninety minutes, they sat in taxis headed for the Indianapolis Municipal Airport, which turned out to be a small, three-story art deco structure on the southwest edge of town.

Inside the building, Mr. and Mrs. James C. Todd of Indianapolis overheard Petey say to her daughter, "Carole, don't take that plane." Carole kept walking toward the gates, where exhausted *Life* photographer Myron Davis sat on a wooden bench waiting for his flight to Chicago. Davis was dozing with his head back against the wall. He had spent a long day trying to keep up with dynamo Lombard. Here he was, a kid, and he had no idea how she managed to be that up. How did anyone maintain such a high level of energy?

He sat there on the bench half asleep, he would remember later, "when I sensed somebody come in and sit next to me. I felt a fur coat pressing against the side of my leg. Well, of course I knew it must be a woman, but I was so surprised when I opened my eyes and here was Carole Lombard sitting right next to me! We were so close together it was almost like we were boyfriend and girlfriend. I was so startled that it made her laugh, and then I laughed, too.

"So we just sat there and talked about a few of the day's events. I thanked her for being so cooperative and letting me follow her around and do my thing. And she said, 'Well, I was happy to do it, Myron.' It was a very sincere personal exchange between the two of us thanking each other for working on a job that we both thought was necessary for the country at that time."

He remembered Mr. Winkler and Mrs. Peters being quiet and gloomy and that "Carole and I were doing all the talking and laughing." And why shouldn't Carole be happy? Two million in sales in one day, and now she got to go home, and in a hurry.

25

The Computer

Mary Anna Johnson's job title read simply, Computer. Long before computers were electronic devices, *people* were computers—those who computed—and at Moffett Federal Airfield in Mountain View, California, Mary worked for the National Advisory Council for Aeronautics, NACA, computing data from wind tunnel tests on new aircraft designs. She had been one of four girls hired for the job straight out of the University of California. At a time when most young women didn't even consider going to college, Mary earned a degree in chemistry that got her foot in the door at NACA. Then she applied for a posted job as the aeronautics librarian and got it. In October 1941 she headed east for three months of intensive training in Washington, D.C., so she could take that new position at Moffett Field in the administration building just constructed.

Finally, she was returning home after three months of D.C. life that included some great memories, the most thrilling just weeks earlier at the White House during the ceremony to light the national Christmas tree. In this time of national crisis so soon after Pearl Harbor, Mary had gone to see FDR and there he appeared on the balcony of the executive mansion. And who was that right behind him? The shocked crowd realized it was Winston Churchill waddling out after FDR. He flashed the V for victory sign he had invented, which drew a terrific response from a mob of surprised

Americans who didn't know Churchill had entered the country.

Now, Mary sat aboard TWA Flight 3 over the blackness of the Ohio night heading west. Flight 3, a ten-month-old DC-3 with the number NC 1946 painted on its right wing, had lifted off from LaGuardia at 11:17 P.M. and made a quick stop in Newark, then landed in Pittsburgh at 2:18, in Columbus, Ohio, at 3:50, and in Dayton at 4:49. Airborne again in this glorified tin can, Mary struggled to sleep at 10,000 feet. She knew they would land in Indianapolis in less than an hour, meaning that sleep, when it came, would be brief and fitful at best, but that was life aboard the DC-3, then described as a "giant airliner" with twenty-one seats for passengers as well as a galley for the preparation of meals. In reality it was, as Mary noted later, "cramped."

Flight 3 touched down in Indianapolis at 5:24 A.M. and was blocked at 5:27, an hour and a half behind schedule because of the requirements of air mail service. Air mail was a big deal, and Flight 3 was an air mail run, picking up the latest priority mail at every stop along its flight path.

On the ground in Indianapolis, Mary noted commotion in the darkness. The hostess announced that a VIP was coming aboard, the Hollywood actress Carole Lombard. Carole and two other people, a worried-looking man and an older lady, boarded the plane and Miss Lombard sat just two rows in front of Mary! The intense man sat directly in front of her! Mary's ticket read Burbank, California, and from there she would fly to San Francisco, which meant she was going to fly as far as Carole Lombard was. Which meant that Mary Johnson was going to be in Burbank when Carole Lombard met up with her husband, Clark Gable. The thrill of it shot through Mary: However many hours in the future, I'm going to see Clark Gable when he meets up with his wife!

At 5:39 A.M. TWA Flight 3, carrying the Lombard party of three, Mary Johnson, and the other passengers, lifted off from Indianapolis into the black Midwestern night. Next stop: St. Louis, Missouri. For Petey, the ensuing 140 minutes amounted to white-knuckled torture. How could she look out the window at the void, not knowing how high up they were? How could she do anything but stare straight ahead at the back of the seat in front of her as Carole held her hand across the aisle and dozed in exhaustion? The rigors of the previous day dictated sleep, but how could Petey sleep? There wasn't one good reason in the world why this damn contraption should stay in the air. She had to expect trouble with every bump and noise in flight as she shivered in the cold of a cabin scarcely warmed by a heater while everyone huddled under blankets.

The DC-3 was an audacious, aluminum beast of an airplane: solid-state, hard-charging, and reliable in any job. Its cabin was not pressurized, which meant conveying passengers in temperatures near that of the air outside, sandwiched between growling, twin 1,200-horsepower engines working on each side of the cabin to keep the sleek ship aloft. Those engines vibrated into the pores of every passenger, every moment. For a woman who didn't want to cruise at 8,000 feet, Petey felt all the cold, vibration, and noise, and every dip of a wing and rumble of a turbulent cloud.

Flight 3 reached Lambert Field, St. Louis, at 6:47 A.M. Dawn was still half an hour away. Lombard and party stepped out of the plane and saw only blackness beyond. There was talk of fog rolling in, so they moved inside the terminal and waited. Carole paced, Petey fretted, and Wink sent a telegram to Gable about the delay and finally admitted they were on their way home by air.

Oh, how that fog did roll in, and Lombard stared out at...nothing. Gray, drizzly, nothing. Finally, at just short of 9 A.M. Carole, Petey, Otto, and the other passengers of Flight 3 stepped out onto the tarmac again and now in fog-enshrouded daylight could see they stood in the middle of nowhere. Maybe it represented the geographic center of the nation or the Bread Basket of the United States or the Garden Spot of America, but just this moment they were absolutely nowhere. Farm fields barely showed through the gauze of the morning, past a couple of older planes parked about and beyond the row of hangers. The weary passengers climbed aboard the DC-3 and waited. When visibility reached an acceptable minimum, finally, mercifully, the Sky-Club sliced its way up through the cottony morning sky, now heading for Kansas City.

An hour-and-forty-five-minute flight got them into Kansas City at ten minutes to 11 A.M. By now all three were beyond dead tired. Dozing on a DC-3 wasn't the easiest of chores, and each felt the shouts, the cold, the bands, the applause, the emotion, and the wintry shadows of the previous day in the marrow of their bones.

The flight crew that had steered the plane from Columbus, Ohio, led by Captain John "Speed" Hagins, a snappy-dressing and lazy-drawled Texan, now stood down, and young, German-born Ernest Pretsch, newly minted TWA captain, took to the Sky-Club with his copilot and air hostess.

Carole, Petey, and Otto grabbed a bite inside the Municipal Air Terminal during a long hour amidst what the *Kansas City Star* described as a "large crowd which awaited the arrival and departure of several flights, all held here or held out of here," and Lombard paced the waiting area as she always paced. At each of these stops, she drank a bottle of Coca-Cola or three if she could find it, and smoked one Camel cigarette after another. A passenger on Flight 3 said of Carole Lombard, "I watched her as she walked up and down.... She was very animated, but I had a feeling she was not very gay, not very happy. I looked at her and had a feeling that she was melancholy."

That passenger, Joseph Szigeti, knew melancholy when he saw it. An accomplished concert violinist who had performed across continents, Szigeti had been born in Budapest of a Jewish family, and as the Nazi threat increased, he and his wife emigrated to the United States just two years earlier and settled in California. He was heading in that direction now on a break from his latest tour, having performed the previous night in Winfield, Kansas. Joseph Szigeti was a classically trained musician. Lombard couldn't look up her nose high enough to see him; he couldn't look down his nose low enough to see her. His impression from her manner and aura—but only in retrospect and after tragedy had struck—was, "I pictured her to be an artist-colleague of mine."

Passengers of Flight 3 boarded again at 11:30 A.M. and by now fifteen of nineteen seats were occupied, and luggage—thanks in part to the bags and trunks of the Lombard party—spilled over from the luggage compartments and the overheads. "When I boarded the plane," said Szigeti, "I noticed that on both sides of the aisle up in the front just back of the cockpit, luggage was stacked." It was standard airline procedure to block off the front row of seats on commercial flights for cargo when loads grew too large.

The plane flew the next leg to the Wichita Municipal Airport, another hour-plus in the air, landing at 1 P.M. Another agonizing two hours was spent on the ground in Wichita, and by now the Hollywood trio was numb from the experience of trying to get home. On the plane Mary Johnson got a new seat-mate, Genevieve Brandner, a young army wife from Holton, Kansas, who was celebrating her thirty-third birthday. Genevieve settled into her seat and onto the plane walked Carole Lombard.

"Is that—" she began.

Mary assured her that it was. Brandner put two and two together about as fast as the human computer sitting in the next seat, and now Mary had somebody who could share the glee of what lay ahead in Burbank.

The Sky-Club took off for Amarillo, Texas, and the trio of war-bond travelers in seats eight, nine, and eleven endured another two hours in the air, touching down at 3:11 P.M. local time for fuel. One hour on the ground followed, giving Wink ample time to send a Western Union telegram to the MGM publicity department stating that the plane was experiencing what seemed like endless delays and not to expect arrival in Burbank before 8 P.M. California time.

At Amarillo two military men boarded, their gear adding to the pile at the front of the cabin near the cockpit. A civilian boarded here as well, a young woman of twenty-four with coal-black hair and striking movie-star looks. Lois Mary Miller Hamilton, from just outside Detroit, had been a stenographer before marrying 1st Lt. Linton D. Hamilton of the U.S. Army Air Corps seven months earlier. Now the Army wife flew west from Detroit to meet up with her husband. Anyone looking at Lois, and everyone noticed a looker like Lois, knew at a glance that this was a woman with class. There was something about her that said good upbringing, and smart girl, and big future. Mrs. Lois Hamilton settled into seat seventeen for the long trip west.

At 4:10 P.M. Flight 3 roared into the sky heading west out of Amarillo for Albuquerque. Two more air hours passed, and the plane again changed time zones; Lombard and Winkler dozed while Petey listened to the drone of those big engines and felt the penetrating cold of the air at 8,000 feet.

For the excited young pair sitting two rows behind Carole Lombard, Mary Johnson and Genevieve Brandner, one thought occupied their minds and one thought only: Every single minute that goes by, we are getting closer to seeing Clark Gable.

26

Stranded

Warren E. Carey, the Senior Air Safety Investigator of Civil Aeronautics Administration Region Six, had completed his frantic taxi ride from the Hotel Amarillo out to English Field, the remote Amarillo airport, and now awaited an American Air Lines DC-3 that would pick him up for the hop to Boulder City, Nevada. There the plane would arrive after dawn, which was critical since Boulder City didn't have a lighted runway.

Carey knew as much as there was to know about the crash west of Las Vegas. The TWA man in the station had related that Trip 3 from LaGuardia to Burbank had refueled at the Western Airfield in Las Vegas and taken off in the dark and had gone down fifteen minutes later near a mountaintop and had caught fire. A Western Air pilot had flown over and confirmed it. Carey wanted to believe there could be survivors since nobody had yet reached the crash site and determined for sure that all were lost. The crash had occurred above the snow line and snow helped lessen any impact, and yet—

He heard a plane overhead. It was the 4:00 A.M. flight and it was more or less on time. Wait a minute—he heard some commotion at the American Air Lines desk and that damn plane flew over and kept going. The American man told him that because of winds on the runways, the American plane had been forced to continue on and not stop for passengers.

So much for his flight to Boulder City.

Warren sat there in the quiet with his suitcase, hat in hand. Fine thing: A man has a job to do and no way to get there to do it. Well, he had three choices: talk to the TWA man, the American man, or the Braniff man, and that's what he did, in order, and finally learned that Braniff had the next flight in, heading for Fort Worth, which was in the wrong direction, but at least he wouldn't be in Amarillo any longer, so Fort Worth sounded fine to Carey. He knew there would be American flights from Fort Worth to Los Angeles and home, and he could figure out a flight from Los Angeles or Burbank to Las Vegas or Boulder City. Or if need be, he could drive to Las Vegas. He handed over his bag for the Braniff ticket agent to tag, and he hoped.

The sun came up. Warren ate some breakfast and then called Wilma and woke her up. He kept close tabs on the TWA desk for updates. From the radio he learned that Carole Lombard's mother had been aboard the downed plane, and that the fifteen Army personnel on board were Air Corps. Army fliers, just as he had been an Army flier in the last war. It got to him a little, thinking about brothers in arms going down that way. And Carey was reminded that Carole Lombard was married to Clark Gable, the most famous movie star of all.

Carey considered the ramifications of this fact, that Hollywood people were involved, and this would draw the press, and additional scrutiny from the President on down, and plenty of questions and demands for answers.

It was Warren Carey's job to determine why crashes occurred. It had been such a tremendous problem in the late 1930s, with airlines springing up and taking to the skies with no rules or regulations, and their planes plummeting to earth and killing people. Congress took action by establishing committees to investigate these crashes and by creating the Civil Aeronautics Administration, which FDR then split into the Civil Aeronautics Authority and the Civil Aeronautics Board. The first crash involving this new investigative branch, the CAB, had occurred on August 31, 1940, when a Pennsylvania Central Airlines DC-3, designated Trip 19, had plummeted to earth during a thunderstorm after takeoff from the Washington, D.C., airport, killing twenty-five, including a U.S. senator from Minnesota. When investigating air crashes, Carey always started with the most obvious cause and worked from there. In the case of Trip 19, lightning had been observed in the area; it was the obvious cause and in the end that's what the CAB had determined, that lightning had struck and disabled a brand new Douglas DC-3, which then fell out of the sky.

But from what Warren Carey knew so far about the TWA crash, admittedly not a lot while sitting in the middle of a prairie, the causes weren't so obvious. Weather out of Vegas had been clear, with light winds, which should have meant a fine night for flying, all of it by visual reference. Carey had flown out of McCarran Field often enough to know there were lots of visual references for night flying, despite the fact that Vegas sat in desert.

Or were there enough references? As he sat and waited for the Braniff plane to come in, Carey turned over in his mind those new regulations about signal beacons. If those critical navigational aids couldn't be extinguished on fifteen minutes' notice—which represented the warning time for civil defense personnel that the Japanese had launched a carrier-based attack on the U.S. mainland—then the beacons were ordered to be extinguished permanently. And with mountains as rugged as those in the High Desert above Los Angeles, well, that could be an obvious cause of a crash.

But the commercial pilots were slick and knew their business. Hell, they had been the ones who taught new Army fliers of 1941 how it was done this past year, so, beacons or no, that TWA pilot should have been fine. Should have. There was another obvious concern, even in clear weather and VFR conditions, and that was sabotage. Carey was certain that airplanes would be sabotaged in this war—it was the dirtiest possible game but leave it to the Axis powers to resort to something like that. He had been preparing himself to see evidence of sabotage in commercial air disasters, and he wondered if a day, two days down the road this would be it.

The Braniff DC-2 approached the terminal and eased to a stop. Warren Carey began to pace. He would fly southeast down through Texas to Fort Worth, and then head west to Los Angeles, and by the grace of God, this evening he would have a meal in him at his own house, and get a hug from his own wife, and if necessary take his own car north through the desert to Las Vegas, where he would begin to look at all possible causes for the loss of Trip 3, from the obvious to the obscure.

And in the meantime he said a prayer that they would find the crew and passengers alive.

27

The Glamorous Life

Alice Frances Getz was always special, the last of four born to Fred and Katie Getz of Kewanee, Illinois. The Getzes had thought Alice would be a Christmas baby, but she didn't steal the show from Santa and arrived a respectful two days later, on December 27, 1916. Smart and wise beyond her years, Alice always had her eye on the horizon, because that's where the planes were. After a family move from Kewanee to nearby Mineral, little Alice would stand and stare with all the concentration of young Charles Castle and, mouth agape, watch the airships pass over. At age eleven, in 1928, she made her first flight in a plane and decided then and there that she must have a career in aviation.

Mineral, Illinois, at this time was an American small town lost in the vast open spaces of farm country, a town that had consistently numbered 275 people for a century. Fred Getz had run a farm until he retired in 1930; Katie taught school. Both insisted that their kids must get an education, and Alice happily obliged because of her goal. Always a popular girl, she became president of her class all four years of high school, then valedictorian; never mind her graduating class totaled nine students.

By now, air transportation had gone commercial, and a new career field had opened up. In a man's world where few women this side of Amelia Earhart flew planes, Alice set her sights on becoming an air hostess. In those days only trained nurses could become flight attendants—one didn't know what might happen 10,000 feet in the air—so Alice trained to become a nurse at St. Luke's Hospital in Chicago, graduating in February 1938. She became an obstetrical nurse at St. Mary's Hospital in Racine, Wisconsin, then at Cook County Hospital in Chicago.

At the beginning of 1939, twenty-two-year-old Nurse Getz saw an advertisement for stewardesses from American Air Lines. *Are you a registered nurse? Between five-feet-two and five-five? Between 100 and 125 pounds? Between the ages of twenty-one and twenty-six? If so, join us in the air!*

Four hundred girls responded to the ad; six were chosen. Alice Frances Getz was one of the six, and all embarked on a crash course, not in serving coffee, tea, or milk, but in aeronautics, air traffic control, radio transmissions, meteorology, airplane loads and determining center of gravity, timetables, food service, and company organization. Upon Alice's graduation, American Air Lines had a wait list for hostesses, but TWA snapped up the dark-haired, browned-eyed, five-foot-two-inch, 119-pound Alice Getz, and suddenly she was living the glamorous life at 10,000 feet on the Chicago to New York line of TWA flights in the sleek new DC-3s.

TWA air hostess Alice Getz had it all: looks, a warm personality, an education, and now money and fame. She bought herself a yellow convertible, and in her tailored uniform with a smart jacket, pencil skirt, heels, and cap set rakishly on her head, she became the celebrity of Mineral and turned heads wherever she went, from O'Hare in Chicago to LaGuardia in New York. In just two-and-a-half years she had racked up more than 300,000 air miles, and her photo regularly made the local newspaper, the *Kewanee Star Courier.*

Alice was an athlete who enjoyed horseback riding and golf. Pretty but not beautiful, Alice drew the attention of the opposite sex with her personal warmth and a devastating charm in all circumstances. One male passenger recalled that "on a flight to Tucson, she was putting a dinner tray on my lap. My hat fell on the floor and as I reached to pick it up the cigarette in my hand burned a hole in her silk stocking. She let out a yell and everything spilled." He went on, "I bought a couple of pairs and gave them to her on the return trip. She didn't want to take them saying, 'It's all in the game. It was my fault not yours.'"

Now, at twenty-five, her personnel file thick with similar platitudes from passengers with all manner of troubles she had remedied, Alice found herself holding hands with Army Air Corps 1st Lt. Robert Burnett in a cab heading for Albuquerque Municipal Airport, suitcase at her feet. She had agreed to take the flight of another hostess, which caused no small unhappiness for Robert because he had flown an AT-6 down from Phoenix so they could spend time together, and now that time had been whittled away to nothing. Then again, part of the reason he loved Alice was that Middle America reliability of hers, stepping in when needed. He would be counting on that same spirit from her for the rest of their lives, so how could he complain now?

The cab pulled up to the curb. Alice stepped out, and Robert slid across the seat and stepped out with her. Neither cared for good-byes, and what was the worst that could happen—a few days' delay before they would meet up again back here in Albuquerque or maybe in Salt Lake?

They shared a young lovers' kiss, and Alice knew she had to dash because TWA Flight 3 was due in at any minute from Amarillo, and she needed to meet up with the flight crew. She reached up and kissed her flier good-bye one last time, and he stepped back into the cab for the ride to the Army base next door to the airport.

Alice had been besieged by all manner of suitors—suitors enough to occupy her mind on any flight, any layover, any time. There was sweet Bob Hix with whom she rode horses in Phoenix. And there was Vernon Ode, known by everyone as "Bud," the young repairman with big ideas for the future who looked more like Gary Cooper in *The Virginian* than Gary Cooper did. She had just played golf with Bud on the previous Sunday in Van Nuys, but oh, how young Bud was, just twenty-two and living with his folks. He had positively deluged her with gifts at Christmas, from a bedroom suite to imported cologne to five pounds of chocolate, and he couldn't understand her reticence, but then Bud hadn't been introduced to Robert Burnett, who had asked her to marry him and, well, what was a girl to do? She had fallen for Robert hard and knew he was about to shoot up the ladder to senior rank in no time at all. They had yet to set a date but engaged was engaged, and she had to figure out a way to break the news to Bob and to Bud.

With all this on her mind, she entered the Pueblo-style airport station and inquired about the status of Flight 3 at the TWA desk. It wouldn't be in for at least two-and-a-half hours, she was told. No! She wished she could get in touch with Robert before he flew back to base; instead she sighed and accepted that she had time on her hands, so she spun the postcard rack and smiled at the thought of her family reading a postcard about this latest escapade. She had sent lots and lots of postcards in the last two years, and she enjoyed bringing home souvenirs from all those exotic spots she visited, whether it was New York City, St. Louis, or Los Angeles. She loved seeing the delight on her parents' faces at her gifts and brought things for older sisters Marie and Ruth, and brother Fred and his wife Elsie and their daughter Doris.

She looked up and here came TWA Capt. Wayne Williams, who was about the calmest, most highly skilled pilot in the fleet and an unabashed flirt. Captain Williams was also about the happiest pilot alive, having waited ten years for an assignment in the Western Division and finally getting it two months ago—making him as much of a joy to fly with these days as ever. She had worked with Williams often on the Chicago-to-New York routes. Just a month ago she had gotten a Christmas card from Wayne and his wife, Ruby. On it was a drawing of a DC-3 roaring low over the desert, startling a roaming cowboy and his horse. In the background loomed high mountains. It was a strange sort of Christmas card but expressed the captain's delight at the transfer west.

With Williams walked the kid, Morgan Gillette, one of the newer copilots. Morgan was Alice's age, but she felt older somehow, maybe because she was on her second career after nursing in two hospitals in two states. As a nurse, well, one saw just about everything. Too much sometimes.

Gillette had a New England accent and seemed to come from money. He was smart and funny and soon would make a fine captain. The three of them sat together and killed time waiting for their ride to come in from Amarillo. Williams told of attending a wedding in Long Beach the next day and said he wanted to get home to Ruby up in Reseda at the five-acre ranch they had just bought. But it looked like he would be better off staying in Long Beach, which was the terminus of Flight 3, given the need to get the pilots home. In his nasal New Hampshire twang Gillette said he would soon meet up with Joan, his fiancée and a Hollywood girl from a well-to-do family—Joan's father was an engineer at Douglas Aircraft in Santa Monica, the company that manufactured the DC-3s Gillette flew every day. The wedding was only a week away in Los Angeles on January 24, and Morgan admitted to already feeling the nerves. Then Alice broke the news to the two of them that Robert had popped the question and she had said yes, which meant that the entire flight crew had weddings in their future.

Alice remembered that Wayne had been hospitalized to remove his tonsils. He talked about the ice cream he had eaten; Gillette wondered if the extra weight would throw off the center of gravity of the plane. All three had good reason for some laughs as they looked forward to the upcoming flight on this, the easiest leg of any along the transcontinental Trip 3 route since weather from

Albuquerque to the final stop in Burbank was usually quiet, and today would be no different. Just four and a half hours of air time separated Williams and Gillette from a weekend off. Alice could think only of meeting up with Robert again and the quality time they would share during her week-long vacation in February.

Alice noticed that there were other Army Air Corps fellows spilling out of airship transports outside and congregating in the station because their uniforms reminded her of Robert. And the Air Corps men certainly noticed her.

It was a growing clot of men across the way, all smartly dressed in tan shirts and khaki pants, with neckties, polished shoes, and the yellow patch of the Air Ferrying Command, the empennage of an airplane on a globe, on the shoulders of their uniform jackets. There must have been thirty of these men now, each with a parachute and other bags. All belonged to the U.S. Army Air Corps Ferrying Command and were making their way west by hitching rides on whatever planes, military or civilian, could carry them. Their mission was as important to the war effort as any that existed in mid-January 1942. These were the men who flew bombers just released from the assembly line in Southern California to embarkation points to the east, either to the New York area, or on to Canada and England. After delivery the fliers would meander back to California to start the process all over again. In this case the Ferrying Command had delivered its planes to Montreal, Canada. No question about it: These were critical personnel.

First Lt. Hal Browne, Jr., took notice of the pretty TWA stewardess across the floor, but Hal was married and he knew Patti wouldn't appreciate him looking too hard. Hal thought about seeing Patti this evening and their infant son, Hal III. It seemed certain the reunion would happen now since they had just been given priority to bump civilians from the TWA ship coming in.

Browne's copilot, 2nd Lt. Kenneth Donahue from Massachusetts, had no problem giving Alice some attention. Hal and

Kenneth had become friends these past months as they flew new bombers from the manufacturer in Los Angeles to various destinations near the war in Europe. Come to think of it, their training in flying the big four-engine ships had taken place right here in Albuquerque, at the Army air base next door. Sitting there ogling the stewardess, Kenneth Donahue noticed a TWA pilot and copilot sitting with her and wondered if they had been part of the Army training program of 1941. TWA had worked with the U.S. Army to establish the flight school here and donated its pilots as instructors on handling the big bombers coming off the assembly line.

It wasn't a bad life for the Army guys, ferrying planes around. Sgt. Fred Cook knew that. Fred of the easy North Carolina drawl and impeccable manners had already made sergeant at age twenty-one, a source of great pride for his ma; his dad was dead, but he would have been proud too.

The father of 2nd Lt. Charles Nelson was deceased as well, and Charlie, who had both military school and college in his background, had hesitated before enlisting because he didn't want to leave his mother, Margaret, alone back home in St. Cloud, Minnesota. Another in this pack of young men at the Albuquerque Airport hailed from Minnesota. Second Lt. Stuart Swenson had enlisted the day after Christmas 1940 after being out of work most of the year. In less than thirteen months he had clawed his way up from air cadet to copilot on the bombers and had just gotten married.

Second Lt. James Barham of Waco, Texas, had been in the Army going on four years after working in the Texas Highway Department. A warm and friendly guy, he had become an excellent flier, and everyone said he was destined for big things.

They all loved to fly or they wouldn't have enlisted in the Air Corps, and ferrying planes around got them to Canada and overseas to England, where the shooting war had already begun. That certainly made an impression on these young boys of twenty or twenty-five, flying military planes into a war zone, but here they all were, still alive to tell the tales, and the experience they had picked up would come in handy now because soon, all knew, they would be in the middle of the shooting war themselves. Just then, they heard the distinctive purr of a DC-3 coming in for a landing.

The passenger agent at the TWA desk, Ed Knudsen, was looking at all the Army airmen with the phone to his ear and suddenly slammed it down. He felt himself covered in perspiration. The boss in Kansas City had just issued an order to deplane all the civilians coming in from Amarillo to make room for the Army Air Corps personnel now crowding the station. He hurried outside and pushed the aluminum stairway out onto the runway as the plane was guided in to a stop and blocked. He guided the stairs up to the cabin door and locked them in place, and then climbed up. As soon as the door swung open and the hostess appeared, Knudsen pushed her into the plane and swung the door closed behind him.

"May I have your attention, please!" said Knudsen, shouting past the stewardess with as much authority as he could muster. Fifteen startled faces stared back. "I have just received an order from TWA headquarters. All civilian passengers on this flight are to be removed in favor of military personnel with priority status. Will the civilians on the plane please follow me into the station so I can make arrangements to place you on later flights west!"

Knudsen saw commotion among the passengers up ahead in the seven rows of seats. He heard a woman's voice; he heard cursing. Then a short, heavy-set man rushed up the aisle toward him. The man appeared nervous, with dark circles under his eyes.

"Listen," said the man, "my name is Winkler."

Remembering the voice of the boss in his ear, Knudsen called to the other passengers in his most commanding voice, "Please feel free to proceed into the station. I'll be right in." The passengers began to file past and clomp down the steps, and Knudsen returned his attention to Mr. Winkler, who stood there resolute.

"We can't get off this plane," asserted this man. "We—my party—are traveling as part of a—a—national defense program. Fundraising. For the war effort."

"I don't know anything about that, Mr. Winkler," said Knudsen. "All I know is that I was just issued an order to remove civilians from the plane in favor of Army personnel."

"Well," said Winkler with an odd, knowing look on his face, "I think you will find that the three of us will be continuing on to Burbank—one way or another." He pulled out a limp handkerchief and swiped it across his face. What Ed Knudsen saw in the man Winkler wasn't a smug expression at this remark, more one of weariness and resignation.

Knudsen turned to show Winkler out of the plane and noticed the hostess cleaning the galley. Ed also noticed a passenger, an elderly woman, who had remained in seat nine. Winkler noticed Knudsen noticing the woman. "Oh, that's Mrs. Peters," said the nervous man. "She doesn't wish to go inside at this time."

"But," said Knudsen, "she's going to be in the air three hours or more to the next stop."

"It's best to just leave her alone," said Winkler with a sigh, and the two men stepped off the plane and walked inside an airport station now teeming with people. Walking past to hurry out and into the plane was the replacement hostess, the pretty one who gave Knudsen and Winkler a disarming smile as she walked past. It was TWA policy that a hostess couldn't leave a plane assignment until her replacement had come aboard.

At a quarter past four on Friday afternoon, passenger agent Knudsen returned to the TWA counter knowing there would be hell to pay from the passengers who had just been bumped, but he didn't expect to meet the icy blue eyes of movie actress Carole Lombard glaring from three feet away as he stood at his station. Ed attempted to encapsulate his recent phone conversation with Kansas City for the benefit of the TWA passenger, but she cut him off with something about being just a few hours from her own bed in Encino and nothing was going to stop her now.

Carole Lombard beheld the perspiring, fair-haired man about her age and wasn't about to let him dictate the rules. She didn't like throwing her weight around and playing movie star, and tried to be pleasant and muster whatever of the ol' Lombard charm remained after raising a flag, opening a recruiting station, entertaining state governors, leading 12,000 people in song, staying up all night, and flying 1,500 miles. But the earnest approach got her nowhere.

She turned to the *Do you have any idea who I am?* approach. Another dud. Then she moved from plan B to plan Z: *So these men are critical to the war effort? Well, I just sold two million dollars worth of war bonds in one fuckin' day and I'm on official government business so you can kiss my fuckin' ass* approach. And she felt free to drop the names of the string-pullers who had suggested the ride on the plane in the first place, and asked for a phone so she could make some calls that would convince Mr. Whoever He Is not to try to pull rank on her. She could even call Howard Hughes, boss of TWA. This argument gained traction. Under the red-hot, red-faced Carole Lombard glare, Knudsen relented. Carole and Otto were given permission to reboard Flight 3; Petey had never left it.

Then Lois Hamilton, the striking brunette Army bride, edged up to the counter. Quietly she said, "*Please* let me go on. I haven't seen my husband in so long." As the fireball watched, Knudsen could only nod an OK to the forlorn Army bride. Lombard found herself thawed by the moment; suddenly Knudsen became human.

Joseph Szigeti, the musician, was bumped as were Mary Johnson, the NACA researcher determined to lay eyes on Clark Gable, and her seatmate, Genevieve Brandner from Holton, Kansas, along with Mrs. Florence Sawyer, a widow from Portland, Maine. But the movie star and her entourage had fought and won. *Nobody* was going to keep Carole Lombard off Flight 3.

Amongst the waiting crowd of Army Air Corps personnel,

each with a parachute along with duffels of flying instruments and personal gear, 1st Lt. Robert E. Crouch of Bloomfield, Kentucky, stood looking out the window at the adjacent Army air base. Then he turned around and spotted one of his pilot instructors at the base, Captain Williams, an old Army flier and a damn good pilot. Many of the TWA captains had been devoting time to training the Army fliers here at Albuquerque in everything from piloting to instrumentation to meteorology, radio operation, mechanics, and briefings. How Crouch admired the knowledge and experience of the TWA men. He had wanted to be an Army flier since he was a kid, but as long as his mother lived, he dared not even speak of it. She didn't want him in the service and she certainly didn't want him in the air, but then Mom had died, and he enlisted after two years studying aviation at the University of Alabama. Flying was something a guy was called to do; not just Crouch, but all these boys. Now, Lieutenant Crouch was senior man of the group.

Senior *commissioned* officer, that is. Nobody in the pack had more length of service in the Army Air Corps than Sgt. Al Belejchak, who stretched his lanky form out on a hard wooden chair and waited with the others. Al had enlisted in 1934, right after high school, to escape the fires of home. Many boys his age were told they would end up in hell, but Al had been *born* there—that's what North Braddock, Pennsylvania, was in 1934: hell on earth. At all hours, steel mills along the Monongahela River spat fire and belched smoke into skies that never showed blue. The air stayed brown all the time, brown and acrid, just like the river, which flowed a rusty brown up toward Pittsburgh a few miles away. Every breath of air, every sip of the drinking water, came with a dose of poison. The Belejchaks lived high up in a hollow above the Edgar Thomson Works of United States Steel, where Al's father George was a boilermaker. Options were few for people like the Belejchaks, so Al had enlisted, then grown tired of Army life and tried the mill but ended up back in the Army. His dad had never gone to college, and his mother Mary came off the boat from Czechoslovakia and had stamped out Al and four other kids with the precision of Andrew Carnegie's mill. They all had to eat, so it was off to the mill for Al's dad and brother, but Al just didn't take to the life, and now he flew the world in clean, blue skies and could behold Pittsburgh safely from the air and marvel at its fiery brown grotesqueness far below.

Beside Belejchak sat two privates, Marty Tellkamp from tiny LaMoille, Illinois, and Nicholas Varsamine—everyone called him Nicka—from historic, picturesque Woonsocket, Rhode Island, a stone's throw from the Atlantic Ocean and a world away from the harsh realities of Al Belejchak's steeltown. Tellkamp of Illinois, once a paperboy for the *Kewanee Star Courier*, had recently torn up the gridiron at Mineral High, the same small-town high school where glamorous air hostess Alice Getz had once been valedictorian. Nicka loved to fix things and the Army Air Corps had lots of things to fix, so he enlisted right after New Year's 1941. Now he was flying all over the place with these great guys learning about the new bombers. In a very short time he would become a non-commissioned officer and, he hoped, obtain reassignment to Europe, where he could fix very important things.

Radioman David Tilghman, another staff sergeant, hailed from a fine, big family from tiny Snow Hill on the Maryland eastern shore and was moving up through the ranks fast. A few chairs over, twenty-seven-year-old Cpl. Milton B. Affrime sat reading the newspaper about war in Europe and the Pacific. Milt also hailed from Pennsylvania but the other side of the state, Philadelphia, son of an immigrant father from Russia and an immigrant mother from Austria. They had settled in a Russian corner of Philly, and his father Daniel had been a doughboy in the Great War. The Affrime men were all short and slender, which made service in the Army Air Corps a natural for Milt, but right now he worried about his father, who had just lied on his draft card, saying he was fifty instead of fifty-six, and five-foot-eight instead of his true five-foot-three. The old fool might actually get himself drafted and end up serving in a second world war as he had served in the first. Daniel was a proud man, a Russian Jew who had sought a new life in America and loved America. Now, here was Hitler and this terrible new threat against the Jews, and Milt's father was going to go over there and single-handedly set things to right at age fifty-six. Milt sat there thinking his father was crazier than any other father. Any sane man of fifty-six would want to stay out of a war, but this one lied to get in the middle of it!

Nearby, twenty-two-year-old Lt. Frederick J. Dittman of Oakland, California, gazed out at the gleaming silver DC-3. Dittman, a broad-shouldered, round-faced newlywed with a bride waiting in Long Beach—a girl he married on Christmas Eve—had just learned he was bumped because the movie star's party of three was staying aboard the plane. "I've never been on a big airliner," sighed the Army flier who had been in service only a year and two weeks. His eyes raked along the shiny fuselage with red script reading *The Lindbergh Line*, and on the tail were evocative words. SKY-CLUB. It put him in mind of plush seats, a hot meal, a cocktail, and good-looking stewardesses handing out pillows and candy. He sighed, "One of these days I'd like to see how it goes."

Lt. Burton K. Voorhees held a seat assignment on Flight 3. This old man of twenty-eight and veteran of four-plus years in the service glanced over his shoulder at the big Sky-Club, and then he held out his ticket and shrugged his shoulders. "Take my seat," he told the burly Dittman. "I've ridden them."

Dittman was stunned. "You sure?"

"Sure, I'm sure," said Voorhees. "I'll get the next ride. See you back in Long Beach."

"Thanks!" said Fred Dittman, taking the ticket and picking up his small mountain of gear by shoulder straps and handles and lugging it toward the door.

During the just-ended melee, the old flight crew and the new met amidst the clot of Army fliers and the movie star's party. In his prominent German accent, which reminded people of Sig Ruman, the Hollywood character actor, Capt. Ernest Pretsch briefed Williams and his copilot, First Officer Gillette, on the condition of the ship, the heavy cargo load, and the passengers. Williams and Gillette prepared to board Flight 3 but paused when they saw TWA agent Knudsen working numbers and sweating profusely.

The TWA man looked at Flight 3's new pilot and explained that with the Army personnel, fifteen of them and their gear—and there was a lot of gear—and the movie star and her bags and trunks—and there were a lot of bags and trunks—and 338 pounds of dinner service that would be dished up in the air, Trip 3 was well over the 25,200-pound maximum provisional gross weight permitted by the Civil Aeronautics Authority. They had been trained to average passengers at 170 pounds each, but that wasn't going to work in this case. Knudsen maneuvered a slide rule in his shaky fingers as Williams shrugged and suggested they simply use the actual weights of the passengers, which must be less than the 170-pound average, and maybe the ship would be deemed airworthy.

Knudsen liked this idea. The Army boys tended to be smaller of frame; that's one reason why they were fliers—because they could fit inside cockpits and gun turrets. He asked the military men who was in charge and was pointed to Lieutenant Crouch. Knudsen asked Crouch to obtain the true weights of his men, which Crouch did, coming back with a tablet and pencil and reporting that his men averaged almost exactly 150 pounds each. Knudsen jotted this number down and that was easy enough, 150 times the fifteen of them. Then he walked over to Carole Lombard and asked for her weight. Carole shot the passenger agent a murderous glance and barked, "115." He asked passenger Peters and passenger Hamilton, and the three women together totaled 401 pounds. When he obtained passenger Winkler's weight, the total combined passenger weight calculated to within thirty-one pounds of what TWA required. So Knudsen rounded down, and suddenly the airplane's gross weight fell within regs. The agent turned to the pilot, relieved, and Williams gave him a *What did I tell you?* gesture.

Carole Lombard watched this exercise, and smoked cigarettes, and fumed, knowing she still had five more hours ahead of her by air, calculating the time she might actually see Encino. If she was lucky, ten tonight. More likely eleven.

Captain Williams had time on his mind as well. None of TWA's pilots could match this flier's experience, which included schooling in flight with the Army Air Corps and the U.S. Naval Air Service in the 1920s. Then he flew commercial airmail routes across the American Midwest, which had led him to a one-day portrayal of fictional Jimmy Donnally for an exuberant eight year old at the Springfield airport. It was a stint that suited Wayne because with almost 13,000 hours in the air, including 1.4 million air miles for TWA from 1931 on, he knew he could fly any*thing*, any*where*, but this afternoon luck was against him. Trip 3 had reached Albuquerque more than two hours behind schedule owing to all those earlier delays. Now, with this full load of passengers and overload of cargo, he would need refueling halfway to Burbank, ideally in Boulder City, Nevada. But Pretsch told Williams of strong headwinds, and a glance at his watch told him that, no, they couldn't use Boulder City because that airfield had no lights, and they'd be forced to land after dark. Williams told First Officer Gillette to write up a flight plan west to Kingman, Arizona, and then northwest to Las Vegas, the desert terminal surrounded by mountains. Vegas featured lighted runways and even though refueling there meant a later time into Burbank, Williams had no other option.

As the chaos caused by the Army personnel and their gear continued, Gillette hastily consulted his reference materials for compass readings and altitudes. Gillette hailed from Burlington, Vermont, and had caught the flying bug at age seventeen to such an extent that his grandmother had bought him an airplane. Now twenty-five, he was bright, had scored very high on all ratings, and would rise to fleet captain within a year. Gillette scribbled sets of numbers and handed his flight plan to Ed Knudsen. Then Williams and Gillette headed outside with glamorous Alice Getz to the DC-3 sitting quietly on the runway. Meanwhile, Knudsen still fretted over the center of gravity of Flight 3 with a full load of passengers and all that baggage. It wasn't his job to check the numbers on the captain's flight plan, so he signed the paper and set it aside—just one more document in a growing stack of documents.

The crisis had passed. Williams and Gillette squeezed into the cockpit of the gleaming Sky-Club as Getz prepared to serve a full meal to the nineteen passengers.

Fuel was added to the capacity allowed by the heavy load of passengers, baggage, and cargo, which meant a limit of 330 gallons. The cargo compartments, forward and rear, were crammed, and parachutes and duffel bags were piled high behind the cockpit and lashed in place under a tarp.

Inside the station, Ed Knudsen called passengers to the door of the station, and the Air Corps fellows fell into line by seat assignment. Squarely in the middle of the group and conspicuous by a lack of green and khaki clothing and ramrod-straight posture stood Carole and Wink. Knudsen led the group out onto the tarmac, watched as each climbed the steps into the plane, and waited until Alice Getz had taken a head count and confirmed that all nineteen passengers were in their seats and accounted for. Finally, Knudsen ended the most hectic twenty-six minutes of his life. He watched as Getz closed the cabin door, and at 4:36 P.M. the engines powered up and Flight 3 headed out to the runway, where it took off at 4:40 into the setting sun, heading west.

Carole Lombard had thrown her weight around and gotten her way; Petey continued to white-knuckle it at 8,000 feet, and Otto sweated out the moments along with her and attempted to rationalize away last Saturday night's premonition about impending disaster aboard an airplane. So many takeoffs and landings. So many chances for something to go wrong, and yet they kept taking off and landing, and he kept clawing his way closer to 1106 North Wilton Place, his cozy home just off Santa Monica Boulevard.

One row behind Carole and Petey sat baby-faced Sgt. Bob Nygren of Dunbar, Pennsylvania. Bob occupied seat twelve, the window seat in the right-side single row of seats. Bob sat behind the quiet old lady who was receiving Miss Lombard's attention during the long hours in the air. Directly behind Bob sat older brother Ed, perhaps cursing the fact that he was a couple rows removed from a real-life movie star.

The Nygrens hailed from the sticks of Fayette County, Pennsylvania, in the rural southwestern part of the state, and had certainly never seen any sort of famous personality before. Ed had just turned twenty-five and was always mechanically inclined. He had been all over the country since enlisting in the Army Air Corps in 1936. They sent him to Langley Field in Virginia and then to Chanute Field in Illinois, then back to Langley and on to Long Beach to begin ferrying planes when war seemed a certainty.

Bob had seen how well Ed was doing and how much he loved the service, so Bob enlisted too, straight out of Dunbar Township High School. Whereas Ed was a mechanic, Bob became a radioman, and their claim to fame back home was that they had never been separated from the time Bob finished basic training. Today, Ed took second seat, and there was Bob trying his best not to stare at Carole Lombard's legs. All Ed had to look at was a nervous, perspiring guy with slicked-back hair who looked like some sort of gangster. This fellow would lean forward to talk to the movie star occasionally, and she would turn her head a bit and respond without turning all the way around.

And so it went for 550 air miles, with both Ed and Bob Nygren feeling pretty darn lucky to have a story out of this trip to Long Beach that they could tell Dad and everyone back in Dunbar for the rest of their lives.

Back in Albuquerque, Mary Johnson clung to the memory of watching Carole Lombard walk out to the plane and up the steps. To Mary there was nothing more awful than the heartache of knowing that now she would never see Clark Gable, king of the movies.

28

I Won't Be Coming Home

At about 6:30 P.M. California time on January 16, Jill Winkler pulled her car into the parking lot of the Burbank Air Terminal and there spied Gable's convertible. She eased into a parking spot next to his and later said, "Clark was like a happy kid anticipating Carole's homecoming. He jumped out of his car, came over, opened the door of my car and invited me to come join Carole's brother Stu and himself."

He ushered her into the backseat and sat beside her. Out of a portable bar Gable poured drinks for three. They sat and drank and talked for a while, searching the skies for any passenger planes in case the TWA flight had thoughts about sneaking in early.

He told them about the telegram from Will Hays and what a hit Ma had been in Indianapolis. He giggled about the gags he had spent the week preparing for Ma, like the life-size mannequin lying on her bed, waiting. The prop boys had built it to his specifications, complete with an erection big enough to draw a gasp and hopefully some giggles from Mrs. G. Ma and Pa had never spent eight straight days apart, and he wanted her to know just how much he missed her, and he needed her to understand that he felt bad about the blow-up—as bad as Clark Gable could feel, as a matter of fact.

As far as they knew, Carole's plane was due by seven, but seven came and went and sometime later a car drove into the lot. It was Larry Barbier from the MGM publicity department. He hurried over to report that the studio had received a telegram from Wink in Texas that more delays had occurred along the route, and the plane wouldn't be in before eight and might be quite a bit later than that. Barbier said he'd go into the terminal and obtain updated information.

Jill Winkler said, "We sat in the car talking and getting more nervous as time went by." Darkness had fallen but the air was warm, and they continued to sit in the convertible and watch the skies. Finally, Barbier appeared again, walking out of the terminal building, illuminated by the lights of the parking lot. They watched him walk slowly in their direction, stiffly, strangely, like a man who was drunk and trying to imitate sober. It was a different person from the one who had gone inside.

They heard a plane overhead and the three people in the car looked up toward it, excited at the Lombard party's arrival. They watched the plane circle and come in to land. It wasn't TWA.

When they had nothing further to look at on the runway, they returned their attention to the man beside the car, who stood there, trying to speak but stammering, his words making no sense. The plane—was down—an emergency landing—somewhere—Las Vegas—somewhere. Barbier said he was sure it was fine, just a routine maintenance issue.

"Looks like they'll be at least an hour and a half late," he said. "Why don't you go out to the ranch, and the moment I get any definite news about its arrival, I'll call you and you can hop right over." What Jill didn't know, what Barbier could not reveal, was that he sensed trouble by the behavior of the airport men, who "were evasive about where the plane was, [and] when it was due to come in."

Jill looked at Clark. Gable shrugged that it was fine with him, and he drove Jill and Tootie away. Clark knew how pissed Ma

Left: Carole Lombard begins her acting career in 1925 at age sixteen. Below: An unretouched photo reveals the scars on her cheek, eyebrow, and upper lip.

Above: In 1927 Carole poses at Mack Sennett Studios to promote her short subject *The Girl from Everywhere*. A curl hides the scar on her left cheek, and bangs dip over the scar in her left eyebrow. Right: Elizabeth Knight Peters, better known as "Petey," poses with her daughter at the time of Carole's 1931 wedding to William Powell. [Douglas Cohen Collection.]

Top: Carole's brother Fred (left) stands with bridegroom Stuart and his new wife, Rosemary, at their wedding ceremony in 1933. Carole and husband William Powell serve as witnesses— and divorce within months. Above: In summer 1934 Russ hovers over Carole during dinner at the Biltmore, and she remains aloof. [Both photos from the Marina Gray Collection.] Right: Meanwhile, as she dates Russ steadily, Carole is also chummy with her ex. [Douglas Cohen Collection.]

Above: Carole leases a bachelorette house on Hollywood Boulevard and makes it party central. Below left: Countless bathing suit poses help her sell the sizzle. Below right: Screenwriter Robert Riskin offers a change of pace—masculinity, humor, and no commitment. [Marina Gray Collection.]

Above: On June 9, 1937, Clark Gable, Carole Lombard, Walter Lang, and Madalynne Field arrive at Wee Kirk O' the Heather chapel at Forest Lawn Glendale for Jean Harlow's funeral. [UCLA Library Special Collections.] Below: Carole and Clark sit with Alice Marble as she waits for a tennis match to begin in 1938.

Above: Jill Winkler had danced on-screen under the name Lucyle Keeling, seen in a publicity still for the 1935 Warner Bros. musical *Broadway Gondolier*. [Marina Gray Collection.] Below: Clark Gable with his right-hand man, Otto Winkler.

Above: Four players in the Mt. Potosi drama pose together at the press conference announcing the elopement of Lombard and Gable in spring 1939—Otto, Carole, Clark, and MGM publicity chief Howard Strickling. [Nazoma Ball Collection.] Right: Petey celebrates with the happy couple. [Douglas Cohen Collection.]

Above: An MGM photographer captures bliss in an extensive photo shoot at the Gable ranch in 1939. Below: In March 1941 the Gables visit Arcadia's Santa Anita Racetrack. [Douglas Cohen Collection.]

A Showman's Dream!

GABLE and TURNER
to sell with
EXPLOITATION

THE GREATEST BOX-OFFICE TEAMING OF THE YEAR! A MAGIC TICKET-SELLING COMBINATION!

W. R. FERGUSON
Manager of Exploitation

Above and left: Lana Turner enters the picture and forms an incendiary new love team with Gable at MGM. Below: Carole hits rocky career times as seen here with director Garson Kanin during production of *They Knew What They Wanted* at RKO Radio Pictures.

Above: By December 1941 strain is visible in the faces of the Gables during dinner out. Said one friend, "She probably screamed at him every six, eight weeks, and he was a good boy for a while." The diamond and ruby clips visible on her left shoulder will be taken to Indianapolis. Gable will wear a portion of one of the clips in a locket around his neck after her death. Below: At the end of December the Gables attend a meeting of the Hollywood Victory Committee where Clark is elected president. [Douglas Cohen Collection.]

Above: Carole and Robert Stack rehearse under the direction of Ernst Lubitsch on the set of *To Be or Not to Be*. Right: Carole shoots a scene in the mock-up of a cramped airplane cabin similar to a DC-3. [Both photos from the Douglas Cohen Collection.]

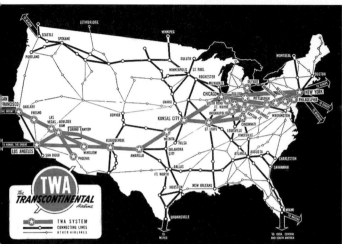

Above: The luxurious TWA Sky-Club DC-3. Left: The routes flown by TWA. [LostFlights Archive Collection.] Below: TWA air hostess Alice Getz sends home photos of the glamorous life flying around on DC-3s. [Doris Brieser Collection.] Bottom: The 1941 holiday card of Wayne and Ruby Williams features a startled cowboy watching a DC-3 flying low over a desert with mountains in the background. The crash of Flight 3 will involve all these elements. [LostFlights Archive Collection.]

Right: Petey and Carole arrive at the Chicago train station to begin a day with the media. Otto is partially visible behind Carole's right shoulder. [Douglas Cohen Collection.] Below: Petey and Carole pose at Union Station in Indianapolis for the beginning of a day of bond-selling activities. Beside Carole is Indianapolis Mayor Reginald H. Sullivan and Will Hays, overseer of the Motion Picture Production Code. [Foster Photos Collection, Indiana Historical Society.]

Above: Upon arrival in the plaza of the Indiana State House, Carole poses with cadets from the Culver Military Academy. Below: On the platform with other dignitaries, she awaits the start of ceremonies that will be broadcast nationally on radio. [Foster Photos Collection, Indiana Historical Society.]

Above: Carole and the other dignitaries autograph the first shell fired by American forces in the Great War. Visible are *Indianapolis Star* publisher Eugene C. Pulliam, Otto, Indiana Governor Henry F. Schricker, Alex Arch, Arthur Braxton, Carole, Will Hays, and Mayor Sullivan. [Foster Photos Collection, Indiana Historical Society.] Below: Carole urges the crowd to show the V for Victory.

Above: Carole moves inside the State House for an hour of bond selling at a furious pace. [Douglas Cohen Collection.] Below: As she settles into a routine, Carole chatters away as J. Dwight Peterson, organizer of the event (end of table, holding papers), enjoys the scene. [©2013 GoodKnight Books. All rights reserved.]

Above: From the second-floor balcony of the State House, the photographer Myron Davis captures the excitement of the bond sale. Right: After a furious hour, Carole escapes down a back stairway for her next appearance. [Both photos ©2013 GoodKnight Books. All rights reserved.] Below: Next, she raises a flag inside the atrium the Claypool Hotel, which opens a recruiting office. [Bass Photos Collection, Indiana Historical Society.]

Above: After a tea at the governor's mansion, Carole changes into a gown and shares dinner with other VIPs in the Empire Room at the Claypool Hotel. Left: Mingling follows, with Otto always close at hand. Below: Petey looks on at far left as Carole meets and greets after arrival at the Cadle Tabernacle. [All photos ©2013 GoodKnight Books. All rights reserved.]

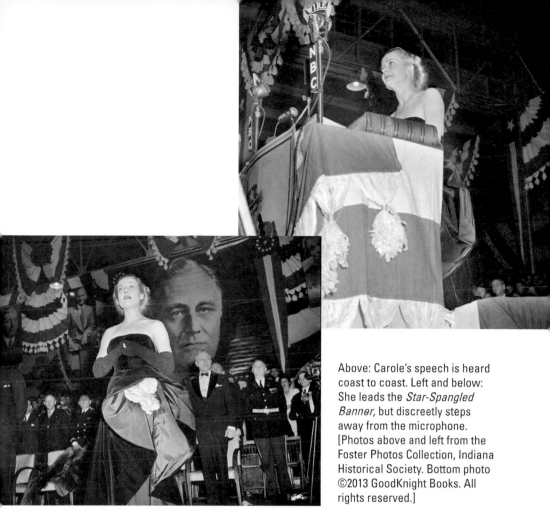

Above: Carole's speech is heard coast to coast. Left and below: She leads the *Star-Spangled Banner*, but discreetly steps away from the microphone. [Photos above and left from the Foster Photos Collection, Indiana Historical Society. Bottom photo ©2013 GoodKnight Books. All rights reserved.]

Above: Petey and Carole pose for one last set of photos at the Claypool Hotel. [Douglas Cohen Collection.] Below left: Among the Army Air Corps fliers heading west toward Long Beach is 2nd Lt. Fred Dittman. Below right: Mary Anna Johnson, the human computer, is about to meet up with Carole Lombard on the tarmac in Indianapolis. [Savoie Family Collection.]

Above: Jack Moore's rescue party stands on this spot and faces the imposing cliffs of Mt. Potosi, which they must scale on foot. The crash site is marked below the crest. Left: The second wave of rescuers attempts to deal with the terrain. Below: The Saturday morning edition of the *Los Angeles Times* hits the streets with hope of rescue remaining.

Los Angeles Times

EQUAL · RIGHTS

LIBERTY UNDER THE LAW · TRUE INDUSTRIAL FREEDOM

MAdison 2345
The Times Telephone Number

IN TWO PARTS — 28 PAGES
Part I — GENERAL NEWS — 16 Pages

TIMES OFFICE
202 West First Street

VOL. LXI   CC   SATURDAY MORNING, JANUARY 17, 1942.   DAILY, FIVE CENTS

Carole Lombard and 21 Others on Airliner Believed in Crash

Allies Deal Heavy Blows in Malaya

R.A.F. Strikes Hard as Lines Form for Singapore Showdown

SINGAPORE, Jan. 16. (P) Eager Australians and other fresh empire troops dealt costly blows to the Japanese in Southern Malaya today and the R.A.F. struck its hardest blows of the six weeks of the conflict as the British command organized a final defense for the showdown battle of Singapore.

Battling the invaders along a shortened line, rested imperial forces were reported to have knocked out 14 Japanese tanks and 10 armored cars along the west coast above the plains of Muntara.

JOYFUL SCOUTS

The Australians, who had moved into the lines with partly Thud-blood armor, reported they had rolled back...

Five More Japanese Vessels Sunk by U.S.

Three Transports and Two Cargo Ships Victims of Admiral Hart's Asiatic Fighters

Times Pacific War Summary

The Allies scored impressive victories on several of the Pacific war fronts yesterday which included the announcement by Admiral Thomas C. Hart that the United States Asiatic Fleet had sunk five additional Japanese vessels—three transports and two cargo ships.

This brought to a total of 25 the number of Japanese warships smashed to date by American naval and marine action.

What was interpreted as one of the most encouraging reports of the day was the slowing up of the Japanese offensive on the Malayan Peninsula.

The situation in this and other zones of action in the Pacific, is summarized from United Press and Associated Press dispatches, included:

1.—The Imperial British defenders of the Singapore approaches— bolstered by eager Aussies— dealt costly blows to the invaders along a shortened line and most important of all, the R.A.F. was in such strong action as to suggest either that considerable reinforcements had arrived or that much aerial strength had heretofore been held back.

Navy Combs Pacific for Enemy Fleet

Deadly Force of Sea and Aircraft Hunts in Vain for Japanese Armada

BY TOM YARBROUGH

WITH THE UNITED STATES PACIFIC FLEET, Jan. 16. (P)—Somewhere in mid-Pacific this deadly force of warships and planes has patrolled hundreds of thousands of square miles the last few days, almost entirely without incident.

A small number of enemy submarines was reported seen. What happened to them remains the Navy is not officially in the open, in any officially in the open on time and is in harmony with operational secrecy.

The hunting hasn't been the goal. None of the shooting has been target practice. No active Japanese force has appeared in these waters since Dec. 1.

ON MISSING PLANE—Carole Lombard, who, with her mother, was reported among 19 passengers on T.W.A. Skyclub plane feared to have crashed.

Plane Missing Near Las Vegas

Actress' Mother and 12 Army Men Also Aboard Craft Believed to Have Burned on Mountain; Clark Gable Charters Plane to Join Search

Missing several hours, a 21-passenger T.W.A. Douglas Skyclub airliner with 22 persons aboard, including Carole Lombard, actress-wife of Clark Gable, was believed to have crashed last night about 30 miles west of Las Vegas, Nev.

Pilot Wayne Williams last reported from his plane at 7:07 p.m., a few minutes before residents of the mountain area reported hearing an explosion and seeing a fire about five miles west of the Blue Diamond mine, located 15 miles west of Las Vegas.

Also among the 19 passengers and crew of three aboard the ship were Miss Lombard's mother, Mrs. Elizabeth K. Peters, and Otto Winkler, Metro-Goldwyn-Mayer studio publicity man.

ARMY GUARDS AREA

Shortly after word was received of the reported crash, T.W.A. officials in Los Angeles were informed that the United States Army had ordered a special guard set up about the area.

Twelve members of Army personnel were aboard the ship.

Above: Lyle Van Gordon walks into this catastrophic scene the morning after the crash. Scorch marks stain the cliff where the fireball burned. This photo is part of the set shot for the Civil Aeronautics Board and retains the official labeling. [Trans World Airlines (TWA) Records (K0453), The State Historical Society of Missouri.]

Above: Lyle and Elizabeth Van Gordon pose with Mt. Potosi behind them. [Van Gordon Family Collection.] Below: Remains of passengers are wrapped in army blankets and set aside. Soon the right wing (at center of photo) will be moved to reveal several crash victims, including Carole Lombard. [Trans World Airlines (TWA) Records (K0453), The State Historical Society of Missouri.]

Photo taken from
poition near point of
impact, looking down
on remains of wreckage
of tail section.

Above: Official photos show, at top left, the bodies of Army personnel that had been thrown clear of the wreckage and burn area. Below: A circle in ink marks the spot where the nose of Flight 3 hit the cliff wall. [Trans World Airlines (TWA) Records (K0453), The State Historical Society of Missouri.]

View taken from west
to east showing grade
of cliff and point of
impact. (indicated by
inked circle.)

Above: The notation "top" marks the impact point of the nose of the plane, which is embedded in the cliff. Cables trail down from the spot, while at far left the remains of the instrument panel hang free. [Trans World Airlines (TWA) Records (K0453), The State Historical Society of Missouri.] Right: Crash investigator Warren Carey stands on a ridge above the crash site and draws this sketch of the location of wreckage and crash victims.

PLAN AT LEVEL OF IMPACT POINT
APPROX. 10 FT. ABOVE BASE OF CLIFF
Elev. Approx. 7600'   X = Victims
No Scale - Approximate Only

SKETCH SHOWING DISTRIBUTION OF WRECKAGE
T.W.A. ACCIDENT- POTOSI PEAK- NR. LAS VEGAS NEV.
JAN. 16. 1942 - NC 1946- Pilot-W. Williams

Sketch by W. Carey.

Remains of right wing wedged against cliff.

Above: The right wing is photographed before it's moved to reveal bodies underneath. [Trans World Airlines (TWA) Records (K0453), The State Historical Society of Missouri.] Right: Weary recovery team members take a break. [LostFlights Archive Collection.] Below: The body of Carole Lombard is lifted by ropes from the crash scene.

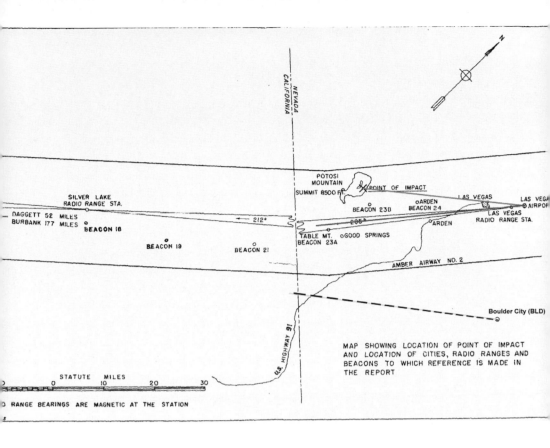

MAP SHOWING LOCATION OF POINT OF IMPACT
AND LOCATION OF CITIES, RADIO RANGES AND
BEACONS TO WHICH REFERENCE IS MADE IN
THE REPORT

RANGE BEARINGS ARE MAGNETIC AT THE STATION

Above: The CAB report shows that Gillette's compass heading from Boulder City (dotted line) is correct; from Las Vegas, a fatal error. Right: Alice Getz shares a happy moment with Capt. Wayne Williams as they stand beside a DC-3. [Doris Brieser Collection.]

Above: The crash site in recent times. A great deal of wreckage litters the mountainside, and human remains are frequently found. Right: In August 2016, after nearly seventy-five years, 2nd Lt. Kenneth Donahue, a copilot in the Army Ferrying Command who boarded Flight 3 in Albuquerque, finally makes his way from Mt. Potosi to be with family in New England. [Maureen Green Collection.]

Above: Clark Gable encamps at the El Rancho Las Vegas casino and motor hotel on Highway 91 south of Las Vegas. Below: From left to right, MGM VP Eddie Mannix, a shell-shocked Gable, and close friend Al Menasco emerge into the light of day on January 20.

Above: Early on the morning of January 21, caskets in shipping crates are unloaded at the Pomona train station. [Carole Lombard Archive Foundation.] Below: Clark Gable says good-bye to his wife and mother-in-law as they are interred in the Great Mausoleum at Forest Lawn Glendale.

Above: At Wasson's department store in downtown Indianapolis, where Carole Lombard had been scheduled to appear on the morning of January 16, a window display now serves as a makeshift memorial. [Foster Photos Collection, Indiana Historical Society]. Below: In August 1942 Clark Gable decides to enlist in the U.S. Army Air Forces; friends claim he does this because he wishes to die in an airplane, as his wife had. [Marina Gray Collection.]

Above: Major Gable bravely faces cameras at the launch of the Liberty Ship *Carole Lombard* in January 1944, flanked by Fieldsie and Irene Dunne. Below: In November 2007, Edwin Lewis of NASA and Dion DeCamp of the Civil Air Patrol, two vastly experienced pilots, crash a Cessna T182t into Mt. Potosi and set off a fireball despite the latest in avionic technologies. [LostFlights Archive Collection.]

would be at all the delays and now this latest for mechanical trouble. He would need to wring her neck anyway for taking the plane at all against everyone's orders.

At the ranch Jean Garceau was waiting to welcome Carole home. About hearing that the plane had made a forced landing, Jean said, "We were not duly alarmed, because Carole's plane had been down once before when she was returning from location. She'd laughed and made a big story out of it."

Clark's valet, Martin, served drinks in the living room for the group assembled: Clark, Tootie, Jean, and Jill. Conversation was quiet and grew ever more awkward as time dragged on.

"Soon the gate phone rang," said Jill, "and Martin came in and told Clark that Mr. Mannix and Mr. Wheelright from the studio were coming in." Don McElwaine, also from the studio, waited outside. Hearts stopped and restarted at two very high executives from MGM stopping unannounced at the ranch on a Friday night. "Clark opened the door and greeted them," said Jill. The two men walked in stone-faced and the mood grew black at once. "They told Clark that the studio had chartered a plane," said Jill, "and that they were going to look for the downed TWA airliner. Clark asked me to come along with them, but I declined as I told them I would wait to hear from the airport, as I felt sure they would be in, and someone should stay to talk to them."

The downed TWA airliner. Gable looked at his guests and they looked at him and saw the color drain from his face, and those canny Gable eyes showed something just the far side of fear. He started to speak, found nothing coming from his mouth, and followed Eddie Mannix and Ralph Wheelright out. Jill and Jean could see Stuart considering what he should do, and then he bolted out the door after Gable.

Jill stayed behind as agreed upon because she still expected Otto and Carole to burst into the room. So she sat in a chair and the quiet of the room gave her time to think. Did she count the months she and Otto had been married? Did she cipher it in days? She sat there in silence and Jean didn't bother her. Jill remembered that Otto had said, "If we fly, I won't be coming home," with tears in his eyes. He was talking about a plane trip, and not just any plane trip but a plane trip on this job.

The telephone next to Jill in the living room rang and she gave a start. She picked it up and a female voice wanted to speak to Mr. Gable. Jill said that Mr. Gable was not available and the voice said: "Will you please give him this message. We have positive word now that the plane crashed and went up in flames."

Jill Winkler later said that she thought she had hung up the phone; she would never be certain.

At the Lockheed Air Terminal at Burbank Airport, Larry Barbier took a call from his boss, Howard Strickling, instructing that Barbier contact Art Kelly, who chartered planes, and to find a pilot. Kelly provided a Western Air Express chartered DC-3, and a call to stunt flier Paul Mantz led to another call to stunt pilot Don Hackett, who hot-footed it over from his home in nearby Encino to Burbank airfield to operate the ship that would take the king to Las Vegas.

The MGM limousine swerved up by the wing of the plane, and Gable climbed into the plane with his entourage. They sat there. Gable's skin crawled over his bones, but nothing happened. No engines spooled. Mannix stepped off the plane and there stood an airport official, clipboard in hand. "Mr. Gable must sign for the plane or it won't be taking off," said the official to Mannix, who shouted that this was an emergency and MGM was good for the goddamn plane. "Gable must sign for it!" shouted the official back.

Mannix, a very rough character, grabbed the clipboard and pen. "This'll be good for the price of the goddamn ship," he growled and shoved the items into the man's hands. The official looked down at scrawled words: *E.J. Mannix, Executive VP MGM*.

Engines now coughed and sputtered to life. Gable wanted to

speed up time, to get airborne and get to Las Vegas and get into action. He felt the plane begin to inch forward, the growl of the engines now filling the cabin from each side. The plane started down the runway and suddenly Clark heard the voice of someone in the plane. "Who's that? It's Jill!"

Out the window, Jill Winkler could be seen running onto the tarmac, mouthing a scream and waving her arms. With her was Howard Strickling, who had finally made it from Olympia, where he had been visiting family. The engines quieted and Captain Hackett turned his ship about and found the spot where Strickling and Winkler stood. The hostess opened the door as the engines sputtered to silence and the plane eased to a stop.

Strickling usually had a mouthful to say. Gable knew Strick to be a bright guy, brilliant really, the kind of guy who stuttered because his mouth couldn't keep up with a rapid-fire brain. Strick always talked in a burst, in a rush, but now as the other men pulled him onto the plane without waiting for steps to be wheeled into place, Strickling gave Gable a wary glance and said nothing. Ripped away from a weekend with the family as he was, Howard seemed to understand that the best thing he could do now was keep quiet. The men lifted Jill into the plane awkwardly, and the hostess sealed the door.

Gable guided Jill by the shoulders to a seat and then plunked down beside her. He couldn't make eye contact. He couldn't talk. He could only sit and listen to the engines cycling up again and wish to God that he could *will* the goddamn plane to get to Las Vegas. Now.

Out the window he looked through blackness as the plane took off and headed north. Below he saw the lights of Burbank and Glendale fade away, and the plane lifted high to clear the San Gabriel Mountains. Then the ebony void of desert swallowed the plane whole for the longest hour of his life. He smoked cigarettes one after another. Not a syllable was uttered inside the plane.

They say that at the moment of death, the experiences of a person's life flash through the mind. This wasn't Gable's point of death, or was it? The torture of the plane ride aged him. Did he see their life, their entire life together, flashing before his eyes? That sculpted Lombard face, that voice, that goofy grin with her tongue between her teeth and her eyebrows raised when she had gotten him good with one of her gags. The early days at her place in Bel Air, the hunting trips to Canada and Mexico, her coaching of his dance moves for *Idiot's Delight*, buying the ranch and riding the horses and tinkering with the tractor, running lines for each other after dinner, the endless Selznick shoot—oh, how she had stuck by him through that year of hell on *Gone With the Wind*. Did he relive the elopement and the hours in that damn rumble seat with Otto driving? Otto. Christ, Otto too. He had never had a better friend, really he hadn't. Never a more loyal lieutenant. Wink was a guy who would take a bullet for you.

Or die doing his best to protect and serve your wife. Oh God.

Nobody knew if there were survivors on the mountain, or maybe they did know and they weren't telling Gable. He looked at the faces of Mannix and Wheelright for clues. Did they know for sure? No. If something had happened, if there was news, about... her, the plane would be radioed, right? But nobody made eye contact with him, and that was a bad sign.

Ma was the toughest broad he had ever known, tougher than he was certainly, and if anyone could survive a crash landing it was her, and she'd be bossing around the ones that could walk and tending the ones that couldn't. She was a hard one, all right, and nothing could stop her. And yet, here he sat on an airplane when he hadn't expected to be flying, listening to the drone of engines, the ominous silence in the cabin, feeling temperatures getting chillier every minute. And the faces of the men he knew so well. Grim, on edge, silent.

"He was so tense," Strickling said of Gable on that flight. "You knew you shouldn't talk to him. You knew not to say 'It's going to be all right' or 'I'm sorry.'"

The hostess brought around blankets. Gable put his arm around Jill to warm her; he didn't say anything; neither of them did as the Western DC-3 charter flew on.

At this moment Clark Gable revealed nothing to the others in the plane, but then he had always been a closed book and always would be, an immaculately dressed, obsessively clean person who expended his energy living the image of what Clark Gable was expected to be, which meant that now he must be what the others needed to see. It wasn't something he thought about or affected. He was just…himself.

Ma was the first woman who ever knew and accepted the wounded narcissist and helped him to become some semblance of a human of genuine warmth. But then Ma was a rescuer, and her incredible energy had maintained the task of spoiling Gable for six years now. How many times had she flown off the handle at his lack of communication and screamed at him and slammed doors and cussed his ears into bleeding just trying to get him to open up, which was something he just couldn't manage for her? He just couldn't. He knew he was a handful, but he had long ago accepted the reality of life as the king of Hollywood and all that meant for himself, for the women he had to satisfy, and, of course, for Ma. He had just accepted that he was living the life he was meant to live. He was Narcissus, with Ma cast in the role of her life as Echo.

And now what was he to do, with her plane down somewhere between Las Vegas and Burbank?

Finally, the passengers felt the DC-3 begin to descend, and the engines quieted a little. Gable could see lights on the ground. Dread must have filled him; he would step off that plane and not know what to do, and he hated that feeling, the helplessness and incompetence of just not knowing what was the right thing to do at an important moment. He had always been that way, as if at some level he realized he was made of spun glass, and it was his big secret and nobody else knew it but him. But Ma knew. Oh, sure she did, and somehow she loved him all the more because the glass could chip or crack or shatter into a million pieces if mishandled. But the biggest secret of all was that when that happened, she would get down on hands and knees and with utter patience pick up every shard, large and small, and put him back together again. The gal who couldn't sit still, who paced every floor, who exploded in tirades of profanity and had the patience of a cobra would become serene for him, as if somebody had thrown a switch and she was a different person, if it meant helping Pa get through some little thing that troubled him.

He couldn't find fault with Ma except she gabbed too much, so why did he feel compelled to step out on her? Why had he stepped out on every woman going back to Franz Doerfler—women with genuine qualities, good qualities? As much as he was capable of loving, he loved Mrs. G, but he needed the others for reasons even he would never understand. To him it was like breathing, walking, eating breakfast. It was something he *had* to do, and somehow she seemed to know that, and perhaps even understood. Well, most of the time, anyway. Not quite about Virginia Grey, though, and not at all about Lana.

Even Pa had to understand what the experience of Lana meant to him. The Lana thing meant what Crawford had meant, but more, because at the time of Crawford he had been thirty and now he was forty and what they called "middle-aged." And a hot little number of twenty-one, the biggest sensation in the pictures, still found him to be the cat's pajamas. Well then, he had to do his best not to disappoint. He owed it to the kid, and to himself, because who knew about age forty-two or forty-five and God forbid fifty. Would he even be able to get it up at age fifty? Then Ma could be content because the king had been put out to pasture, not to stud but just to graze.

Outside the window the forward landing lights snapped on, and Hackett eased the plane down, down. Wheels touched with a bang, and they were on the ground in Las Vegas, Nevada.

The Western Air Express ship taxied up near a hangar where police cars awaited. He followed the MGM executives off the plane and shivered in the bitter-cold air. Ma had just been here, just a little while ago, and now she was out *there* someplace, in the cold and in the dark. It was after one in the morning, and voices were hollow and dry. The police officers introduced themselves, shook hands with the entourage, and offered seats in their warmed cars for the drive to police headquarters.

He looked at their faces for clues, all these cops and politicians, but they were so many masks, faces behind masks, avoiding eye contact as much as possible, not saying anything important about where Ma was. He heard something about a command post, something about rounding up search parties to put into the mountains, something about the location of the plane being pinpointed. But nobody would say anything about Ma and how she was. It was enough to scare any man like he'd never been scared before.

29

There's No Rush

Lyle Van Gordon kept climbing through the snow and the cold. He swiped at the tears clouding his eyes, tears produced by the winds and the snow blowing into them. His nose was clogged and it was hard to breathe, and deep within him was a general weariness, his bones aching from every bump and bruise from the rocks of 2,000 feet already climbed. But something deep inside kept him climbing up, up, over places he wondered if any human had ever trodden, through deep snow and over fallen timber.

There was that smell again: burning wood as if in a campfire, and he wiped his nose, paused, and breathed, and watched clouds of his own breath on the mountain air and sensed—nothing. But in another few steps there was that aroma, burning wood, evoking images of survivors of the crash huddled around a fire for warmth. Exhausted as he was, he forced himself to wade on through the white, up a deep dry wash in the mountainside. He was tired and hungry, and he needed to urinate but hadn't allowed himself for hours because Lyle Van Gordon needed to be up the mountain so he could save people.

He sensed that he must be nearing the peaks. He didn't know this for any sensible reason, but something about the terrain and his own mind led him to believe that he was near the end of his search. The smell of the burning wood lured him, and he imagined warmth ahead, a fire to ease what he thought must be frostbite after hours in the snow. Then came another pungent odor. He didn't know it then, but Lyle would soon be shedding some innocence. Life was hard for Nevadans, but nothing could prepare him for what lay just ahead.

It was exhausting, plowing two feet of snow aside with every step. So terribly exhausting. He pushed on and waded his way past rotting tree trunks and boulders, until finally, up the ravine, he could see what he imagined was a metal structure. He rubbed his face through frozen gloved hands and scooped mouthfuls of snow for the water it held and sat there enjoying his long lead over the others. His stomach was empty after expending everything to climb the mountain, and he hadn't prepared for two feet of snow. He couldn't even remember the last time he had eaten a full meal, so long it had been that he anticipated the climb and then embarked on it. He struggled for breath in the thin air of Potosi Mountain, so thin, so cold, all alone where no men had been, not since the snow anyway. A part of him deep inside didn't want to stand or go any further because a part of him knew. Just stay here and rest a while. There's no rush. But really, there *was* a rush and there were lives at stake, and he strained to raise himself to a standing position. Ahead through clouded eyes he saw something blue. He could make no sense of it because this was January in the desert, but he saw blue amidst the white of the snow and the brown of the timber. He set one foot in front of the other and climbed toward the blue.

There was an explosion, and he ducked. It was—what—birds?

Yes, birds. It was blue jays. Flocks of blue jays took to the air, the strangest sight he had ever seen, their wings snapping to motion at once and producing that sharp sound. Blue jays way up here where he had seen no beast, not even a rabbit or a mule-deer.

Now the birds started shrieking in a wild cacophony, talking to one another, scolding the human for intruding. In another ten, twenty yards he gazed heavenward and above him, ahead not too far off, he saw burning cedars, aflame not at ground level but up a good fifty feet. Smoldering. It was the odor he had caught on the mountain breeze way down below.

He pressed on. Then, yes! Yes! He could see a metal structure. Climbing, pushing aside deep snow, up he struggled, and he thought to himself that the surface of the snow was perfectly smooth and glistened like diamonds where the sun hit it, meaning that he had gotten here first. He had gotten here to see the tail section of the plane, gleaming silver and beautiful in the morning sun, and the color and the reflection gave hope of rescue and people who were alive and resilient and grateful.

"Miss Lombard?" he called out, his voice thin and lonely.

But the higher he climbed, the more his heart fell. The silver tail of the plane sat upside down in the snow, dismembered amidships and burned black in places, ribs showing in others. Van Gordon leaned over to read inverted words on the tail fin. SKY-CLUB. Past the tail, up the rise to the right of him, he saw what appeared to be a green rock in the snow. No, not a rock; a man. And then another. Men in military overcoats. Two, no three of them, sprawled about in the snow, face down, face up, odd angles, all of them dead and frozen to the spot.

After the hours, the effort, and the hoping, Lyle Van Gordon found his limbs unresponsive. He stumbled against rocks that he couldn't see under the blanket of white. He struggled past the belly-up tail of the plane. Nearby, the trees gave an occasional pop and crackle, and smoke wafted into the morning air. But now he didn't find the scent of cooking pine to be at all fragrant.

The Bull thought to look up and his mouth hung open. All those blue jays up there, flapping limb to limb, impatient, annoyed, calling out to the visitor below. And what was that up there with them? Caught on tree limbs all about and moving in the breeze were crazy things. Fragments of aluminum, opened suitcases, pieces of clothing. What was that, swaying there in the breeze, a fur coat? And there above him, a brassiere, and he stared at it until his eyes watered and suddenly he was weeping, looking up at a brassiere of all the crazy things and crying his eyes out.

The quiet of the morning became oppressive. He was all alone and did not want to go a step further. Instead he backed off and waited for the others. If only there was something he could do for anyone, any survivor, but there wasn't anything for him here but death. By accident he looked into a blackened pile of debris directly ahead below a cliff and there he couldn't help but see three charred bodies. They *had* to be bodies because there were heads and shoulders and torsos and they seemed to be still sitting in their seats, but they had been hacked so oddly, with chunks of them gone. He backed off some more, and waited a long while until Deputy Moore came up, and then the others.

Jack Moore grew wary when he saw Van Gordon, the powerful man sitting on a rock and slumped, forlorn. Moore took some steps in a forward direction, up the hard terrain of deep snow and steep mountain, past the Bull, and he walked into hell. Ahead he beheld what looked for all the world like the city dump. Luggage everywhere; the twisted fuselage of the plane, a tangled mass of aluminum, wires and cables, seats, shattered glass, random hunks of engine, and melted rubber. Wedged in here and there were passengers, or rather, what was left of passengers; pieces of passengers. Bodies that had so recently been human were now nothing but blackened clumps of bone and tissue. People burned to a crisp, including some still in their seats in a big pile of debris. All around in rugged terrain, in the midst of rock and snow and twisted metal, he beheld arms, and legs, and heads. The rescuers had found what granite cliff could do to a plane and its occupants at a couple hundred miles an hour.

The pungent smell in the air he and the others had encountered now made sense. It was no longer the clean campfire scent of pine and cedar; it was burned flesh smoldering from the knot of fuselage at the base of the cliff, and from lazy traces of steam wafting up from wreckage that lay crumpled ahead, with NC 1946 painted in large red letters and numbers outlined in black on one of the silvery wings now leaning against the cliff wall. Oh, that stench; it must have been the horrid smell that drew the blue jays, now calling from above, insistently, mockingly, hundreds of birds above them looking down on the foolishness of humans and their flawed flying machine.

All about in the snow, what snow hadn't been melted away, was oil and blood in beads and splashes and puddles and lakes.

The six weary, sickened men climbed to the base of the cliff that rose up before them, blackened for ninety feet straight up. There was no easy place to stand on the steep incline. Deputy Moore rested hands on knees and gasped, struggling for a deep breath, or any breath at all; the baked earth revealed a hodgepodge: crockery, shards of glass, contents of suitcases, bits of flesh, twisted metal.

Death.

Lyle Van Gordon turned and faced down the mountain. He could see Las Vegas, glistening in its normalcy and life, far off in the distance. In other circumstances this would have been a spectacular view of a beautiful morning. He put his head in his hands and just sat.

Deputy Moore asked if anybody could see her, if they could recognize Carole Lombard. It suddenly seemed strange to hear a human voice in this vile place. No one answered. No one but the angry blue jays. The rescuers didn't want to look anymore and find out what had become of the movie star.

Moore had to figure a way to get word down the mountain that all aboard the ship were lost.

Robert Griffith of the Las Vegas Chamber of Commerce knew that the story here was a worldwide FLASH. The death of Carole Lombard and its effect on Hollywood in general, and on her husband, King of the Movies Clark Gable, in particular. But Griffith didn't care. He was a rescuer and a man, and he hurt for the passengers of this plane, for Lombard and all the others on board, the pilot, the copilot, those soldiers lying back there in the snow. All of them. Such a way to die.

The men shared a thought in the long silence: This wasn't just about Lombard and her husband. All these poor people lying about this place had mothers and fathers. Some had sisters and brothers and wives and children.

Even the courageous, hardened band of Nevadans who had struggled for hours up the most unforgiving mountain in the west and found the plane a hundred others sought—all six of these men needed a moment. Some broke down. Others knelt in prayer. The birds above settled, and silence deepened and the moments passed until Deputy Sheriff Moore remembered his duty. He asked for two who were willing to stay with the wreckage, but the band was all in and he knew it.

Finally, Moore said he would stay with the wreck of the plane until other rescuers arrived, and he asked for one other volunteer. He didn't expect any takers, but Bondley said a simple, harsh, "Yah," and all six helped to get a fire going. The others gave Moore and Bondley all the food they had left in their pockets. Moore handed over his car keys and said to get word to the sheriff. Then the two deputies watched the crestfallen four others descend from the scene, Van Gordon, Griffith, Otto Schwartz, and Jack Hart. The two who stayed knew the horror the others faced: It had been hell getting up and now it would be hell getting back down, especially as they swallowed the bile they all felt rising from a scene none were prepared to see up close, despite their best intentions.

Three hours later, after many slips, falls, scrapes, cuts, and smears of blood in the snow, the four descending rescuers finally made contact with level ground once again. Wearily they eased into their vehicles and drove down to Goodsprings. Griffith sent a wire up to the Clark County Courthouse in Las Vegas. At the Pioneer Saloon, a reporter sidled up to the four shell-shocked men, their faces painted in grime and skin stretched tight by God only knew what. The reporter asked what the men had discovered. Had they found the plane? Jack Hart said, "We found it. Sure. It was a tough climb. I guess I don't care to say any more about it."

"It was pretty awful," Otto Schwartz allowed. "Me, I think I'll go to bed."

30

Caring Enough to Climb a Mountain

The Gable party of six was driven from the police station in dark of night past the southern edge of town and into desert. There along Highway 91 they found the brightly lit—even at two in the morning—El Rancho Vegas motor hotel. It was, in fact, the only hotel and casino in the entirety of Las Vegas, the first of its kind and genesis of later empires. A main structure housed the casino, restaurant, and opera house. Behind it in a broad semicircle stood sixty-three rooms motel style. El Rancho Manager Ernie Hawes met the group upon arrival, no matter that it was the middle of the night, and personally showed Mr. Gable into the best bungalow in the place. Hawes put the MGM men on both sides of Gable, Mannix in an adjoining room, and Gable remained as he had been since the ranch: bewildered. It was the middle of the night and nothing made sense and he looked about him at his room and began to pace. The walls were done in a cowboy motif, and he paced by them and smoked and paced and smoked and waited—he didn't even know what he was waiting for. For some stranger to come in and tell him his wife was dead? Time dragged and he was tired and angry and couldn't see straight, but he went on pacing and smoking. When he ran out of cigarettes, more appeared for him. Who brought them, he didn't know. He couldn't think. He could only pace the room that was like a cage, back and forth, back and forth.

How could he think about the past week and not conclude that everything happening now was his fault? Ma wanted to get home as fast as possible and that's why she had taken the plane. She had been ordered by the government *not* to take a plane because of what might happen, and she had taken the plane and it *had* happened. All because of the fight they'd had and her frustration with him, sometimes wanting to split his skull because he couldn't communicate with her like she needed him to because he didn't know the words to say. They had fought about Lana, but was it really about Lana or about Ma being sick to death of the way he was. She would say: If only she knew what to do, what to say, how to hold him, what to bring him, how to please him; if only he would *tell her* what he needed, she would do it for him, but he didn't know how to say what she needed him to say. If he wanted a scotch and soda he could ask, but anything deeper just brought disconnection.

The dawn kept not coming. He loved his liquor, and here he stood next to a building full of the stuff, and all he could manage was lighting one cigarette with the other and pacing, in silence, alone, with five of the closest people in the world to him just a few yards away in surrounding rooms. Inevitably, he thought about Otto, his go-to guy, because how many times on this long evening and night had he wanted to get Wink in to take care of things, but Wink was with Ma. It was a train wreck of awful.

Finally, he couldn't stand it anymore and threw away his cigarette and stormed outside and demanded to be taken to Carole Lombard, and taken right now. His friends tried to pull him back into his room, but he wrestled free and demanded: Take Me to My Wife. Right This Minute.

He found himself in a car, with Mannix on one side and Wheelright on the other. The car was moving, driving south along the highway, in the black of night with Ernie Hawes of the El Rancho at the wheel. It was a long drive, very long and very dark, in a large vehicle full of people, and he was seated in the backseat between the MGM men who seemed to be holding him down so he wouldn't lose his mind and start flailing his arms. He didn't know what to do. How did one deal with a situation like this? With a wife missing and presumed, what? Dead? A best friend minding the wife and also lost? There were no rules and nobody who knew what to do, and he was among those people not knowing, and it unnerved him.

The car finally turned off the southern highway and headed in another direction, west, he figured. There was no telling about the scenery with the blackness on either side of the car but the road made lazy bends this way and that, and finally they reached lights from a town and pulled up at a sheriff's station. There were mountains behind the town, high peaks, and he knew that only because the grip of night began to slacken, and the faintest light hit the peaks.

There was some conferring outside the car, and Gable sat and waited, and then a car pulled out in front and led Hawes up a dirt road, a frozen dirt road, in the dark. On they went, the two-car caravan, and the road grew rougher. Gable drew breath in and out, and far off he could hear murmured words, muffled voices, men not wanting to displease the king because he might lop off their heads, but the car was moving, which was the important thing, and Gable had to figure that every foot of ground they covered was getting him closer to Ma. The car progressed behind the sheriff's car ever slower up this bad road that kept getting worse until the jarring and banging of the car on the road brought some focus, with the car retching violently and his big, hard head hitting the ceiling again and again. It was as if he was being slapped, as if someone was smacking that face distorted with rage and fear back into the features of Clark Gable until he was once again inside himself and could breathe. Things started to make sense and he, Clark Gable, would have to feel his way through and determine how he should act and what he should do next. The terror lay in the fact that his wife had taken on the role of handler, and when his wife wasn't around Wink was the handler, but now she wasn't here and neither was Wink; they were out *there* someplace, in the dusky gray of morning, and he needed her back at his side so she could help him figure out what to do, and when to do it.

The veil of night lifted during that torturous car ride to reveal the desert of Nevada, the rugged terrain, the brown earth, the cactus, the Joshua trees, and off to his left, a mountain. A very tall mountain. Very tall. The tallest of all that were in sight, and nearly straight up, practically a wall right beside the car, rising—how high he didn't know—two thousand feet? Three thousand?

Ernie Hawes' car rolled to a stop with a high-pitched squeal of brakes, and after all that pounding, the vehicle had aged since they had climbed inside an hour or more earlier.

The sun was up now and it was cold, dry cold, and their breath was visible in clouds of vapor. Gable stood beside the bad dirt road with a few parked vehicles and men about, rough customers in cowboy hats, some Indians, and some older prospector types, and sheriff cars and police cars, men conferring, campfires, maps, activity. Horses, maybe a dozen of them, stood snorting and protesting, and it took him back to the ranch and riding with Ma over their twenty acres as they would gaze off at the San Gabriel Mountains.

Through the course of the night, it had seemed at times that nobody cared about the plane and its passengers, that everyone was just killing time, but here he beheld a tremendous caring, a tremendous dedication and love. Maybe there was room to hope after all.

The policemen kept talking to him, explaining, their voices calm, respectful. They were *handling* him, but that was OK because he was used to being handled and liked it because it meant he had less to do himself and less to think about and fewer decisions to make. The plane was above them, they told him, above the cliffs directly ahead. They pointed high, past a prominent rocky outcropping almost directly up that caught the morning sun and gave a glow that looked like angels but was really the sunrise light hitting cactus that grew out of the ledge. It was beautiful in the light, and maybe it was a sign that Ma was up there alive. Waiting.

Just past that ledge, they told him, they figured the plane was resting. It was such a tranquil word. The plane was *resting*.

Minute by minute his moods swung. He wanted to get up there; he had to climb, but they told him to be patient and to wait. Time passed, with the cold so many needles penetrating skin. Finally, he told anybody within range that he couldn't stand it anymore, and he heard Eddie Mannix's voice in his ear saying to calm down, to let the professionals do their job. He always had paid heed to Eddie; Mannix was a dangerous man, he knew. He heard Strickling in the other ear in that rat-tat-tat way of his, stuttering through it. It'll be all right, Clark. You belong to MGM, and you can't go climbing mountains when you aren't dressed for it and you don't have a horse to ride. Look at all these men. This is their job, not yours.

But to Gable, nobody moved fast enough. Everything was happening so slowly, as if in a bad dream, and he needed things to move faster. Goddamn it, he was going to climb up there, and he was going to find his wife.

That's exactly what he did. Clark Gable broke free of the men who would have held him back, and he started up the well-worn trail that everyone else was following, that everyone nodded toward. He hiked up, up, ever up a long rise. There were times the trail took him into a dry wash and he climbed boulders, and pulled himself up by dead tree limbs, but his progress was generally up toward Ma. Dead limbs speared him and he slipped on the rocks, but all of a sudden he had crossed the snow line and climbed on. After the time waiting in his car in the parking lot in Burbank and the time waiting on the plane and the time waiting at the El Rancho, now he was doing something with his body, his flesh and his bones, and it was wonderful. It was incredible. It was a feeling to tell Ma about when he found her. Wouldn't she be proud of her husband? He cared enough to climb a mountain.

Overhead, he heard an airplane, flying low in the sky, a steady hum of a sound overhead. All of a sudden the altitude hit him, and the smoking, and the lack of a meal. Gable was gassed. He stood in a chasm with rocks ahead, and rocks to the left, and rocks to the right, and giant cliffs looming above. He panted. His eyes watered. He ached from the climbing that he only now realized he had done. He looked around and was in the middle of nowhere. He leaned against a rock to catch his breath, waiting for his head to clear. Slowly his senses returned. Mannix, Wheelright, and the cops caught up with him. The two MGM men gasped for air, doubled up, dressed in blazers and fedoras, dress pants and dress shoes way up in the wilds of Nevada.

The sun was higher in the sky. It was late morning somehow, but nothing made any sense and hadn't for hours and hours. The policemen stood by, but nobody interfered with Gable because maybe they were putting themselves in his place and thinking, what if it were my wife up there? No force in the world could hold me back.

As they collected themselves, there was activity ahead. Men were struggling down the mountain, civilians, descending through the snow, slipping and sliding and stumbling down the sheer slope. The police officers rushed forward, half to meet them and half to catch them before they shot on past. They weren't far off, sixty feet maybe, but they were out of earshot, exchanging words, vapor trails of information and effort in the air. The men kept talking. The three from MGM really felt the cold now because if they stopped for even a minute, the air knifed inside any exposed spot in outer clothing and ignited the sweat clinging to flesh underneath.

With those cliffs rising high behind them, the police officers approached the civilians. The cops didn't look like handlers anymore. They were not smiling. Their faces were tight and their lips were pinched.

A policeman matching Gable's height stopped before him. "Look, the plane has been found, Mr. Gable. There are men up there now guarding it, and there are parties on the way."

If only the cop would stop speaking. If only the Hollywood men could be allowed to hold on to some hope a little longer, and in their minds she could be alive a little longer. After all, they lived in a world of make believe. Please, just let her be alive a little while longer. But they knew what was coming next and, oh, just not to have to hear it. Police officers moved in around Gable, a physical presence to hold him up if needed. Just in case. Everyone was still so respectful, every minute. Respectful and so poised it was enviable.

"I'm sorry. I'm very sorry. There are no survivors."

31

The Entire Gang Showed Up

Mary Johnson, the human computer who had been bumped in Albuquerque, caught the next flight out to Burbank with her three companions five hours after Flight 3 took off without them. Mary again sat beside Genevieve Brandner. On the way into Burbank, Genevieve listened to the radio with an earphone and heard about the missing plane carrying Carole Lombard as Mary slept beside her. Genevieve rushed back to tell the hostess on her flight, who ordered silence about the news until the plane had landed so as not to create a panic. Sitting there as the ship made its final approach, Genevieve had time to think about the fact that on her birthday, she had been spared the fate of those poor people.

At touchdown Genevieve roused Mary Johnson and told her that Flight 3 may have crashed. After they got off the plane, Mary remembered, "The two of us and the other two who had been bumped [Joseph Szigeti and Florence Sawyer] just kind of huddled together in the airport, in complete shock."

Asked when he had learned about the crash of Flight 3, Robert Stack said, "I was walking out of the Hollywood Palladium. I was with my date, and we had been dancing. I heard a newspaper crier on the street corner. It was the *Los Angeles Times*, and he was calling out, 'Carole Lombard in Plane Crash!'" Stack's eyes filled with tears remembering it. "I saw it in a newspaper headline," he said, "and I couldn't believe it."

All Hollywood learned that way, as the stars and the technical people of the studios spilled out of the Trocadero, Ciro's, Club Mocambo, Grauman's Chinese, the El Capitan, and all the other nightspots in town. With a war on, with so many men about to go away to fight, the partying now had purpose. More than ever before, people sought getaways.

In all cases the story was the same. Bundles of newspapers hitting the street. "Jack and I had had dinner with some friends at Chasen's," said Mary Benny, "and had sat talking until the wee hours of the morning. When we got outside to wait for our car, the man who put the papers in the small news rack in front of Chasen's was just delivering the Saturday edition." There screamed that headline and, said Mary, "I thought Jack was going to drop right there on the sidewalk."

Said Margaret Tallichet Wyler, "I just couldn't believe all that vitality was gone. All that vitality, and beauty. It was just terrible."

"I went to my room like a sleepwalker," said Alice Marble, "and slumped in a chair, dry-eyed, staring into space. This couldn't happen. Losing Carole was like losing a sister. We had such a wonderful kinship, an intuitive understanding of each other. I loved being with her because she was caring and fun and had become my closest confidante."

Famous (some would call him infamous) Hollywood columnist Jimmy Fidler said, "It came suddenly, flashingly, as the woman herself had always come and gone in life: Carole Lombard killed in air crash. It came so abruptly that not until hours later did its full impact strike Hollywood. For at first, you see, the movie colony did not believe the news flash. 'Carole Lombard dead?' people echoed. 'Impossible! She's too alive!'"

Despite the evidence, the film people clung to hope, because nobody *could* believe it. Carole Lombard couldn't be dead, not this girl so full of gags, full of mischief, screeches, and squeals. Not the party girl. Not the girl so intent on paying her taxes, the girl who took over public relations at the Selznick Studios one day under a sign that read, DANGER: LOMBARD NOW AT WORK.

Within six hours the story had crossed the wires to every corner of the nation and beyond. Newspapers screamed the headline in three-inch letters. Radio brought every available detail of the location, the passengers, and the search, and despite all the facts, for Clark Gable and the Galahads who had climbed to rescue her while clinging to boyish hope, there never had been hope, not from the moment that Arthur Cheney had piloted his Western Air Express DC-3 over the crash scene and reported the blaze and the terrain.

So now Gable knew. Mannix, Strickling, and Wheelright led him back down the mountain, and all of a sudden he had gone from the strapping and broad-shouldered hero of the movies, from Rhett Butler, to frail and disoriented. He had gone from not knowing to knowing. It took a while to lead him back to the cars, and they made the long drive down to Goodsprings and back to the El Rancho Vegas.

They got Gable back in his room, and nobody wanted to leave him alone; they took turns staying with him. He was mostly quiet but would murmur things, now and again, like a reflex, softly, to break the quiet.

"Ma's gone." And, "Who would have thought?" And, "Do you think she suffered?" And, "Why her?"

He asked for liquor and they brought it to him. He drank. He ate nothing, but he set about consuming as much of the liquor in stock at the El Rancho as humanly possible, and he smoked, and he looked out his window at the ragged, snow-covered peak of Potosi Mountain plainly visible to the southwest. She was up there with Otto and Petey. How could this have happened?

He heard that Jill had become hysterical when given the news. He heard that the entire Gable-Lombard hunting gang showed up at the El Rancho. Freddy and wife Virginia had driven up. Fritzy, Ma called him. Suddenly, the motor hotel in the middle of nowhere crawled with people who loved Clark and Carole, and he would see none of them. He stayed in his room and grieved.

Jack Benny had been up all night and entreated his brother-in-law, nicknamed Hickey, to drive him to Vegas. They set out with Jack in a stupor, mumbling about Lombard. They drove eighty-five miles to San Bernardino and in frustration Hickey said, "Look, Jack, there's absolutely nothing you can do. Even Clark is just waiting. We might be in the way!"

Jack thought it over. "OK, Hickey," he said. "Let's turn back."

Spencer Tracy had also gotten wind of the situation, packed a bag, the most important cargo being three bottles of Chivas Regal, Gable's favorite. Tracy hopped in his car and didn't turn back. He drove six hours through the Mojave Desert to be near the friend he called "Big Moose," knowing there was nothing he could do but offer moral support and maybe share some drinks.

By now Maj. Herbert Anderson, second in command at Mc-Carran Field, had received several official requests for assistance in the form of Army trucks and personnel to secure the crash site and begin to recover bodies. He conferred with the sheriff and then detailed twenty-one men under the command of Lt. William B. Hunt with four trucks to proceed up Ninety-Nine Mine Road at 5:30 A.M. Sunday. The men would climb to the site, relieve the two county guards up there now, and lead the recovery effort of the crash victims who had been aboard Flight 3.

32

Groaning Pines

Thomas J. Devlin worked for the *Los Angeles Examiner*, and Tommy was on a mission. Devlin had heard about the crash and driven up to Vegas not because of Carole Lombard. Yes, he knew Lombard and felt bad for her and her mother, but Devlin sought his pal from the city beat, Otto Winkler. Devlin had followed the progress of the bond tour in the papers and planned to meet up with Wink afterward and maybe write a story about the former newsman and the movie star pitching war bonds and stamps.

Devlin had gone up the mountain on horseback with a posse of cowboys, including the old Piute Indian, Jim "Tweed" Wilson. They rode over one mountain, down into a valley, and up a second sharp rise to where they could see smoke from the fire built by Moore and Bondley. Devlin said that the group "went as far as the horses could go. Then we tethered the horses, and started up on foot, and about several hundred yards up, why, some of the party started dropping out, and then perhaps a thousand yards farther up to really rough going, why, the rest of them built a campfire and dropped out."

Devlin and Dan Campbell from Goodsprings pressed on because Devlin believed that if the situations were reversed, and Winkler was down *here* and Devlin up *there*, Otto would have done the same thing.

Devlin and Campbell climbed until they reached a vertical wall and clawed their way up that, at which point the terrain finally relented, and they found a long, gentle snow-covered slope leading straight to wood smoke and finally to a roaring campfire. Devlin said of Jack Moore and George Bondley, "I believe only one of them had a coat, and they had two sandwiches, and two tangerines, and a small piece of cheese for food. It was getting dark around that time. They had no blankets.... I identified myself to them, and told them I would like to take a look at the crash, and I assured them I would touch nothing, and perhaps 150 or 200 yards to the left of their fire, I came upon the crash."

Tom Devlin stood there and the enormity of the moment hit him. He had covered the crime beat for years, so he had seen some awful things. He had stared down at shotgunned bodies, at strangulation victims, at gun-to-the-mouth suicides. He had slipped and fallen in pools of blood at car crashes; he had smelled the rot of dead vagrants under bridges. He had seen it all. Now he saw this.

He couldn't believe the utter violence reflected in twisted airplane spread all over. Some of the scrub cedars in front of him still burned; they rocked and popped in the wind and their odor was pungent. From where he stood on an elevation with the wreck below in a sort of a bowl, he could look across and see suitcases and a pile of something on the ledge at the top of the oil-smeared cliff, seventy-five or a hundred feet above all the other debris, as if the plane had hit with such force that stuff was vaulted *up*. He could see bodies on a lower cliff, and down in the snow. He thought he could see some more inside what appeared to be the mangled fuselage, but he couldn't be sure. He didn't want to be sure. He knew Otto was in there somewhere, and he didn't care to remember his friend this way.

"What're ya doin' here, Wink?" said Devlin aloud, to no one. The snow deadened his voice, and it sounded so strange in his own ears. "This is no place for you, my friend." The wind kicked up and blew acrid smoke his way. It smelled of oil, and of flesh.

He stared into the blackened carnage. "I wish we could vamoose, go down the hill, and get a drink." He paused. "I'm buyin'." The wind blew again and the pines creaked and groaned high above. Devlin thought of a hundred happy moments with Otto Winkler, and knew this was too good a guy for the world to lose. Tears flowed down Tommy's face. He swiped at them with his gloved hands and by the time he turned back toward the guards, he was stone-faced again. Reporters had to be that way.

Tom Devlin walked away from the wreckage, wading through his own tracks in deep snow.

He found his companion, Dan Campbell, waiting with the guard. Dan had given Devlin time alone with the man he had come to find. Devlin and Campbell savored the warmth of the big fire for a few moments, but it was at least three o'clock now and the sun was sinking, and if they wanted to get off the mountain they would have to head back right this minute. Devlin looked at Moore and Bondley, two very tough men to take on this duty, with one jacket between them, little food, and a long night ahead. He thanked them for their kindness in letting him walk over. He said that he knew a guy on the plane, and they said they were sorry. Tommy offered them the coat off his back in exchange for some moments with Wink and they declined.

Then he and Campbell headed back down, leaving Jack Moore and George Bondley to their vigil, all alone in two feet of snow, eating their meager rations by calculation, eating snow for water, and endlessly feeding their fire to keep from freezing. They had no fear of looters or villains of any sort, not up here, not making that climb. Nor were there wolves or coyotes or bears and, in fact, they saw evidence of no creatures up here at all, not even jackrabbits. It was a sad place to be, and when the wind blew, the pines would groan and crack as if to lament the recent tragedy and the poor humans ground to pieces in that airplane. The heat from the fire would lure the men to doze. Then their discomfort would snap them back to consciousness, and their empty stomachs would protest. They'd scoop up some more snow to eat and doze again and repeat the process through an endless night. The fire remained a demanding companion, a greedy consumer of timber that kept them in motion for more wood, more wood.

It was strange that just across the way there were twenty-two people at their final rest, including the famous movie star, Carole Lombard. Jack and George had wandered over now and again at various times while it was still light, after Devlin and Campbell had shuffled off, and viewed the wreck, viewed the carnage, everything frozen up now so that the smoldering odor of seared flesh, what they had smelled when they reached the site hours earlier, had gone. They gazed up at the belongings hanging from the branches of the trees. The sight brought sadness to them to the point that they had to retreat again. Such a way to end your life, way up here in this godforsaken place.

The long solitary hours made them wonder if they might perish up here with the others, forgotten by the people down in Las Vegas, where there was civilization. They had been hoping that TWA or the Army would learn of them from Van Gordon and the others and drop supplies. The sound of every plane in the distance renewed hope, but no supplies came. They could see the lights of the city far off, and they imagined their homes, their warm beds, their warm wives, and the meals they should have eaten but hadn't.

But Moore and Bondley had not been forgotten. A powerful force formed down at McCarran Field as feds and TWA men converged on Vegas: The Civil Aeronautics Board had scrambled men from Kansas City, Atlanta, and Los Angeles; men like Warren Carey. A postal inspector headed north from L.A. and another southeast from San Francisco; the FBI sent men. A contingent from TWA flew up from Burbank.

At dawn on Sunday, January 18, this army of men set into motion, and the trail blazed by Lyle Van Gordon and Jack Moore suddenly became well-traveled. Corduroy was laid to strengthen the mining road. A bulldozer cut a new road up the long rise by the course that Gable had taken the day before. A series of ropes were tied off along the line of ascent to help the soldiers and investigators hoist themselves up, and marks were put in the trees to guide the way.

A posse of sixty men set off along the ridges of Potosi, a much longer route but less treacherous. All headed up to the scene to try to make sense of something horrific and so seemingly random. The feds and airline officials and reporters in the massive group had one overriding question they all wanted an answer to: Why?

33

Unfixable

Edgar J. Mannix, age forty-nine, had done the bidding of Louis B. Mayer as an MGM vice president for years to the extent that he had acquired a nickname, "The Fixer." Mannix had the look of an aging prizefighter about him, or as Ava Gardner described later, "He had a face like a raw potato in shades, that's how I still remember him." Mannix's body was thick and New Jersey tough; he was a one-time bouncer at Palisades Park who had drifted into the movie business and served Mayer and MGM as equal parts henchman and business associate. The man at MGM he most resembled was Bert Lahr, the Cowardly Lion. But there was nothing cowardly about Eddie Mannix.

Gable liked Eddie as a drinking buddy who could really put away the booze. Mannix had stepped in and helped to fix a lot of bad situations for Metro over the years, none worse than the pistol-to-the-head shooting of Paul Bern not long after Bern had married Jean Harlow. According to prominent researchers it was murder, covered up by Mannix and Howard Strickling to protect MGM's property, the girl affectionately known around the lot as The Baby. Then had come the shocking death of Harlow herself with its medical malpractice and the slow poisoning of the Baby's delicate body.

Not that Eddie merely protected MGM in cold-blooded fashion. "If Mannix felt that a loyal employee had signed a contract that paid him less than he was worth," said Louis B. Mayer biographer Scott Eyman, "Mannix would tell them to pick up an extra $100 for expenses from the cashier's office each week. Nothing was ever put on paper about such arrangements; they were just Mannix's way of doing business."

Now, ensconced at the El Rancho Vegas with Gable, Mannix found himself amidst a mess that he didn't quite know how to figure. The new Gable-Turner picture, *Somewhere I'll Find You*, had two days of film in the can, and there was no question it would go dark. God only knew when Gable could pull himself together and return to work at Culver City.

Of more immediate concern was the fact that Gable's wife, not even a Metro employee, mind, still lay inside the smoldering wreck of a plane on a mountaintop nobody could get to. The cops kept talking about a plan, but from where Mannix stood at the El Rancho, nobody actually had a plan, and the whole time Gable was drinking himself stupid until finally, mercifully, later on Saturday he had passed out.

Early Sunday morning Gable regained consciousness, looking almost dead himself, and finally agreed to eat something. Then Clark heard that investigators were organizing to hike up the mountain, and he growled that he was going along to get Mrs. G. That's what he called her this morning, Mrs. G. He would find her for himself, and he was already saying he wasn't leaving town without her. In fact, he wasn't leaving town without all three of them, Ma, Wink, and Petey. He was a funny kind of haywire this morning, pasty skinned, unshaven, his eyes swollen and bulging in their sockets. He had a tremor, the kind that comes with a high fever, and it took two hands for the king to get a cup of coffee to his mouth. That scene in *Gone With the Wind*, the one where an unshaven Gable had cried in front of Olivia de Havilland, that was *nothing* compared to Gable this morning. No, he wasn't one for tears, but he was quiet, hung over, and strung tight. Strickling had been correct that the best thing was to give Gable some distance, but not leave him alone.

Howard Strickling knew the score about Clark Gable: "The most wonderful and the most beautiful and the greatest thing—the only real happiness he ever had in his life—was gone. 'Cause they had planned for years. They had plans on how she was going to do this and how he was going to do [that] and... they had it all planned out."

At best Gable was now adrift and the question of the moment was, would Clark even survive this?

Now, the MGM men had to head off this new disaster because what if Gable went up there and fell off the goddamn mountain, and there would go the studio's biggest star and most important financial asset. Simply put, Clark Gable was worth millions to Metro Goldwyn Mayer. Over the course of his career to come, twenty million at least and probably more.

Mannix, Strickling, and Wheelright were all in Gable's room trying to reason with Clark that there was nothing he could do now that it had been determined there had been no survivors, so what would be the point of even trying that inhuman climb? In fact, why would he want to see his wife in the condition they would undoubtedly find her in? Why not remember her as the beautiful girl she had been in life? No. Gable wouldn't cooperate. No, he needed to be up there and he needed to see to her recovery and—

"I'll go," said Mannix. Two simple words that headed Clark Gable off at the pass.

"Eddie and I will both go," said Wheelright without even a decent beat that the script called for.

Mannix had to wonder if either of them could really climb up there; he had heard nothing for the past thirty-six hours other than how brutal and unforgiving that mountain was. He wasn't a kid anymore and his waist had been growing and parts were sagging that hadn't sagged before, but he wasn't The Fixer for nothing, and this is what he did at MGM and what he would do now.

He and Wheelright didn't even shop for appropriate clothes better suited for the outdoors; they just set out for Goodsprings and the base camp where they found a steady stream of men heading up toward the cliffs; dozens of men dressed warmly and carrying as much in the way of provisions as they could lug on their backs. The place crawled with feds, Civil Aeronautics investigators, postal inspectors, FBI guys, and Army personnel, not to mention TWA men, reporters, photographers, miners, cowboys, and of course, the coroner.

It was an experience the MGM Fixer would never forget, and he spent it clawing at the earth, coughing up his lungs, gasping for air, climbing ropes, clinging to trees, and toppling over against rocks. His leather gloves did nothing in that cold, and he lost the feeling in his fingertips. It was four hours straight up and by the time he had ascended above the last of the cliffs, his clothes were torn to what seemed like ribbons.

Then all that he had just experienced seemed like nothing, because he had reached the crash site and even a Jersey kid who had seen his share of stiffs could not be prepared for what met his watering eyes now, at just about noon on Sunday, January 18.

34

I Still See It in My Dreams

Just ahead of ten in the morning, Jack Moore and George Bondley, the two lonely, hungry, freezing guards of Flight 3, had finally been relieved. Army men arrived first and gave Moore and Bondley biscuits and Spam to eat, and they accepted it willingly before stumbling back down the way they had come for the sleep of their lives. On the way they dodged men of all shapes and sizes, men with the luxury of ropes and ladders, and saw in the faces of the newcomers the same physical punishment, the same shock, that they had experienced on the previous day's climb.

Army personnel with loaded rifles now took position around the crash site, at the top of the cliffs above, on either side of the wreck, and in the ravine below. Inside their newly created perimeter, the various functionaries went to work. The CAB men got their first look at the shattered plane and the cliff. There was no telling why this catastrophe had occurred until they understood how it had occurred. What was the attitude of Flight 3 as it struck the cliff? Was the ship in level flight? Were its engines working? What was its airspeed?

The TWA men had questions of their own. A definite flight path existed for the run from Las Vegas to Burbank. Fly south past Goodsprings and then bank south-southwest so that the highest terrain encountered would be 5,800 feet. And at a cruising altitude of 9,000, there was never a problem. But for reasons no one could understand, Flight 3 had taken off and flown due southwest, directly into the highest peak between Vegas and Los Angeles. From McCarran Field, the mountain was clearly visible thirty-three miles distant; from the mountain, McCarran Field and Vegas were clearly visible thirty-three miles distant. So what the hell had been the problem? It became imperative to locate the flight plan of the pilot and copilot, which would have been kept in the cockpit and might explain how Captain Williams had been so far off course. TWA also wanted to locate the engines and propellers so they could tell their story about the operation of the drive systems at the point of impact. If the motors worked at impact and if it had been Williams alone making a mistake, liability would be entirely on the company, and that would displease Mr. Howard Hughes. But if an engine were nonfunctional or a propeller had failed, then there would be blame to go around.

The postal inspectors stepped carefully around bodies and body parts to recover U.S. mail that had been carried on the plane, and there had been sacks and sacks of it. Some had been consumed by the fire, but some of it had been placed in the rear baggage compartment, and this clump had been thrown clear. The collection of this mail would begin after the entire area had been photographed and crash debris located and marked.

The FBI representatives had the most sobering questions to ask. They were physically visible to the press that day and yet their work was *in*visible; while newspapers reported the names of all the other feds involved, the FBI men weren't discussed at all because their big question could impact national security: Was Flight 3 sabotaged? This was wartime and the nation had already been struck a cruel blow at Pearl Harbor, and the activities of fifth columnists were known in some cases and unknown in others. The plane had been serviced in Albuquerque, only a few hours' drive from the Mexican border, and the Nazis were quite active in Mexico, just beyond U.S. reach. FBI men had already set to work checking the identities of other passengers who had left the plane on previous stops and might have planted a bomb. They studied one man in particular, violinist Joseph Szigeti, a man with a heavy European accent who seemed all too willing to surrender his seat to airmen in Albuquerque.

The FBI also wanted to know how secure the plane had been upon refueling in Las Vegas. It remained on the ground for thirty-one minutes, leaving plenty of time for disruption to occur. Was it mere coincidence that this plane had gone down carrying fifteen vital U.S. Army Air Corps personnel and a Hollywood star on official government business for the war effort? Mr. J. Edgar Hoover and the Federal Bureau of Investigation very much wanted to know the answers to these questions.

But the crash scene presented a worst-case scenario. The growing contingent stared at the steep ravine carpeted in wreckage, pieces as long as fifteen-foot wing sections and twenty feet of empennage, and as small as a dime, smaller, after the catastrophic explosion of the plane against the cliffs. John Collings, TWA superintendent of operations out of Kansas City, stared in awe at the twisted, blasted, mangled remnants of aluminum and steel and the bodies and pieces of bodies spread out before him. "This is the most completely obliterated crashed plane I have ever seen," he murmured.

On Saturday the bodies had not been touched once Moore had determined that all were dead. But right away on Sunday morning Clark County Deputy Coroner D. G. Lawrence faced a horrifying reality with the first bodies he reached: Against all reason, there might have been survivors of the crash of Flight 3, if only help could have gotten there in the first hour—those three fliers who had been thrown clear into deep snow after the plane had broken in two amidships. It was conceivable that they had been concussed on impact, and one or two may have kept breathing before boiling from the heat of the fire, expiring from their injuries, or freezing as night clamped down upon the scene.

Lt. William Hunt of the Army Air Corps began the collection of bodies, leading his detail from McCarran Field. Already, Eddic Mannix had visited Major Anderson at McCarran to urge in the strongest possible terms that the first bodies removed from the scene must be Carole Lombard and her mother, Elizabeth Peters. Eddie Mannix was a jovial enough man on the surface, but something sinister lurked just beneath the surface. Not even a major in the United States Army was going to say no. It would not have mattered in any event, because MGM corporate out of Culver City had already been heating up the phone lines with Washington to ensure that the remains of Mrs. Gable and Mrs. Peters were given all due respect. Studio bosses were, after all, practical men, and they needed their asset Clark Gable back within the arms of the studio family, and his terms for leaving were clear: Ma, Petey, and Otto must be with him when he departed.

One of the civilian volunteers that day working on body recovery under Lieutenant Hunt's direction was Harry Pursel, a wholesaler from Las Vegas. "When we first arrived, there were several bodies lying clear of the wreckage," he said of the Army personnel, some of which had no obvious signs of injury, "and which we picked up." The first of these bodies lay in deep snow—those that the coroner thought might have survived the crash. Then up on the cliffs a bit, the team found two more Army men splattered onto rock. These men were wrapped in brown army blankets and laid aside, and the search for one particular body, that of Carole Lombard, was on.

The recovery team climbed up the steep slope and crossed the fire line from snow to charred earth, the result of the three-hour gasoline and oil fire of tremendous ferocity that had been seen for miles. Inside the fire line were five more charred bodies, more or less intact, and it seemed as if they too had spilled out when the plane cracked in two. As grisly as the idea would have seemed even a day earlier, Lieutenant Hunt fell to all fours and examined each body, and it appeared from their military-style buttons, attire, and general body features that all five were Army Ferrying Command personnel. But it was getting harder to make a determination.

Harry Pursel helped to characterize the nature of the crash when asked later if seat belts were still fastened around the passengers. He responded, "You couldn't *find* any belts."

Warren Carey, chief investigator for Civil Aeronautics Board Region Six, had finally made his way from Amarillo to Fort Worth to Los Angeles, then had gotten home, showered, dressed, and climbed in his car for a six-hour drive through the desert to reach the base of the mountain. Then he had climbed to this spot: the ledge above the wreckage. There he sketched the large and small pieces of the plane and the contours of the land, marking with an X the bodies as they were recovered. The feds were doing all they could to preserve the evidence for later determination of what the hell had happened up here thirty-six hours earlier.

Mannix had struggled onto a scene unlike anything from motion pictures. Wheelright had fallen out of line and Eddie was alone now, barely holding himself upright by hugging pine trees and gasping for a decent breath in the thin air of 7,800 feet above sea level as he watched the military personnel, federal agents, and civilians crawl over the junkyard of a scene like ants swarming an anthill. He saw the Army guys wrapping some bodies in brown blankets and Mannix had to scramble over and ask Lieutenant Hunt, had they found Carole Lombard? No, came the answer.

It was ominously quiet except for the constant clinking of metal. Shattered aluminum met every footfall, tumbling against rocks and more aluminum in a constant, maddening tinkle, like nightmarish wind chimes. It was the only sound most of the time, as the men were too tense, too focused to utter a word, working as they were in a human butcher shop. Each knew he must do the one thing he didn't want to do: Search every dark place, every crevice, every shadow and examine each victim to locate the once-beautiful, once-vibrant, and once-very-much-alive Carole Lombard.

The search team struggled up the forty-five-degree-angled mountainside of loose shale, limestone, and twisted metal and approached the cliffs where the plane had impacted. They knew the exact spot because the smashed nose of the plane stuck out from the rock. To the left of them in a twisted mass of aluminum lay the fuselage and only parts of bodies could be seen there, ground to bits large and small, and the search team didn't want to think about the task of dealing with *that*. Instead they stared at sections of the right wing leaning against the base of the cliff. They headed toward the wreckage to attempt to move it but were stopped. The Civil Aeronautics men wanted more photos, so the searchers stood down while a series of stills were taken of the scene.

Finally, the search detail reached the center section of the right wing. Painted in red on the silver aluminum of the ten-foot wing section laying against the cliff wall were the giant letters NC 1946.

Among the reporters on the scene was twenty-six-year-old Gene Sherman of the *Los Angeles Times*. Sherman had a way with words that he would use to cover the war in the Pacific on the front lines in 1944 and 1945 with his column "Pacific Echoes," and he would earn a Pulitzer Prize a generation later for his coverage of drug trafficking between Mexico and southern California. Sherman painted a chilling picture of the mountaintop that Sunday morning: "The totally demolished, luxurious Douglas DC-3 'Sky-Club' presented a grim, sorrowful picture on its rocky resting place. Wreckage was scattered in a radius of 500 yards and some of the victims were strewn around the waist-high snow. Bits of the plane, personal effects of the passengers, including handkerchiefs, overcoats and other apparel, were strung from the branches of stunted pine trees like macabre Christmas ornaments."

Associated Press photographer Ira Guldner said, "The big ship was shattered to pieces against this big rock cliff. Some of it still clung in a crevice. Bodies of the victims and oil made dark splotches on the white snow. Some of what we saw is too gruesome to talk about."

"As fast as we located the bodies," said Pursel, "we would take them and wrap them in the blankets and prepare to take them out."

Gruesome work indeed. A cowboy named Tommy Young, one of the civilian volunteers, described the task facing the Army detail and the civilians that January Sunday: "There was just parts of bodies everywhere you looked, everywhere. At first we tried getting bits that went together, but reached a point where we was just grabbing pieces and stuffing them into bags." Army blankets weren't effective for pieces of bodies. The most convenient receptacles available were mail bags hauled up the mountain by the postal inspectors to secure mail that had survived. Of the collected remains, said Young decades later, "Some went down the mountain with two left legs in the same sack. I've never seen nothin' like that before or since. I still see it in my dreams sometimes."

They climbed the steep slope, so steep the men fell and stood upright and went down again, landing on wreckage, bodies, and parts of bodies. The higher they climbed, ever closer to the point of collision, the bodies grew more indistinct, smaller pieces or burned torsos or bodies crushed by impact. Ahead of them now rose the jagged cliff, burned black in places from the fire, and splattered in other places with oil.

Against the cliff lay parts of wing. Prior to moving the wing the men found five victims who had been hurled forward by the force of impact and gone straight into the cliff at nearly 200 miles per hour and then dropped to the base. So many sacks of potatoes.

Pursel and Pat Clark, owner of the El Rio Garage in Las Vegas, worked with the Army detail to lever aside a section of wing to see what lay underneath. There they found three bodies. One of these appeared to be male, and two seemed to be female. A general commotion ensued, not something uttered in a shout but none-theless communicated on some inaudible frequency among the assembled men on the mountainside, like the vibrations that ac-company an earthquake. Men drifted or skittered across the steep surface and stumbled or slid or fell to congregate in a single spot, looking down at two burned bodies on the rocky earth. "Some of the bodies seemed to have almost been cremated," said a reporter. One of the two they beheld near the wing had been burned beyond all recognition but had a smallish appearance that they guessed to be female. The other that lay beside her had also been subject to the funeral pyre, but there was something about it, something dis-tinctive and familiar and oh, so repulsive, for the grievous damage done. Scorched by the fire, multiple fractures to every bone of her body, including the skull.

"I don't think she was over five feet from the wall of the moun-tain," said Pat Clark. "She was buried in the snow."

The body was carefully turned over. Underneath her Pat Clark found a half-charred envelope and retrieved it. He held in his hand crumbling bits of paper that fell apart by the second. It was, said Gene Sherman, standing alongside Clark, a belonging of Carole Lombard, "schedules of her personal appearances to promote the sale of Defense Bonds in her home state of Indiana, correspon-dence between her and her studio and data on a radio program to have been given on behalf of Latin-American countries." Pat Clark dropped the papers and fragments of papers into Hunt's gloved palms. He recognized their importance at once, looked up, and saw Eddie Mannix. Hunt motioned him over. They looked down on what was left of the poor souls found under the wing. A fire that had risen hundreds of feet had burned above them for three hours, and yet the aluminum wing and the snow had shielded the remains to some extent. The one body, Mannix could make nothing of. It was little more than blackened bones, but the other—

The left arm was missing and the head clung to the body by

just a thread of blackened tissue. Ralph Wheelright would identify the body later at the mortuary in Las Vegas and said he could imagine, despite multiple facial fractures, "the general contours of her face." Hints of that square jaw and high forehead remained, although seared into leathery relief. Eddie Mannix would make the identification of the mortal remains of Carole Lombard by "her hair. The top of her hair was still on her." And a patch of it remained blonde. PR man Howard Strickling—who spent Sunday keeping a weather eye on Gable and did not climb Potosi—would call it "a single wisp of blonde hair," but there was nothing quite so poetic to be found on the mountainside this day.

They all stood there, all the recovery men, in a circle in the oppressive silence and shivered in the cold. Somebody thought to ask for a silent prayer for all those on board the crashed airliner, and especially for a brave woman and patriot, Carole Lombard.

Mannix only now remembered: her wedding ring. Where was her wedding ring? Gable would want that, but the left arm was gone. He looked about him at utter chaos, utter destruction. There was no telling where the ring had ended up.

Impossibly, something red on the torso of Lombard's corpse caught Mannix's attention. It was a jewel. A ruby, part of the matching diamond-and-ruby clips that Lombard always wore attached to her clothing. Everybody who knew Lombard knew those clips; they had been part of her look since Gable had presented them to her and went with her to all social occasions. Mannix reached down and as best he could, as carefully, his fingertips numb, he retrieved the quarter-sized fragment and slipped it in his pocket.

Suddenly, the most important search was over. Carole Lombard had been found and confirmed dead, and the newspapermen in the group made a mad dash down the mountain to communicate the news as the Army detail and civilian volunteers went on with the task of gathering up bodies, a chore they would relive in nightmares for the remainder of their lives.

35

The Fatal Flaw

Fiction about the recovery effort at the crash site of Flight 3 endures today, all of it generated by Howard Strickling, proving his reputation as the top publicity man at MGM. Strickling would write that Mannix had stopped at a way station on the mountain to telegraph news to Gable of the identification of Lombard. Strickling then invented a touching scene in which MGM man Don McElwaine approached Gable in his room at the El Rancho. Strickling's version, run verbatim by the press, stated:

"Bad news?" said Gable to McElwaine.

"I'm afraid it looks hopeless," McElwaine replied.

"God," moaned Gable.

"What," asked McElwaine, "are you going to do?"

Gable shook himself, as if to shoulder away the shock, and replied that he would remain here until the bodies of his bride, her mother, and Otto Winkler, his press agent and close friend, were brought down.

Strickling also broadcast far and wide that Gable had been a rock for all of his pals who had journeyed to Vegas and congregated at the El Rancho, and even had befriended rescuers and offered to buy dentures for a toothless old prospector who had helped to search for the plane.

But Gable did not "shoulder away the shock" because Gable

was too occupied being in shock to function on Sunday, January 18. In his warm and quiet bungalow at the El Rancho Vegas, Eddie Mannix told Gable that he had seen and identified Carole's remains. Then he placed in Gable's hand the piece of jewelry he had recovered. Gable looked down at it, at only a battered fragment of one of the two clips, which spoke of the violence of his wife's death. It brought to mind once again the question he had been asking for almost two days: Had she suffered? Did she know?

Mannix had been where the plane had crashed and he had heard enough from the experts crawling over the scene to be able to meet Gable's gaze and tell him, "She never knew what happened."

The king nodded and eased over to the window to gaze at the peaks of Potosi Mountain far off to the southwest. Eddie and Ralph had been up there and seen everything and now Ma really was dead. The hunk of platinum and gemstones, heavy in his hand, proved it. He had been crazy to hold out hope anyway, but that's what a crazy mind will do, imagine your wife stumbling through the snow for help after the crash of her plane, but this wasn't *Lost Horizon* and people didn't walk away from scenes like that. People died in scenes like that. Ma had died, and now she was gone and she wasn't coming back. Ahead was just blackness. Imagining the barn and the fields without her, the house without her, the station wagon—life itself without her. She was just gone, and it seemed all of a sudden like forever that he had even seen her, heard her. It wasn't even nine days ago, that Friday morning when they had fought, screamed, slammed doors, hated, and been so goddamn sure of themselves that they hadn't even said good-bye. He knew he had hurt her, as she had hurt him. The two tough guys had mauled each other and retired bloody to their corners, as they so often did, just nine days ago. Now they would never have another chance to maul each other because Ma was gone for good. She had placed a curse on him by leaving this earth without saying good-bye, without properly making up, and there was nothing he would ever in this life be able to do about it. Oh, sure, they had exchanged telegrams, they had spoken on the phone, and he had sent flowers. But she was up on that mountain and dead because she had been too impatient to get back home and make up, or get back home and check up, and that was the end of it. Dead and gone.

It had never seemed that her impatience might be a fatal flaw. He had seen it many times, in many ways. She was a charge-ahead-and-take-that-hill kind of a girl who feared absolutely nothing, but a little fear now and again would have done her some good. She didn't seem to fear Lana because she would show up on the set and glare right through Lana and just be there, and the girl would go to pieces, but maybe Ma feared Lana after all because she felt compelled to be there on the soundstage in the first place and menace the poor kid.

He stared off at the snow-capped mountain, the one that had killed his wife. There it was, no mistaking it, standing there in the glare of late afternoon sunlight. Mannix and Wheelright were trying to warm themselves and were feeling every scrape and bruise from their trip. Before heading down from the crash scene, Mannix had spoken with Lieutenant Hunt, and it seemed clear that the two bodies discovered together were Carole and Mrs. Peters, and they were being brought down the mountain right this minute.

But thirty-three miles distant at the crash scene, all was not going well. There simply was no easy way to get the bodies out. With the mountain's inhuman angles and sheer drops, they couldn't be taken out the way the men had come up. A team of cowboys and prospectors had determined that the only course was to hoist the bodies up the cliff to the peak of the mountain ridge where horses and mules would haul the remains along a circuitous route that traversed dangerous precipices and eventually eased down the mountain and met with trucks four miles off.

Carole Lombard's body was placed delicately in a brown Army blanket, as was that of Elizabeth Peters. Both were bundled securely, and after hundred-foot ropes were dropped from the heights above, the blanketed bodies were lashed to these ropes and then hoisted by a team of men to the waiting horses and loaded on their backs. Carole Lombard had loved horses and ridden the range in Encino; now her last ride would be frozen and ponderous aboard careful animals led by men on foot, stepping gingerly at the edge of thousand-foot drops. The remains of seven Army Air Corps personnel, those least mangled in the crash, were lifted up the same way and also loaded on pack animals for the somber procession down the mountain. The rescuers found it to be tense, exhausting work that produced fear and frostbite as darkness closed in.

By the end of the day, with guards poised to spend the night at the scene, thirteen crash victims remained, although Lieutenant Hunt already knew that he wouldn't be able to produce thirteen bodies. To reach a final count of twenty-two, he was going to have to match twenty-two of something, whether it was heads or left feet or some other parts, because the simple fact was that he couldn't scrape together anything approaching twenty-two complete bodies after a crash like this.

36

The Complication

Jack Benny did not perform his scripted Sunday night program, the most listened-to radio show in the nation. Big-band music filled the slot. The news of Lombard's death had shattered the gentle comic—he and Carole were due to meet up at the sneak preview of *To Be or Not to Be*, which he knew during production would be "the best picture I ever made." The preview was to have been Monday evening at the Academy Theater in Inglewood. Now, it would never happen, and Benny shared the nightmare of Gable, Robert Stack, and so many others.

Benny could never talk about the death of Carole Lombard; it was too personal. The closest he could come was to speak of her in his memoir, of a New Year's Eve party at the Benny home given by Mary Livingston. Benny had fallen asleep during the festivities and awoke at nine o'clock the following morning. He said: "The party was still in progress, although only four revelers lingered on. They sat on the floor sipping champagne. They were telling stories and laughing their heads off. The four people were Honey and Don Ameche and Carole Lombard and Clark Gable. They had never left. Mary couldn't have been happier. It was the best New Year's Eve party I've ever been to. All six of us went into the dining room and had popovers and scrambled eggs and bacon and the most delicious coffee you ever drank.... It was a real good party."

That was long ago in a different world, a world without Joshua trees and cactus, parched earth and killer granite. At 9:00 on the evening of Sunday, January 18, Carole Lombard's burned and mangled body lay on a gurney next to another bearing the remains of Elizabeth Peters. Seven other bodies, including the Army boys who had been tossed into the snow, lay on the floor at the Garrison Mortuary at 515 Fremont Street in downtown Las Vegas. No photographers were present out of respect to the live king and his dead queen, although reporters milled around the front of the building and shared notes, smoked, drank coffee, and waited.

Within the city, Eddie Mannix and Howard Strickling exerted pressure on Clark County authorities to keep the process moving to get the bodies officially identified and released for a return to Los Angeles, while MGM corporate did the same from Culver City. To achieve this feat, an inquest must be conjured up for the two sets of remains. Strickling had tracked down the dentist who had worked on the teeth of both Carole and her mother and had their dental records flown directly to Las Vegas in anticipation of the identification process.

Forest Lawn Glendale was on alert for a funeral service to take place on Wednesday, and the thought was to inter Carole and Petey in the Great Mausoleum, a magnificent edifice with a stained glass mural of the Last Supper and an eighty-foot spire. The structure, half church and half fortress, nestled into a Glendale hillside, and here rested for eternity the remains of Marie Dressler, Russ Columbo, Irving Thalberg, and Jean Harlow. It was the "in" place for the Hollywood crowd to be laid to rest.

At ten Sunday night, Deputy Coroner Lawrence convened a hearing at the courthouse to officially identify Carole Lombard and establish a cause of death. Three citizens of Las Vegas sat in as jurors, and a stenographer took the oath and prepared to take statements. Present were Roger Foley, attorney for TWA, Eddie Mannix and Ralph Wheelright, Mahlon Brown, coroner of Las

Vegas Township, Major Anderson of the Air Forces, and Harry Pursel of the rescue party.

Mannix had been asked to go to Garrison's Mortuary with Wheelright and identify the body one more time. Ralph asked the attendant if he might cut a lock of Lombard's hair for Gable and the attendant supplied scissors. Wheelright placed the unburned snip of hair in an envelope, but then realized that the shock of it might put Gable over the edge. He didn't tell Gable what he had done; later he would place the envelope in the care of Jean Garceau.

At the inquest Mannix stated how he had made the initial identification on the mountain, principally from her blonde hair and the shape of her face. Harry Pursel was asked to explain the process used to retrieve the bodies from the crash site and to confirm that, yes, these two had been found under the wing of the doomed plane. Wheelright testified that Carole Lombard's personal papers had been found near the body. Then the coroner's staff confirmed that the dental charts of Carole Lombard of Encino, California, matched the teeth of the body in the next room. The panel decided on language stating that Carole Lombard had met her death "as a result of injuries sustained in a crash of a TWA liner en route from Las Vegas to Los Angeles."

Carole Lombard was agreed to be a native of Fort Wayne, Indiana, and, said the panel, "about thirty-two years of age." Somewhere, Lombard was smiling because she had managed to shave a year off, one of her inside jokes, as admitted to Garson Kanin.

Back at the El Rancho, Howard Strickling kept close tabs on Clark Gable during the stated time of the inquest. The king still refused to see the many friends who had traveled to Las Vegas. Only Spencer Tracy was allowed in, and the two of them sat quietly and drank. Tracy was the perfect companion on an occasion like this, a gruff man, a hard drinker, and a cynic who could curse the fates right along with his devastated friend and mean every word of it. But underneath the hard shell was the sensitive soul who could charm on the screen. Tracy was a friend or he would not have driven 350 miles through the desert to find Gable, and Clark needed a friend right now more than he could admit or even understand.

Over at Garrison's on Fremont Street, attention had turned to the formality of identifying Elizabeth Knight Peters, poor Petey, mother of Carole Lombard, and establishing a cause of death. Then both bodies could be released into the custody of Clark Gable and shipped back to Los Angeles by train the next morning, and Mannix and Strickling could be shed of this godforsaken desert town. No offense against Gable and his dead wife, but life had to go on and after a certain time Gable would return to work and sooner or later find himself a new wife and hopefully make several hit pictures. Of course, Mannix would never say this to Gable's face because Gable had big fists capable of breaking jaws, but to Mannix, business was business and this most definitely was business.

The entire process to declare Carole Lombard dead at the courthouse had taken about fifteen minutes, and now there was a lull and some murmured conversation. Most everyone was exhausted; almost all the people in the small room had made at least one trip up the mountain in the last thirty-six hours.

Deputy Coroner Lawrence eased up from his chair with a grimace, shuffled into the hallway on stiff legs, and there a man from Garrison's awaited. In a minute Lawrence came back into the inquest room. There had been a complication, he explained. The dental records didn't match—the body brought down the mountain with Miss Lombard was *not* that of her mother, Elizabeth Peters.

This was the last thing Mannix wanted to hear, and the epithets resounded through his brain. Another goddamn day in Las Vegas, Nevada, waiting for the yokels to scrape up more bodies and bring them down the mountain. Sure, he had liked Otto Winkler just fine, but Mannix would have had no problem boarding the train with Lombard and Peters and letting Otto trail along later. Poor Wink was long past giving a damn. Mannix could assign Wheelright or somebody to stay with Jill Winkler for the transport back to Santa Monica. Business, you know. Mannix always believed you played the hand you were dealt, so at around eleven o'clock he shrugged his burly shoulders, peeled himself off the hard wooden chair, smoothed his rumpled pant legs, and led Ralph Wheelright into the cold air of Las Vegas, where Ralph had to deal with the press and catch them up on the inquests. But as Mannix lit a cigarette he could content himself with the fact that at least he didn't have to climb a mountain the next morning, which meant he would sleep well that night.

37

Just a Few Yards Apart

Monday morning Carole, Petey, and Wink should have been returning to Hollywood on the City of Los Angeles. Instead, Monday's edition of *The Hollywood Reporter* featured a black wreath along with portraits of Lombard and Winkler and the simple headline, **Good-bye Carole**. On page two was written, "Carole Lombard died in the line of duty. She was the first casualty of show business in this world war. She was in active service on a mission in defense of the United States—selling Defense Bonds—when death suddenly overtook her in the skies. Carole and twenty-one others who died on that Nevada mountainside are all listed as Soldiers of Their Country.'" A half-page box on page five purchased by the Screen Publicists Guild bore the inscription, "We salute OTTO WINKLER for gallant civilian service to his country in the line of professional duty." Across Hollywood, in all the soundstages, a five-minute silence was observed in their honor.

Back at the crash scene, work went on. The various investigative teams, feds and TWA corporate, had spent Sunday puzzled over the crash of Flight 3 and on Monday the mystery deepened. Wright Aeronautics, manufacturer of the two twelve-cylinder Cyclone engines on NC 1946, sent Clyde Burkett up to the scene from North Hollywood, and he arrived on Monday morning to inspect the engines for signs of failure. By that time most of the bodies and body parts remaining on the mountain had been collected and laid in neat rows at the edge of the ravine away from the crash. Still, Burkett had to step gingerly around a pudding of crash debris mixed with spatters of blood and bone and tissue fragments as he was pointed to the right engine, which lay up near the cliff wall in front of the right wing.

Burkett could not believe the ferocity of the crash as reflected in twisted metal covering the mountainside as far across and down the steep slope as the eye could see. He found two blades of the right propeller still attached to the hub and trapped under the right wing. The blades were bent in such a way that it was clear the right propeller was spinning at the instant it hit granite. Burkett let out a sharp breath—that solved fifty percent of the problem right there, because if an engine had failed and Wright was found to be at fault for this crash, there would be hell to pay with *all* the airlines, not just TWA, and with the families of the passengers and the United States Army. He found the third propeller blade from the right engine half melted ten feet away by the cliff wall.

Burkett looked around the frozen mountaintop for the left engine, but it was nowhere in sight. He asked one of the Civil Aeronautics men if he had any idea where the left engine might be found, and the CAB man led him across the ravine, past the inverted tail section, past the center section of the left wing, across and down a mountain slope so steep that Burkett just sort of butt-slid where he wanted to go. Walking was difficult; breathing was difficult. Just being up there was oppressive because of the obvious violence of what had happened, the fire and destruction and death. As much as anything, the pall for most of the men on the mountain had something to do with Carole Lombard. Many of the newspaper reporters and photographers had known her in life and could call to mind a story—a break she had given them, an exclusive, or the time she had touched an arm or given a hug or made eye contact and somehow managed to convey to a guy a feeling that was indescribable. To these news people she was as sexy as it got. Not painted-up, lacquered movie-star sexy but flesh-and-blood Real Woman sexy. And everything she did, everything, was at top speed. She moved fast, talked fast, thought fast, cussed fast. Nobody could keep up with her, but then nobody really tried; they were all too drunk from just being around a dish like Lombard.

Now every newspaper in every home in the land and on every newsstand in every town screamed headlines about the dead movie star and ran her picture, and here in this hellish foreign place was where it all had happened. Where fireball Carole Lombard had finally come to rest in another kind of fireball.

Burkett also found it a dangerous place as he stepped around twisted, jagged fists of metal higher than his head. He had to watch what he grabbed onto and what he scraped against. Finally, a good seventy-five feet from the right engine he saw the strange sight of the left engine and nacelle, propellers and hub still attached, lying face down on the steep incline looking for all the world like a beached whale. How the heck that one-ton monster had ended up way down here he couldn't imagine. He looked up at the cliff directly above. Either the explosion had knocked it down here, or, more likely, it had ricocheted off the cliff and been hurled this far away. Basic physics: action, reaction. A long portion of the left wing had tobogganed down the hill thirty feet past where Burkett and the CAB man stood and now rested against pine trees, but the engine and nacelle had broken off and come to rest here. Uphill from the spot, the engine had bled parts—cylinders, pistons, valves, and gears. And there was a long smear of oil.

The CAB man stood by waiting for Burkett's assessment of the left engine, and Clyde edged down past the length of the nacelle to the propeller hub facing down the mountain. The left engine propeller blades showed the same deformities, the bending and scraping of spinning metal against rock. Both engines were in full operation at the moment of impact, no question about it.

Up at the base of the cliff, TWA chief pilot Waldon Golien stared at the scars in the scorched cliff wall, indentations where the left wing, the left propeller, the nose, and the right wing and propeller had struck. He looked back over his shoulder at Las Vegas through clear, cloudless sky and could, and could not, imagine what had happened. Flight 3 had power-climbed from McCarran carrying a heavy load of passengers and cargo and flown on a beeline to this spot. The left wing had hit the cliff first and levered the fuselage into the cliff in sort of a bang-bang, which meant that the flight crew and passengers had forewarning of, what, a split second of what was about to hit them. The result was spread out below him in a junkyard of aluminum and steel. What he couldn't figure out was what had possessed Wayne Williams to assume this course. The Sky-Club was seven, eight degrees off the standard course out of Las Vegas—everyone knew you headed south and then turned southwest over Goodsprings to Silver Lake and Daggett. He knew Williams to be a good pilot. Hell, Williams' left-seat time surpassed Golien's by 3,000 hours! And Golien had personally checked Williams out on this route and the other routes and landed with him at Vegas and took off with him for Burbank and checked him out there as well. He knew this pilot to have a steely eye and a rock-steady hand, and the crash made no sense at all.

Across the thirty-three miles of clear blue desert sky, as Golien puzzled and pondered, Clark Gable stepped out of his El Rancho bungalow into the harsh, low sun of Las Vegas in January. Strickling had convinced him that he had a duty to perform, to pick out caskets for Carole, Petey, and Otto. So yes, now that he knew what he must do, he appeared in a dark suit and tie and hid behind sunglasses, and Mannix and Strickling had warned that a photographer would be present at the El Rancho but it was a good one and wouldn't intrude. Strickling knew that tasteful photos of a grieving Gable would be golden for box office, and so he had permitted the action.

Mannix and Strickling led Gable to a car where they were driven up Highway 91 three desert miles to the Garrison Mortuary. Nearby loomed seedy casinos, but Gable didn't see them. He and his handlers arrived at the mortuary and slipped inside. Las Vegas mayor and local undertaker Hal Garrison, who had led a futile search for the plane less than three days earlier, met them and personally led Clark Gable through the showroom of caskets, explaining the various price ranges. Gable reasoned that she wouldn't be kept underground—the Great Mausoleum had already been decided upon—so there was no reason to spend extra money on frills. Gable made his choice, three sharp-looking gray steel caskets, and then he was asked the most difficult question of his life: Do you want to view the body of your wife and spend some time with her?

Suddenly, Clark felt the electric jolt that Ma was here, that they were close, just a few yards apart, and that she was dead. Dead. Which meant that she wasn't here at all; the woman—wife, friend, lover—was gone. He remembered the words of Mannix and Strickling, what was it, forty-eight hours earlier? Gable chose to remember Ma in life and not in death. No, he had no interest in spending time with the body. He was whisked out of the mortuary and back into the car for the drive south to the El Rancho.

Back at the motor court, Gable had an idea, and the king summoned his friend Al Menasco to take him on a drive out in the chilled desert. Menasco was a pilot in his forties that Gable met during production of one of his pictures, *Test Pilot*, in 1938. Today a pilot would be especially important to Clark, one of those joyriders who took to the skies, like that captain who had steered Flight 3 into the cliff. Al was the kind of man who knew things, an engineer, a Great War veteran, and maybe he could help Gable to understand what had happened.

Strickling was startled by the request for a drive in the desert but figured he should support the decision because Clark Gable had finally decided to do something other than sit and stare. Strick-

ling and Ernie Hawes watched Clark and Al climb into Hawes' car
and pull out, heading south on Highway 91.

Al took it easy on the drive. They followed the signs pointing the way to the Blue Diamond Mine and pulled off the road
within sight of the entrance to the facility. Before them loomed
the twin-peaked mountain that Gable knew so well now, knew by
sight, the mountain that had swatted Ma out of the sky. It stretched
up so high that it looked close enough for him to reach out and
touch, but really it was ten miles off past the desert flatlands and
beyond the foothills, this snow-covered giant mocking Gable as he
stood by the side of the road with cars whooshing past. His mind
was with her, and he didn't stop to consider the sight that might
greet passers-by, the king of the movies standing by a car in the
desert, lost and helpless and anything but heroic. He was just a
man now, chopped into little pieces by grief, standing there hum-
bled by that goddamn mountain as if its mighty grip had crushed
his knuckles and driven him to his knees.

He stared and he stared—they said the plane had hit in the
saddle of the mountain between the peak on the left and the one
on the right. They said you could see the spot, the ravine and the
burned patch of earth and melted snow, and he squinted the famous Gable squint and tried to see, and it was then he felt as much
as saw a movement out of the corner of his eye, half hidden by
the rim of his sunglasses. He feared photographers; he feared fans
pressing close for an autograph. He looked to his left.

Horses eased closer. No, not horses. Donkeys. Oh yeah, he
remembered something that Ernie Hawes had called as Gable and
Menasco had departed the El Rancho, something about looking
out for the wild burros. Hawes had said to stay away from the
burros because they want food and they bite. Now, Gable had to
smile because he had been worried about intruders, and these creatures cared nothing about Hollywood or movie stars crashing into
mountains. Their lack of concern, or rather their focus on other

matters, such as their empty bellies, allowed Gable to lift a few pounds of the load off his back and hand it to the beasts of burden wandering closer with a snort and a rustling of hooves.

There were eight wild burros in the pack, or whatever it was that burros traveled in, and they all minded their business but stole glances at the visitors to see if anybody was reaching into pockets and producing food. If they recognized Clark Gable, royalty in their presence, they gave no indication. In fact, their interest was transitory; they seemed to sense right away that these weren't tourists, and they drifted off with barely a sound.

Gable had already forgotten about them. He stared up at the goddamn mountain, the one that had pounded him down and wouldn't let him up. Gable said to Menasco, "What do you think happened up there?"

The question startled Al, who couldn't escape the importance of it. They were, after all, this small band of people at the El Rancho Vegas, standing on a world stage, and it was better if nobody glanced down at the footlights or at the vast, faceless audience out there watching. Menasco gave a shrug of his shoulders and said that the plane had flown up there and crashed, and word was that nobody had seen it coming and nobody had suffered.

Gable stared a long time at the mountain, long past the moment when Al realized that the marrow of his bones had frozen. But that was all right, because Gable needed to be doing something besides smoke and drink, and right this minute he wasn't doing either as he stared at the mountain. He just stood there, and he might as well have been on another continent for how far off he was. The sun was lower in the sky when Gable turned back to the car and got in, closed the passenger door, and sat there. It was over. Al Menasco opened the driver's-side door and slid in, started the engine, and headed back toward Las Vegas. He couldn't think of a single thing to say, so he didn't say anything at all, and they drove back to the El Rancho in perfect silence.

38

All in a Day's Work

As Gable cast his far-off gaze at the mountain, Lieutenant Hunt still commanded his team at the crash site, and he looked down at two sets of female remains, or at least at remains that his team reasoned were female. This was Hunt's second day on the mountain, and he was so tired. Exhausted from the climbing and the altitude and far more bone weary from the pressures of doing everything just right for his commanders, military and otherwise.

Hunt got word this Monday morning that dental records had confirmed the body found with Carole Lombard and brought down the mountain with her yesterday was not that of Elizabeth Peters, the second most important VIP to find and identify on the mountain. It was, by process of elimination, that of Mrs. Lois Hamilton, a young bride who, it was said, had been on the plane because she was traveling to visit her husband, a first lieutenant in the Army Air Forces. Dental records had confirmed her identity.

Lieutenant Hunt looked down at the two females before him in the snow just as a man wrenched his way through and past the clot of rescuers. He was an Army officer with silver wings on his chest so a flier, dark haired, his nose and cheeks flushed with cold.

Robert Burnett had begged, borrowed, and stolen to get there. He had cajoled his way from Falcon Field in Mesa to McCarran, and he had trudged every inch with the rescue party up the mountain to find his fiancée, Alice Frances Getz of Kewanee, Illinois, and now here he stood. He gasped for breath and looked down at the butchered body lying there in the snow and scorched earth. It was almost as if he beheld a miniature of her, shrunken there before him on the frozen earth. She had been larger than life, that glorious personality and a warmth that had charmed men from coast to coast, and now here she lay, in a fetal position with her head resting on her hands, as if in slumber. For an instant Lieutenant Burnett prayed that maybe this wasn't Alice lying there in a lump, but he knew it was. He looked down upon her features, blackened and weathered in death, but her features all the same. He wiped his eyes clear and there, on the breast of the blackened corpse, he saw the wings of a TWA air hostess that had been seared into flesh when her uniform had become one with her body in the funeral pyre.

As Burnett stood above her, the others reared back a little as if to say, Who *is* this guy? They held their places in a tableau for a long moment. Then Robert crumpled, down to his knees, and then he fell onto his butt and sat there beside the body. His eyes raked across the trees, the snow and the rocks, and the desert valley. His reeling mind whipped him backward just a few days when they had been together. The moment pounded his head like a wave at high tide: *What was the worst that could happen?*

The other Army fellows watched the new guy wipe his nose on his sleeve as he cried his eyes out. It became clear to them slowly in ones and twos: This fellow knew this girl. Then: This fellow *loved* this girl. They did their best to shut themselves off from him, and pretend he wasn't there, to give him his moment.

The man in charge, Lieutenant Hunt, didn't have time to watch a fellow officer dismantled by grief. There was work to do. The search team knew with certainty who Alice Getz was, and they had figured out Mrs. Hamilton. That left the charred remains of Elizabeth Peters, Lombard's mother, as the final female on the flight and therefore the body lying forlornly at Hunt's feet. Imagine living a whole lifetime, growing up, marrying, raising a famous daughter, probably being in high society, then getting on a plane, and ending up...here. So that was the score, the critical female bodies lying before the group of rescuers. Process of elimination of male bodies on the mountain had yielded the identity of the only man who had not worn a uniform of some sort, either Army or TWA, on the evening of January 16. Hunt glanced down at his clipboard and introduced himself to Mr. Otto Winkler, press man from MGM and Carole Lombard's companion on the doomed airliner.

The body of the civilian male, burned to a crisp, with only stumps of arms and legs, lay right in front of the Army lieutenant. Peters and Winkler were the most important bodies to be moved today and as soon as possible, although Lieutenant Hunt was mindful of the grieving brother officer sitting there in the snow.

Hunt stepped gingerly away from the other man, wiped his nose on the back of his gloved hand, and ordered the bodies to be bound in blankets for the trip up the cliffs to waiting horses. As he saw them hoisted, Hunt found it an immense relief to be able to cipher things out this far, to have the key bodies identified, and he felt pity for the others, the pilot and copilot and hostess and the Army boys who had been drawn and quartered in the crash. They didn't have a powerful studio in Hollywood or generals in Washington looking out for them. They were just...casualties.

Finally, the bodies had been conveyed up on ropes and were out of sight, and Hunt felt physical relief that he was done with them. Things moved fast now—or, if not fast, at least they moved. His men had figured out that two of the bodies at the base of the cliff were the pilot and copilot. Scrutiny of charred sinew had revealed remnants of TWA uniform in both cases. Hunt didn't know which was which, but at least he knew he had accounted for the entire three-person flight crew.

The sun was low in the sky and it would be dark soon, but at least Peters and Winkler would be on their way to Garrison's for identification and inquests. All his men had felt the burden of official pressure from both coasts and keenly wanted to be done with the grisly task of scooping up frozen bits of human and lugging them about like groceries. Now that the Hollywood people had been attended to, he could see to ending this mountaintop drama, with only one significant problem: Through various means he could identify nineteen bodies, or parts of nineteen, and there were just miscellaneous pieces of three others; the pieces were Army personnel, and these pieces might never be positively identified. He knew he couldn't promise anything to Major Anderson other than accounting for a representative part from each of the twenty-two people aboard Flight 3. And he really couldn't even do that with any certainty.

Hunt was long past counting the minutes and hours on the mountain. This was a hell of a way to make a living, securing the scene of an air disaster, and as the sun sank and the air began to bite into his skin, Hunt heard an ungodly sound echoing up from the deeper ravine. He stopped and listened. It was the shriek of a banshee, blood-curdling screams, and not too far off. In a moment one of his men ran up holding a walkie-talkie.

The voice projected through the walkie was panicked: "The pack animal with the bodies has taken a fall! I don't know what to do!" Hunt shuffled through the snow and took control of the unwieldy talking box. He tried to ask what was going on. The G.I. at the other end of the line babbled; the horse's name was Cotton, and he had taken a wrong step in deep snow and gone down the precipice. Two bodies were aboard. The important bodies. The horse had slammed into a rock, broken a leg, and was wedged between that rock and a tree at the edge of the cliff. Something needed to be done now! Hunt didn't even know if he had authority to order the animal destroyed, but the distant screams stabbed right into and through him.

"Shoot the horse!" he said into the walkie-talkie. "Repeat, destroy the animal!"

"We don't have sidearms, sir!" cried the soldier.

"Use a knife. Anything. Just do it!"

The screams went on, echoing endlessly. God help us, thought Hunt. Then they changed; grew yet more agonized. Finally, all again grew quiet. He knew he needed to get up there, and he asked for the location. As he stumbled across steep mountainside, he knew he was in trouble now. It was the very definition of snafu. The bodies of Peters and Winkler had crashed. Again. They now lay off the trail, no horse to get them out; they were still, after seventy-two hours, trapped on the mountain. And there wasn't anything that Clark Gable or Major Anderson or the President of the United States could do about it with winter's darkness closing in fast.

Hunt fought the urge to feel sorry for himself. It sure wasn't easy being an officer. He knew he would be in for it the instant he had been ordered onto this job, and he knew it again now. The bodies of Peters and Winkler were far beyond caring about grievous damage done by a fall down a mountain and being rolled over by a thousand pounds of thrashing beast. They had already been slammed into a cliff at 180 miles per hour. This was just one more complicating factor in an already problematic exercise in forensics. Finally, Hunt found the scene of the mishap, where one of his men had been lowered by a rope down the mountainside, where he had cut free the bodies of Peters and Winkler. The unlucky horse lay a bloody mess and hung by a thread next to a thousand-foot drop.

"Cut him free," called Hunt to his man on the rope and down the horse went.

Later there would be international headlines: **New Tragedy on Mountain: Horse Killed as Bodies Fall off Cliff**. But for Lt. William Hunt, it was all in a day's work of victim recovery on Potosi Mountain.

39

The Little Boy Was Gone

Two special Union Pacific train cars had been ordered by MGM for the return of the grieving king and dead queen from Las Vegas to Los Angeles, including a car that would offer Clark Gable complete privacy as he traveled back home with the coffins of his wife and mother-in-law. By now, after dusk on Monday, he was sleepwalking. In the past twenty-four hours he had returned to something resembling the Gable that people knew. He had showered, multiple times in fact, shaved, and dressed in a new suit and shirt that had been brought in for him, and was ready for the trip home. But Mannix was worried and so was Strickling. The man was aging before their eyes and appeared a decade older than the wide-eyed movie star they had surprised at Encino the previous Friday. His skin was hanging and his face ashen, the result of three days of anguish, and chain-smoking and drinking, with precious little food consumed.

Gable was prepared to leave the El Rancho. In fact, he had checked out before he even checked in, but Clark had already made it clear to anyone who would listen that he couldn't return to the ranch. They had seen Gable lots of ways—happy, jovial, bemused, angry, offended, cold, prickly, and gruff. They had never seen him *old*, this barrel-chested man's man. And they had never seen him skittish. For the first time the veneer was gone and the swagger and smirk with it. It was as if somebody had yanked the script off his lap, and he didn't know his lines or the character he was supposed to play. In place of Clark Gable, King of Hollywood, an awkward, shy, middle-aged man sat before them, gray of face and dead in the eyes.

"I can't go back to that lonely house," he said over and over.

The entire MGM and Gable party at the El Rancho were ready to pull up stakes. They all awaited a mere formality, for the bodies of Petey and Otto to be trucked in to Garrison's, formally identified, and released after the inquest. In fact, it was dark now, and where were the bodies? Shouldn't some word have come by now? Gable would be driven up to Garrison's to climb in the hearse with Carole's body. Mannix would go with Petey in another hearse, and Wheelright would accompany his friend Otto and widow Jill in a third. They would be driven to the train station under cover of darkness and moved into the private car. Mannix, Strickling, and Wheelright would ride the train with McElwaine and Tootie, while Freddy, Spencer Tracy, and the many friends who had migrated to Las Vegas drove back home. A double service for Carole and her mother would take place on Wednesday at Forest Lawn, and admittance would be by engraved invitation only.

Finally, the phone rang as expected. Strickling picked up the receiver as Mannix rose to head out to his waiting car for the trip to the courthouse and the Peters-Winkler inquests. As Strickling listened on the phone, he put a hand out to Mannix: Halt. By the time he hung up the phone, Howard's face was as gray as Gable's.

He could barely choke out the words. The important bodies had *not* been brought down. There had been an accident; they were being brought out by horse and the animal had fallen off some cliff or other, and it had been too close to dark so the Army had kept the bodies up there. Strickling ordered Wheelright to get on the phone at once: train station in Las Vegas, train station in California, Forest Lawn Memorial Park.

Gable's reaction was predictable; he was mute, just nodded to himself, and sat and stared at nothing. At memories. At ghosts. At something no one else in the room could see.

As Strickling would try to sum up later, "The boyishness he had, you know. The little boy was gone."

The men came to grips with the fact that the siege had not ended and would drag on. Mannix ordered food to be brought in, again, and each man made a call home to alert his wife of this new delay. Moments like this brought it home to Gable anew: He didn't have a wife to alert anymore. It had taken this catastrophe to make him understand what he once had, and what he now didn't. He saw a familiar piece of paper beside the overflowing ashtray on the coffee table in front of him. He picked up the paper. It was a telegram from the president of the United States. He read the words for about the twentieth time:

"Mrs. Roosevelt and I are deeply distressed. Carole was our friend, our guest in happier times. She brought great joy to all who knew her and to the millions who knew her only as a great artist. She gave unselfishly of her time and talent to serve her government in peace and war. She loved her country. She is and always will be a star, one we shall never forget nor cease to be grateful to. Deepest sympathy, Franklin and Eleanor Roosevelt."

Hadn't he and Ma just been at the White House, at the Capitol, the Washington Monument, and Mount Vernon? Ma had been bouncing off every wall, thrilled as a kid, her enthusiasm downright contagious, and she kept saying in that fevered pitch of hers how they had talked to the President and First Lady "pretty as you please." How intensely Ma had sat and listened to Roosevelt's speech about the threat of the Axis powers. It was just a moment ago; he could almost reach out and touch those conversations. Could almost reach out and touch her. It was as if the echo of her voice bounced off the walls of the El Rancho.

She really was something, Ma was. He knew that. He did. He

loved having Carole Lombard on his arm because she was a fab-
ulous-looking dame. What would the kids call her, a pipperoo?
But much more than that, he gloried in having Carole Lombard
on his arm because she believed she belonged there. As if she had
been born to it, like royalty was born to it. When they were in
the spotlight together, she was never the clown, but rather she let
the lights and flashbulbs and attention wash over her and her chin
would go up just a little and her smile would be serene and there
was a knowing set to her face that said, "Yes, he is the king but
don't forget that I am the queen." It was funny how she ran that
motor mouth except at public occasions when she would clam up
and the image would take over. At those times she understood that
less was more. She kept people guessing and became mysterious.
She really was something.

How could he ever set foot in the ranch again without her?
The ranch where they had fought their last fight. The ranch where
they had *not* said good-bye. He was a lost soul and his friends and
handlers knew it. Word got out to reporters, and soon the whole
world knew via the newspapers that Gable had "turned from a
swashbuckling, carefree prankster into a depressed, grief-stricken
recluse by the tragic death of Carole Lombard."

40

Flying with Full Acceptance

On Tuesday morning, Lieutenant Hunt finally took the last of the bodies off the mountain and led his exhausted, half-frozen twenty-one-man detail back to barracks. After they had gone, the CAB and TWA men remained. TWA's Waldon Golien knew that with Hunt's group gone, the official recovery of bodies and other evidence had ended. As he would later report: "After the last man of this detail left the scene of the accident, I made a final inspection that covered the area as thoroughly as I thought possible at the time. During that last inspection I found a number of additional pieces of mail. I also found parts of bodies that had not been uncovered by the searching party. I placed all material found in sacks that I carried with me."

Warren Carey, one weary investigator after days in airports, in his car, and on the mountain, had looked over the crash scene all day Sunday, then Monday, and now stood there again, marveling at the destruction.

Carey had always wanted to learn to operate a flying machine, God knew why given the devastation now before him. He had gotten his chance in the Army in the Great War. Now in middle age he still held a captain's reserve commission, although he'd been flying commercially since 1928. He had accrued 4,300 hours of left-seat experience by the time he stood on Potosi Mountain. Car-

ey knew he was a decent pilot, yet the captain who had flown Flight
3 into this mountain, Wayne Clark Williams, had piled up three
times Carey's cockpit hours. It was inconceivable that a man this
experienced could make such a fatal error, and yet pilots did steer
their planes into hills and mountains and even flat fields because
it was just too easy to become confused up there, in a cloud deck,
in weather, watching the forty-six panel instruments and minding
more than one hundred instruments, switches, and controls in all.
Just a split-second error could be fatal.

Carey had gone over this wreck for three days with Safety Bureau Inspector Jack Parshall out of Kansas City and George Cas-
sady, chief of the air carrier branch of the CAA out of Santa Monica. They didn't want to rush to any judgments, and they certainly
didn't want to put the finger on an innocent pilot. They were just
making observations and gathering facts, and what they knew so
far was, as Carey would later report:

> Inspection revealed that the aircraft had, while in full level flight,
> collided with the lower part of an almost perpendicular granite cliff
> approximately 90 feet high on the northeasterly slope of, and approx-
> imately 500 feet below, the 8,304-foot summit of Potosi Peak. This cliff
> was 33 air miles southwest of Las Vegas Airport, the point of last de-
> parture. The aircraft was completely demolished at impact.
>
> Examination disclosed the nose section of the aircraft telescoped
> and impinged upon the face of the cliff. All instruments and cockpit
> controls were demolished or destroyed by the fire which followed the
> crash. The right wing tip outboard from the aileron recess was tele-
> scoped inward by contact with the projecting ledge of rock. The right
> center section with fuel tanks, completely melted, lay at the base of
> the cliff. The left center section with fuel tanks, demolished but un-
> burned, also lay at the base of the cliff below the point of impact of the
> nose section. The outer left wing with ailerons attached, the whole
> completely telescoped, lay approximately 75 feet down the rock slope

at the base of the cliff. Its leading edge bore clear impressions corresponding to newly broken projecting rocks on the cliff face. The points of impact of both the left and right wings, clearly visible on the rock wall by fresh breaks thereon were in a level position compatible with the position of the nose section which remained at point of impact. The tips of several pine trees located on the rocky slope approximately 50 feet from the base of the cliff were slightly below the point of impact. None of these trees were broken. None bore any indication of contact by the aircraft.

Both engine nacelles were completely demolished and fresh breaks in the face of the cliff indicated the point of contact of each engine.

The right engine, with nose section demolished and propeller detached, was found on the slope under the right center section. It was badly shattered and its aluminum parts were melted. Its propeller with two blades remaining in the hub was found nearby. These blades were broken and scarred as by contact with solid object. The third blade was pulled out at the hub and completely melted.

The left engine, following impact, rolled approximately 40 feet down the rock slope. Engine and nacelle had been driven backward into the left center section at impact before breaking clear. The rear portion of this engine was demolished. The propeller with blades attached remained in place. All three blades were broken 12 to 24 inches from their tips and scarred as by impact with a solid object. This engine was also damaged by oil fire.

The fuselage was shattered and destroyed by fire with the exception of the empennage which was found inverted approximately 30 feet down the rock slope. The left elevator and stabilizer were torn off but found in the wreckage. So far as could be determined all control wires were intact.

Landing gears were bent and distorted beyond any possibility of accurately determining their position before impact. That portion of the wing flaps remaining on the right center section were retracted.

Fresh oil blotches covered the face of the cliff to a height of 73 feet above the point of impact of each engine.

Baggage and miscellaneous small parts of the aircraft were thrown over the top of the cliff 75 feet above the point of impact. Bodies of victims were in general found to the right of the point of impact. The bodies of four victims, all army personnel, were thrown clear of the burned area.

All radio equipment and instruments were completely destroyed and owing to the demolition of the aircraft it was impossible to determine any settings or readings at time of impact. However all component parts of the aircraft were found and nothing was discovered which indicated engine or mechanical trouble prior to impact.

Warren Carey, Waldon Golien, and their colleagues covered the crash scene from every angle for days, in the snow and cold, and their minds worked every moment. They made mental notes of every boulder, every tree, every piece of wreckage. Flight 3 had crashed on a night with what Western pilot Arthur Cheney called "unlimited visibility." The doomed airship had two engines under full power and hit the cliff so level that not even the treetops just down the slope were touched when it flew over. Its cockpit had been completely destroyed so that no flight plan could be found and no gauges could be read. Its flight crew had radioed the wheels-up time, but then nothing that might have indicated trouble.

According to witnesses on the ground, this plane had flown with great assurance and full acceptance straight into the highest peak between Las Vegas and Burbank, a snow-covered mountaintop that both the pilot and copilot should have seen from miles off. That pilot had flown over the north-south road out of Las Vegas, Highway 91, which would have alerted him that he was going the wrong way. Pilots flying the Las Vegas to Burbank run at night used headlights on the highway to know they were flying safely south and past the mountains. Fly along Highway 91 to

Goodsprings, then bank south-southwest, and safety was assured. Instead, Williams had flown not due south but rather southwest over the highway and over the town of Arden, and its signal beacon warning of the mountain ahead. Even if he and Gillette had seen the mountaintop at a mile's distance, a simple banking maneuver would have taken them back to McCarran Field in fifteen minutes. But there was no indication that they even thought to act.

Flight 3 was off course by miles. If Williams had flown south to Goodsprings, a cruising altitude of 6,000 feet would have gotten these people home. Hell, if they had been flying 500 yards farther to the left, they'd have missed the mountain. Carole Lombard would have met her husband. The Army fliers would have been safely back in Long Beach. The flight crew would be in the air today. Instead, all now amounted to statistics down at Garrison's Mortuary. Warren Carey wanted to know what had happened. He felt an obligation to those people, and to every man and woman who would next step into a DC-3. If it was pilot error, he wanted to know; if it was mechanical failure, he wanted to know; if it was sabotage, he wanted to know. The bodies had been removed, but he still saw reminders. A lump of tissue here, a bloodstain there. Each bit of their corporeal selves gave them life again, and suddenly they looked over his shoulder, putting questions into his head, nudging him here, coaxing him there, and day upon day at the crash site, he wanted to know the answer. What happened on TWA Flight 3?

41

The Under Side

Louella Parsons reported on Wednesday, January 21, that Fieldsie and her husband Walter Lang had waited at the Encino Ranch for the return of Clark Gable and that "comfort to Fieldsie is the belief that Carole would have chosen to go as she did—when she was on top."

All around this little pocket of drama in the lives of Hollywood people and the families of the other crash victims, a much larger drama gripped hundreds of millions: world war. Air, sea, and ground forces of the United States and its allies learned about the wages of this new conflict the hard way, going head-to-head with Japanese imperial forces in Malaya, Burma, and the Philippines. A new name grabbed headlines, Gen. Douglas MacArthur, and geography-challenged Americans scrambled to atlases to learn the whereabouts of a place called Bataan, where a quarter of a million crack Japanese troops under Lt. Gen. Masaharu Homma seemed ready to wipe out MacArthur and his defenders of Bataan province. Off the U.S. east coast, from dozens to hundreds of souls a day went to Davy Jones' locker on defenseless ships of all sizes courtesy of German U-boats that often came within easy view of beaches from Long Island to Florida. War carved vicious wounds the length of the American heartland, from San Francisco and Los Angeles, where attacks were rumored daily, to the Outer Banks of

North Carolina, lately known as Torpedo Alley.

Who had time to stop for long to ponder a dead movie star? Two days earlier, Pittsburgh editorialist Florence Fisher Parry acknowledged how wonderful Carole Lombard had been in life, particularly the size of her heart in proportion to a diminutive body, but, said Parry as she witnessed the furor of the press to cover the plane crash, "There was something bizarre, almost frightening, in this exhibition of sensationalism. It seemed incredible that the people of this country, plunged as we are in a life-and-death struggle for survival—let no man call it less—could let ourselves exhibit such disproportionate emotions! We are at war," she declared. "We need every trained flier. Fifteen of these airmen, most of them officers, died in the crash that killed Carole Lombard. Look at the newspaper headlines. What about them? Our sons, lovers, husbands?"

The Army boys on Flight 3 had lived and breathed right along with Carole Lombard, but Hal Browne, Bob Crouch, Fred Dittman, James Barham, Kenneth Donahue, Charles Nelson, Stu Swenson, Dave Tilghman, Ed Nygren, Bob Nygren, Al Belejchak, Fred Cook, Milt Affrime, Marty Tellkamp, and Nicka Varsamine had indeed passed into glory as an anonymous list of casualties in a new war. A high officer of the Ferrying Command who agreed to speak to the press on condition of anonymity said, "They were eager to go anywhere, any time. They were the cream of the crop."

One reporter who asked for a quote about how the Army personnel had been overlooked drew this response from the officer: "All of these men were top-notchers. Their deaths are a big loss, felt by all of us. They were some of our oldest crews. They were doing a tremendous job."

Clark Gable didn't need any reminding that nineteen others had been aboard that plane beyond Carole, Otto, and Petey. He knew what the families must be going through. Gable also knew damn well there was a war on and that events related to Flight 3 were newsworthy. He could see the reporters and photographers in his peripheral view, and he despised them now as he had always despised them. Luckily, most feared him so they kept their distance, and if they didn't fear the king, they certainly gave a wide berth to MGM's fixers, Mannix and Strickling.

At the same time as bombs were exploding in the Philippines and torpedoes in the Atlantic, early on a business Wednesday in Pomona, California, a train pulled into the station. Very early. Several grim men in suits stepped off a passenger car with no fanfare. At the center of the group, Clark Gable hid behind sunglasses and moved within the ranks of the other men with the efficiency of the Secret Service. They whisked him into a waiting limousine and drove him off. Just behind, three wooden shipping crates, each containing a gray steel casket, were unloaded from the train with alacrity, slid into three hearses, and driven off in the wake of Gable's lead car.

The nondescript procession headed west, over the Arrow Highway to Arcadia, home of the Santa Anita race track, one of the places that Clark and Carole loved to frequent. The idea of where they were, Santa Anita, was driven home for Gable when the procession picked up Colorado Boulevard—how he and Ma loved to take his convertible to Santa Anita with the top down and speed and laugh their heads off back in the carefree early days of their courtship.

At long last the procession reached Forest Lawn Glendale, and the limousine pulled in at the offices just inside the main gate. For Gable, the memories were inescapable: Thalberg's funeral, and Harlow's, and Carole's passionate reaction to both. Her desire for no such spectacle if she went first, how quiet she had been, quiet and sad. Was sad the word? That day for Harlow, there was also fury, confusion, and hurt, all mixed with sadness in a combustible cocktail within Lombard's five-foot-four body.

Ma's will dated August 8, 1939 expressed her wishes clearly

enough: "I request that no person other than my immediate family and the persons who shall prepare my remains for interment be permitted to view my remains after death has been pronounced. I further request a private funeral and that I be clothed in white and placed in a modestly priced crypt in Forest Lawn Memorial Park, Glendale, California."

The wish to be clothed in white was a nod to her Baha'i faith, which also called for no embalming, and movement of the body limited to one hour's journey from the place of death. As for no cremation, another Baha'i tenet, well, even the higher powers had been overruled on that one.

Gable walked into Forest Lawn's Glendale offices and there Jean Garceau laid eyes on her boss for the first time in five days. She would remember "one of the saddest moments of my life. I was shocked to see the change in him. He seemed to have aged years, was hollow-eyed with grief and loss of sleep."

Those in attendance got down to business right away. Forest Lawn's representatives offered Gable a private end-of-corridor vault like Harlow had, and Thalberg. He was told of the prestige and of the security that these spaces offered. He asked for the cost. He was given a number. No, he wanted three wall vaults anywhere that offered consecutive spaces so that Carole and Bess could rest together and later he could rest next to Carole. Someplace that people couldn't have easy access. He was asked if he had a preference of locations within the Great Mausoleum. He said anywhere with some privacy. Oh, and anywhere away from Russ Columbo.

Then Gable was presented the option, by official Washington, of a military funeral complete with flag-draped coffins, caissons, and a twenty-one-gun salute.

Said Jean Garceau, "I was privy to Carole's will and knew of her desire for a simple funeral, with expense kept within the bounds of good taste, and no publicity. She'd even specified the order of service and the Bible texts to be read. Quietly, I outlined her wishes to

Clark and he quickly vetoed all other funeral suggestions, ordering things as Carole wanted them." Garceau's confidence in Carole's wishes allowed Gable to turn down the D.C. offer of a military funeral. He knew what his wife wanted, and it wasn't a high-profile burial with guns a-blazing.

Final decisions were made, crypts were chosen, and easy as the king pleased, the service was set for four that very afternoon, January 21. Gable shook hands with the Forest Lawn staff and walked outside into an overcast Wednesday morning. He continued to hide behind sunglasses and stepped into a limousine to be driven to the home of Al Menasco in San Gabriel. There he counted out three hours before returning to Forest Lawn for the simplest funeral service in the history of Hollywood stardom. In the meantime, Fred Peters' wife, Virginia, had been asked to supply white gowns in preparation for the burial of her mother-in-law and sister-in-law—it had been Petey who had gotten her daughter interested in Baha'i. The younger Mrs. Peters secured these garments and brought them to Forest Lawn Glendale, and as her son Fred III would say decades later, his mother helped prepare the bodies for burial, but, "there were no remains in the coffins. They put gowns in the coffins. That's what was buried in the graves."

Virginia had expected to see bodies in those steel-gray caskets, but met instead remains that had been devastated and lay in body bags. She did not assist in placing a gown on Carole's body or Petey's, as per their wishes, but rather set gowns on top of the bodies inside the caskets, which were then closed for the last time.

Several dozen people, each having received an engraved invitation, passed a police checkpoint at the bottom of the long drive inside Forest Lawn Glendale and gathered at the hilltop Church of the Recessional for the twin funerals of Carole Lombard and Elizabeth Peters at four o'clock on Wednesday, January 21, 1942. Gable was driven by limousine up a private drive to a side church entrance and slipped into the eight-pew private Family Room, which directly faced the sanctuary at a ninety-degree angle from the congregational seating area. It was an old tradition, the Family Room, and offered total privacy in grief.

As he sat down, an organ played softly and the view devastated him: Right there ten feet away sat the steel gray caskets of his wife and his mother-in-law, in a V shape and draped in blankets of gardenias. About the altar sat dozens of floral arrangements of different shapes and sizes—vivid bursts of color in a bombardment from every corner of motion pictures. Gable sat with his father, William, and stepmother, Edna. Howard and Gail Strickling sat on a pew nearby. Gable conversed with no one before or after. The organ stopped playing. Reverend Gordon C. Chapman of Westwood Community Methodist Church began to speak.

Attendees in the church chamber included Fred and Virginia Peters; Stuart Peters; Carole's girlfriends, Fieldsie, who was with her husband Walter Lang, and Dixie Pantages Karlson, accompanied by her husband Phil; Jean and Russ Garceau; William and Diana "Mousie" Powell; Myrna Loy and her soon-to-be ex-husband, producer Arthur Hornblow, Jr.; Zeppo and Marion Marx; Spencer and Louise Tracy; Carole's new agent Nat Wolff and his wife Edna; Clark's close friends Al and Julie Menasco and Harry and Nan Fleischmann; Jack and Mary Benny, who sat with Ernst Lubitsch and his wife Vivian; Fred and Lillian MacMurray; Gable cronies Buster and Stevie Collier, Phil and Leila Berg, Norris "Tuffy" Goff—who was Abner of Lum and Abner radio fame—and his wife Liz, and Andy and Dorothy Devine; Eddie Mannix and his common-law wife Toni Lanier; and Louis B. Mayer. There were also many of Petey's friends in attendance. A dozen members of the press "came not as newspapermen," said United Press correspondent Frederick C. Othman, "but as friends and mourners."

Said a reporter, "There was no music. Miss Lombard would not have wanted it. Floral tributes, including two large United States flags made of red and white carnations and blue cornflowers, lined the chapel. None of the bouquets bore cards…. The Reverend…said a brief prayer. He read the 23rd Psalm, then a poem." The poem, by Grant Colfax Tullar, was one of Carole's favorites:

> My life is but a weaving
> Between my Lord and me;
> I cannot choose the colors
> He worketh steadily.
>
> Oft times He weaveth sorrow
> And I, in foolish pride,
> Forget He sees the upper,
> And I the under side.
>
> Not til the loom is silent
> And the shuttles cease to fly,
> Shall God unroll the canvas
> And explain the reason why.
>
> The dark threads are as needful
> In the Weaver's skillful hand,
> As the threads of gold and silver
> In the pattern He has planned.
>
> He knows, He loves, He cares,
> Nothing this truth can dim.
> He gives His very best to those
> Who chose to walk with Him.

Fieldsie had written a short sentiment that was read by Reverend Chapman. It stated: "Only those are fit to live who do not fear to die, and none are fit to die who have shrunk from the joy and duty of life. Those whom we have come to honor and, in God's name to bless, never shrank from life, but welcomed it—welcomed life and its every aspect—loved life and were responsible to both its duties and its joys…. Each believed steadfastly in the glorious life to come."

The Baha'i prayer for the dead was recited, and then silence fell. Reverend Chapman said the benediction. The pallbearers were called: Fred MacMurray, Buster Collier, Nat Wolff, Al Menasco, Harry Fleischmann, Walter Lang, and Zeppo Marx stood and moved to the dark gray steel coffin of Carole Lombard. The mourners stood; Carole's casket was lifted and carried from the chapel. A collection of Petey's friends bore hers out. Sobs and sadness filled the Church of the Recessional, and then slowly the mourners wandered out into the graying dusk.

Fred and Stuart Peters stood outside and watched the caskets of their mother and sister as they were borne to twin hearses for the drive to the Great Mausoleum. The caskets were taken to waist-level, side-by-side crypts in a private section called the Sanctuary of Trust with Gable, Fred and Virginia Peters, and Stuart Peters watching as each casket was carefully lifted to its crypt and pushed inside. Word was out that Carole and Clark had fought—and why. The Peters had nothing to say to Gable this day; they seethed quietly and held him responsible for the destruction of their family.

According to UP's Othman, Gable "left the cemetery at sunset, alone in the backseat of a rented limousine. His fans and Miss Lombard's, numbering by now perhaps 100 at the gates, glimpsed him hatless, with chin in hand, as the car purred away."

42

Even the Unfortunates

Jill Winkler's short stretch of life with her "Winkie" had been charmed, and there was no question that the Winklers were part of the Hollywood fabric. Wink took care of MGM's elite and the elite relied on him, trusted him, and loved him. Not only Gable but others like Walter Pidgeon and Lana Turner. Of course, Gable counting on someone wasn't an easy thing because Gable was a demanding man, and he wanted Wink within arm's reach, within the distance of a shout every moment the king was on the lot, and within the reach of a telephone the rest of the time. As difficult as this was, the pressure relentless, the trade-off for Jill was—Clark Gable, for God's sake! Gable was, bar none, the most famous movie star in the world and probably the most recognizable face in the world, more familiar than FDR or Einstein or Hitler. And Jill's husband worked directly for the king.

Then, there was the other royal to serve, and that was Carole Lombard. Carole had a down-home breezy loud boisterous charm about her that was just…love. She loved the people she was close to and if you were Carole's friend, she had your back and would fly into a rage on your behalf at any insult. Gable's charm was different. It was really all about Gable in some way. He'd make that sparkling eye contact and any girl would want to just giggle, he had that way about him, and he didn't like to talk about himself and would rather talk about whomever he was with. He called Jill "honey" like he called all good-looking women honey. Lombard was a brass band; Gable was a crooner who didn't even need music.

And this famous duo had called Otto and Jill Winkler friends. The elopement caper had forever bonded the four, which had been a glorious thing and led to picnics and dinners at the ranch, where the Winklers were among the chosen few. Carole famously said she didn't much like to entertain and certainly never, ever wanted a guest to need to spend the night, and yet the Winklers were welcome and Jill and Carole were girlfriends. They shared secrets.

Yes, the world had been a happy place for Jill Winkler for three glorious years. Then it had turned dark in an instant, what was it, five days earlier? Six? The air, the faces, the sky, and the clouds: dark. The days dragging into nights. Dark. She would recall that last dinner on North Wilton when Otto had revealed his premonition about his death by air. She would flash back to the frantic Gable-chartered DC-3 taking off from Burbank. "It seemed to shoot straight up into the sky," she remembered. "It was such a beautiful night. I looked out of the window at the twinkling stars above. I thought my mind must be playing tricks on me, that this was just a bad dream. It couldn't be happening this way.... As the plane reached its proper altitude, I began to realize this was not a bad dream—that we were indeed on a sad mission to Las Vegas and to the scene of the fatal crash."

At 3 P.M. on Thursday, January 22, 1942, Jill Winkler took her place in the Family Room at the Church of the Recessional. Jill's sister, Hazel, sat in the pew behind her with husband, Joe Roznos, and their daughter, Nazoma, age twenty-two. Otto had a sister, Clara, and she was there. They looked out at the steel casket ahead. None of them knew who was out in the main part of the chapel, but they could feel the force of a large crowd—MGM people from the brass on down, Louis B. Mayer, Sam Katz, Benny Thau, Eddie Mannix and Toni Lanier, Lana Turner, Ann Rutherford, Virginia

Grey, Nelson Eddy and wife Ann, Rosalind Russell, and the entire publicity department. "Many of Winkler's former cronies and friends from the metro dailies were there," said *The Hollywood Reporter*, "as were fifty members of the Los Angeles police and civic officials who knew Winkler during his twelve years on the *Examiner*." Even some of the unfortunates showed up, guys to whom Wink had given a break when he was a reporter on the beat.

Yesterday, the church had been less than half full, so disinterested had Lombard been in funerals and so strong had been the impression made by 250 Harlow mourners sucking the air out of a small chapel in the heat of June. It had taken a police cordon to keep people away yesterday; today the church was packed past its capacity of 155.

Just as the service was about to start, the Roznos contingent heard the outside door open and in tiptoed Gable, moving as a dark-suited blur up to the front beside Jill. Her family members exchanged glances and no one said a word, but there was king of the movies Clark Gable, thin, pale, his skin hanging from his bones, a shocking sight, the pall of death unmistakable about him. Heavy, sad, lingering death. For a moment Lombard was there in everyone's thoughts as they shared the load he was lugging around, but this was about Otto now, and thoughts settled back only to him.

Gable put his giant bony paw over Jill's cold ivory hands clasped in her lap, and the service officiated by Rev. James Lash, pastor of the Hollywood Congregational Church, began. Comforting words were spoken. Prayers recited. Hymns sung. After a pause, the rich baritone of Walter Pidgeon bounced off the ancient rafters as he spoke simply and from the heart about the guy he knew named Otto Winkler. The living, breathing humans who heard Pidgeon's eulogy melted into the floor of the Church of the Recessional. No one could have heard this testimonial and not succumbed to tears in a trickle or a torrent, because Wink had been a good guy, a loyal guy, who, as was pointed out by his newspaper pals, "never hurt anyone to get a story and yet he always got the story."

"Clark Gable was very grieved," said Nazoma. "He sat in front of me and tore a handkerchief to shreds while the service was going on. This was one of his best friends."

MGM contract player Allan Jones took the podium and sang a melancholy tenor rendition of "Ah, Sweet Mystery of Life," which took the MGM people straight back to the Harlow service down the hill in Wee Kirk O' the Heather when Nelson Eddy had sung the same song.

Finally it was over. Mr. Mayer stood. Howard and Gail Strickling stood. And Eddie Mannix and Toni Lanier. The Wheelrights. The Spencer Tracys. And so many other MGM people filed out into the January afternoon. Otto Winkler's body was borne by pallbearers that included cops, reporters, and publicity men to a waiting hearse and then driven to the Great Mausoleum, as Carole's and Petey's had been the day before. The casket was slid into crypt 8727 in the Sanctuary of Comfort, one floor below Lombard and Peters. Finally, after four years serving Clark Gable at all hours, and experiencing dark premonitions, and trying to wrangle Carole Lombard on a hectic bond tour, and being forced to flip a coin and losing that toss, and finding himself dragged cross country at breakneck speeds that finally broke his neck and the necks of twenty-one others, Otto Winkler began his rest.

A few days later Damon Runyon's syndicated column, "Brighter Side," ran a guest commentary written anonymously by an L.A. reporter, probably Wink's pal Tom Devlin of the *Examiner*, which Runyon used verbatim in a piece that was run coast to coast: "The story of a former police reporter. Just a little guy with a heart so big that it finally cost him his life. The guy I refer to is Otto Winkler, who lost his life in the plane crash with Carole Lombard and carried to eternity with him the love and friendship of everyone who knew him, including the jail bums he helped in his reporter days as well as the big stars and film magnates he worked for."

The column summed up, "Otto had a beautiful wife whose love for him as his for her was as glamorous a love tale as any of Hollywood's publicized romances. Jill Winkler might have been a movie star, too, because she was rising in the ranks when she met Otto and married him. But she gave up her career for the biggest thing in her life. And just when things were the happiest, tragedy came winging its way to crash against the Nevada mountains. And the little guy with the big heart, the man who had written the record of a thousand heartbreaks for the papers, got his own name in print at last."

43

The Cream of the Crop

The evening of the fireball, Lieutenant Voorhees had given Lieutenant Dittman his ticket and felt good about doing a comrade a favor. Now, Voorhees had moved on to his next assignment, and Dittman lay in cinders, leaving behind a young widow who would never remarry.

A single inquest was held for the military men after the processing of the high-priority civilians and the flight crew. Then one by one, the bodies of nineteen crash victims made their way back to grieving families.

As dramas had played out for Clark Gable and Fred and Stuart Peters, and for Jill Winkler and her family, so did they play out for the mothers, fathers, brothers, sisters, wives, children, and sweethearts of eighteen other families around the nation. The mother of Mary Johnson, the computer for NACA, heard about the crash on the radio and believed her daughter dead. Mary arrived safely in Burbank and, knowing that the family in tiny Benicia, California, didn't have a telephone, telegrammed her mother that she was safe. But the Johnsons also didn't have a mailbox and instead, telegrams were inserted in their mail slot at the post office.

On Saturday morning, a heartbroken Anna Johnson walked to the post office and picked up the mail. She saw the telegram, assumed the worst, that it was a death notice for her beloved Mary, and lugged the envelope home with a heavy heart. She asked a neighbor to open and read the telegram—and learned that her daughter Mary was alive and housed in Hollywood luxury at the expense of TWA.

Other families did not fare so well. Especially hard hit was southwestern Pennsylvania, home of Al Belejchak and the Nygren brothers. Fred Nygren, father of Ed and Bob, had served as superintendent of buildings at Leisenring High School for a generation and was one of the most respected men in Dunbar Township, Pennsylvania. Dunbar hid in the morning shadows of the Appalachian Mountains on a spot that once had been frequented by a young George Washington during the French and Indian War. One quiet Saturday morning, Fred answered a knock at the front door of his white frame house. Unfortunately for Fred, who had lost Ed and Bob's mother, Lela, about a decade earlier, that knock came Saturday morning, January 17, 1942.

When he grabbed the door handle and pulled, he saw a neighbor boy and felt a blast of January cold. The boy handed Fred a telegram from the War Department. He opened it with no warning as to what he was about to read: "The Secretary of War regrets to inform you that your sons Staff Sgt. Edgar Allen Nygren and Sgt. Robert Frederick Nygren have been involved in the crash of a civilian transport near Las Vegas Nevada along with 13 other Army personnel. If further details or other information are received you will be promptly notified."

Thus began for Fred and second wife Amelia a weeks-long nightmare trying to get information about how and why Fred's sons had died. Not only had he lost Lela, but their little girl had died in infancy, and now the boys were gone as well.

Fred was damn proud of his boys, especially that they had stayed together from the first, even through three transfers, and both were noncoms at such an early age! They were officers and doing important things for the country. Imagine, local boys from

Dunbar taking the big bombers from Los Angeles all the way cross country to the east coast and some even to England and Canada. Fred would hear the drone of an airplane overhead and wonder if Ed and Bob were aboard.

Pearl Harbor had hit Fred hard. His boys flew combat aircraft, and now there was a shooting war to fly in. He hadn't heard from them since Christmas but didn't think anything of it. He relied on the fact they served stateside and therefore out of harm's way.

Then came the second telegram a few hours later—after Jack Moore, Lyle Van Gordon, George Bondley, and the others had made their discovery—confirmation shot across from Las Vegas 2,500 miles to Fred Nygren in Dunbar, Pennsylvania, that no one survived the crash.

Very soon, a reporter from the *Connellsville Daily Courier* appeared with hat in hand. Fred told him, "Had it happened in a war zone, probably one might have prepared himself for it." It hadn't happened in a war zone, and Fred clearly wasn't prepared. "But we can't decide these things," said the now-childless father. "The choice is someone else's."

The community rallied around Fred Nygren and offered condolences, food, and company. Fred became a celebrity because Ed and Bob had been killed on the same plane as Carole Lombard.

During the long week of body recovery and identification, Fred received a telegram of condolence from Clark Gable and another from Fred and Stuart Peters, and Nygren was struck dumb that these important California people would take a moment from their own grief to send word to others. But then, the crash united all the families of Flight 3; all had lost loved ones in that lonely place on a mountain in the middle of nowhere. And maybe it was something special that Gable had lost *two* family members, and could understand Fred's loss in particular and the fact that two sons had been taken away.

Fred began to wonder when his boys would make their last

journey home and heard sporadically from the Army that identification of the remains was difficult. Finally, Bob was identified
when the last of the victims arrived at Garrison's, but not all of Ed
was found. Ed was one of three that Hunt could never find enough
of to satisfy Deputy Coroner Lawrence. As a result, the United
States Army resorted to the wisdom of Solomon. After the Lombard party, the flight crew, and twelve of the Army personnel had
been positively identified, random pieces of three bodies remained.
Those unidentified were Ed Nygren, Hal Browne, Jr., of San Antonio, and Kenneth Donahue of Stoughton, Massachusetts. With
the permission of the families, including that of Fred Nygren, the
remaining body parts were cremated together and divided in three,
so only a small pile of ashes that possibly once had been S. Sgt.
Edgar Nygren was sent east along with brother Bob when finally
twin coffins arrived in Connellsville, Pennsylvania, on the frozen
Saturday morning of January 31, via Baltimore and Ohio Railroad.

The caskets were taken to McCormick's Funeral Home in
Connellsville, where they lay in state, flag draped, until Sunday
noon, when they were moved to a packed-to-the-rafters First
Methodist Church for the funeral service. TWA was represented, as were the Ferrying Command and the VFW. The president
of the United States sent a message via his secretary, Mr. M.H.
McIntyre, and Lutheran Rev. Dr. William Hetrick said over the
boys, "It so happened in the inscrutable Providence of God that
these two brothers, Edgar and Robert, inseparable in life as children, reared together in this community, of the same church and of
the same school in Dunbar township, hand in hand united serving
their country, should both meet death in this tragic way."

The funeral procession drove several miles over twisting foot-
hill roads, trees barren, ground frozen, sky full of clouds, from
Connellsville to Flatwoods Cemetery, where Ed and Bob were laid
to rest under a rattle of rifle fire in military salute, and another two
casualties of Flight 3 settled in to eternal rest.

Similar ceremonies took place around the nation. Milt Affrime was sent back to Philadelphia for burial in the Adath Jeshuran Cemetery. Milt would have been relieved to learn that his fifty-six-year-old father was never called to active duty. James Barham returned to Waco, Texas, and Hal Browne, Jr., to San Antonio. Al Belejchak was sent east by rail to Braddock, Pennsylvania, for burial in the heights overlooking the steel mills. Fred Cook was shipped to Reidsville, North Carolina, and Robert Crouch to Bloomfield, Kentucky. Fred Dittman went west for burial at Golden Gate National Cemetery in San Bruno, California, where, standing over the grave, a shaken Burt Voorhees related to Fred's devastated bride Violet and other mourners the story of exchanging plane tickets with Fred. Kenneth Donahue was forwarded to family in Maine. Charles Nelson went to St. Cloud, Minnesota, and Stuart Swenson, who had enlisted as an aviation cadet the same day as Charles in the same place, Fort Snelling in Minnesota, was shipped to Los Angeles National Cemetery. Martin Tellkamp returned to La Moille, Illinois, and David Tilghman to Snow Hill, Maryland. Nicka Varsamine from picturesque Woonsocket, Rhode Island, ended up in grave number 23,757 at Arlington National Cemetery.

Lois Hamilton, the Army wife with movie star looks who pleaded with Ed Knudsen to let her remain on Flight 3, returned to suburban Detroit, Michigan, in a child's casket, there was so little left of her. Her cousin, Marie Levi, then a child of nine, remembered a packed gathering of family and friends in the home of Lois's affluent parents, Russell and Viola Miller. They were tough people; there were no tears and instead Marie remembered a resolute acceptance.

The broken remains of Stillman-Morgan Atherton Gillette, copilot of TWA Flight 3, made their way back to Burlington, Vermont. Alice Getz lived the glamorous life for a very short time and left behind fiancé Lt. Robert Burnett and ardent admirers Bud Ode and Bob Hix along with a shattered family, all of whom attended her burial mass at St. Patrick's Church in Sheffield, Illinois. And Wayne Williams, recently TWA's top pilot and a man with a successful present that was certain to become an even brighter future, had already earned scorn because of the spectacular way his ship had gone down. Captain Williams was given a quiet funeral in Kansas City, and his shattered body was cremated, again, and shipped on to his widow, Ruby, in Southern California. Ruby decided to deposit the ashes of Wayne Williams, once known for a day as ace pilot Jimmy Donnally, in Forest Lawn Glendale where they would reside for eternity near what was left of Carole Lombard, Elizabeth Peters, and Otto Winkler.

44

Skyrocketing

Clark Gable knew he could stay at Menasco's in San Gabriel as long as necessary, but after Otto had been laid to rest, he asked Al to drive him home. Reaching Encino on Ventura Boulevard, making the familiar left turn onto winding Petit Avenue, he steeled himself for that last right turn onto the winding, uphill driveway to the ranch.

There in the stillness and quiet, he looked at the house, the garage, the stables, all still there. Just no Ma. Jean greeted him on arrival, and she had asked Gable's permission to have others over, to ease the moment. He said OK, so Strickling and Mannix showed up, and Nat Wolff and his wife, and Harry Fleischmann, and some others.

When Garceau was alone with Gable in her office with the door closed, she handed him the last in the series of love notes Carole had written, a note Jean had held back when the worst happened. The words in careful green ink reconnected his emotions and overwhelmed Gable, and what poured out was something he could never have expected or known he was capable of experiencing. This man who didn't know how to cry when called upon to do so in *Gone With the Wind*, who had then been coached by Olivia de Havilland on the art of tears, this man's man, felt the emotional dam fracture and when control left him, he wept. How awful it was, finally after forty years, to have the head and the heart connected. She had done that; she had cursed him to feel his heart, and then she had gone.

"It's a dreadful thing to see and hear a strong man cry," said Jean, who stood there awkwardly, "lending what strength and comfort I could muster until he was calm again."

Gable had endured the worst: the weekend, the funerals, and now the return to the ranch. He couldn't spend the night there, not yet, so he drove up to Bakersfield with hunting buddy Harry Fleischmann to get his mind in order and prepare. After that, he settled back in at Encino, where Jessie, Juanita, and Martin shared Gable's grief. Garceau kept her distance, and time passed in silence, each of the five of them joined by tragedy and yet separated by it. They remained alone with their thoughts, learning to accept the cavernous emptiness, the lack of screeches and shrieks, gags, kindnesses, and that cat-ate-the-canary smirk. The haunted man walked the farm and let the memories of her wash over him. It was all he had, memories. He would get in his car or on his motorcycle and drive to places they had lived, partied, or sought refuge. The Bel Air house, Santa Anita, restaurants, nightspots, friends' homes. He would drive there and sit, alone, and remember, alone.

He ate at her favorite restaurant, the Vine Street Brown Derby, and Benny Massi said, "He didn't know nobody. He didn't even recognize *me*." At Drucker's Barbershop on Wilshire, the formerly gregarious Gable made his usual once-a-week appearances, and said nothing. "He was despondent," according to Harry Drucker.

Others also experienced the depths of grief. Fieldsie, Allie, Teach, Talli, Billy Haines, Lucy, all felt such pain that it was a struggle to keep going. "When it happened, they all went off alone," said Richard Lang of his mother Fieldsie and the rest of the Lombard gang. "It was such a loss to all of them."

Another kind of loss troubled United Artists, where *To Be or Not to Be* executive producer Alexander Korda faced a dilemma:

What would the company do with this picture, which had been scheduled to sneak preview three days after the crash? As had happened with Jean Harlow, demand for Lombard pictures increased after death. "Such films generally have done exceptional business," stated *The Hollywood Reporter*. The public wanted to see the departed star on the screen again, perhaps out of morbid curiosity, perhaps as a way to deal with personal grief. When theater owners requested prints of Lombard pictures, representatives of producing companies chastised the exhibitors for "ghoulishness." Paramount opted to sit on its seven years of Lombard features. At the same time, Universal sent out old prints of the 1936 comedy *Love Before Breakfast*, and RKO put *Vigil in the Night* and *They Knew What They Wanted* back into circulation, hoping to squeeze a trickle of blood from these two stones.

Dating back to the fight over the title, UA thought *To Be or Not to Be* represented a tough sell anyway. The German army's rampage through Poland had been no laughing matter in 1939, so why should the public see it as a source of giggles now? If anything, Lombard's passing would cast a pall over the proceedings. But the picture *had* to go out. United Artists understood the need to respect the grieving king, and also to steer clear of offending mighty MGM, which could easily accuse United Artists of cashing in on tragedy. The board of directors met in New York and decided to finish final editing of the picture and set it aside for two weeks before issuing a release date.

Jack Benny, who knew he had made a hit thanks in large part to Lombard's generous style of acting, now couldn't bring himself to look at it, to see her up there on the screen, twenty feet tall on a screen of silver and very much alive. When finally the picture premiered in mid-February at Grauman's Chinese, after "a respectful period of time," the Bennys were scheduled to appear on the red carpet to highlight the event. Instead, *The Hollywood Reporter* chastised Benny for driving around and around the block and never entering the theater. Mary Benny walked in alone and watched the picture, and afterward assured Jack that it was all right—it would be all right. Only then would he watch it through, in a projection room, in private. He told Louella Parsons afterward that he was thrilled Mary had liked it so much and that the reviews were positive. "I know how happy it would have made Carole," he said, "and she would have wanted everyone to see our movie. I'm more glad for her sake that most people like it than I am on my own account."

By the third week of February, UA knew it had a hit. **Lombard Fan Yen Skyrocketing 'To Be'** read a trade headline. L.A. area box office was strong, either doubling usual returns or setting house records. By early March, *To Be or Not to Be* was proclaimed as "one of UA's top all-time domestic grossers, and one of the top industry grossers of the year" and opening to "record premiere crowds at all situations throughout the country."

America could giggle at Nazis in Poland after all, if it meant one last visit in the dark with Carole Lombard. Once there in the picture palaces, audiences savored the biting send-up of Hitler and the Nazis, and gasped at a Lombard more radiant and self-assured than ever before. She had been right to do *To Be*, and her next two comedies might have put her back on top. Now, the script that had been written at Columbia with Lombard in mind, *He Kissed the Bride*, would be given to Joan Crawford, who volunteered to take the assignment and donate her entire salary of $112,500 to charities, including the Red Cross, the president's Infantile Paralysis Drive, the Motion Picture Relief Fund, and the Navy Relief Fund. Joan owed that much to Clark Gable.

Lombard and Crawford had always been rivals and never close, and Gable and Crawford had loved and hated over the years, since that first passionate affair, but Joan's gesture now showed genuine respect. When her agent tried to take his usual ten percent for negotiating this particular deal with Columbia, Crawford fired him.

The other feature in the pipeline for Carole, *My Girl Godfrey* at Universal, would be produced in 1943 as *His Butler's Sister*, with the starring role given to popular young singer-actress Deanna Durbin.

By the time *He Kissed the Bride* started shooting in mid-February, Gable was set to return to work on *Somewhere I'll Find You*. He had driven all the places he could drive, including a solo car trip to Oregon, and replaced his tight-lipped silence with the beginnings of a new habit. He talked about her. All the time. To everyone. Said Delmer Daves, "That affectionate love of this girl would come through in his 'remember when's.'" Said Clark's pal Andy Devine, "It was just that any time he'd run into you, it would make him think of Carole. He would talk about her—and only about her."

Gable was slowly moving toward acceptance as February wore on, acceptance of Lombard's passing and of his own guilt in the matter: that last argument and the reason for it, Lana Turner. Yes, he was learning to accept, but his eyes would never look alive again and his hands continued to shake. Strickling said Gable had always been an ambitious man, but now his ambition was gone, never to return. As Jean Garceau put it, "He never reverted to what he was in the early days." But he survived.

45

Mangled

On January 24, 1942, Congress released the results of its investigation into the disastrous Japanese air attack on Pearl Harbor, placing blame squarely on the on-site commanders, Navy Adm. Husband E. Kimmel and Army Lt. Gen. Walter C. Short. With war raging, with the new concept of rationing of sugar, butter, and other goods about to begin, the story of Flight 3 receded far into the background.

However, the number of air disasters involving civilian passenger liners throughout the 1930s and into the new decade had caused Congress to set up a body to study these disasters, and the Select Committee on Air Accidents in the United States investigated the crash of TWA Flight 3, as did the Civil Aeronautics Board. These bodies interviewed TWA personnel who had interacted with the plane, including Las Vegas station manager Chuck Duffy, and maintenance men Ed Fuqua and Floyd Munson, as well as witnesses who had seen the ship fly over, such as Dan Yanich and Ora Salyer, rescuers including Jack Moore, Lyle Van Gordon, and Harry Pursel, and TWA and Western Airlines pilots. Authorities questioned dozens of people in an effort to understand this mystery: On a clear night, a highly skilled pilot had flown his ship straight into a mountainside. True, there was no moon that night, and two of the three navigational signal beacons were extinguished because of blackout rules in place for a month, but somehow the flight crew had managed to avoid visual flight references in plain sight that included traffic on Highway 91 and the one beacon still lit in Arden. And Williams and Gillette seemed ignorant of a compass heading that directed them straight into the mountain.

No "black box" cockpit voice or data recorders existed in 1942, and the instrument panel had been destroyed, along with all useful logs and other papers located inside the cockpit. Michael McComb of Lostflights Aviation Archaeology, an airline pilot who has investigated this accident among many others, said, "The plane was equipped with an early version of a flight recorder referred to as a flight analyzer. It recorded four things: airspeed, altitude, heading, and vertical velocity (up and down). They were not designed to be crash or fire resistant, so the information on the pen and ink card was probably destroyed in the fire."

In testimony before the Select Committee, TWA pilot William H. DeVries was asked for an opinion about the piloting skills of Captain Wayne Williams, with whom DeVries had flown. "He has a reputation as a very excellent flier," said DeVries, adding when questioned that he believed Williams to be a "cautious aviator."

Two copilots who had flown with Williams confirmed his conscientious approach to the job. TWA copilot Paul Sydney Grave was asked if Williams was prone to reckless flying in mountains. "Well, he was far from being reckless in mountains," said Grave, adding that Williams "was very receptive all the time. If I made any suggestions as to the carrying out of the flight, he was very glad to cooperate."

TWA copilot Paul Bracken called Williams "a very cautious, safe, and able captain" who "was very conscientious; and I'd say that he believed that rules were made for a purpose and they should be abided by."

Grave went so far as to say, "He was a very even-tempered person. He was not excitable at all. He had a great enthusiasm for his work.... I don't believe you would find any person who was more calm in his work than he was."

But the press needed a cause for the accident and on January 28, a story broke that Captain Williams had been fired by TWA in 1933 for what the company called "infraction of company rules and regulations, however, this had no bearing on his ability or skill as a pilot fully capable of flying transport aircraft." The press and public seized on this termination as proof of Williams' incompetence. Records show that, yes, in his early employment with TWA, Wayne Williams had continued to pursue seat-of-the-pants flying that was fine for the Army and for mail runs, but not for passenger trips. But the blemish that had nearly ended his career and caused his termination from TWA involved labor unions. Williams had attempted to unionize the pilots and the company had fired him for it. Then the National Labor Board, newly formed under the administration of FDR, learned the true nature of Williams' dismissal and quickly ordered his reinstatement. TWA was forced to take Wayne Williams back and put him on mail duty until such time that, with a scrupulous record, Williams resumed his status as a pilot of passenger aircraft. According to a TWA report, "From that time forward Captain Williams had logged approximately 8,000 flying hours and had been continually checked by his supervisors. The company has received many favorable comments from passengers in regard to his flying ability and general conduct."

Three days after the newspapers had been led to condemn Williams for negligence based on his 1933 firing, David L. Behncke, president of the Air Line Pilots Association, issued an impassioned statement that received much less attention in the press. In it he pointed to a disturbing trend to "blame the pilot when he was dead and unable to defend himself or point an accusing finger at the actual cause or causes.

"So far as the cause of the accident on January 16 is concerned, it will in all probability never be known, for the only people who actually know what happened are the pilots of the ill-fated craft, and they are dead and all their aboard-plane records are destroyed." Behncke lamented the fact that the accident was being investigated so hastily and that the only way to truly get to the bottom of the crash was "a far more lengthy and thoroughly scientific study."

With a war on, with the crash scene so remote and buried in snow, the federal effort pushed ahead as February began, looking at the plane itself for signs of sabotage or mechanical or structural failure. Because of the violence of the collision and the massive fire, no helpful evidence from inside the cockpit survived, and if the plane *had* been sabotaged, evidence of that had been compromised. The engines and propellers functioned at the time of the crash and the plane was under control—in level flight based on marks in the cliff and by the fact that the craft hadn't even hit the treetops under the belly of the plane before it struck the mountain.

It had been such a dark night on the sixteenth, one of the blackest Major Anderson had ever seen, and testimony conflicted about whether the mountain could be seen at all. Some eyewitnesses on the ground said that it could, others said it couldn't. When asked about visibility of the mountains on a moonless night, Captain Cheney, the man who had flown over the burning wreck of Flight 3, testified, "If the lights in the cockpit are kept low enough you can usually distinguish the mountains within a reasonable distance of them." Of that night in particular, Cheney said, "We climbed to an elevation high enough to clear everything in the mountains and as we got close to it, we could make out the crest of the mountain, which was below us.... The snow on the mountain made it much easier to see the crest than it would have been any other time of the year."

Cheney's mention of the lights in the cockpit led to investigation of TWA policy and standard practice related to the dimming of lights within the cockpit in darkness. The DC-3 windshield reflected light from the controls, reducing visibility of terrain outside the aircraft—like rugged, unlighted mountains. The investigation looked at cockpit lighting. TWA chief pilot Waldon Golien was asked, "Does the reflection from the light on the copilot's paperwork reflect on the inside of the pilot's windshield?"

Golien replied, "Yes, sir. If there are lights on the copilot's side."

"What is the effect of this on the pilot's forward vision?"

"The effect is to reduce the pilot's forward visibility," said Golien. "I would like to add here that it has, for some time, been the practice of TWA copilots to use a small pencil flashlight cupped in the hand in such a way that the light used is confined to only the necessary writing area." Golien previously noted that Williams had logged more than 200 hours of night flying just in the past four months, so he was well familiar with any windscreen glare issues.

TWA and Western Air pilots were asked about use of the radio range, which broadcast a signal that pilots followed to know they were on course and away from high terrain. All the pilots flew by "contact" or Visual Flight Reference (VFR) and if the radio range was used at all, copilots did the listening on headsets. Flying on course gave a steady signal; flying off course gave a different tone. But the weather over Las Vegas in the Mojave Desert was nearly always clear, meaning the pilots found no need to use anything but the lights below for reference on night trips.

The morning after the crash, Waldon Golien flew another DC-3 with a load and center of gravity matching Flight 3 along the same flight path to the scene of the crash and reported that the radio signal was functioning properly. "The signal received in the vicinity of the accident was distinctly an off-course signal," Golien testified, "with no trace or indication of the on-course being in the near vicinity." Was copilot Gillette monitoring the signal on his headset? If so, how did he fail to alert his captain of impending danger?

The regional signal beacons used as aerial navigation aids were given tremendous scrutiny. Because of the danger of air attack by the Japanese, only signal beacons that could be extinguished on fifteen minutes' notice were allowed to be lit that night, which meant that the beacon on difficult-to-access Potosi Mountain and the one near Goodsprings both had been left dark. The Potosi beacon, 23B, located near the crash scene, would have alerted Williams and Gillette to the dangers they faced. The Goodsprings beacon, 23A, would have helped as well, signaling to Williams that the mountains to his right had been safely passed. But then, the lights of houses in Goodsprings should have done that, so why did Williams choose to fly a course to the north and west of Goodsprings, bisecting Highway 91, flying to the north of the Arden beacon and thus clearly the wrong way, and straight toward Potosi Mountain? The other pilots estimated that Williams was seven miles off course in only fifteen minutes of flight time when he hit the mountain, an unheard of discrepancy for a veteran pilot.

Captain DeVries indicated that his practice had been to gain altitude out of Vegas as quickly as possible while flying toward beacon 23A. This way he knew he had flown safely past Potosi. But beacon 24 in Arden was the only beacon lit, leading an investigator to ask, "I am wondering now, if, in your judgment, guiding first to 24 and then going straight on looking for another beacon might have caused him to fly into this mountain."

"Had he done so it undoubtedly would have had something to do with it," said DeVries.

"Do you think he did?" asked the investigator.

"I haven't the slightest idea," DeVries shrugged, and when pressed to speculate on the action of Captain Williams said it was impossible to reconstruct accurately, because, "I don't believe you will find two pilots anywhere who conduct a flight exactly the same."

TWA Capt. Alexis Klotz, who had flown into and out of Las Vegas for fourteen years, described his procedure for departing

Las Vegas to the south at night: "I always have the [cockpit] lights turned down as low as possible, and I always fly for the farthest light I can see…, beacon 24 on the ridge just this side of Goodsprings, and just north of where the accident happened; but by the time you get over the city of Las Vegas you are able to pick up beacon 23A, which is Table Mountain. But I flew that run before we had any beacon lights, and I used to use the town of Arden on the left and the town of Goodsprings. You can always see those lights. As long as you can see those lights that is all you have to get."

Amber Airway Number 2, one of the highways in the sky used by TWA pilots, came into question. TWA regulations did not mandate a particular altitude. Regulations stated only that a pilot must remain 1,000 feet above terrain. A Congressman asked Captain Klotz if he would consider 8,000 feet of altitude out of Las Vegas to be within regulations for Amber Airway No. 2. "I certainly would," said Klotz. Asked to explain, considering that Flight 3 hit terrain on Amber Airway No. 2 but lower than 8,000 feet, Klotz said, "It is very true that you can wander off just a little bit and hit something, and that is what happened. But, as I explained to the other Congressman this morning, we drive down a narrow highway. There is traffic within twelve inches on one side and a gully on the other. It is considered safe. You watch what you are doing."

Transcripts of radio conversations between Air Traffic Control and the plane were routine. No maydays had been issued; just an all clear from Las Vegas along with the departure time.

The weight of the plane at takeoff from Albuquerque and from Las Vegas was scrutinized, and Ed Knudsen, who had adjusted the numbers to allow for takeoff from Albuquerque, was called to explain his actions. Chuck Duffy of Las Vegas also testified. The plane was clearly overweight in terms of passengers, baggage, mail, and other cargo. In particular, the fifteen Army personnel each carried with them full, heavy gear in terms of flight kits, parachutes, tools, and other material.

While the Wright Cyclone G202 engines had plenty of power for a load slightly over maximum, TWA Captain DeVries testified before the House Committee that a heavy load would have affected the rate of climb out of Las Vegas. DeVries had flown into and out of Vegas and knew the capabilities of the DC-2s and DC-3s in the TWA fleet. Of the lift capabilities of Williams and Flight 3, DeVries stated: "The rate of climb varies greatly depending upon the load, the air condition, and many other variables that are possible. He could have 8,000 feet within thirty-two miles under certain conditions, but it is more likely that he would have less with a heavily loaded ship." Flight 3 struck the mountain thirty-three miles from the airport at approximately 7,700 feet.

Temperature was investigated as a possible factor. Did the engines struggle to meet the pilot's climb rate? Said Captain DeVries, "If he is climbing the total distance sometimes due to atmospheric conditions—i.e., heat or cold—if the motors are running hot or there is a tendency for them to overheat it will climb more slowly and keep a higher airspeed to get the cooling effect on the motors...."

Several witnesses were asked about evidence of sabotage. All said there was no such evidence, although the plane had been so mangled and the on-scene investigation so cursory that evidence not obliterated by the crash may have been overlooked. The priority had been to locate and remove the dead movie star and her party so that Clark Gable could return to Hollywood. Yes, the area was secured from looting, but the investigation was by no means forensic in nature. In fact, the last TWA man to leave the scene on Tuesday, January 20, Waldon Golien, reported that he was still retrieving body parts and personal effects up to the last moment and that searchers could continue to do so indefinitely. With so much potential evidence still up there, who was to say if the plane had or had not been tampered with?

What about the soldier that Ed Fuqua, the TWA maintenance

man in Las Vegas, mentioned in his testimony? Fuqua was asked, "At the time that you were working about the airplane and servicing it, did you observe anyone loitering around the airplane that had no right to be there?"

"No, I didn't," he replied. "I don't think there was anybody but a guard up in front where I was but I couldn't tell, I was so busy. I didn't even think to look around."

"Was the sentry a soldier?" he was asked.

"Yes, because I remember checking his [the aircraft's] tanks twice and I think I almost bumped into the soldier once, or something. I know there was a soldier there."

Why was the soldier, who was never called as a witness, standing so close to the plane that the mechanic almost bumped into him? Is it possible that something was done to the aircraft to limit its controllability after takeoff? Calvin Harper had heard what he described as "irregularity of one of the motors." When asked to elaborate, the eyewitness told investigators, "One of the motors sounded perfectly normal, while the other motor sounded just as an automobile motor sounds at times when you have carburetor trouble—when the power goes on a bit and off a bit. In other words, I heard that motor for a minute, and then I couldn't hear it, and then it would come on again." Harper had ridden in airplanes "twenty-five or thirty times" and loved to tinker with car engines in his spare time.

Willard George at the Wilson Ranch stated that "it just sounded as though the engines were racing at top speed. They were roaring."

The nation was gripped by sadness at the death of Carole Lombard in a plane disaster, and yet the nation moved on, so Lombard's value as a target of sabotage was limited. But those fifteen Army Air Corps fliers played a more significant role in the war effort, ferrying brand-new bombers for immediate use against Axis targets.

Nazi spy networks were known to exist only in the northeastern United States and based in and around New York City. In fact, the 80,000-ton French passenger ship *Normandie*, in the midst of being converted to a U.S. troop ship, was destroyed by a mysterious fire while docked at the port of New York just twenty-four days after Flight 3 crashed. The *Normandie* had been sabotaged by German operatives, and Congress, the newspapers, and the American people knew it. Yet the cause was engineered by investigators into an "accident" and not sabotage. So close to Pearl Harbor, the White House would not admit that a giant ship had been destroyed by the enemy on the U.S. mainland. Similarly, if Flight 3 *had* crashed because of sabotage, this fact would have been covered up beginning that Friday night when Burbank told Duffy the situation was "under control." Such a cover-up would have been practical: The United States didn't possess resources enough to provide maximum security to every civilian flight from every airport at all hours of the day and night for the duration of the war. Such extreme measures would have crippled American commerce. Business travelers, including those in government service, would be confined to trains; air mail would cease to be viable. Troops would be diverted from the European and Pacific theaters of war to guard the civilian air fleet.

Accompanying the first team to reach the crash site, the FBI had examined the skin, guts, engines, propellers, and cargo of Flight 3. They went over debris on the mountain, and then investigated the mechanics who had serviced the flight along with the engineering logs, flight crews, and passengers who had died on board or hopped off at various stops.

Calvin Harper's testimony about the flame trailing one engine drew interest from the FBI, as did Jack Moore's statement that upon reaching the crash scene, he saw that "the passengers had been literally thrown through the side of the cabin, which had practically disintegrated after the crash." Moore described "parts of bodies, mail, luggage, and parts of the plane scattered over a wide area." The FBI wanted to know, did sabotage cause the complete destruction of Flight 3?

An FBI report from the beginning of February mentioned a communist informant who fingered Joseph Szigeti as the saboteur: "He probably left something on the plane, probably a violin case which contained something which affected the plane's instruments."

Charlie Hawley, the camper collecting firewood who watched Flight 3 pass directly overhead and at low altitude reported seeing the plane turning slightly to the left, left, left. Were Williams and Gillette attempting to turn away from the mountain, but with limited maneuverability? If this were the case, it raises the question, did the flight crew and passengers know what was about to happen to them? Did they have warning that amounted to minutes and not a mere second or two? And if so, how terrifying were those last moments?

Virtuoso violinist Joseph Szigeti then became the focus of the FBI's investigation. He had first traveled to and performed in the United States in 1925 and had toured all over the world, from his native Hungary to Moscow to South America and all points in between. He was a colleague of the top classical musicians in the world, had performed with Maestros Richard Strauss, Igor Stravinsky, and Eugene Ormandy, among many others, and seemed to live and breathe not murder, but music, all hours of the day and night. He had refused to perform in Germany from 1933 on and had settled with his wife and family in southern California, where he hoped to return aboard Flight 3 before being bumped in Albuquerque. That turn of fortune caused Szigeti to receive the only known message of congratulation about Flight 3, a telegram from Polish conductor Artur Rodzinski celebrating what he called Szigeti's "rebirthday." Szigeti had to agree that "indeed it was."

Not just the Communist informant but many other citizens wrote to authorities certain that the passenger with the foreign-sounding name, Joseph Szigeti, had brought down the DC-3. One even connected the musician to the loss of Pennsylvania Central Airlines Trip 19 on August 31, 1940, and claimed Szigeti had placed something on board the DC-3 at National Airport that had caused a crash killing twenty-five, including U.S. Senator Ernest Lundeen of Minnesota. This was the crash that Warren Carey of the CAB had attributed to lightning.

Szigeti himself stated that he should have been aboard Trip 19 when it crashed in Virginia, but stated that he "had a lot of letters to get off," so he missed the flight. It remains an improbable coincidence that Szigeti was connected with the only two fatal DC-3 crashes of this time period, both of which resulted in the deaths of prominent Americans on federal government business. Yet the FBI could not connect Szigeti with any sinister actions that might have resulted in either disaster.

Not found in surviving FBI information was any mention of Ernest Pretsch, the twenty-nine-year-old, German-born TWA pilot who had lived in his native country to age fourteen and captained Flight 3 from Kansas City to Albuquerque. Pretsch would maintain close ties with his homeland and after the war head up a TWA-Lufthansa joint venture, but he seems never to have been an object of scrutiny by the FBI.

A bizarre twist would be added seventy-two years later in 2013, when the book *My Lunches with Orson* would revisit the thought that Flight 3 had been brought down by the Nazis. In transcripts of lunches between Orson Welles and film director Henry Jaglom, Welles asserted that Lombard's plane had been shot down by Nazi agents "standing on the ridge" who "knew the exact route that the plane had to take." However, such agents would have had to possess this knowledge with several hours of head start to climb the mountain, which they didn't have since the stop in Las Vegas had been necessitated only by darkness falling on Boulder City. One statement by Welles—a friend of FDR—sounded ominous: "The people who know it, know it. It was greatly hushed up. The official story was that it ran into the mountain."

In the end, after following all leads involving Szigeti, examining the wreckage, and looking at the remoteness of Las Vegas and the fact that Flight 3 took off from a U.S. Army facility that appeared secure, the FBI could never pull together enough threads to make a case for sabotage, and the Committee agreed that sabotage seemed unlikely.

Official scrutiny returned to Williams and Gillette when it was stated that Wayne Williams had been assigned to this region—from Albuquerque on west—just two months prior to the crash and had made several trips into and out of Las Vegas, but only one night trip from Las Vegas to Burbank. In addition, Wayne had lost flight time in his new region due to hospitalization related to the removal of his tonsils.

Gillette was shown to be as new to this district as Williams was and had flown out of Las Vegas only twice, once toward Burbank at night. Gillette's flight plan was found in Albuquerque and on it, he had recorded the compass heading and altitude for the intended departure from Las Vegas. But these numbers were incorrect for Las Vegas; he had jotted down the heading and altitude for a departure from Boulder City. For a departure from Las Vegas, this heading took the plane directly into Potosi Mountain at an altitude approaching 8,000, which was too low to clear it.

Williams became a victim of renewed character assassination in the press. Rumors circulated that he left the cockpit to visit with Carole Lombard, and yet Flight 3 was the only ship in the sky at that time and all witnesses were deceased, reducing this claim to pure fantasy since no one could have witnessed him leaving the pilot's seat—an unlikely eventuality in any case given the procedures involved with takeoff and climb to altitude in the first minutes of flight.

The final word was given to James N. Peyton, Investigator in

Charge of the Safety Bureau, Civil Aeronautics Board Region 2, who visited the crash site from January 24–26 and made the following statement that greatly influenced the investigating bodies:

"In my opinion the accident was caused by one thing and a series of contributing factors. As this was the last leg of the trip, it is obvious that the pilot desired to get home or to the Burbank Airport with the least possible delay, and I believe that he intended flying a straight course from Las Vegas, Nevada, to Burbank, California. This would take him considerably to the right of the center of the airway. This is evidenced in one respect by the position or location of the scene at which the accident occurred. It is also my opinion that he had reached his cruising altitude, which, according to flight plan, was 8,000 feet. And probably he struck the cliff at a time when he had leveled off and was making adjustments on his propellers, controls, and manifold pressures, and leaning his mixtures for maximum cruising speeds.

"It appeared to me that the left wing was the first part of the airplane to make contact with the face of the cliff and this wing made a scar on the face of the cliff which was discernible. This point was plotted on the chart by engineers, and indicates an altitude of 7,769 feet above sea level. Making adjustments on the engines from a climbing attitude to a cruising power, it would be necessary to turn the cockpit lights up so that he could see the instruments better, and I believe that that was the condition when the airplane actually hit the rock.

"I heard that there was no moon that night, and it has been my experience flying over the western part of the country in rarefied air on a clear night with no moon that it is very dark. You can see the stars, but the outline of a mountain wouldn't be so prominent to you if you had any lights on to any degree in the cockpit. Although you might not be able to see the stars where a mountain would be, it would appear more as a black void than it would as the shape of a mountain. A contributing factor would be the fact that the route flown from Albuquerque to Las Vegas and then from Las Vegas to Burbank was not according to schedule."

Peyton's statement relied heavily on opinion, supposition, and hearsay regarding key points, particularly his assertion that Williams was, in effect, attempting a shortcut straight to Burbank. TWA Chief Pilot Golien had previously explained in his testimony that shortcutting—which in this case meant flying over dangerous mountaintops and then through restricted U.S. Army airspace—would have saved a mere "three or four minutes." Peyton only supposed that Williams would risk his passengers and crew—and his pilot's license—for a savings of four minutes maximum, although airline pilot and crash investigator Michael McComb said in 2013 on the issue of shortcutting: "Pilots would do that back then just to save a few precious minutes. It was not uncommon, and it was practiced through the 1950s. When air traffic control radar started watching planes en route, then pilots would have to ask to leave course." Why would pilots take such risks? "To keep an on-time schedule," answered McComb, "to make up time if running late, but also to save fuel. Airlines back then were very competitive to please the customer, but also to save money. The big boys were United, American, Delta, Eastern, Northwest, and TWA. All at the time boasted fast transcontinental service."

In stating that the mountain was not visible, CAB investigator Peyton contradicted Captain Cheney, who had flown over Potosi after the crash and reported that the outline of the snow-covered mountain was visible from the air. Capt. Marshall Wooster, piloting Western Air Flight 11 that night, also reported that he could see the mountaintops from 10,000 feet despite the lack of moonlight.

As David Behncke of the Air Line Pilots Association had stated on February 1, long before findings were rendered by the CAB and the congressional investigators, it was all too easy to "blame the pilot when he was dead and unable to defend himself or point an accusing finger at the actual cause or causes." And in this case it was also convenient to cite pilot error since no other cause of the crash could be established, and an official cause would never be found, as Behncke had predicted.

These questions can never be answered: If Williams wasn't looking out his window and flying by the visual references that all pilots used after takeoff from Las Vegas, and if Gillette wasn't looking at visual references or monitoring the radio range, what were they doing for those fifteen minutes? What of the Sperry Automatic Direction Finder that helped the pilot to determine his exact location by triangulating on existing broadcast stations? Was Williams not using it? Was the ADF out of order? Indeed, if Wayne Williams was captaining such a careless ship, how had he survived in the air for fifteen years, 13,000 hours, and 1.4 million miles?

As an air carrier, TWA would remain stumped about the crash. "Actually," began a communication between leaders at company headquarters in Kansas City in May 1943, "there has never been any convincing evidence as to the exact cause of the accident. TWA does not purport to be able to explain how the accident happened; nor do we believe that anyone else can explain it except on a pretty flimsy chain of circumstantial evidence, with most of the links forged out of pure guess."

But in hindsight—the passage of time along with the collection and synthesis of evidence from the investigating bodies—likely conclusions can be made that may solve the mystery of Flight 3.

The trip of January 15 into 16 had been a tumultuous one throughout, with multiple cargo and weather delays. From Albuquerque on it had been chaotic thanks to the necessity of conveying Army personnel. Yes, Williams knew that a sexy movie star was aboard—certainly not the first he had piloted in 1.4 million miles—and he was responsible for the Army fliers, some of whom he knew and had instructed. But testimony revealed that Williams was a steady and calm pilot and especially conscientious to learn about the Western Division. In several ways the deck was stacked against him on January 16. Circumstances forced him into Las Vegas and not nearby Boulder City. The latter was favorable for the nighttime takeoff of an overloaded plane; the former was not.

Departing Las Vegas, Flight 3 was overloaded not by a little, but by a lot, packed as it was with passengers, Army gear, Lombard's trunks, a heavy load of mail, and fuel levels sufficient to deal with contingencies over Burbank. With that load, the ship still climbed at a normal rate toward a cruise altitude of 8,000 feet as per Gillette's flight plan, which he continued to use even though it would work for a departure from Boulder City and not Las Vegas. A correct plan from McCarran Field would have called for a flight path due south with a steeper climb rate to achieve a cruise altitude of 10,000 feet, not 8,000, that took into account the mountains at the right edge of Amber Airway Number 2.

What of the orange streaks of exhaust flame trailing the engines that eyewitnesses had reported to Major Anderson? Cool blue flame was the norm for a DC-3 flying at night, not hot orange. The answer to this question also accounts for Calvin Harper's testimony about the "irregularity of one of the motors." According to Michael McComb: "Orange flame equals a fuel-rich mixture. Blue flame equals a fuel-lean mixture. Since they were climbing, the mixtures were kept rich to facilitate engine cooling. The witnessed power changes or surges might have been adjustments to propeller RPM, which were also adjusted at climb and cruise. I've read in other accidents witness statements saying, 'the engine sounded like it was changing gears,' which was just propeller RPM changes."

With mountains of various sizes surrounding Las Vegas, on an exceptionally dark and moonless night with key navigational aids unavailable, the pilot may have become preoccupied with the issue of the weight and the engines, despite the presence of the lights of Highway 91 and the lights of Arden, including beacon 24.

Another factor was Williams' lack of familiarity with the Las

Vegas-to-Burbank route at night. Since reassignment to the Western Division of TWA, he had flown only once out of McCarran Field at night headed for Burbank. TWA copilot Paul Sydney Grave testified that he had been paired up with Wayne Williams to teach him the ropes for flying in the Western Division. When asked by the House Committee about cockpit procedures followed by Captain Williams in night flying, Grave said, "All the time that I flew with him, why, he liked to keep the plane log and paperwork himself to get more or less in the swing of things out here, because he had not done anything like that out here for some time, and in fact I did most of his flying on most of his trips that I made with him..., and lots of that time, of course, the lights had to be on to do the paperwork." When asked at what point during the course of the flight that Williams entered data into the log, Grave said, "I believe that he entered them pretty close after the takeoff."

Did Williams turn over control of the plane to Gillette so the captain could enter data in his log to better familiarize himself with a Las Vegas departure? Definitely yes, according to Earl Korf, the radio operator on duty in Burbank on the evening of January 16. Said Korf, "I don't believe Wayne was flying the plane on that takeoff. The reason is that all the years I had known Wayne Williams, he always made the radio contacts himself. He knew all the radio operators by name and wanted to make the contacts himself. It was definitely not Wayne who talked to me that night."

That placed copilot Gillette at the controls, and Gillette then would naturally refer to the flawed flight plan that he had created in Albuquerque. With the cockpit lights up to accommodate paperwork and with Gillette confidently steering the ship on course, albeit the wrong course, and climbing to 8,000 as per the flight plan, the copilot would not have been reckoning by the lights of the highway or the signal beacon, and the interior lighting reflecting off the cockpit windows would have obscured views of the looming mountain on the darkest possible night. In this scenario, with Williams confident in Gillette's abilities and filling out his paperwork, he would not have referred to the Automatic Direction Finder and its reference to mountains dead ahead.

The orange flame reported by witnesses as trailing the engines and changes in propeller RPM heard by Calvin Harper serve as testimony of a flight crew stationed in the cockpit (not chatting with Carole Lombard) and hard at work to gain altitude for the passage to Burbank.

Neither Williams nor Gillette seems to have been monitoring the radio range and the on-course signal, but this didn't constitute negligence on their part. The various Flight 3 crash investigations revealed that the standard practice of TWA flight crews was to fly into and out of Las Vegas using visual references only and not instruments or radio signals. No regulations existed for using the radio range, so the pilots simply didn't bother or feel they needed to use it given the nearly constant clear weather around Las Vegas. Captain Williams' fatal mistake was his confidence in Gillette, as he seems to have relied on all his first officers. He might have assumed they were all crack pilots like he was, so he didn't check his copilot's flight plan when it was created during the commotion in Albuquerque, when nineteen Army Air Corps fliers intended to board Flight 3, and Carole Lombard made a successful defense of her three precious seat assignments and Lois Hamilton retained hers. Williams merely *assumed* that the bright and promising Morgan Gillette had filled out an accurate flight plan, and he hadn't.

Don Hackett, who had piloted the Western Air Express charter that brought Gable to Vegas, was interviewed by film historian Richard M. Roberts in the 1980s. "Hackett recalled hanging around the Las Vegas airport with other pilots discussing the crash," wrote Roberts in his interview notes, "and some of the pilots who were used to flying in and out of Vegas commented that the Table Mountain area was a bit problematic for takeoff as it went sharply from 4,500 feet to around 8,000 at that part of the mountain known as Double-Up Peak, and it threw pilots not used to taking off out of Vegas airport." When it was decided that Gable would stay the weekend and wait for the bodies, Hackett was released to take the Western plane back to Burbank. Hackett reported that when he took off for the return trip to Burbank, he realized just how dangerous the mountains were. He hadn't been familiar with the terrain surrounding Las Vegas and didn't know that accepted airways in southern Nevada included jutting mountains within their margins—until he almost hit one.

Said Richard M. Roberts: "Hackett also discovered one more interesting fact on his own takeoff out of Las Vegas.... When he looked at what was then the standard flight map pilots used of the Vegas landscape, the Table Mountain area, specifically the section indicating the altitude jump at Double-Up Peak, was directly on the place where the map folded up, and as the pilots usually did not unfold the entire map in the cockpit when they were flying, Hackett said the altitude jump was easy to miss. These were still the days of more seat-of-your-pants flying and less technical sophistication." To Hackett, it was no wonder that disaster had struck a commercial flight departing Las Vegas in the dark.

Then there was the UFO seen on the nights of January 12 and 13, then not known as a UFO but as "a strange light" observed in the western sky from four miles north of Baker, California, on the flight lane to Los Angeles. The strange light wasn't seen by just anyone; it was witnessed by two Civil Aeronautics Authority men responsible for maintenance to the airway beacons.

John Elmer Furrey, a CAA maintenance manager, was driving on Highway 91 with his assistant in the passenger seat when, according to Furrey, "I glanced to the west and we both noted a light above the crest line of the mountains, which was about fifteen miles distant. This light was a white bright light similar to an eighteen-inch course light, stationary and suspended against the sky as a background, and never moved or varied as long as we could see.

It looked like it was suspended in the sky with nothing to show it could be supported there."

He said to his companion, "What's that light doing there?"

The passenger in the car said, "I don't know. I never noticed it before." The men noted it was round and "many times brighter and larger than a star."

The evening of the crash of Flight 3, Willard George noted a similar light that was "yellow and round in form and hung in the sky like a lantern" and compared notes with the CAA man. In both cases, Furrey realized, the lights "were on the airways directly on course." However, no material evidence existed of the strange lights in the sky, and the investigating bodies could do nothing but note the occurrences and move on to some sort of resolution.

With so many factors at play, some as solid as granite mountains and others as subtle as the folds in a map and lights in the sky, while within the boundaries of the correct airway and following accepted procedures, Captain Williams had struck high terrain. If he had flown 200 yards more to his left, he would have lucked his way clear of the cliffs; if he had flown 300 yards to his right, he would have inched over the peaks. He was 150 or so yards from clearing the mountain vertically. He might as easily have had an "incident," as it's called today in the case of a near miss, as an accident.

For Carole Lombard, some facts can't be disputed. If she hadn't felt so threatened by Lana Turner that she needed to rush home to Gable at breakneck speed on a plane instead of a train, she would have lived. If she had lost the coin toss, she would have lived. If Flight 3 had not experienced cargo delays at several stops along the way, before and after she boarded, and a two-hour weather delay in St. Louis, the plane would have refueled in daylight at Boulder City, and she would have lived. If she had agreed to vacate the plane in favor of boarding three more Army Air Corps fliers in Albuquerque, she would have lived. If the two extinguished signal beacons had been lit, particularly the one on Potosi, she would have lived. For Lombard, changes to any one of these events would have meant life, and a career rebound, and more patriotic acts, and years with Gable at the ranch, and perhaps popularity on television down the road. Instead, she, Elizabeth Peters, and Otto Winkler took up early residence at the Great Mausoleum in Forest Lawn Glendale.

Changes to some of these events would have meant life for the flight crew and the Ferrying Command personnel. Gillette and Getz would have experienced weddings; Crouch could have proven his late mother wrong when she had told him to stay out of airplanes; Browne would have seen his wife and son, Dittman his bride; the Nygrens would have told tales of a plane trip with Carole Lombard; Affrime would have had the luxury of continuing to worry about his crazy father being drafted into the war; Lois Hamilton would have been reunited with her husband.

A bizarre epilogue at the crash scene proved just how hasty and incomplete the on-scene investigation had been. It was almost as if the cashiered Wayne Clark Williams had decided to issue a protest from the grave. On April 14, three months after the crash, with the snows now melted, five Las Vegas postal workers climbed to the site to search for as-yet unrecovered airmail. The wreckage still lay where it had come to rest, speaking to the horrors of that black January moment.

The visitors did indeed find many pieces of mail, some complete and some partially burned. They also found something else. Up at the base of the cliff, near the spot where Lombard and Lois Hamilton had been found, the post office employees stumbled upon portions of a blue TWA uniform jacket. Inside a pocket, intact, was the wallet of Wayne Williams containing his pilot's license and other personal papers, almost as if Williams was saying, "Complete investigation? Hogwash!"

But that wasn't all. A few feet away, the unsuspecting postal workers found a burned human torso.

Recently promoted Col. Herbert Anderson was called; in turn, Anderson made some calls of his own, one of them to TWA, which dispatched three officials to Las Vegas at once. To these officials, Colonel Anderson "expressed the very definite request that this portion of the body be buried at the scene of the crash and that reopening of the inquest and efforts at further identification be avoided if at all possible." Anderson reasoned that the discovery would only rip open the wounds of the grieving families, particularly of the three boys who had been cremated and their ashes divided for burial. This was the official excuse he used with Clark County representatives: sensitivity to the families of crash victims. TWA certainly didn't want more headlines over the crash of its passenger plane, and the government had no interest in its investigation being proven so obviously incomplete.

On Friday, April 17, Clark County Sheriff Glenn Jones, Deputy Coroner Lawrence, and the TWA men climbed to the one place they hoped never to see again. There, said L.W. Goss of TWA, "we found partial remains of a human body consisting of the upper part of the torso and the back portion of the head. This portion was very badly burned on all sides and it was very apparent that any clothing which had been on this portion of the body would have been burned completely. It therefore appeared definitely certain that the portion of the uniform coat which had been found adjacent was not on this body at the time the body was burned...."

In accordance with Colonel Anderson's "urgent request" not to reopen the inquest, the men buried the remains at the scene and the incident never made newspapers. The U.S. Army and TWA now desperately wanted the case of Flight 3 to go away—an unsecured crash scene where artifacts, including human remains, would continue to surface. As Waldon Golien had said, significant articles could be recovered at the Potosi site for years. And since most of Carole Lombard's jewelry remained unaccounted for, looting was inevitable and the mountain far too dangerous for routine travel.

Three days after the burial of the body, a demolition crew recruited by Deputy Coroner Lawrence and sponsored by TWA rushed to the crash site—as fast as one could rush when climbing a mountain hand over hand—and spent four days attempting to dynamite the cliff above the wreck to bury the wreckage and whatever human remains and artifacts lingered there. But the mountain wouldn't cooperate, leading Goss to report that "the blasting operations had been very unsuccessful and that although much of the wreckage had been covered with rock, some of the larger pieces, such as wing sections and portions of the tail surface was still visible." Heavy equipment and a lot more dynamite would be required, meaning a tremendous expense to TWA; at that point the operation was abandoned, and the wreck of Flight 3 was left to time, nature, and the fates.

The scars in the cliff wall made by the nose, wings, and engines of the DC-3 were sufficiently deep that they remained, as did scars on the families of the victims. Fred Peters, who lost a mother and sister, refused to speak about the crash for the remainder of his life, and forbade his son, also named Fred, to fly on airliners.

Following the death of her new husband, 2d Lt. Fred Dittman, Violet Dittman never remarried and felt his loss another sixty-six years, until her death in 2008.

Lt. Linton D. Hamilton mourned the death of his wife Lois as he continued to fly for the Eleventh Air Force, 21st Bomb Group, based in Alaska. Almost a year to the day after the death of his bride, Lieutenant Hamilton and his flight crew were lost at sea in air combat over the Pacific.

Twenty-one years after the deaths of the Nygren brothers, a Citation of Honor of the United States Army Air Force issued to Ed Nygren showed up at their father's house in Dunbar, Pennsylvania. There was no corresponding honor for younger Bob. Five years after that, Fred Nygren joined his first wife, daughter, and two sons in death at age eighty-three.

Alice Getz's fiancé, Lt. Robert Burnett, wrote to Alice's sister Marie: "Every day I picture just what life would be with our darling to share it. I'm lost, Marie, really I am. I didn't realize it could ever be so terribly hard, but I'm beginning to know. It's strange how out of all the people I've met and meet every day, none approaches the ideals Alice held."

Her other beau, Bud Ode, also wrote to Marie of his sense of loss: "Sometimes when I'm having quite a lot of fun and seem to be enjoying life for a moment, something will remind me of her and take me back. There are so many things that remind me of her."

Fred and Katie Getz filed a $25,000 lawsuit against TWA for the wrongful death of their daughter, although they knew this wouldn't ease the pain or bring back lovely Alice, the baby of the family. "My grandfather was never the same," said Doris Brieser, the niece of Alice Getz. "He'd sit every night by the window. He had a cross and two candles on the table and every night he'd pray and he'd sit there and cry about her."

Then there was Mary Johnson, the girl who *knew* she would see Clark Gable at the termination of Flight 3, only to be bumped in Albuquerque. Mary made the local papers for being the girl who lived, who escaped what one headline labeled a "fiery plane death" to serve through the war as a civil servant for the National Advisory Committee for Aeronautics at Moffett Field, California. In the capacity of research librarian for NACA, she received a copy of the preliminary report by the CAB on the crash of the TWA flight, the one she should have died on. She noted that the report said the plane was overloaded and remembered that indeed it was. And she saw that the pilot had taken the wrong flight path.

Mary proclaimed to a reporter in 2002, "I've always been lucky." She said in 2013, as the last remaining passenger who had ridden aboard Flight 3 on its last day, "I was on government travel. I could have said, 'I have to stay on this plane.' But I didn't. I'm not that aggressive."

46

If I Can Do It, So Can You

Carole Lombard and Elizabeth Peters shared many experiences—including dying—and, prior to that, the writing of wills. In the summer of 1939 both had updated those wills, Carole because of her altered marital status and Petey because she had moved from Beverly Hills with Fred, Virginia, and Tootie to a large frame home on North Saltair Avenue in quiet Brentwood. Petey left everything to her three children to be divided equally; Carole, knowing that her brothers would be taken care of by Mother and figuring she would have a long life ahead with Clark Gable, left everything to her husband.

Announcement was made on January 29, 1942, that Petey's will had been read and that her sons would share equally and also claim their sister's portion of an estate valued somewhere in the six figures. Two days earlier, Gable had filed four insurance claims, two to Penn Mutual Life Insurance Company for policies Carole had taken out in 1934 totaling $75,000, one with John Hancock for $25,000, and another with Equitable Life for $10,000.

Carole's agreement to accept less salary in exchange for a percentage of *To Be or Not to Be*, the picture with the name that wasn't box office, ended up netting her estate, and therefore Gable, $57,307 when audiences flocked to see Lombard on the big screen one last time.

The money was little consolation for the loss of Ma, yet it was his legally, and Clark Gable never met a dollar he didn't like. Along those lines, Gable now severed ties with Fritz and Tootie; he had just plain disliked Fred from the start; Stu was tolerable enough as a drinking buddy but not the kind of company that Gable would choose to keep had it not been for Carole. In the eyes of Ma and Pa, the wills of Petey and Carole had been written strategically and the boys had gotten all they were going to get.

Virginia Peters, Fred's wife, telephoned the ranch one day and Jean took the call. She handed the phone to Gable and after a short, brusque conversation, the king slammed down the receiver. He told Jean that the boys expected to be given Carole's clothes, which is why he hung up on Virginia.

Clark Gable chose not to initiate contact with either brother for the remainder of his lifetime. They had unknowingly hit a nerve—upon his return to the ranch, Clark had closed and locked Ma's bedroom with all the contents inside, and he wasn't about to touch it for anyone. As much as the crypt at Forest Lawn was a tomb, so was Lombard's bedroom at the farm, a tomb like those for the pharaohs in Egypt. All that Carole would need for the afterlife remained intact and ready, from her jewelry to her furs, hats, dresses, shoes, purses, hairbrushes, compacts, and lip rouge. Where she had last set them, that's where they would remain—just one more little way Pa could be close to Ma.

In the days after her death, Clark made pals with Carole's dachshund, Commissioner, a dog he had never liked. Clark also continued to feed and care for the doves. Otherwise, he remained a man alone, drifting about Hollywood. When Lucille Ball occasionally heard a motorcycle coming up Devonshire Drive in Chatsworth, she would know the king was stopping by to talk about the queen for a while, and she would accommodate him. She felt that he was a man in trouble and might do himself harm, that he rode that bike "so recklessly," and so she would encourage him to leave the bike parked there so she could drive him where he needed to go. He didn't care; sure, whatever.

Gable returned to MGM to resume production of *Somewhere I'll Find You* with Lana Turner. MGM contract stars Robert Taylor and Franchot Tone were two who experienced shock at the change in Gable, describing him as "bleary-eyed and haggard."

When Gable blanched at the now-ironic title of this picture, MGM changed it to "Red Light," then later changed it back. The story remained a typically sassy MGM action romance covering the outbreak of the world war. Gable stumbled around the sound-stages, a man lost, his confidence shot, trying too hard to cover his grief. His performance was shrill, and in every scene his eyes revealed death and mourning. On the Culver City lot he was hit with a double-barreled dose of reality because yes, Ma was gone, but so was Wink, the man always present on the MGM lot to serve him. Said Howard Strickling of Gable's life in the happy old days, "He'd expect Otto down [on the set] every morning because Otto was his pal. Sometimes Otto would go down on the set and if Clark was busy, Otto would almost cry. They had a great devotion, these two." Gable realized in hindsight what he had had prior to January 16, what he had so taken for granted, and what he had lost, not only a one-in-a-million wife, but a one-in-a-million best friend in Otto Winkler.

Gable finally learned of the existence of the lock of hair that Wheelright had cut at the mortuary. Pa asked Jean to have a locket created that would hold strands of the hair and the fragment of diamond-and-ruby clip recovered at the crash site. He intended to wear it around his neck every minute, day and night, so he could keep Ma right next to his heart.

Everyone on the MGM lot deferred to the grieving man and kept a respectful distance, including Lana. But she refused to experience any guilt over the fact that Clark and Carole had quarreled over Gable's fascination with Turner. Lana later shrugged at the thought and said, "No one forced Carole to take the plane. It was her decision and her decision alone."

Joan Crawford sensed Clark's crushed spirit and invited him over to her home in Brentwood. He went, every night, and sought solace in his once-and-again lover's arms. Crawford was Crawford; there was no one else like her. An original, like Lombard, except Joan was all pretense and sweeping gesture. But oh, how she could comfort him with that silken, empathetic voice and talented body.

He drifted through the months on a sea of booze. He knew he was no longer the man of the Gable brand, and so did MGM. He just didn't give a damn anymore. The studio desired that its cash cow would remain in Hollywood for the duration of the war, but Gable didn't want to make pictures; Gable wanted to die, and the best way to accomplish that was to enlist and go to war in airplanes so that if he got it, he would go down like Ma and be close to her in one final way.

Of Gable's subsequent enlistment in the Army Air Forces, the same branch as those fliers lost with Lombard, Richard Lang said, "I don't think that Clark was patriotically impelled; I think he was *suicidally* impelled, as if to say, if she died I want to as well."

Jill Winkler was similarly lost without her Winkie. Jill's niece Nazoma quit her job at a movie theater in North Hollywood to care for Jill. Said Gail Strickling of Jill, "She couldn't accept this thing. She kept going into these awful relapses." During a low point, Jill escaped her niece's attention and drove to a cliff above the ocean, where she contemplated suicide. "She was sitting there thinking, should I do this or not," said Nazoma, "and was planning to do it when she heard Carole's voice: 'No, Jill, no! Don't you do it!' So Jill backed away and came home and no longer contemplated suicide."

"No," she told her niece, "Carole doesn't want me to do that."

Lombard's forceful presence would come to Lucille Ball in a similar way. In 1951 a thirty-nine-year-old Ball seemed to have worn out her welcome on the big screen and considered a last-ditch, highly doubtful move to television. Her doubts vanished when Carole Lombard appeared in a vivid dream and said, "Honey, go ahead. Take a chance. Give it a whirl."

Gable made sure that Jill Winkler would have a roof over her head and paid for construction of a ranch house in Encino on Louise Drive directly across the street from the Stricklings and just a mile from the Gable ranch. Otto had purchased the lot, but Gable paid for construction, using his own money or under-the-table funding from TWA. Officially, airline president Jack Frye was notified on October 17, 1942, by internal memo that "the passenger liability claims of Lombard, Peters, and Winkler have been settled for a total of $40,000." This shockingly low number did not reflect the July 1942 published results of the House investigation, which ascribed blame for the crash and the "appalling loss" to Wayne Williams. The House also blamed the Labor Board for reinstating the pilot back in 1933.

The fact that the Lombard, Peters, and Winkler claims were settled together indicates MGM's involvement representing the estates on Gable's behalf. For some reason, Clark had signed away his rights to sue the airline and had encouraged the attorneys for Peters and Winkler to do the same. These actions hint at an under-the-table solution to the claims between MGM and TWA that would keep the matter out of newspapers. Said Howard Strickling, cryptically, "Clark refused to make any settlement until they did the right thing by Jill."

On August 11, 1942, almost seven months after the crash of TWA Flight 3, Clark Gable drove his motorcycle over the mile from the ranch to Jill's newly completed house on Louise Avenue where Jill and her niece Nazoma sat eating breakfast; just two turns separated the Gable and Winkler homes. Clark was one day away from being sworn into the Army, and he said to Jill, "Honey, I'm going over there and I don't give a damn if I come back. But if I do come back, you and I will get married." It was something to bank on for two lonely souls adrift, knowing there might be a haven out there somewhere, beyond the pain.

The next day Clark Gable enlisted as a private in the U.S. Army Air Forces. A deal had been prearranged between the War Department and MGM: Gable would complete Officers Candidate School in thirteen weeks and then ship out to England, where he would be stationed at one of the many B-17 and B-24 bases in East Anglia and shoot a feature documentary to recruit machine gunners to serve on heavy bombers. He was now forty-one and looked all that and more after seven brutal months of grief and drinking. Suddenly, he found himself surrounded by men half his age who possessed many times his vitality. The old Gable would have sought favors and cut corners; the new Gable played by the book and began to garner respect. At the end of October, he graduated as 2nd Lt. Clark Gable. A little later, he earned aerial gunner wings and then promotion to captain. Each accomplishment provided some satisfaction—Ma would be proud—but never happiness. The capacity for happiness had left him.

In November Jill wrote to Clark saying she had received her portion of the settlement from TWA. On a postcard he wrote from Panama City, Florida, "Was glad to hear you got everything settled so now the next thing to do is be sure and hang on to it. That's very important." Otto had told Clark often enough how freely she spent money, and the lump sum could go fast. In the postcard, which was dated November 28, Gable worried openly about the potential spending and about her state of mind. "Your place must look very nice by now," wrote the widower. "I hope you don't get too much time by yourself. Keep busy. Clark."

He shipped over to England with the 508th squadron of the 351st Bombardment Group (Heavy), 1st Air Division, Eighth Air Force. In May he took his camera up on a B-17 bombing run over Belgium. On this first mission aboard a Flying Fortress, which should have been an easy "milk run" across the English Channel, an enemy shell fired from a flak cannon shot up through the bottom of the fuselage and punched out the top, missing him by an inch. He learned at once what life was like at this point in the war, with enemy fighters and flak potent and lethal, yet Gable went up again as soon as possible. He would go on to expose thousands of feet of Technicolor film for his documentary about life in a bomber, flying missions more dangerous than anything concocted by MGM. He kept Ma right at hand in that locket he wore around his neck. John Lee Mahin, the man assigned by MGM to look after Gable in the service, said Clark would often touch the locket, which was, he murmured at one point, "All I have left of her."

During his time in England, many men in Gable's group died. When they did, he took it personally. "He would write wonderful, compassionate, connected letters to the families of comrades in arms who had died," said Carole Sampeck. "I've seen some of them. Just beautiful. He could have been spending his time going out and getting laid; that ability to connect with people was something that Lombard gave him."

By October 1943 the Eighth Air Force could no longer stand life with a king in its midst. He was a captain but without the military experience to do much more than fire a .50-caliber machine gun in an Army Air Force that needed its officers to be top-notch pilots, navigators, or bombardiers. And the commotion produced by his presence was counterproductive to an effective war machine. He may have been an Army captain, but he was also a king and had reverted to that rank, wined and dined by top brass and looking for female companionship.

The Army packed Clark Gable up and shipped him home to Los Angeles. He arrived in a smartly tailored U.S. Army Air Forces uniform adorned with an Air Medal combat ribbon, and cans and cans of Technicolor film ready to make his movie. There he learned from Gen. Hap Arnold that there was no longer a need for a film to recruit aerial gunners. The Army had plenty now, which meant that Gable must find another angle for a film that nobody really wanted or needed. Disillusioned, forced to face life after combat at an all-too-tranquil ranch, he set to editing a feature documentary that he knew had become obsolete. It starred the commanders and fliers of the 351st Bomb Group and included General Arnold along with shots of Bob Hope and Frances Langford entertaining the troops in England. Gable collaborated on the editing at MGM and narrated the hour-long picture, which carried the final title of *Combat America*.

In January 1944 Captain Gable in Army uniform attended the launch of a 441-foot, 10,500-ton Liberty freighter called the *Carole Lombard* at the port of San Pedro, California. Irene Dunne christened the ship, with Madalynne Field as matron of honor. Louis B. Mayer and several politicians spoke. Gable was asked to give remarks but as usual declined and stood there weeping as the ship slid into the water.

A new Gable emerged from the process of grief and wartime sacrifice. No, he would not marry Jill Winkler; neither of them really wanted that. He stayed close to Fieldsie for a time and every six weeks or so she would host a party, where the king hung out with Lombard's pals Cesar Romero and Fred MacMurray as well as Ty Power and John Payne. "All actors are children," said Richard Lang, an observer of this gang of five. "The ego and self-importance are always there. I saw them relaxed and they were letting off steam." Gable never lacked feminine companionship, whether it was producer Joan Harrison, model Anita Colby, or the woman everyone figured he would marry, actress Virginia Grey. Everyone knew he had changed, and always the same words described him. Sad. Isolated. Haunted. Alone.

No longer a boy, now a man; no longer self-involved, now the product of five years with Carole Lombard. "It was unbelievable how both characters changed," said Jean Garceau of those five years. "He was pinch penny and worried about everything. She had great assurance and was very generous…. They rubbed off on each other." No one understood just how much, especially Gable, until she was gone.

"It was an epiphany that he had," said Carole Sampeck. "The good part of her lived on in him. She couldn't even get him to really communicate, to give of himself while she lived, but all of a sudden, he got it."

Even acerbic Orson Welles would describe Gable as "terribly nice. Just a nice big hunk of man."

Early in 1945, with Clark a retired Army major, he cracked up his car on Sunset Boulevard; the king was DUI in the middle of the night and taken hush-hush by Strickling's people to Cedars of Lebanon Hospital, where Gable spent days recuperating from a laceration and concussion. His doctor happened to mention another MGM patient at the hospital at that time, contract player Susan Peters, a rising star in the studio system who had been paralyzed in a shooting accident the New Year's Day just past. It was clear she would never walk again, and her spirits were low. The old Gable might have felt sympathy for a moment and then gone on with his day. The new Gable went further and asked to see her.

"I must have startled him," said Peters of Clark Gable, "for at that time I was a bag of bones and had my hair in pigtails which I am told made me look a sharp twelve. I was almost completely hidden by strange bottles, tubes, lamps, and other weird hospital gadgets. But if he was dismayed he certainly didn't show it."

They chatted for a while. The next day Gable sent her flowers.

When she finally returned home from the hospital, MGM arranged for Peters to write a series of articles for *Photoplay* magazine entitled "My Hollywood Friends," and late in 1945 she called Gable asking for an interview. The king had turned down the entire legion of Hollywood scribes since Lombard's death. He simply would not talk to the press or consider talking. But after almost four years, to Susan Peters he said yes and just before Christmas drove to her house in Malibu. There he sat, poised and patient, for questions from the wheelchair-bound waif, who brought up the touchy subject of his wife's loss. Peters described Gable's "loneliness when he spoke of Carole Lombard…, their fishing and hunting trips together and the wonderful times they had. He was leaving on a fishing trip the next day. Fishing trips aren't the same any more but above all he wanted to be away through the holidays."

Flash forward another three years when Gable would seek out a woman named Nedra Etting, whose husband, popular singer Buddy Clark, had been killed in a freak air crash in Beverly Hills. When asked why he had contacted Etting, he explained that he could understand what she was going through. Said actress Ursula Theiss: "I remember Clark telling me about this incident of getting together because both of them were in the same boat. Nedra taught him to turn on the television and look at some old movies of Carole, because she [Nedra] was able to listen to her husband's records. So this is the way they helped each other."

In the old days Gable had been a lot more fun, a big kid, a giggler with Lombard, and now he had developed a compassionate streak that would indeed have made Ma proud—never more so than at the holidays in 1944. Alice Marble had been married to an Army pilot for a year, had gotten pregnant, and then suffered a miscarriage after a car crash. At the Battle of the Bulge, Alice's new husband was shot down and killed in Belgium; she received word during the singing of Christmas carols at a party with friends. Telegram in hand, one that read, "We regret to inform you…," she walked to her room and swallowed a bottle's worth of sleeping pills. She was rushed to the hospital and barely survived.

Back at the ranch, Clark Gable learned of Allie's plight from Teach Tennant. In the old days Carole would have coached him on what to do, but now Gable didn't need any coaching. He acted on new instincts.

In her hospital room, Alice Marble lay there grieving for her husband, believing there was no reason to go on. Life was over. Husband gone. Unborn child gone. The one person who might have been able to understand was Missy Carole, Allie's benefactor who had shared all her confidences, who always knew the right thing to say, the right thing to do, and the right advice to give. God bless. Angels keep.

Carole had given Alice so much over the years, and it had all begun with that letter and its incredible message. If I can do it, so can you, if you fight. But Carole had gone as well, dead almost three years now, and there lay Alice, despondent in a hospital bed.

Suddenly, all was commotion. Nurses barged into the room and surrounded the grief-stricken widow, Alice Marble, with red roses, three dozen of them. Splashes of vivid color surrounded her and she lay there, bewildered. Allie was handed a card. It read, *If I can do it, so can you. Clark.*

Epilogue

High-Energy Impact

On the evening of Thursday, November 8, 2007, a Cessna T182t single-engine aircraft designated as flight 2793 took off from North Las Vegas Airport at 7:05 P.M. on a dark, nearly moonless night. Two vastly experienced fliers sat at the controls, one a NASA pilot and the former Pacific Region Commander of the Civil Air Patrol and the other the Nevada Wing Commander of the Civil Air Patrol. Col. Ed Lewis had served as the Aviation Safety Officer at NASA's Dryden Flight Research Center located at Edwards Air Force Base and flown NASA's DC-8 "flying laboratory" in addition to many other NASA science aircraft based at Dryden. Colonel Lewis and copilot Dion DeCamp had accumulated almost 60,000 hours of flight time between them.

They flew southwest out of Vegas heading toward a science conference in Rosamond, California. November 8 featured fine weather for flying with winds of only three knots, so their flight plan called for visual flight rules—using references on the ground to guide them. Their aircraft was relatively new, with only 300 hours of air time, and was equipped with a sophisticated Garmin G1000 glass cockpit (an integrated flight instrument system composed of two LCD display units) and tracked by sophisticated radar in Vegas and at Daggett control center. Below them, the lights of modern Las Vegas sprawled as far as the eye could see, casinos as mighty as the Luxor and the Bellagio, shopping meccas, and sprouting housing developments stretching to the foothills of the mountains. Their plane flew over I-15, which paralleled the road that had once been Highway 91, and then over Arden and Blue Diamond Road on a night with just broken clouds at 8,000 and high clouds at 15,000.

Thirteen minutes after takeoff, the Cessna piloted by Lewis and DeCamp slammed into the vertical cliff wall of Potosi Mountain and exploded in a fireball seen by residents across Las Vegas. The National Transportation Safety Board final statement about the accident of flight 2793, released in January 2009, sounded eerily familiar to anyone who knew about the crash of TWA Flight 3 so many years earlier:

> The accident occurred during dark night, visual meteorological conditions, about 13 minutes into the night cross-country flight. No lighted roads or ground structures were present in the area to provide ground reference to terrain. One percent of the moon's disk was illuminated. Over the last 6 minutes of the flight, recorded radar data indicated the airplane's average groundspeed was 100 knots and its average rate of climb was 406 feet per minute; an average rate of climb of 600 fpm was required to clear terrain along the flight path. An examination of the accident site indicated that the airplane impacted rapidly rising terrain in a near level flight attitude before descending and coming to rest in a rock outcropping. The resultant high-energy impact forces, coupled with the extensive thermal damage, destroyed the airplane. A post-accident examination of the airframe's structure and engine failed to reveal any pre-impact failures or malfunctions. The airplane was equipped with a Garmin G1000 Integrated Cockpit System, which incorporates a multifunction color display that is capable of displaying terrain elevation information when selected to the Terrain Proximity page. Due to the extensive impact and thermal damage that the component had sustained, it was not possible

to determine if the pilot was using the display to receive topographic data during the airplane's ascent.

Colonel Lewis had been trained on the G1000, but the unit contained a warning that the system could not be relied upon for primary terrain avoidance. It remained the pilot's responsibility to be aware of the terrain at all times. The NTSB determined that the crash was an example of what had become known as Controlled Flight into Terrain (CFIT), wherein a fully functioning plane under pilot control had flown into land or water. Since the plane "was receiving VFR flight-following services from the Las Vegas Terminal Radar Approach Control facility," the radar controller on duty was partially responsible for failing to issue a "terrain-related safety alert, as required by a Federal Aviation Administration order."

Wayne Williams, Morgan Gillette, Ed Lewis, and Dion De-Camp carried to the grave those last moments that had set their aircraft on a collision course with Potosi Mountain. Despite 25,000 hours of flight time, sophisticated, three-dimensional cockpit displays, and the most modern air traffic control support, Lewis had flown straight into the mountain. It was a simple conclusion for investigators who had no other explanation, just as it was back in 1942 when Flight 3 had impacted those same cliffs with the same fiery result.

In some ways the impact of Flight 3 with Potosi Mountain on January 16, 1942, was a crash heard around the world. Carole Lombard became the first Hollywood star to die in World War II and would be joined later by motion picture leading man Leslie Howard and bandleader Glenn Miller, both of whom, like Lombard, met their deaths on airplanes.

Flying was how Albert Belejchak had managed to escape a life broiling in the steel mills along the Monongahela River in smoke-choked Pittsburgh. Flying was how eight-year-old Charles Castle sought to escape the farm fields of Pawnee, Illinois, although he never did, and it turned out that the big adventure Charles had asked God for in 1930 was the biggest of his life. Castle died in Pawnee in 2002 at age eighty-one.

Flying always did well by Burton Kennedy Voorhees, who had given away his seat assignment to help Fred Dittman realize a dream. Voorhees was typical of Barham, Browne, Crouch, Dittman, Donahue, Nelson, and Swenson—top-notch officers and pilots in the Ferrying Command who likely would have shot up through the ranks in the Army Air Forces. But they were gone and Voorhees went on. He lived to see his brother get married sixteen days after the crash of Flight 3. He lived to become a major before 1942 ended. He lived to marry Cuyler Griffith Schwartz, daughter of a former Wyoming senator. He lived to become Lieutenant Colonel Voorhees and take over the Air Transport Command at Consolidated Airfield in Tucson, where in autumn 1945 he coordinated the passage home of thousands of returning servicemen aboard DC-3s and their military counterpart, the C-47. He lived to enjoy a rich and full family life until his death in Sun City, Arizona, in 1984, and always haunting the corners of his mind was that moment in Albuquerque with Fred Dittman.

But Potosi would only grudgingly give up its Flight 3 secrets, and over many decades. In 2014 hikers on Mt. Potosi found remains at the crash site, including part of a skull along with ribs and long bones, and the Clark County coroner's office was called to the scene. Coroner's investigator Felicia Borla used *Fireball* to ground herself in the story, and began a search for living family members of the three servicemen who couldn't be identified—Ed Nygren, Hal Browne, Jr., and Kenneth Donahue. Over the course of a year, DNA samples from all three families were obtained via cheek swabs. Borla made a positive identification after eighteen months, and in August 2016, more than seventy-four years after the crash, 2nd Lt. Kenneth Donahue made one last journey from McCarran International Airport to Hartsfield-Jackson in Atlanta and then to Logan in Boston, with an honor guard present at each location. Finally Donahue reached Biddeford, Maine, where he was buried with honors in Saint Mary's Cemetery.

For Donahue it was a long journey in death. For many "survivors" of Flight 3, those directly affected by the crash, the journey was hard in life. Lyle "Bull" Van Gordon, who blazed the trail that led to the downed airliner on the snowy morning of January 17, 1942, fathered two boys after daughter Nancy and left Goodsprings for Oregon in 1944. He always regretted not taking his gridiron prowess on to college and, after giving up on mining, spent his career working for the power company. A down-to-earth man, he would never discuss his role in the recovery of Flight 3 and when pressed would grumble, "I didn't do anything." Lyle died of cancer in 1978.

Fieldsie was another survivor who grieved for her lost friend Carole Lombard for the remaining thirty-two years of her life. In 1973 she stepped out her front door to pick up the morning paper in Palm Springs and was savagely beaten by a mugger. The incident defeated a fierce woman, and she died in October 1974.

Jill Winkler never came to grips with the loss of her Winkie, instead blocking the memories from her mind. She would go on to lose the home that Carole helped her design and Clark helped her build in Encino, across the street from Howard and Gail Strickling. Jill died in September 1994.

Margaret Tallichet, the young publicity girl at Paramount whom Lombard promoted for stardom, married director William Wyler in 1938 and bore him four children. William Wyler died in 1981 and Talli lived on to 1991 and always fondly remembered her mentor, fireball Carole Lombard, and the wacky publicity campaign of 1937 that led to a few starring roles in pictures—and one of Hollywood's most enduring marriages.

Alice Marble lived through her 1944 suicide attempt and went on to become a tennis instructor like Teach Tennant. In fact, Tennant and Marble became rival teachers for many years until Teach's death in 1963. Among Allie's pupils was nine-year-old future NASA astronaut Sally Ride. "For two weeks I stood at the net, tossing her balls to volley," said the plain-spoken and hard-drinking Marble, "and for two weeks she tried to hit me in the face. I told her parents to find another target." Alice admitted that Teach "would have loved the fight" in Sally Ride.

Alice Marble wrote two books in her lifetime, and both included vivid descriptions of life with Carole Lombard. Tennis great Jack Kramer said in the 1980s that Allie was "the lady who most changed the style of play for women. She introduced the aggressive and athletic style that has led down to the female stars of today like Billie Jean King, Martina Navratilova, and Steffi Graf." In fact, King had been Marble's pupil in the early 1960s.

Said King, "Alice Marble was a picture of unrestrained athleticism. She is remembered as one of the greatest women to play the game because of her pioneering style in power tennis." All of that had been made possible thanks to a whim by Carole Lombard to help a girl in a TB sanatorium. It was an act of kindness that rubbed off on Marble who, said Billie Jean, "always helped others." Alice Marble died in 1990 at age seventy-seven, having taught tennis to new generations until the end of her life.

"If I can do it, so can you," Clark had said to Allie, paraphrasing Missy Carole, but Clark Gable never recovered from the death of the woman he called Ma. His malaise continued and his career suffered. He aged badly, beginning that weekend in Las Vegas. He would keep the ranch that he had created with Ma and he would brood over every inch of it, holding tight to memories of places she had stood and things she had said and done in those spots.

At length, after his brief military career, Gable threw himself into life at the ranch and made it his own for the remainder of his lifetime. Jean Garceau ran it day-to-day and Clark reaped the benefits. He also became the most eligible bachelor in Hollywood and played the field long after the war ended. The fan magazines handicapped the Gable marriage sweepstakes and gave the inside track to longtime girlfriend Virginia Grey. Virginia had never married and, it was said, she insisted on waiting for Clark to ask.

He would marry two more times, but never to Virginia Grey. Maybe she was just too nice, too settled, and not enough of a handful. Instead, he picked two spitfires he hoped would replicate Carole Lombard. Neither did. He married Sylvia Ashley, former showgirl whose marriage to screen idol Douglas Fairbanks, Sr., made world headlines, but this particular spitfire broke the seal on Lombard's bedroom and disposed of its contents. Clark divorced her soon after. His last wife, named Kay, pretended to be Carole for Clark's benefit and used bad language and behaved like a tough broad. But she never had Ma's big, warm heart and managed to alienate most of the people who had been in Gable's life during his years with Lombard. Jean Garceau was dismissed, and eventually the old guard of friends fell away.

Time marched on for the places as well. The Gable ranch, where Carole and Clark spent two-and-a-half tumultuous years, saw its twenty acres sold off by Kay Gable, and today the ranch house and Gable's garage sit pressed in on all sides by other houses, garages, and swimming pools. The Cadle Tabernacle, where Carole Lombard drew 12,000 people on January 15, 1942, and led them in the singing of the *Star-Spangled Banner*, succumbed to the wrecking ball at the end of 1968 to make way for a parking lot.

In a sense, time did *not* march on for Clark Gable, and it caused worry for his Hollywood friends. Steve Hayes remembered occasions with Ava Gardner, who was, if anything, earthier than Lombard and a good deal darker: "When I had lunch or a drink with Ava, I would ask her how Gable was and had she seen him lately. She'd shrug those incredible creamy shoulders of hers and say either yes or no or 'same old, same old,' but then she'd always add something like, 'That poor son of a bitch, my heart bleeds for him.

I mean, here's a great guy, a real sweetheart who's maybe the biggest movie star of us all, Sugar, the fucking king for chrissake, and the poor bastard has nothing to look forward to.'"

Clark left MGM on bad terms in 1954 and became an independent. His last hurrah was the Seven Arts feature *The Misfits*, directed by John Huston and co-starring Marilyn Monroe. It was shot on the other side of Nevada from Las Vegas and Potosi Mountain. It was said that Marilyn's antics on the set of *The Misfits*—her tardiness and neuroses—contributed to the heart attack that felled the king on November 6, 1960, just past the end of production. It began with a sharp pain in his chest as he worked on his car by the garage at the ranch. Ten days later, after it seemed he would recover, Clark Gable died at Presbyterian Hospital in Van Nuys. His funeral was held at the Church of the Recessional, Forest Lawn Glendale, where almost nineteen years earlier he had been forced to say good-bye to Carole, Petey, and Otto. After the service, the body of the fallen king was driven down the hill to the Great Mausoleum. Despite having had two more wives, Clark Gable was laid to rest next to what was left of Carole Lombard, the woman who had loved him, challenged him, made him complete, and left him because of a desperate, uncharacteristic, and irrational need to secure her place in his heart. In a twist worthy of Hollywood, Lombard never learned that she meant everything to Gable. Everything. But he learned it and woke up every morning with this information and went to bed every night with it for the 6,874 sunrises and sunsets remaining in what was, for him, a very long lifetime.

Acknowledgments

My thanks up front to those who helped to deepen the content found in this expanded version of *Fireball*. They include Patricia Hirsch, who provided early information about the magnificent Tuckaway in Indianapolis. Kenneth Keene, late owner of Tuckaway, welcomed us inside for a tour and interview. Elizabeth Kelley Cierzniak conducted research on Carole's Indianapolis activities and the Claypool Hotel. Jennifer Hodge and Rose Wernicke provided a guided tour of the Indiana State House and helped to identify the exact location of Lombard's hour of bond selling. Douglas J. Cohen provided several key documents related to Carole's day in Indianapolis as well as photos used herein. Rosalynn DeFelice gave an eyewitness account of Carole's bond speech. Brian Lee Anderson tracked down and made available a recording of the Cadle Tabernacle speech as well as other key documents. Nadia Kousari of the Indiana Historical Society made available key images for this expanded photo section. Jeannie Clapper lent information related to the Baha'i faith. Felicia Borla of the Clark County coroner's office discussed the case of Kenneth Donahue with me. Maureen Green also discussed Kenneth, who was her uncle, and talked about the emotional experience of his 2016 burial.

The development of this book was pure magic, from long before the climb of the mountain. I would like to thank John McElwee for sitting with me in Columbus, Ohio, and laying out a vision for the book that became *Fireball*, and Carole Sampeck for her expertise and especially for her sensitivity, partnership, and gentle spirit in fulfilling the *Fireball* vision. It couldn't have happened without you, CB.

Many others were essential to this project, and their contributions unique and invaluable: Mary Savoie spent time telling me what it was like to ride on Flight 3 for 1,500 miles the day it crashed, Tom Wilson put me on the trail of Mary Johnson, Marie Earp connected me with the Savoie family, and Spencer and Becky Savoie told me about their incredible mother and shared a hoard of fascinating information about Mary's role in the last flight of TWA Flight 3; Jim Boone provided intrepid leadership in the climb of Potosi Mountain; researcher Ann Trevor unearthed great treasures, including the TWA crash files and the House transcripts and, ultimately, the long-sought FBI file on the crash; Marina Gray made many incredible research finds on the people aboard Flight 3 and helped to secure the Myron Davis photographs; David Phillips (a great guy) made it possible to land the photos of Myron Davis for this book; Steve Hayes gave his time and extra effort to reminisce about his friends Clark Gable, Lana Turner, Ava Gardner, Franchot Tone, and Robert Taylor; Lyn Tornabene donated her research materials to the Academy and thus made them available to me for this book; Marie Levi and Donita Dixon shared information about their cousin, Lois Mary Miller Hamilton; Burton Brooks helped to connect me with Doris Brieser, who reminisced with me about Aunt Alice (Getz), and she and Cindy Lightle shared their amazing family scrapbook; Steve and Doug Van Gordon provided photos and information about their father, Lyle, and mother, Elizabeth; Nancy Myer gave insights on Lombard and Gable; Stacey Behlmer and the staff at the Margaret Herrick Library at the Academy of Motion Picture Arts and Sciences generously and patiently helped Mary and me comb the archives with emphasis on the Lyn Tornabene collection; Mike McComb made available the CAB transcripts and key photos, and lent his aviation and research expertise to the project; David Stenn provided guidance, leads, and research on both Gable and Lombard; Nazoma Roznos Ball spent hours on the phone with me talking about Jill and Otto Winkler and made available Jill's original manuscript detailing the events leading up to the bond tour and the night of the crash; Mike Mazzone lent his expertise on John Barrymore and the production of *Twentieth Century*; Fred Peters III spoke with me about his father, Fred Peters, Carole Lombard's brother; Robert and Rosemarie Stack and their dog, Hollywood, shared their home with me on a memorable day as Bob reminisced about Carole; Debra Sloan-Shiflett went with me that day and helped with research on Lombard; Sharon Berk created another terrific book design; David Boutros and the University of Missouri-Kansas City conserved and made available the TWA files pertaining to the crash of Flight 3; Scott Eyman discussed with me the concept of *Fireball* and lent his expertise on both MGM and Ernst Lubitsch; James V. D'Arc shared his knowledge, energy, and enthusiasm about the project; Jeff Mantor, Mike Hawks, and the Larry Edmunds Bookshop provided friendship and support; Richard M. Roberts supplied his notes from interviews with stunt pilot Don Hackett; Neve Rendell lent perspective on Clark Gable; Jack El-Hai graciously granted permission to use portions of his blog about the Lombard FBI file; Robb Hill gave advice on climbing to the crash site and *Las Vegas Review Journal* news articles pertaining to the crash; Bob and Kathy Basl worked their magic to recapture the splendor in camera negatives created by Myron Davis; and Val Sloan provided her usual Photoshop wizardry. Lastly, I would like to thank Mary Matzen for taking on Potosi, walking up to the Encino Ranch, sitting with me at the Lombard and Gable crypts, researching at the Academy, reading this thing not twice but three times, and in all ways helping to make *Fireball* the book it needed to be.

Chapter Notes

1. A Perfectly Routine Friday Night

Accounts of the events of January 16, 1942, by Thomas Parnell, Charles Duffy, Ed Fuqua, and Floyd Munson were found in the Civil Aeronautics Board (CAB) official "Investigation of Accident Involving TWA Trip 3, Aircraft NC 1946, which occurred near Las Vegas, Nevada, January 16, 1942," Docket No. SA-58 (known throughout the Chapter Notes as "CAB investigation"), and in "Hearings Before a Select Committee on Air Accidents in the United States House of Representatives, 77th Congress, Second Session on House Resolutions 125 and 403, Executive Hearings in Las Vegas on January 21–33, 1942 and in Los Angeles January 23–27, 1942" (known as "House investigation").

2. Perpetual Motion Machine

Biographical information on early Carole Lombard came from a variety of sources, including Larry Swindell's biography, *Screwball*, which was written in 1975 when a number of Lombard's friends and relatives were still alive. Periodicals and files at the Margaret Herrick Library of the Academy of Motion Picture Arts and Sciences provided a wealth of material, including the Lyn Tornabene Collection of research gathered in writing her 1976 biography of Clark Gable, *Long Live the King*. Tornabene's audiotaped interviews with many notables from 1973–75 are available for study, including that of Delmer Daves, who spoke at length about his relationships with both Lombard and Gable.

3. The Radiating Halo

Descriptions of the Blue Diamond Mine, the village of Blue Diamond, and Mt. Potosi were based on my visits to the sites. The testimony of Yanich, Harper, and Salyer was found in the CAB investigation and House investigation transcripts, as was the story of Charlie and Ruth Hawley. Quotes by eyewitnesses received wide coverage in news stories that appeared within twenty-four hours of the accident as reporters struggled to make sense of the crash.

4. The Long Road

Various accounts covered the surgical procedure on Carole Lombard's face, and information about her subsequent treatment and recovery was taken primarily from the article "Scars That Glorified" by Agnes O'Malley, which appeared in the June 1929 issue of *Motion Picture Classic*, and from other allusions by Lombard to the accident. The article "Sophisticated at Sixteen" by Carter Bruce in the July 1931 issue of *Modern Screen* also helped. As for the spelling of Fieldsie's last name, for generations it has been spelled Fields with an *s* on the end, but all official records spell it without an *s*. The Academy Library houses Lyn Tornabene's audio interviews of Richard Lang and Margaret Wyler. My interviews with Lombard archivist Carole Sampeck in the fall of 2012 provided fresh perspective on the encounter with Joseph P. Kennedy. Contemporary articles at the Academy fleshed out the Lombard of this time; the Hughes and Liveright stories were unearthed by Swindell. Jill Winkler's niece, Nazoma Ball, provided perspectives on Carole Lombard and Jill in a series of interviews I conducted with her in 2012 and 2013. The relationship between Lombard and William Powell was widely chronicled in contemporary magazines. Robert Stack's memories of Carole Lombard and Clark Gable were collected in my conversations with him on the phone and in Bel Air as well as in his memoir, *Straight Shooting*.

5. A Long and Grim Weekend

An understanding of the geography of southern Nevada, including Ninety-Nine Mine Road, the village of Goodsprings, and the Walking Box Ranch, was obtained during my explorations of the area. The papers of the CAB investigation contained transcripts of the radio conversations between Flight 3, Las Vegas Air Traffic Control, and Burbank. The story of Thomas Parnell was taken from his testimony before the CAB and House investigations.

6. Merely Physical

Communications between Carole Lombard and Russ Columbo revealed their complex relationship. These were published in the 2002 biography *Russ Columbo and the Crooner Mystique* by Joseph Lanza and Dennis Penna. Their research revealed a tempestuous pairing unlike that described in previous biographical work and cast doubt on the often-repeated story that Lombard had described Columbo as the love her life to Noel Busch of *Life* magazine. My conversations with Greenbriar Picture Shows web host John McElwee and Barrymore expert Mike Mazzone helped to put *Twentieth Century* in proper perspective, and the account by Howard Hawks of working with Lombard and Barrymore on the picture appeared in Richard Schickel's *The Men Who Made the Movies*. Lombard's perspective was found in the article "Perfect Abandon for Carole Lombard" by William Fleming, which appeared in the June 1934 issue of *Shadoplay* magazine.

7. A Perfect Flying Experience

The experiences of Capt. Art Cheney were found in his testimony before the CAB and House investigations, as were transmissions between the ground and the Western Air vehicles in flight that evening.

8. Inflexible Fate

Coverage of the shooting of Russ Columbo was provided by the *Los Angeles Times*, with Lanza and Penna providing depth and perspective in *The Crooner Mystique*. Lombard's comments on the matter were found in a somewhat sanitized article, "We Would Have Married," by Sonia Lee in *Movie Classic*, December 1934. Descriptions of the Church of the Blessed Sacrament resulted from my visit to the site.

9. Jimmy Donnally Lands His Plane

I first discovered the story of Wayne Williams and Charles Castle while reviewing contemporary coverage of the crash of Flight 3 by the *Pittsburgh Press* in an article entitled "Flier Fulfills Hopes of Child: Pilot Killed in Crash Gave Illinois Boy Ride in '30." From there the trail led back to newspaper coverage of the Charles Castle story in Illinois newspapers from June 1930. In particular, a full account was contained in a three-column story syndicated nationally and entitled "Boy Makes Hero of Mail Aviator: Achieves Ambition to Ride with Idol and Is Now Official Mascot."

10. Calculated Mayhem

The views of George Raft were expressed in Lewis Yablonsky's 1974 Raft biography. The William Haines story was courtesy of Larry Swindell. Descriptions of Lombard's new tennis lifestyle came from an insightful in-person interview of Alice Marble by Lyn Tornabene that is available in the Tornabene collection at the Academy Library, with supplemental information in Marble's two memoirs, *The Road to Wimbledon* and *Courting Danger*. The comment by Swami Daru Yoganu was found in Paramount press materials dated 1936. Lombard's parties were covered widely by the press and photographers, mentioned in numerous movie star memoirs, and encapsulated in articles, including "How Carole Lombard Plans a Party" by Julie Lang Hunt, which appeared in the February 1935 issue of *Photoplay*. The story of Ernst Lubitsch's first involvement with Lombard was courtesy of Scott Eyman's 1993 Lubitsch biography. A history of the Mayfair Club was obtained from the 1985 book *Out with the Stars* by Jim Heimann.

11. Flight 3 Is Down

The testimony of H. Lyle Van Gordon was found in the CAB investigation and that of his wife Elizabeth in the House investigation. Lyle's sons, Steve and Doug, provided information about their parents, particularly Lyle, who climbed a mountain in an effort to save lives. Chuck Duffy, the TWA man in Las Vegas on the night that Flight 3 stopped there, was interviewed by both CAB and House investigators.

12. A Man in a Man's Body

Lyn Tornabene's comprehensive biography, *Long Live the King*, is the starting point for any conversation about Clark Gable. My visits to Gable's birthplace, Cadiz, Ohio, and vicinity also helped. Original quotes about Gable and Lombard by Howard Strickling, Gail Strickling, Ursula Theiss, Delmer Daves, Richard Lang, Harry Drucker, and Benny Massi were obtained from audiotape recordings in the Tornabene collection at the Academy. One of Gable's fast-cars-and-fast-motorcycles friends, Hollywood actor and writer Steve Hayes, provided perspectives on Gable that are sprinkled throughout this book. The story of Gable and Loretta Young comes from many sources, primarily Judy Lewis's 1994 memoir, *Uncommon Knowledge*. Tales of the Lombard pranks and publicity stunts were described in "Subject: Lombard" by Claude Binyon, which ran in the January 1940 issue of *Photoplay*, and Elizabeth Wilson's "It Looked Good for a Laugh at the Time" in the

January 1941 issue of *Silver Screen*. Carole's Bel Air menagerie was described in many print pieces, including Julie Lang Hunt's "The Utterly Balmy Home Life of Carole Lombard," which ran in the February 1937 edition of *Motion Picture*.

13. The Plane That Fell

Calvin Harper described his movements on the night of January 16 to the House panel. The story of Willard George is problematic. George is the only witness who claimed to see Flight 3 circling over the foothills and bobbing up and down prior to impacting the mountain, as if there were "a fistfight in the cockpit." Nobody at the Blue Diamond Mine saw that, the Hawleys didn't see it, and the fact that Flight 3 impacted the cliffs while in perfectly level flight all but disproves George's testimony before CAB investigators, and yet in other regards, he speaks credibly and is difficult to ignore as a witness. Investigators concluded that George was looking at Western 10 as Captain Cheney dipped his wing to get a better look at the crash while circling the wreckage. Major Anderson testified before both the CAB and House panels.

14. Somber Hymns and Cold Marble

American newspapers carried the story of Clark Gable vs. Violet Norton, and FBI files on this case were consulted as well. David Stenn's excellent biography, *Bombshell*, provided grounding on the career and relationships of Jean Harlow. Contemporary newspaper accounts provided background on the funeral, and my backstage visits to Forest Lawn Glendale were helpful as well. An article by Kirtley Baskette covered the Birdwell-created story of Lombard's week as publicity chief of the Selznick Studios. Lyn Tornabene interviewed Margaret Tallichet Wyler about her time with Lombard, and I listened to that audio recording at the Academy. A March 1937 *Movie Mirror* article by Jack Smalley entitled "Lombard Creates a Glamorous Rival" was also consulted.

15. Hoping Against Hope

Accounts of first responders in and around Las Vegas were found in the *Las Vegas Review Journal* and *Reno Evening Gazette* and also in testimony given to CAB and House investigators.

16. Certified Bombs

Both *Long Live the King* and *Screwball* provide descriptions of Gable's lifestyle and proclivities, and these were supplemented by my own interviews with people who knew him and by reviews of source interviews in the Tornabene collection, particularly the interviews with Howard and Gail Strickling, Ursula Theiss, Delmer Daves, and Jean Garceau. The "bombing" of MGM with leaflets was covered in the press of the day, which proved to be a much more reliable source than anecdotes recounted decades later. The saga of production of *Fools for Scandal* at Warner Bros. was uncovered in my thorough review of the production files at the USC Warner Bros. Archives in Los Angeles. The story of Lombard and her tax bill was picked up by the wire services and covered in newspapers large and small.

17. The Plain, Black Night

Maj. Herbert Anderson's trek across the desert is contained in the CAB investigation and more in-depth examination was located in the House investigation.

18. Malaise

Details about the Gable-Lombard ranch were found in an article by Ida Zeitlin called "At Home with the Gables," which appeared in the August 1940 issue of *Picture Play*, and in another by Adele Whitley Fletcher called "How Clark Gable and Carole Lombard Live" from the October 1940 issue of *Photoplay*. Additional information was supplied by Jean Garceau's *Dear Mr. G.* and my visits to Encino and the ranch. Descriptions of Lombard's pregnancy at the end of 1939 were found in contemporary news-papers and magazines. Accounts of the Atlanta premiere of *Gone With the Wind* abound; Alice Marble talked about the experience of accompanying Gable and Lombard to Atlanta in her memoirs. A description of the Selznick-Fleming feud was given by Howard Strickling to Lyn Tornabene on an audiotape at the Academy, and the Richard Lang interview addressed Gable's adultery. MGM got some mileage out of the "disappearance" of Carole and Clark in wire stories that made page one of newspapers in January 1940. Garson Kanin wrote a chapter about Lombard in his book *Hollywood* and recounted several of their conversations. Newspapers covered the trip of the Gables to Washington and Baltimore, with coverage so extensive that it was possible to trace the physicians and their specialties. Garceau's account was found in *Dear Mr. G.*

19. Road King

Warren Carey answered questions from CAB and House in-vestigators in detailing his attempts to reach the crash site.

20. A Flame to Many Moths

Don Worth's article "Will Carole Lombard's Marriage End Her Career?" in the July 1939 issue of *Modern Screen* magazine looked at the star's struggle to balance career and home life. Garson Kanin's reminiscence of Lombard in *Hollywood* was invaluable as a character study. Quotes by Lucille Ball about Lombard were found in *Lucille* by Kathleen Brady, *Lucy in the Afternoon* by Jim Brochu, and *Ball of Fire* by Stefan Kanfer. Insights about Lana Turner were provided by Steve Hayes, a Turner friend and confidant. Turner's memoir *Lana* was also consulted, although in that volume she de-nied any sexual liaison with Gable. Robert Stack opened up to me about Lombard during my face-to-face interview with him about their long association and making *To Be or Not to Be*. His memoir, *Straight Shooting*, provided more information. Lombard's concept of profit participation was recounted by Kyle Crichton in a February 1940 issue of *Collier's* and touched upon in Scott Eyman's Lubitsch biography. Jack Benny's experience making *To Be or Not to Be* was recounted in Mary Livingstone Benny's book. Details about the planning of the bond tour appeared in contemporary newspapers and in the writings of Jill Winkler.

21. Fool's Errand

Details of the passage of the first responders to the base of Potosi Mountain were found in the CAB Report, and descriptions of the terrain were based upon my climb over Van Gordon's route.

22. The VIPs

Details about Otto Winkler were courtesy of Jill Winkler's niece, Nazoma Ball, with additional information provided by Howard and Gail Strickling. Jill Winkler's manuscript, "Flashback into Oblivion," supplied by Nazoma Ball, provided insight into Otto and Jill, details of the elopement of Lombard and Gable, and a description of the last visit of the Winklers to the Gable ranch. Jean Garceau's *Dear Mr. G.* described the notes written by Carole to Clark, and my interviews with Carole Sampeck—and hers with Jean Garceau—put those notes in context. Howard Strickling, Robert Stack, Richard Lang, Fred Peters III, and others confirmed that the Gables had quarreled prior to Clark's departure for New York City and Carole's for Indianapolis. Newspaper articles detailed Lombard's whistle-stops en route to Chicago. Myron Davis's reminiscences about working on the bond tour were taken from a 2009 interview by Dean Brierly that appeared in *B&W* magazine—Davis bird-dogged Carole from Chicago on, and provided confirmation that she flew to Indianapolis on Wednesday rather than take the train on Thursday. Details about Carole's visit to Tuckaway resulted from a site visit and interviews with its owner, Kenneth Keene, who learned the story directly from Nellie

Meier's niece, Ruth Austin. An interview with Indianapolis native Rosalynn DeFelice revealed her eyewitness account of Lombard's Indiana State House appearance. The memoir of Will Hays gave a peer-to-peer account of his dealings with Carole Lombard. A two-page itinerary from Governor Schricker's files provided detail about Carole's schedule for January 15, 1942, and my tour of the State House and match-up of Davis photos with the interior of the building promoted an understanding of what happened where.

23. Gleaming Silver

Descriptions of the first ascent of Potosi and passage into the little valley below the crash site, where debris fell, were based on my climb led by Jim Boone over the rescuers' route. Testimony by Lyle Van Gordon and Jack Moore appeared in the CAB investigation, and their efforts were chronicled in the *Las Vegas Review Journal*.

24. The Coin Flip

Evidence contained in press coverage indicates that Lombard's decision to fly home was a spontaneous one made in Chicago or Indianapolis. Of greatest interest is a wee hours of January 16 conversation between Carole and Petey overheard at the Indianapolis airport by Mr. and Mrs. James C. Todd of Indianapolis. Petey begged Carole not to get on the plane, indicating that the decision was a recent and controversial one. This story, under the headline, "Mother Warned Carole Lombard," hit the wire services with other first reports about the crash. The coin flip was also widely covered in newspapers. Myron Davis described his airport meeting with Carole in the *B&W* interview.

25. The Computer

Mary Johnson Savoie recounted her remarkable story of riding 1,500 miles with Carole Lombard aboard Flight 3 in my interviews with her in September 2013. Mary's family provided several newspaper articles spanning 1942 to 2011 that confirm the accuracy of her recollections. The actual flight times, landing locations, and crew listings of Flight 3 for January 15 and 16 were found in TWA files located at the University of Missouri-Kansas City. Joseph Szigeti's experiences as a passenger on Flight 3 were recounted in a January 18 story in the *Salt Lake Tribune*.

26. Stranded

Warren Carey's ongoing attempts to proceed to Las Vegas were covered in the CAB and House investigations.

27. The Glamorous Life

Details on the life of Alice Getz were related by her niece, Doris Brieser, and other facts were found in the family scrapbook, including articles clipped from the *Kewanee Star Courier*. Details on Wayne Williams and Morgan Gillette came from TWA files and from obituaries. Careful research in local newspapers yielded vignettes on the Army airmen aboard Flight 3. Ed Knudsen was questioned by both CAB and House investigators about events during the tumultuous layover in Albuquerque. The story of Fred Dittman and Burton Voorhees appeared in wire coverage of the crash. The large amount of gear with the pilots was listed in the TWA files and seat assignments for each of the people on the plane were provided by TWA.

28. I Won't Be Coming Home

Jill Winkler's manuscript, "Flashback into Oblivion," provided her perspective on learning of the crash and the flight to Las Vegas. Howard Strickling's version of the story was found in Lyn Tornabene's audiotape interview. The story of the confrontation between Mannix and the official at Burbank airport appeared in the April 1942 issue of *Photoplay* in the Ruth Waterbury article

"What the Loss of Carole Lombard Means to Clark Gable." Identification of Don Hackett as the charter pilot was made by film historian Richard M. Roberts, who provided me with his notes from an interview with Hackett conducted in the 1980s.

29. There's No Rush

A visit to the crash site provided perspective on the terrain and the experience of anyone trying to negotiate it. Lyle Van Gordon's testimony concerning his first moments with Flight 3 was found in the House investigation. Jack Moore's testimony was found in the CAB investigation. Articles in the *Las Vegas Review Journal* provided details, and crash photos in the TWA files showed exactly what Jack Moore's team found on the morning of January 17. Transcripts of the coroner's inquests also yielded valuable information.

30. Caring Enough to Climb a Mountain

Extrapolation of Gable's thoughts on Saturday morning, January 17, was based on extensive study of the subject. His exact movements in the Vegas area were difficult to pin down, but finally an AP story recounted his attempt to climb the mountain, with word reaching him en route that the effort was futile. His path was covered during my climb of the mountain.

31. The Entire Gang Showed Up

Robert Stack recounted for me during our time together his memories of the moment he learned of Lombard's death. Mary Benny's reminiscence was found in *Jack Benny*, Margaret Tallichet Wyler's in the Tornabene audio interview, and Alice Marble's in *Courting Danger*. In *Dear Mr. G.* Jean Garceau talked of Gable's fixation on whether Lombard realized she was going to die and what happened in the moment prior to impact. Other accounts touched on his fear that she knew. The Army response was found in Major Anderson's testimony before the CAB.

32. Groaning Pines

The story of the rescue party in which Tom Devlin traveled was related by John F. Cahlan in "Story of Plane Hunt Told by Writer," which appeared in the January 19, 1942, issue of the *Las Vegas Review Journal*. Devlin's odyssey was also covered extensively in his testimony at the coroner's inquest concerning the remains of Otto Winkler.

33. Unfixable

Scott Eyman's *Lion of Hollywood* and E.J. Fleming's *The Fixers* provided background on the very colorful Eddie Mannix. Accounts of the remarkable and unlikely ascent of Mt. Potosi by Mannix and Wheelright, neither of whom were equipped for such an effort, physically or sartorially, were taken from press coverage.

34. I Still See It in My Dreams

Various accounts of the search for crash victims, including that of Harry Pursel, were taken from the coroner's inquest held the evening that Lombard's body was found. Pursel also testified before the CAB and House investigations. The accounts of Sherman and Guldner were printed in the Monday, January 19, issue of the *Los Angeles Times*. Tommy Young's account was given to Carole Sampeck, and she provided it to me. In general, a surprising amount of grisly detail made the wire stories that appeared in newspapers from coast to coast.

35. The Fatal Flaw

The Strickling version of Gable's reaction to the news of Lombard's death is found in wire stories planted by MGM. The story of goings-on at the El Rancho Vegas was compiled from many accounts. Major Anderson and Lieutenant Hunt testified at the coroner's inquests regarding the challenges faced by the recovery team as they attempted to identify and remove remains.

36. The Complication

Jack Benny's story about the New Year's Eve party was recounted in *Sunday Nights at Seven* by Jack and Joan Benny. Transcripts of the inquests for each of the crash victims were provided by Carole Sampeck and the Carole Lombard Archive Foundation. Death certificates were secured by Marina Gray.

37. Just a Few Yards Apart

All the important "trades" from the time of the crash were reviewed at the Academy Library for coverage of the deaths of Lombard, Peters, and Winkler. Clyde Burkett and Waldon Golien testified before the CAB. Gable's movements were tracked by the press, including the drive with Al Menasco to the foot of the mountain and the speculation about Ma's last moments. Tornabene's *Long Live the King* also mentioned the desert drive. My experiences in the terrain visited by Gable and the roads traveled enhanced the descriptions.

38. All in a Day's Work

Newspaper accounts chronicled the difficulties of Lieutenant Hunt in identifying crash victims and told the story of the unfortunate horse in graphic detail. Testimony by Hunt at the Clark County coroner's inquests provided additional information about his extraordinary challenges over those days.

39. The Little Boy Was Gone

Press accounts and personal reminiscences of his friends and colleagues filled in all blanks about the grief of Clark Gable, the ongoing planning for his return from Las Vegas to southern California, and his understandable trepidation about life at the ranch minus his wife. Steve Hayes also helped by recounting conversations with his friends Franchot Tone and Robert Taylor. FDR's telegram appeared in newspaper stories.

40. Flying with Full Acceptance

Waldon Golien's final search of the crash site was described in an internal TWA memo. Warren Carey's testimony was found in the CAB report, where he also read his crash-scene report into the record. The struggles of the investigators to understand the crash of Flight 3 were seen in all proceedings of both investigations. Even more than seventy years after the crash, questions linger about the events of January 1942. Why had this happened? What was the pilot thinking? What did the passengers experience?

41. The Under Side

Newspapers of the day looked at the crash from every angle, including scrutiny of the lost Army fliers. Coverage of the return of Gable and party to the Los Angeles area was provided by the Associated Press in multiple articles and also by the United Press in the article "Clark Gable Takes Wife's Body Back to Los Angeles." Jean Garceau discussed the meeting at Forest Lawn Glendale to make funeral arrangements in *Dear Mr. G.* The last will and testament of Carole Lombard was consulted for specifics about her final wishes. Fred Peters III recounted the incident in which his mother placed gowns inside the caskets of Carole Lombard and Elizabeth Peters. The best and most complete report on the funeral of Carole Lombard was contained in the *Los Angeles Times* on Thursday, January 22, 1942. Frederick C. Othman also provided outstanding coverage for United Press. Descriptions of Forest Lawn's Great Mausoleum and Church of the Recessional were based on my observations during multiple visits to Forest Lawn Glendale, including private tours.

42. Even the Unfortunates

Jill Winkler's manuscript, "Flashback into Oblivion," provided valuable insights into the relationship of the Winklers and Gables. The best coverage of the Winkler funeral was found in the Hollywood trades. Damon Runyon's syndicated "Brighter Side" featured the editorial that was almost certainly written by Thomas J. Devlin, which also yielded perspective on Otto Winkler. Nazoma Ball, who had met Otto and who attended his funeral, gave a great deal of her time to this project and detailed that difficult day.

43. The Cream of the Crop

The *Daily Courier* in Connellsville, Pennsylvania, provided extensive coverage of the Nygren story; the *Pittsburgh Press* covered Belejchak. My June 2013 interview with Lois Hamilton's cousin, Marie Levi, and Marie's daughter, Donita Dixon, provided details about the Hamilton funeral. Accounts of Alice Getz's funeral were found in local newspaper obituaries and in the family scrapbook, and the story of Captain Williams appeared in the TWA files.

44. Skyrocketing

The Strickling interview by Lyn Tornabene contained information about Gable's return to the ranch; more came from *Dear Mr. G.* The press also dragged the grief of the king out for popular view. United Artists' handling of *To Be or Not to Be* was covered in both *The Hollywood Reporter* and *Variety*. The former noted Benny's strange behavior at the picture's premiere, and Mary Livingstone Benny alluded to it in *Jack Benny*. My conversations with Robert Stack and Steve Hayes covered the change in Gable, and Lyn Tornabene's chapter in *Long Live the King* captures it perfectly. Prior to release, *He Kissed the Bride* was retitled *They All Kissed the Bride* because censors thought *He Kissed the Bride* sounded too suggestive. I used the original title throughout because this was how both Lombard and Crawford knew the project.

45. Mangled

A review of this chapter by Michael McComb of Lostflights Aviation Technology led to valuable refinement of its conclusions.

Transcripts of the CAB and House investigations were used extensively throughout the book, and particularly in this chapter. The August 1992 issue of *TARPA Topics*, the magazine for The Active Retired Pilots Association of TWA, contained comments by radio operator Earl Korf about Wayne Williams not being at the controls. Wire stories were consulted regarding the blame placed on Williams as a result of his 1933 firing by the company. The American public needed a scapegoat, and TWA was put in the awkward position of needing one as well. Its practices were revealed to be lax—wide flight lanes, a lack of regulations about minimum altitudes above terrain, no rules about use of the radio range, and especially a cavalier attitude toward the takeoff weight of its planes. While TWA made a public display of standing behind its pilot, privately, as revealed in company files, the airline fed Williams to the lions. Richard M. Roberts' notes from his conversations with Don Hackett were especially helpful. The official investigations noted how close Flight 3 was to escaping disaster, horizontally and vertically—and my site visit to the crash site confirmed this information. The stories of finding evidence in the spring thaw and of the attempts to dynamite the crash scene were documented in the TWA files. Interviews with family members of some of the victims helped me understand the crash aftermath. The FBI file on Flight 3 was finally provided by D.C. researcher Ann Trevor after my Freedom of Information Act failed to locate the file. The documents show that investigators scrutinized Joseph Szigeti, who was fingered by anonymous informants offering tips about his involvement in the 1940 crash of Trip 19. But nothing concrete about Szigeti could be found. The file also revealed rich detail about the UFO sighting and brought rancher Willard George back into focus. George's testimony is all over the board, saying Flight 3 was out of control as he observed it, but the facts show the plane hit the cliff in straight and level flight. That makes his report of a UFO as questionable as his other testimony. But the officially filed report of the CAA man is troubling since he saw a large, bright, white, round light hanging in the sky in the flight lane just a few nights before the fatal crash. Willard George independently reported exactly the same light visible in the flight lane on January 16 (as confirmed by Furrey upon hearing what George had to say). A March 6, 1942 memo has surfaced from J. Edgar Hoover to the special agent in charge of the case asking for a review of the "peculiar lights" seen by Furrey and George, but the FBI files contain only Furrey's original document. Attempting to build a UFO case on the testimony of Willard George is problematic; on cross-examination during the House investigation of the crash, George broke under rigorous questioning and admitted he wasn't sure about his own timeline and whether Flight 3 was behaving oddly, or if what he really saw was Western Flight 10 surveying the scene. The case of Furrey and George adds another layer to a fascinating mystery of odd lights in the sky near where Flight 3 crashed.

46. If I Can Do It, So Can You

Coaching by David Stenn helped me sort out the estate issues. Stenn also provided his notes on conversations with Nazoma Ball and Fred Peters III, which led to my conversations with each. Legal documents and press coverage told the story of the estates of Lombard and Peters, and unpublished notes in the Tornabene collection provided details about the strained relationship between Gable and the Peters brothers. Fred Peters III added more insights during my interviews with him. Tornabene's interviews with Howard Strickling revealed the affection between Gable and Winkler; Nazoma Ball confirmed it. Recent discovery of the postcard written to Jill by Clark in November 1942 provided new insights. Steve Hayes described the reactions of his friends Robert Taylor, Franchot Tone, and Ava Gardner to changes in Gable. Richard Lang and Robert Stack touched on Gable's suicidal impulses. My interviews with Nazoma Ball detailed Jill's life after the crash. Press coverage and *Long Live the King* provided details of Gable's military career. Howard Strickling talked of the DUI and of Gable's meeting with Susan Peters, and her article in *Photoplay* recounted Susan's side of the story. Alice Marble's *Courting Danger* provided the story of Gable's gesture in 1944.

Epilogue: High-Energy Impact

I learned of the crash of Col. Ed Lewis's Cessna T182t while working as a contractor for NASA Aeronautics and was dumbfounded to find that he and his copilot, Dion DeCamp, had crashed into, of all places, Mt. Potosi, Nevada. NTSB records provided all necessary details of the crash and investigation. The story of Burt Voorhees was sifted from newspapers that followed the course of his life. The discovery of Kenneth Donahue's body was recounted in a Biddeford, Maine, newspaper article with additional information obtained through conversations with Felicia Borla of the Clark County coroner's office and Donahue's niece, Maureen Green. The course of Lyle Van Gordon's life was summarized by his sons, Steve and Doug. The fate of Madalynne Field was described by her son, Richard, in the Tornabene interviews. Descriptions of Jill Winkler's life after Otto were based on the Strickling interviews and my conversations with Nazoma Ball. Margaret Tallichet Wyler's interview with Lyn Tornabene was insightful as was Alice Marble's. Alice was one interesting character. She sat with Tornabene reminiscing with a cigarette in one hand and a mixed drink in the other. Getting a handle on Gable wasn't easy. He was a simple man, and terribly complex, from his early self-centeredness to his obsessions. Through the course of writing *Fireball*, I came to the conclusion that Clark Gable was, in his way, a hero. A flawed hero, but a hero nonetheless. The king could have become a bitter recluse; instead, he made his life count for something, in part through quiet good deeds of the type that he believed would have made Carole Lombard proud.

Selected Bibliography

Benny, Jack and Joan Benny. *Sunday Nights at Seven: The Jack Benny Story*. New York: Warner Books, 1990.

Benny, Mary Livingstone and Hilliard Marks with Marcia Borie. *Jack Benny: A Biography*. Garden City, NY: Doubleday, 1978.

Biskind, Peter, Editor. *My Lunches with Orson: Conversations Between Henry Jaglom and Orson Welles*. New York: Metropolitan Books, 2013.

Breuer, William. *Hitler's Undercover War: The Nazi Espionage Invasion of the U.S.A.* New York: St. Martin's Press, 1989.

Civil Aeronautics Board. Investigation of Accident Involving TWA Trip 3, Aircraft NC 1946, which occurred near Las Vegas, Nevada, January 16, 1942. Docket No. SA-58. Washington: Anderson Stenotype Services, 1942.

Evans, Peter and Ava Gardner. *Ava Gardner: The Secret Conversations*. New York: Simon & Schuster, 2013.

Eyman, Scott. *Ernst Lubitsch: Laughter in Paradise*. New York: Simon & Schuster, 1993.

Eyman, Scott. *Lion of Hollywood: The Life and Legend of Louis B. Mayer*. New York: Simon & Schuster, 2005.

Fleming, E.J. *The Fixers: Eddie Mannix, Howard Strickling and the MGM Publicity Machine*. Jefferson, NC: McFarland & Co., 2005.

Francisco, Charles. *Gentleman: The William Powell Story*. New York: St. Martin's Press, 1985.

Garceau, Jean with Inez Cocke. *Dear Mr. G: The Biography of Clark Gable.* Boston: Little, Brown and Company, 1961.

Gehring, Wes D. *Carole Lombard: The Hoosier Tornado.* Indianapolis: Indiana Historical Society Press, 2003.

Hays, Will. *The Memoirs of Will H. Hays, Indiana Lawyer – Political Genius – Postmaster General – First "Czar" of the Movies.* New York: Doubleday and Company, 1955.

Heimann, Jim. *Out with the Stars: Hollywood Nightlife in the Golden Era.* New York: Abbeyville Press, 1985.

Kanin, Garson. *Hollywood.* New York: The Viking Press, 1967.

Lanza, Joseph and Dennis Penna. *Russ Columbo and the Crooner Mystique.* Los Angeles: Feral House, 2002.

Lewis, Judy. *Uncommon Knowledge.* New York: Pocket Books, 1994.

Marble, Alice with Dale Leatherman. *Courting Danger: My Adventures in World-Class Tennis, Golden-Age Hollywood, and High-Stakes Spying.* New York: St. Martin's Press, 1991.

Marble, Alice. *The Road to Wimbledon.* New York: Charles Scribner's Sons, 1946.

Matzen, Robert. *Carole Lombard: A Bio-Bibliography.* Westport, CT: Greenwood Press, 1988.

Meier, Nellie Simmons. *Lion's Paws: The Story of Famous Hands 1937.* New York: Barrows Massey Publisher, 1937.

O'Brien, Pat. *The Wind at My Back.* New York: Avon Books, 1967.

Ott, Frederick W. *The Films of Carole Lombard.* Secaucus: Citadel Books, 1972.

Rath, Jill Winkler. "Flashback into Oblivion." Manuscript.

Schickel, Richard. *The Men Who Made the Movies: Interviews with Frank Capra, George Cukor, Howard Hawks, Alfred Hitchcock, Vincente Minnelli, King Vidor, Raoul Walsh, and William A. Wellman.* New York: Atheneum, 1975.

Select Committee on Air Accidents in the United States. House of Representatives. Seventy-Seventh Congress, Second Session. Investigation of Air Accidents in the United States. Washington: Government Printing Office, 1942.

Sragow, Michael. *Victor Fleming: An American Movie Master.* New York: Pantheon Books, 2008.

Stack, Robert with Mark Evans. *Straight Shooting.* New York: Macmillan, 1980.

Stenn, David. *Bombshell: The Life and Death of Jean Harlow.* New York: Doubleday, 1993.

Swindell, Larry. *Screwball: The Life of Carole Lombard.* New York: William Morrow, 1975.

Szigeti, Joseph. *With Strings Attached: Reminiscences and Reflections.* New York: Alfred A. Knopf, 1947.

Tornabene, Lyn. *Long Live the King: A Biography of Clark Gable.* New York: G.P. Putnam's Sons, 1976.

Turner, Lana. *Lana: The Lady, the Legend, the Truth.* New York: Pocket Books, 1982.

TWA files on the crash of Trip Number 3, January 16, 1942. Conserved at the State Historical Society of Missouri.

Wellman, William A. *A Short Time for Insanity: An Autobiography.* New York: Hawthorn Books, 1974.

Wighton, Charles and Gunter Peis. *Hitler's Spies and Saboteurs.* New York: Charter Books, 1958.

Ziegler, Connie. *Life By Design: The Meiers of Tuckaway.* Commercial Article by the Priority Press, 2016.

Index